Social Inequality in Oaxaca

Conflicts in Urban and Regional Development

a series edited by John R. Logan and Todd Swanstrom

Social Inequality in Oaxaca

A History of Resistance and Change

ARTHUR D. MURPHY
ALEX STEPICK

Foreword by Henry A. Selby

Temple University Press
PHILADELPHIA

Temple University Press, Philadelphia 19122
Copyright © 1991 by Temple University. All rights reserved
Published 1991
Printed in the United States of America

The paper used in this publication meets the minimum requirements of American
National Standard for Information Sciences—Permanence of Paper for Printed Library
Materials, ANSI Z39.48-1984 ∞

Library of Congress Cataloging-in-Publication Data
Murphy, Arthur D.
Social inequality in Oaxaca : a history of resistance and change /
by Arthur D. Murphy and Alex Stepick ; foreword by Henry A. Selby.
    p.   cm. — (Conflicts in urban and regional development)
    Includes bibliographical references and index.
    ISBN 0-87722-868-X (alk. paper)—ISBN 0-87722-869-8 (pbk. : alk. paper)
    1. Oaxaca de Juarez (Mexico)—Social conditions.   2. Social classes—Mexico—
Oaxaca de Juarez.   3. Neighborhood—Mexico—Oaxaca de Juarez.   4. Community
development, Urban—Mexico—Oaxaca de Juarez.   I. Stepick, Alex.   II. Title.
III. Series.
HN120.O29M87   1991   91-7453
305.5'0972'74—dc20   CIP

To Cecil R. Welte
and the people of Oaxaca

Contents

Illustrations and Tables

Foreword

Once Oaxaca gets hold of you, it is hard to get away. I have certainly found it that way, as I enter my third decade of association with the city and region. For many of us who have lived and worked there and studied the fascinations of the place, Oaxaca is simply one of the most charming places we have been: good, although not high, living, among some of the most pleasant people in North America.

The two authors of this book have lived in and studied the city since the early 1970s. When they arrived, hair was in and never grey; we were all learning about computers, and trying to get the Oaxacans to cooperate in the daunting exercise of modeling their lives. The authors remained to spend two decades exploring how the city of Oaxaca worked, starting as most urban anthropologists do in one tiny *colonia popular* and working their way out of it, constructing a truly interdisciplinary approach and analysis.

This book incorporates many of the lessons that social anthropologists, sociologists, political scientists, and economists have learned in the last twenty years. When this all started, American behavioral science was still in vogue, and a neo-Boasian attentiveness to texts and data informed their work. An uninspected modernization theory was more or less taken for granted by anthropological practitioners. In opposition to behavioral science models, Mexican (and Latin American) social science was developing its models of the world system and dependency relations that were to undo modernization theory, even as the latter was triumphing in the applied academe and development circles of North America. Both approaches tended to presume that urbanization was a modern phenomenon that had peculiar effects on newly arrived migrants from seemingly traditional rural villages. They differed primarily in assessing who and what forces initiated and benefited from the increased urbanization seen during the second half of the twentieth century.

Murphy and Stepick were influenced by both of these major theoretical approaches, but the true significance of their work emerges from their commitment and sensitivity to the complex, often confusing, realities of Oaxaca. In the beginning they studied both villagers and city folks to find out how they thought about their lives, and in particular, what they said about moving from village to town, and then from the city of Oaxaca to other cities in the republic and to the United States—much as Oscar Lewis followed his subjects from Tepoztlán to Mexico City. The ostensible topic of their project was why people and their families moved about (the cognoscenti called it "migration," as though people were birds). Studies, like the one that started the authors off in Oaxaca, were designed to understand how people conceptualized their priorities and how their priorities ordered their activities. Generally they discovered, as Murphy and Stepick did, that people knew what they were doing, gave a fair amount of thought to it, and used the resources available to them to get what they wanted out of life. This approach often ignored the question of the production and availability of resources; as one informant revealed, after he had fully explained the rational basis for his staying in Oaxaca, the only thing he wanted in return for the interview was a job in the United States.

The authors would readily admit they learned a good deal from the early projects. Perhaps the most important lesson was that computers and models and technical apparatus could not reflect the complex relations between enduring structures and situational responses. And so they stayed in the city of Oaxaca, and twenty years later we are fortunate to have this book.

The book is deceptively written. Like good art, the reader is not aware of what went into it. Good writing does not enumerate its sources, except obliquely, and good writers seek out the right example, without revealing how they found and crafted it. But I know what went into the book and its abundance of nuanced and telling examples. Standing behind it are three and a half doctoral dissertations (two by the authors, half by a colleague who included material on other parts of Mexico), and two random sample surveys of the city: the first in 1977, a two-shot quota sample of more than 1,550 households that was the pilot for a national urban study and which covered 53 neighborhood subtypes of the city, and the second in 1987, of 600-odd households. From 1975 to the present, continuous study has allowed the authors to carry out hundreds of hours of interviews and brought them into close association with the important citizens of the city, as well as with academic institutions and scholars in the area. While this continuing twenty-year sociological study was going on, Richard Blanton, Steve Kowalewski, Laura Finsten, and Gary Feinman completed important archaeological settlement-pattern studies that Murphy and Stepick incorporated into this book, providing a needed historical dimension to the political economy of Oaxaca. This cross-fertilization reveals Oaxaca's long urban history, refuting the notion that villagers are new to urbanization and require long years to adjust to the city.

This historical perspective is unusual in urban studies and gives us a long view of urban development that reveals cycles of isolation followed by incorporation into national and international systems. The authors show that as Oaxaca became incorporated, first into the imperial "project" of the prehispanic period, then the colonial project, the modernization project of the Porfirian period, and the nation-building project of the Revolution, social and economic inequality became more marked in the city and its region. Oaxaca's integration into outsiders' schemes favors the accentuation of inequalities and hierarchy, as well as the accretion of wealth by the city's favored groups and classes. Likewise, when Oaxaca and its region become isolated and disengaged, they return to a more egalitarian arrangement. If this sounds like the *dependentista* lemma that the most dynamic periods of development in Latin America were precisely those when it was cut off by war or economic depression from North America and Europe, this is no coincidence. But here there is a difference: while isolation decreased inequality, it did not produce overall economic growth. Rather, the smaller amount of wealth was more evenly distributed.

Within this broad thesis, the authors reveal a constantly evolving, complex play of social forces in which individuals and groups constantly battle to survive and prosper. The breadth and rich detail in capturing these efforts to adapt within broad enduring structural constraints truly distinguishes this work. The authors' narrative ends approximately with Mexico's crisis in the early 1980s. The finding by Murphy, Morris, and Winter that in the decade between 1977 and 1987 the percentage of households with no access to job-related fringe benefits had risen from 40 percent to 60 percent reinforces one of the central theses presented in this book (Murphy 1991).

My own research indicates that the current crisis seems permanent to many Oaxacans. While a primarily nonlocal elite continues to prosper, just as at the end of the nineteenth-century reforms and the twentieth-century revolution, the majority of Oaxacans protest and struggle against the city's growing inequality. Interviews with working-class people between 1987 and 1990 revealed one well-informed subject who knew that official sources were reporting a rebound in the economy of about 3 percent in 1989–90, but who skeptically invited the finance minister to visit him and his friends to inform them why they hadn't rebounded. Another subject echoed the sentiments of many and said, "the crisis is permanent"; a third was more stoic, saying, "Crisis? What crisis? There has always been a crisis around here!" (Selby 1991).

Whatever citizens' opinions about the crisis, incomes have been reduced. Women have gone into the work force in unprecedented numbers: washing clothes, making and selling tortillas and other prepared foods, going door to door selling used clothing, domestic work. One woman was taking home the equivalent of less than $10 (U.S.) a month working as a full-time domestic and living with her son, a student in the (postsecondary) preparatory school; her medical problems had compelled her to borrow money from her employer, who deducted it from her wages of $25 (U.S.) a month. A man was living off what he earned from selling used comics to schoolchildren, along with month-old sweets that were no bargain at a penny a pound. He ate no meat any more, but it did not bother him; he had no teeth and lived on the equivalent of thirty-five cents (U.S.) a day.

At the same time we found households who were well organized and surviving comparatively well, maintaining a standard of living not much worse than before the crisis. Their families were small, but married sons and daughters all lived together in a single *solar* (house site). One woman's great pride was her children, and her *atole,* which she served to the interviewers. When she was in Oaxaca she sold *atole* to her neighbors and worked at laundering when she could. Her principal income came from minimum-salaried work as a *rezagadora,* a culler of tomatoes, in Sinaloa, a thousand miles from home. Hard work, badly paid, and not even all the tomatoes you could eat. (The tomatoes went to the pigs. "Pigs before people!" she declared, merely one of the daily, structural insults to human dignity that the poor suffered in the Mexico of the crisis, but that was going to change.) She was a neighborhood leader of an opposition party, the Partido Revolucionario Democrático; soon she was going to meet the great Cuauhtémoc Cárdenas. She didn't know when, but she was going to meet him, and then, by God, there was going to be some social justice in this country.

This same woman had already stood up to the authorities. She had gone to the governor's office when they had shot her predecessor, an activist student leader, two years earlier and called them "asesinos." They didn't dare touch her; she had too many friends in the neighborhood. But they could attack her family; one son-in-law was in jail awaiting trial on a trumped-up rape charge; another was unemployed because he couldn't get permission to start up a mechanic's shop outside his house and was forced to sell used clothing from door to door, and take whatever casual jobs he could find. They had tried to dislodge her, take away her house site, and harassed her daily, but she was more than enough for them. A magnificent woman, and a fighter. There were three families in her *solar.* She lived with her unmarried children, while her son lived next door with his wife and two children, and her married daughter lived in a third house with her husband (still in jail after two years) and their four children. Lovers came and went, as did other relatives, and the population of the *solar* ranged from thirteen when everyone was there, to seven when she was in the north. Even though she had no money in reserve, hers was a success story because she had managed to keep her family together, cooperating and collaborating and sharing, even though they all kept separate households.

Some of the successes are failures. María Lourdes was one: she had gone as a child to Oaxaca, sent by her imperious father from a Mixtec village twelve hours away to go to secondary school in the state capital. She had been miserable and alone and frightened there, but had met this wonderful boy, and they decided upon graduation to live together as a married couple. She got pregnant, and with the crisis there were no jobs. He panicked, and left her in Oaxaca with an aunt who might look after her. She was desperate, angry and frightened once again, especially as her aunt had never approved of her husband. There was a fight and María Lourdes went to live in a tiny, wooden one-room shack, most of which was taken up by a double bed. She was hungry. The baby came early. She went to the hospital, where the baby was born, and they asked her what she was going to name her baby boy. "Nothing," she replied, "I don't even want to own that I have one." The hospital orderlies named him Charlie, after an American perfume sold the length of Mexico. When we met Charlie and María, she had a job in the medical school cafeteria where (when the school was in session) she earned a thousand pesos a day (seventy-five cents, U.S.), could eat all she wanted at dinner time, and keep Charlie with her. Out of session—which was frequent because of strikes, vacations and suspensions—she had no money and no food.

She fought back. A friend from the medical school told her that she had heard of a wonderful scam: they were giving scholarships to bilinguals who had finished secondary school to help them become bilingual school teachers. Did she speak Mixteco? Did she ever! She applied and was accepted. She finished the difficult course, where as a mother of age twenty she had to attend boarding school and wear uniforms and leave Charlie back in the village. But it didn't matter—it was a way out. She graduated, not with highest honors, but she did graduate. Then the game began. The graduates would have to wait for their certificates; they were being issued by the *secretaría* in Mexico City. Months went by and no certificates. The graduates became angry, and along with other teacher movements in Mexico they went to protest in Mexico City at the ministry of education. Still no certificates. The bureaucrats wore them down, and finally they ran out of money and patience and went home. For a while she went back to the village in the mountains and cultivated some land her father had way out in an *agencia*, far from the village center, all by herself. We asked her whether it was difficult to do men's work, to get along without a man in the village, with the clear implication than we thought it was. "Men," she snorted, looking at the three well-dressed ones sitting on the bed interviewing her, "what liars they are! They tell you that it's so hard to plough and to work with the yoke of oxen, and it's not at all; it's easy. The only time it's hard is when you hit a big rock, and they don't find that easy either."

Back in Oaxaca City we asked about the loneliness of being alone, being young, vigorous, and without a man. What did she do, how did she manage? Another snort, *"Pero hombres, hay bastantes!"* she responded, to indicate that there wasn't any shortage of male lovers either and that most of them were worthless.

These are some of our stories about life in Oaxaca today. What is missing from the stories is exactly what this book provides, the historic and social context. Murphy and Stepick catch Oaxaca at a special time in its history. When the illustrious works of theory in the academic disciplines have faded, when Foucault is a footnote and deconstruction derided, books like this one will still be valuable. A portrait of a city during the most difficult period of its country's recent economic history.

HENRY A. SELBY
Austin, Texas

Acknowledgments

This is truly a work of shared proportions. While our primary interests are not entirely coincident, each of us participated equally in the writing and editing of every chapter. We cannot assign senior and junior authorship and share equally the responsibility for the final product. We are also incalculably indebted to two professional but unpaid editors: Ginny Howard served as our initial editor and critic; Carol Dutton Stepick scrutinized the manuscript at a later state. This book would have never been finished nor possess what coherence it does without their dedicated attention.

During our twenty years of work in Oaxaca, we have incurred personal debts to innumerable individuals and agencies. Above all, none of this work would have come to pass without the unflagging faith and support of Henry Selby, who first introduced each of us to Oaxaca. We also owe a particular debt to the research team that conducted the surveys of Oaxaca and to the National Institute for Community Development (IN-DECO) for permission to use data in this and other publications. Ingeniero Jose Luís Aceves, then director of the Oaxaca INDECO (Instituto Nacional para el Desarrollo de la Comunidad y de la Viviendo Popular) office, encouraged and supported our work at every turn. Ignacio Ruíz Love, Ignacio Cabrera, and Aída Castañeda participated in the original survey and in many discussions in which ideas presented in this book were developed. Earl W. Morris and Mary Winter designed much of the 1987 survey and have helped give the data a dynamic quality they would not otherwise have. As always, Manuel Esparza, first as director of the Oaxaca regional center of the Instituto Nacional de Antropología e Historia (INAH) and later as director of the Oaxaca state archives, has been most helpful during the course of our field work. His experience with the city and state of Oaxaca, coupled with a willingness to share his knowledge, make him an invaluable source of information and support for any social scientist working in the city.

Cecil Welte, of the Oficina de Estudios de Humanidad del Valle de Oaxaca, opened his library to us. It is impossible to number the times in Oaxaca when we and other social scientists, faced with a question concerning the history, demography, or geography of the city, have said, "Let's ask Cecil." Shortly, we would be in his office, where he would either have the answer at hand or would patiently lead us through his library in search of the data we needed. His generosity and good humor are legendary.

Those who provided us with unlimited hospitality and invaluable insight into their lives can never be adequately thanked. We wish especially to extend our gratitude to Adela Otera, Agustín Gallegos, la familia Gutiérrez, Fermina Aquino Cruz, Isaías López Antonio, Arturo Solís, Gilberto Bolaños, Maria Fabían, la familia Pacheco, as well as the people of the *colonias* San Juanito, Benito Juarez, Linda Vista, and Riberas del Atoyac. Each has been patient to a fault as we asked impertinent questions about their households, their neighborhoods, their city, and their state. A special thanks must also be given to the two thousand households in the city of Oaxaca who participated in the 1977 and 1987 surveys. They let us into their homes and talked frankly about their situations. They remain anonymous, but in a real sense are the direct subjects of this book.

Steve Kowalewski, Laura Finsten, Francisca Gutíerrez, María Luisa Acevedo, and Aída Castañeda read portions of the manuscript and provided critical guidance. Martha W. Rees was particularly important in introducing us to aspects of Latin American literature and theory. Much of the theoretical coherence is due to her intervention. Gisela Weis-Gresham did her usual fine work producing the illustrations. We must also acknowledge the intellectual contribution of the many students, friends, and colleagues who have participated in classes, conferences, seminars, and discussions with us. In many cases they have read portions of the manuscript and provided valuable comments.

Research is not free and in the course of our years of work in Oaxaca we have incurred many debts. We wish to acknowledge the support of the National Science Foundation, the Fulbright-Hays program, the National Institute of Mental Health, the Latin American and Caribbean Center and the School of Arts and Sciences of Florida International University, the Institute of Latin American Studies at the University of Texas, the Dean Rusk Center of the University of Georgia, the University Research Committee and the Institute of Environmental Studies of Baylor University, and Georgia State University.

Finally, it is customary for the authors to acknowledge their long-suffering families. We would like to thank those who have sustained us in our extended effort to tell the story of the people in a city we hold dear. That we are still friends and colleagues is due in large part to the support of those around us.

Acronyms

CFE Comisión Federal de la Electricidad
CIESAS Centro de Investigaciónes y Estudios Superiores de Antropología Social
CNC Confederación Nacional Campesina
CNOP Confederación Nacional de Organizaciones Populares
COCEO Coalición de Obreros, Campesinos, y Estudiantes de Oaxaca
CORETT Comisión para Regularización de la Tenencia de la Tierra
CTM Confederación de Trabajadores Mexicanos
FEO Federación Estudiantil de Oaxaca
FONAPAS Fondo Nacional para las Actividades Sociales
FONART Fondo Nacional para el Fomento de las Artesanias
FOVI Fondo de Vivienda
FUCOPO Fusión Cívica de Organizaciónes Productivas de Oaxaca
IMSS Instituto Mexicano de Seguro Social
INAH Instituto Nacional de Antropología e Historia
INDECO Instituto Nacional para el Desarrollo de la Comunidad y de la Vivienda Popular
INEGI Instituto Nacional de Estudística Geografía e Informática
INFONAVIT Instituto del Fondo Nacional de la Vivienda para los Trabajadores
INI Instituto Nacional Indigenista
ISSSTE Instituto de Seguridad y Servicios Sociales de los Trabajadores del Estado
PRD Partido Revolucionario Democratico
PRI Partido Revolucionario Institucional
SEP-INAH Secretaría de Educación Pública–Instituto Nacional de Antropología e Historia
UABJO Universidad Autónoma Benito Juárez de Oaxaca

Social Inequality in Oaxaca

1

Introduction

In this book we present a contemporary ethnography of social inequality in the Mexican city of Oaxaca, capital of the state of the same name. The city lies at the nexus of the three arms of the valley of Oaxaca, about 300 kilometers (186 miles) south of Mexico City. Outside Mexico, Oaxaca is known primarily to those interested in either illicit drugs or prehispanic ruins. The region allegedly produces some of the best marijuana and hallucinogenic mushrooms in North America and waves and waves of *jipis* (pronounced *hee-pees*) have descended upon the area since the mid 1960s. Archaeological mounds literally dot the countryside, and perched just above the contemporary city of Oaxaca are the magnificent ruins of Monte Albán.[1]

Within Mexico, Oaxaca is noted predominantly as a city of pleasant colonial charm surrounded by seemingly bucolic peasant villages inhabited by Indians, many of whom still maintain native dress and language. The valley's altitude of 1,550 meters (5,075 feet) moderates what would otherwise be hot tropical temperatures, producing a pleasant climate with a mean temperature of 65 degrees Fahrenheit and low humidity. The concurrence of the summer rains with the year's highest temperatures cools even the hottest days (Rodrigo 1983).[2]

None of these famous features however, constitutes the core of this book. Rather, we the authors have come to appreciate and understand Oaxaca as a set of seeming paradoxes. Behind its attractive appearance and quaint charm the city and the valley are a crucible collecting all the forces buffeting modern Mexico, the forces of change and continuity, conflict and peace, and most important, rising and falling material standards of living and evolving socioeconomic inequality. The vast majority of its inhabitants earn an inadequate wage, a small minority earn a comfortable living, and an increasing proportion lie between these two extremes. Protest and violence have repeatedly engulfed the city as local

1

elites have sought to isolate it from change while the masses have demanded their concerns be addressed.

All of these forces mix in one of Mexico's most isolated, least
developed cities and regions. The very features of old-fashioned quaint-
ness reflect Oaxaca's separation and underdevelopment. Early this century, after nearly four hundred years among Mexico's preeminent cities,
Oaxaca fell from the list of the nation's top twenty urban settlements. It is
now a secondary city in every respect. It is not among Mexico's top twenty
cities in population, its level of economic output and industrialization are
among the lowest of all Mexican cities, and it has produced virtually no
notable national political figures in the twentieth century, nor does it
possess a significant voice in national political affairs.

It is also a city in which thousands of households quietly and reso-
lutely try to adapt, to survive, and to pass on something of themselves to
their children. In this respect, as anthropologists, we have witnessed a
remarkable continuity and sameness in the daily lives of the majority of
families, households, and neighborhoods. Poor neighborhood communities, called *colonias* or *colonias populares* in Mexican Spanish, continue
to work to obtain potable water, convenient bus service, and recognition
of legal status by the municipal authorities. Each Sunday, here and there
in the city, *tequios* (communal work parties) meet and with pick and
shovel undertake the process of building roads, pathways, and stairways
up mountainsides that seem impassable to the North American observer.
All in all, the colonias change so slowly that it may take a decade for an
outsider to notice. Mexico's economic boom of the late 1970s touched
and improved the lives of many, while the crisis of the 1980s struck
everyone. Yet in many respects the lives of ordinary people seem little
different from the way they were when we first arrived in the early 1970s.

These conditions and contrasts form the thrust of this book. Our
intent is to describe and understand the conditions of social inequality in
Oaxaca and Oaxacans' effort to adapt to them. We focus on social inequality because it has characterized the region's society for more than two
millennia and we believe that in one form or another it is one of the most
fundamental problems that its inhabitants confront daily. We define social
inequality straightforwardly as differential access to and possession of
material goods, that is, material hierarchical stratification. By this definition, increased inequality can occur at the same time that everyone is
materially improving; in that case, some may simply increase their possession of material goods at a faster rate than others. We argue that this has
been the recurring case in Oaxaca. At certain times in history, the city
and region have produced more goods in the absolute and everyone's
standard of living has increased, but some have become disproportion-
ately better off, capturing a higher proportion of the increased wealth.

By focusing on social inequality, we do not imply that material goods
form the sole basis for human existence or social analysis. Indeed, social,

cultural, political, and economic variables are important, too, both in themselves and in their relationship to inequality. Many of them accordingly enter into our analysis. We describe family relations, gender roles, political struggles and strikes, and the history of Oaxaca's relationship to the national and international economies, among other topics.

Our approach to social inequality has been strongly influenced by our experiences in Oaxaca. Both of us have developed strong emotional and personal ties to the city. We have seen our own godchildren grow from preschool toddlers to parents with their own offspring. We have seen families struggle to survive, fight and bicker, love each other, and generously and graciously extend hospitality and share their lives with us. Because of the nature of our academic careers, we have spent almost as much time in Oaxaca since 1971 as in any other city and have deep friendships with people of all classes in the urban area. We have lived and worked among the poorest of Oaxaca's poor and at other times have lived in middle-class areas, working and establishing friendships with members of the local bureaucratic elite.

These experiences have taught us a lot. We came to know intimately the struggles of Oaxacans to survive and improve their living conditions, and we came to appreciate and understand the impediments they confront. We shared many people's frustrations and failures to overcome material deprivation. We marveled at and admired their ability to continue the struggle in spite of the ravages of inflation or the more particular tragedies of unemployment or sickness and death. Above all, we developed a deep appreciation of the dignity and sincerity of the Oaxacans we know, a dignity and sincerity that has persisted through and risen above poverty and strife.

Our fieldwork led us to understand the profound meaning in an Oaxacan cliché, *uno tiene que aguantarse* (one has to adapt, to withstand). Inequality, poverty, or personal tragedy are not viewed by the Oaxacans we know as products of their own failures. Rather, they are conditions externally imposed, enduring and pervasive conditions that few are likely to escape. Some indeed may rise above their poverty to enjoy a life of less pain and struggle, and individuals must work hard if they are to succeed. But poverty itself is not an individual's responsibility, and social inequality is neither a superficial nor a passing phenomenon.

To accomplish our analysis of Oaxacan social inequality, we attempt to wed the two primary foci of urban anthropology, the broad macro perspective and the micro, in-depth investigation. The macro provides an anthropology *of* the city; the micro, an anthropology *in* the city. The approaches are, or at least should be, complementary in the study of a particular urban society such as Oaxaca. The macro approach furnishes the conditions, the forces influencing the micro, while the micro gives life and substance to the macro.[3]

The macro approach best captures the holistic view, the city as a critical unit with specific functions within a wider complex society. In urban anthropology's macro approach, the city and the people in it are not so much of intrinsic interest as they are a reflection of regional and global socioeconomic forces in complex societies, both historic and contemporary. The focus is on the wider context and the effects that context has on a particular urban system and the residents in it.[4]

The macro approach of urban anthropology, however, is not sufficiently developed to provide a specific focus on particular factors. In examining Oaxaca's linkages to its surrounding environment and the effects those linkages have on the city, we take our direction from political economy, which also asserts that a city's internal structure and events in local communities cannot be explained entirely by variables peculiar to the locality.[5] In exploring the precise nature of that impoverishment we also draw guidance from the numerous studies of urban Latin America that focus on political mobilization, urbanization and squatter settlements, and the informal economy.[6]

We employ the macro approach in the book's first half to establish the historical foundations and contemporary structure of Oaxaca's socioeconomic inequality. We conceive of the history and structure of socioeconomic inequality described in the book's first half as both creating and limiting the resources and forms of adaptation available to those residing in Oaxaca. They are what Anthony Leeds (1968) termed the "locality," the sum total of all forces with which a population contends.

We begin our macro analysis of Oaxaca in Chapter 2 by constructing the city's social history. Based on the extensive work by archaeologists and historians of Oaxaca, we discover two constant themes and two cycles that have conditioned Oaxaca's present social system:

Constant Themes

Urban centers in Oaxaca have endured for over two millennia.
Marked stratification has consistently characterized these societies.

Cycles

Recurringly, the urban centers have been engaged and disengaged with a broader system.

During periods of engagement, social inequality increases along with externally induced efforts (usually only partially successful) to reduce Oaxaca's political autonomy. With disengagement, social equality and political autonomy increase.

We conclude that on the eve of the contemporary era, the pattern and structure of socioeconomic inequality had changed little since the end of the colonial era.

The remainder of the book, based upon data we collected ourselves, examines the contemporary era, which we define as beginning about 1950. Chapter 3 explores the structure and differences among Oaxaca's distinct neighborhoods. The city's landscape most obviously and visibly reflects the city's historical and contemporary social inequality. In the contemporary era the central state, that is, the federal government, has assumed an increasingly important role in determining Oaxaca's social geography.

Chapter 4 examines the recent partial transformation of Oaxaca's socioeconomic structure of inequality. We survey Oaxaca's economy from three complementary perspectives: the kind of economic activities present, the conditions of work in those activities, and the results for individuals and households of that work. We conclude by discussing the implications of current conditions for Oaxaca's social class structure.

The second half of the book, beginning with Chapter 5, presents our description and analysis of Oaxacans' reactions and adaptations to the contemporary structure of inequality. Urban anthropology's micro approach focuses narrowly, examining an individual, a well-defined subpopulation, a set of networks, or a problem such as migration. Our task in the second half is to delineate the range of specific activities and the particular conditions that provoke Oaxacans' social responses to inequality.

In Chapter 5 we begin the micro approach by examining collective responses to Oaxaca's social inequalities. We find two distinct types of class-based activities: intraclass responses, particularly local elite efforts to resist the central state's incursions, and interclass conflict focusing on working conditions. We also address voluntary organizations, concentrating on a less sensational, but for Oaxaca's masses a more broadly important form, neighborhood political organizations. Throughout we emphasize four themes: (1) cycles of core–periphery conflict, first between the local elite and the central state, then between the masses and the central state; (2) cycles of regime tolerance and repression of challenges to the structure of inequality; (3) the trend toward the increasingly important role of the state in managing conflict and in attempting to address some of its causes; and (4) the constant pragmatic instrumentality of the participants in political activities, that is, how their activities take into account the structural realities of local inequality.[7] This awareness of structural realities includes, most importantly, assessing the real power of the central state and its tolerance of challenges.

We devote Chapter 6 to the role of the family and household in Oaxacans' adaptation to social inequality. We seek to establish that the household and family, not the individual, form the cornerstones of Oaxacan social life. We then examine the role of *compadrazgo* (godparenthood) in incorporating others into the family and household through a web of reciprocal rights and obligations. The final section analyzes the similarities and differences among households in each of Oaxaca's four income groups.

Chapter 7 presents four life histories, one from each of Oaxaca's four income groups. The life histories fill out the broader picture painted in the preceding chapters, describing each family's material conditions, migration history, employment, the dynamics of family and household structure, gender relations, and political involvement. They reveal the struggles and accomplishments of four families, the obstacles and opportunities each has faced, and their responses and efforts to adapt to Oaxaca's socioeconomic inequality.

In the concluding chapter we reexamine and reflect on the overall nature of Oaxaca's socioeconomic inequality and the relevance it has for understanding urban Latin America. We are modest in our theoretical intentions; while our descriptive sweep is broad, we do not attempt to create new theories or even test existing ones. Our thrust remains ethnographic, that is, descriptive and concrete, to convey to the reader the most important realities of life in the city of Oaxaca.

Methodology

This book is based on three types of data: previously published information; a 1977 random-sample survey of city households directed by Murphy, and another in 1987 codirected by Murphy, Earl W. Morris, and Mary Winter; and extensive participant observation and interviewing by both authors. The wealth of study of the area has allowed us to rely heavily on the primary work of others, including the Mexican government particularly and the innumerable social scientists who have studied in the Oaxaca region—beginning in 1929 when a road was cut to the top of Monte Albán and Alfonso Caso began work on that magnificent archaeological site. The famous anthropologists Bronislaw Malinowski and Julio de la Fuente went to Oaxaca in 1940 to study the indigenous marketing system. Over the past forty years John Paddock and the University of the Americas and the National Institute of Anthropology and History have served to integrate the activities of various institutions, including the Stanford Field School, the University of Texas at Austin, and the University of Michigan Museum. The investigators also collaborated with Mexico's National Institute for Anthropology and History (INAH), the School of Sociology at the University of Benito Juárez (UABJO), the Center for Advanced Studies in Social Anthropology (CIESAS) and the Office of

Popular Culture. Oaxaca has become one of the few places in the world where social scientists from all disciplines have worked and exchanged ideas on a wide range of historical and contemporary issues; our debts to these prior works are detailed in our bibliographic essay, Further Reading, following the notes.

Our ethnographic research in the city of Oaxaca began in 1971 with an anthropology summer field school, and one or both of us has returned every year since then. We have accumulated over sixty months of field time in the city. In that period of time are included eight-month stays for each of us in 1972, a thirteen-month field session in 1976–77, nine months in 1987 for Murphy and in 1990–91 for Stepick. Our roles during that time have ranged from field school student to research project director, dissertation fellow, consultant on urban research projects for the National Institute for Community Development (INDECO), directors of field schools from our own institutions, and continual visitors of friends and fictive kin *ahijados* (godchildren) and *compadres* (cogodparents). At least one of us witnessed and on occasions even participated in the political activities discussed in the book. We personally and deeply know all the individuals and families who provide illustrative examples and again witnessed and often participated in the recent experiences they describe.

The 1977 random sample survey was generated under the auspices of INDECO. This survey consisted of two phases. Initially, using information gathered from expert informants (government agents, local social scientists, and politicians who know the city) the research team developed a general picture of the city with respect to such variables as climate, population growth, spatial configuration of the city's growth, types of land tenure, patterns of land use, and so forth. On the basis of this information, architects on the research team developed a map of the social areas of the city taking into account land tenure, history of the colonias and presumed occupations and income levels of the people living in them. This information was confirmed by walking every street of the city, checking data with neighborhood residents, and refining the city's divisions into various areas. A stratified, random sample of these areas was drawn and a survey instrument was administered to nearly fifteen-hundred households. In 1987 a restudy of the city was funded by the National Science Foundation and codirected by Arthur D. Murphy, Earl W. Morris, and Mary Winter. These data provide the basis for the statistical work reported here.[8]

2

A Social History of
Oaxaca

Stunning landscapes, archaeological monuments, colonial architecture, and indigenous handicrafts characterize contemporary Oaxaca. The
various monuments left by prehispanic rulers and their Spanish con-
querors draw thousands of tourists to the area each year to see its impressive past and quaint present. The past and present are, however, more
than coincidentally related. Oaxaca Valley, where the contemporary city
lies, has been a regional center for more than two thousand years, a legacy
that has conditioned, and in some sense even created, contemporary
social and economic reality. Highly stratified inequality, cycles of economic expansion and contraction, and struggles between local and national interests—all of which are reflected in the landscape, monuments,
and handicrafts—have characterized Oaxaca for millennia. They are
rooted in the environment and the history of the region.

Marked stratification has characterized each of the societies pre-
dominating in the area over time, from Monte Albán during the prehispanic era, to Spanish colonialism, and modern integration with the
Mexican national system. We focus on one particular form of stratification, social inequality. As indicated in Chapter 1, we define social inequality straightforwardly as differential access to and possession of material goods, that is, material hierarchical stratification. By this definition,
increased relative inequality can occur at the same time that people are
obtaining more material goods. During some periods of Oaxaca's urban
history (when Oaxaca was most deeply engaged in the broader world
system, especially from 1750 to 1810), the production of goods increased
rapidly and the common standard of living appears to have improved. Yet,
at the same time, the standard of living of some people improved much
more rapidly than that of others, enabling some to acquire and consume
considerably more material goods. Thus, while absolute material well-
being improved for the vast majority, relative social inequality (by this

9

measure) still increased. During other periods (generally those of disengagement from the broader world system) the region's production of goods apparently decreased and the common standard of living declined. Simultaneously, relative inequality among those in Oaxaca appears to have declined. Thus, the vast majority were worse off during these periods in absolute terms, but perhaps better off in terms of relative social inequality, at least as measured by the production and consumption of material goods.

We use the accumulation and consumption of material goods as our measure of social inequality for two reasons. First, and most important, it exposes the important trends and cycles in Oaxaca summarized above. Second, the broad sweep of our analysis limits the range of comparative data so that the only feasible operational definition is one concerning material goods. Material remains are virtually all that remain of Oaxaca's prehispanic history, and for the five hundred years since the arrival of Europeans the best available documentation also refers to material goods. Material disparities are certainly not the only significant dimension of social inequality; other aspects of stratification, such as prestige, may be critically important and we wish that such data were available for the twenty-five hundred years of Oaxaca's urban history. Our concentration on material stratification nevertheless reveals critical conclusions in spite of its theoretical and empirical limitations.

In this chapter, we divide Oaxaca's history into three eras: the prehispanic, the colonial, and the period from Independence to the twentieth century. For each period, we describe its political economy, social geography, and the resulting social structure.

Prehispanic Settlement

The roots of Oaxaca's social inequality reach deeply into Oaxaca's past, into the origins of prehispanic civilization. Long before the arrival of the Europeans, the Zapotec people of Oaxaca leveled a mountaintop and built a civilization around the ceremonial center at Monte Albán. Although the city's size and its control over the surrounding countryside waxed and waned, its dominion lasted more than a thousand years. Even after its demise, another half-millennium of urban civilization passed in the valley before the arrival of Spanish civilization in the early sixteenth century.

Bordering the central Mexican highlands, the state of Oaxaca lacks any extensive plateau (see Map 2.1). Rather, it consists of rugged mountains with narrow valleys and an even narrower coastal plain. The major topographic feature of the state is its verticality. The western and southern portions of the state are dominated by the Sierra Madre Occidental and the Sierra Madre del Sur. These two ranges merge in the Mixteca Alta,

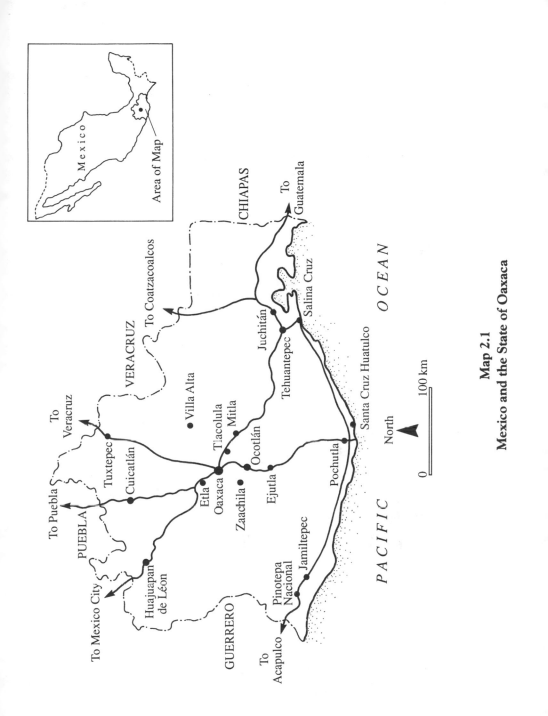

Map 2.1
Mexico and the State of Oaxaca

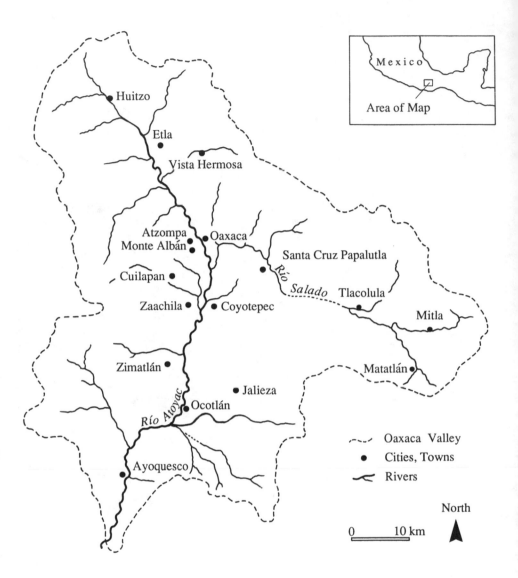

Map 2.2
The Valley of Oaxaca

Table 2.1
Oaxaca's Prehispanic Urban Population

	Major City*	Inequality
350–200 B.C.	17,000	High
200 B.C.–A.D. 300	10,200	Low
A.D. 300–500	16,500	High
A.D. 500–750	25,000	High
A.D. 750–1000	16,000	Low
A.D. 1000–1500	13,573	Low
A.D. 1500	4,500	

*Until A.D. 750, the major city population listed is for Monte Albán. The major city population listed for the A.D. 750–1000 period is Jalieza. For A.D. 1000–1500 it is Cuibán. The A.D. 1500 figure is for the Aztec garrison at what subsequently became the city of Oaxaca.

forming one of the most convoluted and rugged regions in a nation known for its mountains. The northern portion of the state is formed by the Sierra de Oaxaca, sometimes known as the Sierra de Juárez after the Indian president of Mexico who was born there (Rodrigo 1983).

Tucked between these three mountain ranges the Y-shaped valley of Oaxaca is the only large expanse of flat arable land in the entire southern highlands of Mexico (see Map 2.2). Frost is rare, making it possible for farmers in the irrigated southern reaches of the valley to plant three crops a year. These favorable conditions for milpa cultivation (maize, beans, and squash) have made agriculture the basis of Oaxaca's economy for more than three thousand years.

About 500 B.C., at the juncture of the three arms of the valley, the beginnings of the grand city of Monte Albán appeared, overlooking the area that came to be the contemporary city of Oaxaca. From its inception, local urban society underwent numerous cycles of expansion and contraction (Table 2.1). Settlements grew, declined, and expanded again. Monuments were built, enlarged and refined, and then abandoned. During some periods the quantity of material goods increased while quality simultaneously decreased. In tandem with these economic cycles, society was alternately more or less stratified. The population oscillated more or less inversely to social stratification in the valley. In short, as the population of the major urban center increased, socioeconomic equality decreased.

Measuring inequality is always problematic, but it is especially so for ancient times in which few or no written records exist. The rough measurements in Table 2.1 are borrowed from archaeologists who rely upon the distribution of material remains. When Monte Albán came into being, two types of inequality arose: among settlements and within single settlements. In comparing settlements, the measurements reflect differences in private and public structures, for example, the size of buildings and quality of materials used. Settlements such as Monte Albán had numerous large, impressive buildings presumably used for ceremonial purposes and are thus judged to be considerably more affluent than farming villages. Within settlements, excavations of living sites reveal that some individuals and households at Monte Albán and other urban sites consumed more nonlocally produced goods, ate more venison, the principal source of animal protein, and were more likely to have relatively well-made and nicely decorated pottery. Thus, Monte Albán, the major urban center for most of the pre-Columbian period, reveals vacillating levels of social inequality associated with its population size.

These differences among both communities and households were most developed when Monte Albán's population peaked, about A.D. 500–750 (see Table 2.1). During this period, material goods, particularly pottery, were much more concentrated in Monte Albán and other administrative sites, while the amount of pottery declined in farming communities. Moreover, numerous elaborate residences were constructed at Monte Albán and spectacular monumental architecture completely enclosed the main plaza. In general, when Monte Albán's population declined (as it did in the period following its founding, 200 B.C. to A.D. 300 and after A.D. 750), so did inequality, while the quality of locally produced goods improved. In the era after Monte Albán's founding, the better trade goods were distributed more equally, and highly decorated pottery reappeared. Following Monte Albán's collapse in A.D. 750, inequality among settlements also decreased as a more even distribution of ceramics shows. Thus, during the prehispanic era social inequality existed both between the emerging urban areas and the surrounding rural regions and among households within urban areas (Blanton et al. 1981).

Surviving indigenous documents also provide an indication of other dimensions of social inequality at the end of the prehispanic era. Inequality in indigenous society was clearly based upon heredity; at the top was an hereditary aristocracy headed by a cacique, or head ruler, who came from a separate royal lineage and wielded virtually absolute power. There was also a large class of landholders who exercised a type of private land ownership. Much of the land nevertheless was held and farmed communally by commoners, serfs, and slaves (Figure 2.1).

Unfortunately, these indigenous documents provide a glimpse only of the relatively brief moment before the Spanish conquest. We cannot use them to determine if the observed relationship between population and relative material social inequality is associated with other social structural changes over the two thousand years of prehispanic urban civilization in Oaxaca. We can conclude that on the eve of the Spanish conquest, the Oaxaca Valley had already gone through two thousand years of cycles of urban growth and decline and accompanying decreases

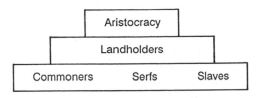

Figure 2.1
Oaxaca's Prehispanic Social Structure

and increases in relative material social inequality. Furthermore, there appears to be strong support for the relationship between urbanization and inequality: the larger the society's central city, the more unequal the society both within and among settlements.

The Colonial Era

Oaxaca's colonial era can be divided into three periods: a brief period, from approximately 1521 to 1575, of engagement with the broader colonial system; a long period, from approximately 1575 to 1750, of disengagement; and a final short, but intensive reengagement, from approximately 1750 to 1810. As in the prehispanic epoch, this cycle of engagement–disengagement–engagement was associated with increasing, decreasing, and again increasing social inequality. Throughout the entire colonial cycle, the fundamental substructure of the economy of the city and the surrounding region remained constant: peasant agriculture focused on a service and marketing city. Spanish *peninsulares* (that is, settlers born in Spain) assumed roles similar to that of the aristocracy in the prehispanic period, while criollos (Spaniards born in the New World) were most likely to be landholders. Mestizos assumed an intermediary position, and native Indians (with the significant exception of the former noble class) were subordinate to all others. While the hierarchy remained relatively constant throughout the three hundred years of the colonial era, the basis for social stratification gradually evolved from individual and family heredity to economics.

Brief Engagement and Extended Disengagement

When the Spaniards arrived in the valley in 1521, they easily conquered the territory. They soon discovered, however, that it was difficult to extract resources from Oaxaca for themselves and the Spanish crown. As a result, the city soon became a colonial backwater with a small population and little economic diversity. This section discusses the numerous Spanish attempts to reorganize the local economy as they had done in central Mexico. We then discuss the city's demographic evolution during this period and finally the evolution of its social structure.

Two competitions characterized Spanish economic endeavors. First, almost as soon as the conquest was over, came conflict between the Spaniards and the native indigenous population. Within months of con-quering central Mexico in 1521, Hernando Cortez sent Francisco de Orozco with thirty cavalry, eighty foot soldiers, and four thousand Indians to explore and conquer Oaxaca. The war of conquest in Oaxaca lasted one week and comparatively little blood was shed. The Zapotecs capitulated without a fight, while the Mixtecs[1] and Aztecs offered sparse resistance.[2] To induce the Indians to give up the fight, the Spaniards offered a peace agreement that included recognition of the rights of the caciques, a concession that later helped insulate Indians in Oaxaca from the extreme ravages of colonialism (cf. Chevalier 1963: 189, 193). Although the fighting ceased, indigenous groups in Oaxaca (and elsewhere) have con-tinued to resist Spanish control and abuses until the present day (Chance 1989).

The second conflict was between locally resident Spaniards and the Spanish authority located in central Mexico. Cortez wanted Oaxaca's agricultural wealth to be channeled to him and his family and not to other Spaniards; he actively but ineffectively discouraged others of his country-men from settling in the area and thus initiated the first contest in a continuing struggle between local Oaxacan and Mexico City elites. After Orozco had conquered the valley of Oaxaca and founded a Spanish settlement at Huaxyacac, Cortez ordered Orozco and his soldiers to aban-don the newly founded settlement and proceed south to the Pacific coast to establish a settlement there. The soldiers, however, preferred the temperate highland climate of Oaxaca to the torrid coast and returned at the first opportunity. They settled next to the Aztec garrison, naming their village Tepeaca. Oaxaca's geographic isolation deterred Cortez from enforcing his will, and by 1526 the settlement had a population of about fifty families and was officially designated a villa by the Crown.

Cortez, however, did not give up. In 1529, while he was in Spain, the Spanish king granted him control of much of Oaxaca's territory. Meanwhile, the colonial government in Mexico City, petitioned by the Spanish residents of Oaxaca appointed an alcalde mayor, the highest Spanish official in a local district for the city. They further redistributed some of Cortez's Oaxaca encomiendas.[3] This initiated a long series of court battles between Cortez and his descendants and the Spanish settlers of Oaxaca. Again, the city's geographic isolation granted de facto control to the local residents regardless of the court's decisions. The appointment of the alcalde mayor also initiated another persistent trend: apart from minor posts, political offices were almost always given to Spaniards from Mexico

City with the requisite political connections. After Independence in the early nineteenth century and through the twentieth century, the officials were no longer Spanish, but they still tended to have stronger ties to Mexico City than to Oaxaca.

For a brief period, Antequera de Oaxaca, as it was called during the colonial era, was a significant way station, the most important one south of Mexico City, both for the overland route from Mexico City to Guatemala and briefly for the overseas route from Mexico City to South America. Antequera de Oaxaca was the only significant city within an area of nearly one hundred thousand square kilometers (nearly forty-thousand square miles), and cacao and wine merchants frequently used it as their home base. Locally produced hides and wheat were shipped to Guatemala, Puebla, and Mexico City. Cotton cloth from the highland Oaxaca villages of Jamiltepec and Villa Alta was traded to Mexico City, Puebla, and as far away as the mines of Taxco, Guanajuato, and Zacatecas. Until the last quarter of the sixteenth century, the primary trade route to South America passed through Antequera de Oaxaca and on to the Oaxacan port of Santa Cruz Huatulco, allowing Oaxaca to supply wheat to the west coast shipping fleet (see Map 2.1).

The Santa Cruz de Huatulco[4] port and an associated shipyard were established by Cortez (Gerhard 1960); he was not, however, so lucky at shipping as he was at conquering. The first ship to leave Santa Cruz Huatulco in 1526 disappeared over the horizon never to return. A second vessel, sent to find the first, foundered, killing the captain and forcing the few survivors to travel around the world via India to reach Spain. Two years later Cortez turned his attention to sailing to Central America. His luck there was only marginally better. He managed to establish an incipient trading relationship, but the length of the trip and the lack of preservation techniques caused the cargos of wheat, cheese, port, and other products to spoil. The enterprise ended within two years. The port continued to function for some years longer and, because of its position between the port and Mexico City, Oaxaca's importance in New Spain was second only to the capital.

The struggles between Cortez and settling Spaniards, however, ensured that early Oaxaca did not prosper. Fifteen years after its founding in 1529 its population had declined from the original eighty to only thirty Spanish men. Oaxaca was far from unique: by 1540 almost all the original Spanish settlements in New Spain had declined as the conquistadors and settlers returned to Spain or the Antilles or continued on to Peru.

In the last quarter of the sixteenth century, Acapulco, closer to Mexico City than the Oaxacan port of Santa Cruz Huatulco, became Mexico's principal west coast port. The rise of Acapulco obliterated Oaxaca's long-distance trade and left the city in relative seclusion. Oaxaca was further eclipsed by Puebla, which remained a significant way station on the route from Mexico City to Veracruz, the port of embarkation for Spain.

Spanish attempts at manufacturing in the Oaxaca region were few and ill-fated. Industries, such as mining[5] and silk production,[6] flourished only briefly. Oaxaca's current wool and cotton weaving industry (discussed in Chapter 4), which began as part of the sixteenth-century silk industry, is all that remains of the first Spanish attempts to industrialize the valley.

Added to these economic difficulties were demographic calamities. Although the Spaniards abandoned Oaxaca soon after establishing it, the indigenous population in the surrounding countryside diminished swiftly. In the valley, as throughout New Spain, the Indians were struck down in overwhelming numbers by invisible agents: measles, smallpox, typhoid, chicken pox, and mumps. Because the New World had never experienced these before, indigenous populations had no immunity. In the sixteenth century epidemics swept through Oaxaca every fifteen years and, through the next two centuries of the colonial era, they were only slightly less frequent. In the seventeenth century Oaxaca had four serious back-to-back epidemics: in 1642, 1643, and 1648, and a final one from 1692 to 1695. The eighteenth century saw five epidemics.

On the eve of the conquest, the population of the valley numbered approximately three hundred fifty thousand Indians. By 1568 (forty-seven years after Spaniards first entered the valley) the population had declined to one hundred fifty thousand and by 1630, to a nadir of between forty and forty-five thousand, nearly a 90 percent drop in just over one hundred years.[7]

Perhaps the greatest impediment to Spanish economic success in Oaxaca was the indigenous society's ability to maintain control of its land. Unlike in central Mexico, the early Spaniards in Oaxaca controlled and reorganized the native society more indirectly than directly. At the end of the colonial period, the indigenous population in Oaxaca still retained control of about two-thirds of the valley's agricultural land, and only three or four villages had become satellites of Spanish haciendas, the large landed estates.[8] As a result, the primary function of the city of Oaxaca was to provide services and become a focal point for the local market of agricultural products, a function that Monte Albán had earlier served and which Oaxaca has continued for centuries.

Because of the Indians' firm control of the land surrounding the city, the Spaniards never succeeded in amassing huge landed estates in Oaxaca, as they did in most other parts of Mexico, nor could they establish a solid, hereditary landed elite. Instead, Spanish land tenure in the valley was unsteady and estates were seldom profitable. Individual families gained control of small farms and urban properties only to lose them, usually within a single generation. Their elite status sprung far more from their Spanish descent than from any economic basis.[9]

While individual Spanish economic activities stagnated, one institution prospered, the Catholic Church. The Church was the wealthiest colonial Oaxacan institution and had far more extensive landholdings than any other Spanish group in colonial Oaxaca. It established itself early in Oaxaca: during the conquest in 1521, a priest accompanied the soldiers to say mass for the Spaniards, and soon after various Franciscans followed to settle permanently. The Dominicans, who later became dominant in the area, arrived in 1528, and the bishopric of Oaxaca was established in 1535, with the city as its seat.

Throughout the colonial period, Church landholdings expanded. The Dominicans were the first order to make a concerted effort to expand their holdings in Oaxaca, a practice that quickly spread to all churchmen in the valley. They also initiated an ambitious building program, completing twelve religious establishments by the end of the sixteenth century. By 1792, monasteries and convents owned 870 houses in the city of Oaxaca, most of which they rented out. It is still almost impossible to walk more than two blocks in the colonial city without encountering a church building.

The social geography of early Oaxaca was much like that in other Spanish colonial cities, indeed, the same architect who had laid out the cities of Veracruz and Mexico City also developed its city plan. Even though the cathedral faces away from the central plaza, the design met the Spanish ideal of a central plaza surrounded by a grid pattern. Apparently, the Spanish settlers simply razed the Aztec garrison and built the new city on the same site and the former ceremonial and administrative center of Huaxyacac became what is now the hub of the city's downtown market. Cortez's local representatives soon built a house, which Cortez never visited, adjacent to what had been an Aztec temple. A small group of Spaniards built houses surrounding the central plaza, while the Indians were pushed to the edges of the Spanish settlement into the adjoining towns of San Martín Mexicapan, Santo Tomás Xochimilco, and Jalatlaco on the site of the original Spanish settlement of Tepeaca (Map 2.3). The first buildings were almost all of adobe with thatched roofs, though a few of the better-off residents built dwellings of stone, gathered from nearby quarries, in the style of Spanish houses—rectangular dwellings surrounding a central patio where fruit trees and other plants grew.

Apart from churches and a few government buildings, the only public projects undertaken in the colonial era were water-related. In the middle of the sixteenth century, Oaxacans constructed an embankment to control flooding of the Atoyac River. Two centuries later the river had two bridges over it. In the mid 1700s an aqueduct was completed from San

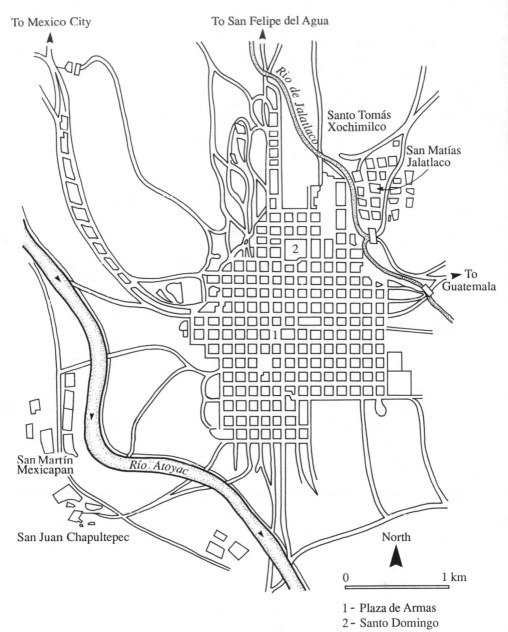

To Mexico City

To San Felipe del Agua

Río de Jalatlaco

Santo Tomás
Xochimilco

San Matías
Jalatlaco

To
Guatemala

San Martín
Mexicapan

Río Atoyac

San Juan Chapultepec

North

0   1 km

1 - Plaza de Armas
2 - Santo Domingo

Map 2.3
The Colonial City of Oaxaca

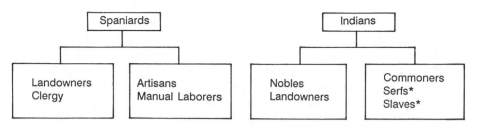

*These indicate social positions that existed in a previous epoch, but not in the present one. Serfs and slaves existed in the prehispanic epoch, but were eliminated in the early colonial period.

Figure 2.2
Early Colonial Oaxacan Social Structure

Felipe del Agua, a village approximately five kilometers (three miles) to the north. Infrastructure beyond this was discouraged by the frequency of massive earthquakes, which averaged about three per century and forced the complete rebuilding of most churches and other large buildings (Gay 1881a, 1881b).

The city's social structure was typical of Spanish colonial society (Figure 2.2). The social hierarchy was divided into two principal groups clearly and rigidly divided by ethnicity (Olivera and Romero 1973; and Seed and Rust 1983). White Spaniards ranked above a steadily increasing urban Indian population. The Spanish community made a second distinction between the small number of landholders and clergy, on the one hand, and the remaining Spaniards who worked as artisans or at other manual occupations on the other (McCan, Schwartz, and Grubessich 1979).

Three factors, however, irretrievably confounded the scheme. First was a distinction between the Spanish-born peninsulares and the criollos, born in the New World of pure Spanish descent. Peninsulares tended to dominate both politically and economically.

Second was an increase in the offspring of mixed descent (McCan and Schwartz 1983). Oaxaca had few Spanish women, but the Spaniards freely took Indian women, at first as concubines and later as wives. Their illegitimate offspring created social-classification problems. In the early years, the children of Spanish men and Indian women were classified according to the relationship between the parents. If they lived together openly, the children were likely to be identified as Spanish; otherwise, the children generally assumed the identity of Indians. With time, the numbers of mixed offspring were so great, they required separate classification. Non-Indians in seventeenth-century Antequera were classified by eight socioracial terms, and the terms for individuals of mixed descent were myriad. Throughout the colonial period, society gradually accepted mestizos and frequently granted them legal parity with whites—particularly as economic criteria replaced racial ones. While a person's racial classification depended mainly on what he or she could get away with, the nonwhites (with the exception of the surviving indigenous nobility), along with many criollos, clustered in the less prestigious manual occupations. Nonwhites could socially interact and, in many ways, become part of the elite, but they never attained elevated positions in the Church or government.

The third factor was the slow and unintentional transformation of the foundation of social differences from heredity to economics. By 1560, the Crown required each adult Indian male to pay eight silver reales annually. The only way to raise the money for the quotas was by selling goods outside the Indian economy in the Spanish colonial economy. The incorporation of Indians into the Spanish cash economy laid the groundwork for the eventual dissolution of racial divisions in society and the corresponding construction of economic class divisions.

Intensive Reengagement (1750–1810)

For one period during the colonial era, Oaxaca emerged from its economic isolation and became intimately linked to the broader colonial economy (Tabulse 1979). During this brief period economic activity flourished, the city's population expanded, social inequality increased, and external elites tried to wrest control from locally resident elites.

From the mid 1700s until the advent of Mexico's independence during the early 1800s, Oaxaca was perhaps Mexico's most important economic region. It was the center of cochineal production, a red dye made from crushed, dried insects that live on the nopal, or prickly pear, cactus. Until the advent of chemical dyes about 1850, cochineal was the strongest red dye in the world, about ten times stronger than the dye derived from the kermes insect of the Mediterranean region, and was avidly sought by northern Europe's burgeoning textile industry.

The first shipment of Oaxacan cochineal to Spain was made in 1526. European merchants soon took an active interest in its production and distribution. The powerful Fugger banking and commercial house placed agents in major European ports between 1550 and 1600 to monitor Spain's cochineal trade. The dye first arrived in Antwerp in 1552, in England in 1569, and in Amsterdam in 1589.

Cochineal did not assume paramount importance as an export, however, until the eighteenth-century development of a prosperous textile industry in Britain, Holland, France, and Spain. This increased demand, combined with the Bourbon reforms in administering the Spanish colonies and a monopoly on cochineal production granted to Oaxaca in 1745, thrust Oaxaca firmly into the world economy, transforming it

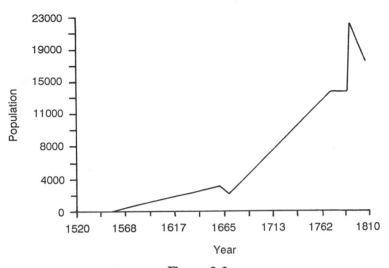

Figure 2.3
Oaxaca City's Colonial Era Population

from a small, backwater colonial city into a bustling commercial export center. The demand for cheap cotton goods among the Indians and urban poor throughout New Spain stimulated a rapid expansion of the clothing industry. By 1792 Oaxaca had more than five hundred cotton and silk looms. More than 40 percent of the employed non-Indian males worked in the commercial textile industry. The city grew from 6,000 inhabitants in 1700 to 18,558 in 1777. A smallpox epidemic in 1796 reduced the population to 17,599, but a 1797 census recorded a peak population of 19,062, making it the third-largest city in New Spain (Figure 2.3).

Cochineal also produced a wealthy elite (about 5 percent of the population) that consisted mainly of cochineal merchants (70 percent of whom were peninsulares), high government and clergy officials, and owners of large estates (Figure 2.4). Descriptions of the colonial era emphasize the wealth of the elite and their lavish lifestyles; undoubtedly, this extravagant affluence reflected increased social inequality. Below the elite, the middle stratum consisted of professional and skilled workers, constituted about 20 percent of the population, and contained both criollos and mestizos. The professions were particularly attractive for criollos and mestizos because they offered a potential avenue to power in a system dominated by Spanish peninsular merchants and government administrators.

The remainder was a large semiskilled and unskilled labor force composed mainly of mestizos and Indians with a few criollos, many of whom worked in one of the city's numerous textile factories. Indians continued to form a critical portion of Oaxaca's labor force, as masons,

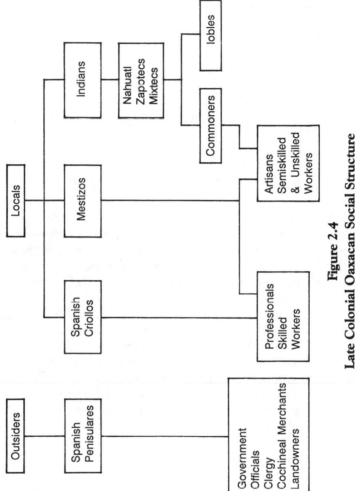

Figure 2.4
Late Colonial Oaxacan Social Structure

bakers, tailors, and shoemakers, most working in shops owned and managed by non-Indians. They also formed an important part of the city's craft guilds. But the division between Indian nobles (caciques) and the balance of the Indian population persisted. Like Indian nobles in central and northern Mexico (Gibson 1964), those of Oaxaca retained social and economic status above the common Indians throughout the colonial period. They spoke Spanish fluently, dressed in European clothes, and lived within the city itself.

Among urban Indians, ethnic identity appeared to decline, once independent neighborhoods were absorbed by the city. Jalatlaco, a Nahuatl-speaking community adjacent to the city, became mestizo (see Map 2.3). Nevertheless, the Spanish diligently attempted to seal off the Indians from the rest of the community, shunting them to the least desirable locations, such as the marshy area close to the Atoyac River (Chance 1975, 1976, 1978, and 1981; Chance and Taylor 1977, 1979).

Outside the city, as detailed by Hamnett (1971), rural Indians were impoverished as they were forced to cultivate cochineal (Salazár 1982), sell it below market price, and buy unneeded goods at above-market prices, leaving little land or time to plant and harvest food crops. The riches brought by cochineal gained the political attention of Spain, and led the central authorities to reinitiate efforts to reduce the political autonomy that had first emerged nearly three hundred years earlier in the battles between Cortez and the other Spanish settlers. A political appointee, the alcalde controlled the cochineal trade. He was always a peninsular, but he also resided in Oaxaca, far beyond the effective reach of the colonial bureaucracy. The post of alcalde mayor contained nearly limitless possibilities for corruption and self-enrichment. Potential alcalde mayores actually bid for the position. The alcalde mayor profited not only from the absolute control of cochineal trade, but also from his ability to force indigenous residents to trade goods for the cochineal (Young 1978). Spain attempted to reform the alcalde mayor by eliminating the office and replacing it with another that would be more closely tied to Spain. However, as had occurred with Cortez's disputes with the early Spanish settlers, the colonial government in Spain could not exercise forceful control, and the corruption and abuse continued until the cochineal trade declined with the onset of Mexico's War for Independence in 1810.

In sum, the nearly three-hundred-year colonial era expressed the continuation of trends identified in the two-thousand-year prehispanic epoch. The region experienced cycles of economic and population growth followed by decline. A brief period of engagement and prosperity developed from Oaxaca's intermediary role in trade between Mexico and South America, but the rise of Acapulco, the geographical isolation of Oaxaca, and demographic collapse all contributed to Oaxaca's general isolation from the Spanish colonial system from the latter part of the sixteenth century to the mid eighteenth century. Accordingly, overall economic production, especially within the city, was minimal and social inequality was reduced.

The cochineal period from the mid seventeenth century until the beginnings of the War for Independence in 1810 reversed these conditions, producing Oaxaca's greatest growth, both economically and demographically. This period saw as well its most pronounced social inequality, an inequality reflected in housing and material consumption as it had been in the prehispanic epoch. A primarily Spanish-born elite enjoyed lavish life-styles, while those of the other occupants apparently improved little (and the rural indigenous population suffered). Cochineal also engendered another contest between the local and external elites, reminiscent of the struggle between Cortez and the Spanish settlers of Oaxaca. The local elite was again aided by Oaxaca's geographical isolation; not only was Oaxaca across an immense ocean from Spain, but it also had formidable mountains shielding it from the colonial capital, Mexico City. Neither Spain nor Mexico City could control their political representatives, the alcaldes, who personally thrived through corruption and greed. Local political power (although vested in nonlocally born officials) prevailed.

While the city's primary economic function as a service center to a surrounding, primarily peasant agricultural region remained constant before, during, and after periods of integration, social relations of production shifted from head taxes and forced labor (which existed in both the prehispanic and early colonial period) to a thoroughly cash economy with wage labor. By the end of the colonial era, at least one important change had occurred: the basis of social stratification had gradually evolved from heredity to economics.

Independence to the Twentieth Century

While tremendous transformations convulsed the rest of Mexico throughout the nineteenth century (independence, the confiscation and distribution of Church property, the entry of foreign capital, and revolution), Oaxaca only vaguely reflected these changes (Pastor et al. 1979). The cochineal boom marked the last time that Oaxaca was of primary importance in Mexico; for a century and a half after the decline of cochineal, Oaxaca and the surrounding region alternated between violence and relative calm. Throughout, with a brief and partial exception in the late nineteenth century, Oaxaca remained economically isolated and socially stable. We divide this period into four parts: Independence to the Reform, a period of disengagement; the Porfiriato, when Oaxaca was engaged with the broader system; the Revolution that again severed

Oaxaca's outside links; and the "institutionalized" revolution, when Oaxaca was economically isolated and the central state established a political dominance characterized by indifference towards the region.

Independence through Reform, 1810–1875

Beginning in 1810, the War of Independence saw the opposition of elite interests, the royalist Spanish peninsulares, who wanted Mexico to maintain ties with Spain, and the Mexican-born criollo rebels seeking independence. The independence struggle and the years of instability that followed meant death, destruction, and economic disaster, with no social change for the majority of Oaxacans. Although the Spanish peninsular merchant and colonial government elite abandoned the city, eliminating the top layer from local society and definitionally reducing local relative inequality, the majority did not benefit.

When a militia brigade of fifteen hundred men left Oaxaca City in 1810 to fight the insurgents on the state's southern coast, Spanish capital fled in the opposite direction—to Mexico City and on to Europe. The small mining operations in Oaxaca's northern mountains were bought by Englishmen who promptly went bankrupt. A group of English merchants entered the cochineal market in 1817, causing some hope among local merchants. But the continued struggle between independence and loyalist forces stifled all external commerce in the state. Guatemala expanded its cochineal production in the 1820s and soon replaced Oaxaca as Europe's major supplier. Newly adopted national policies of free trade brought in cheaper foreign goods, and Oaxaca's textile industry virtually disappeared. Oaxaca's manufacturing production was reduced to small quantities of *aguardiente* (distilled alcohol), pulque (a fermented drink), and soap, all for local consumption. Weaving, pottery making, wood carving, cabinetmaking, and metalworking were all practiced in the city, but productivity was lower than in the eighteenth century. The primary economic function of the city returned to being a regional commerce and service center for the surrounding market-based peasant economy.

During this period, Oaxaca's elite paradoxically defended national conservative interests, while producing some of the nation's most distinguished liberals.[10] Soon after Oaxaca had proclaimed its state constitution in 1825, the first legislature established the Instituto de Ciencias y Artes (Institute of Sciences and Arts), which opened its doors in the city in 1827 (Benítez 1975; UABJO 1990). Chairs in the institute have been held by many who later became nationally prominent, including Oaxaca's native sons and Mexico's two most famous presidents, Benito Juárez and Porfirio Díaz. The institute was closely allied with the progressive segment of the clergy, and in the second half of the nineteenth century was a leading center of liberalism in the country. While locally the Church supported its establishment, the institute fostered the development of the men and ideas that were to dispossess it of its wealth and power.[11] Graduates of the institute filled the power vacuum in Oaxaca City created by the exodus of Spaniards.

Throughout the first half of the nineteenth century, liberals controlled the state, but were internally divided into bitterly antagonistic radical and moderate factions (Falcone 1977). Fighting between the liberal factions often filled the city's streets as control alternated between the radicals, who were mostly upwardly mobile mestizos, and the moderates, who came largely from the more established criollo families. Maintenance of the military became the state's primary expense. Taxes for the middle and upper classes were heavy, while mestizos and Indians were pressed into work gangs and armies for both sides.

Between 1848 and 1852, when Benito Juárez assumed the state governorship, political calm briefly returned to Oaxaca. His administration concentrated on transportation, building bridges throughout the state and improving the road north to Tehuacan, which continued on to Mexico City. With some Italian investment in the northern mountains, mining reappeared, and coffee was introduced in many of the areas where cochineal had formerly been cultivated. English investors also established a textile and a hat factory in a village close to Oaxaca City, Vista Hermosa, and another village, Atzompa, reemerged as a pottery center.

But following Juárez's governorship, the national political struggles between liberals and conservatives and the War of Reform again engulfed Oaxaca, continuing virtually without respite from 1853 until 1876.[12] Rape, plunder, assassination, murder of prisoners, and unchecked destruction of property characterized the actions of both sides in the conflict. Economic activity became impossible, and soon hunger became a more pervasive danger than the warring troops.

When Maximilian's French interventionist army arrived in Oaxaca in 1865, the forces were welcomed by many who hoped simply for an end to the constant fighting. To solicit support, the French army not only provided money to the city, but also ordered the distribution of meat among the city's poor and initiated public works projects. Nevertheless, instability soon returned as loyal Mexican liberals fought to expel the foreign invaders.

These political and economic conditions were also reflected in the city's social geography, its demography, and its infrastructure. In the nineteenth and the beginning of the twentieth century, the city's population again vacillated as had the valley's principal urban areas in both the prehispanic and colonial eras. During this period, however, population trends responded less to the natural disasters of disease and earthquakes and more to social and economic forces. In the wake of the War for Independence, as cochineal production declined and the city's looms

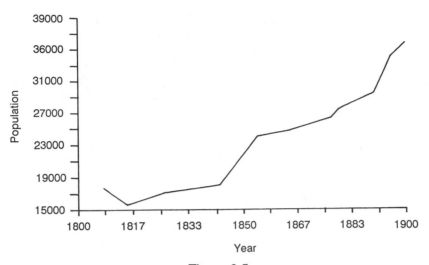

Figure 2.5
Oaxaca City's Nineteenth-Century Population

disappeared, the city's population declined by nearly 20 percent, to about sixteen thousand. Oaxaca's wealthiest residents had been Spaniards involved in cochineal trade who quickly abandoned the city, leaving only a few wealthy families, including an Englishman who became the local moneylender and financier.

The political turmoil of the early nineteenth century did not swell the city as the disease-induced demographic catastrophe had done in the early seventeenth century. Population grew only gradually throughout the nineteenth century and early twentieth century at a rate of slightly under 1 percent a year. The most significant jump occurred when Benito Juárez served as the state's governor. Political calm caused the city to grow. In spite of two large earthquakes, one in 1845 and another in 1854, the city grew by one-third in the twelve years from 1843 to 1855, an annual growth rate of 2.5 percent per year. The city also apparently fared better during the War of Reform than it had during the War for Independence. It managed to maintain the same population and even grew slightly.

Oaxaca's economic isolation and doldrums were reflected not only in the city's population and infrastructure, but in its social structure, in which the old elite and those immediately subordinate to it became the top of the social hierarchy. With the War for Independence, the top elite—the Spaniards associated with cochineal, the few large landholders, and high government and church officials—departed. There remained virtually no foreigners. Those who had been on the fringes of the elite—criollo and mestizo merchants, professionals and some landowners—found themselves at the top of the local social hierarchy without having increased their wealth at all. Of these, probably the most important were the professionals; most had origins in the elite, but a significant minority were upwardly mobile individuals of whom Benito Juárez, who came from a rural indigenous village, is an archetype. The lower levels of the social hierarchy were largely unaffected by the war. They were not impressed into military service, but they were taxed to support whatever side currently controlled the city.

An elite equivalent in this period to the peninsular Spaniards involved in cochineal never fully developed in Oaxaca. In many other parts of Mexico the confiscation and distribution of Church property during the Reform and the promotion of capitalism and foreign interests during the Porfiriato, the subsequent thirty-year dictatorship of Porfirio Díaz, produced an extraordinarily wealthy elite and correspondingly poor rural and urban masses. Oaxaca superficially seemed similar, but a closer examination reveals that it only dimly reflected these national trends.

In Oaxaca, as in the rest of Mexico, the Reform did divest the Church of its real estate wealth. The government took over the properties of the monasteries of Santo Domingo (G. Hernández 1988), Carmen Alto, San Francisco, San Augustín, La Merced, and the oratory of San Felipe. But relatively few Indian communities lost access to their property. As throughout the colonial era, Oaxaca's rural indigenous population successfully resisted incursions and domination by outside forces. In 1858 there were only eighteen haciendas in the central district of Oaxaca immediately surrounding Oaxaca City, and of these, seven had been Church owned (C. Berry 1981: 145).

In all, the reform disentailed 1,436 properties in the central district of Oaxaca, the majority of which belonged to the Church (B. Berry 1981: 156). But ownership of land following the Reform was as unstable as it had been during the colonial period. In 1867 almost half the former Church properties remained unsold. Depressed economic conditions and the state's isolation discouraged investment from the outside and little local capital was available. Moreover, the heavy taxes and forced contributions levied on real estate throughout the battle of the Reform further discouraged real estate investment. In contrast to central and northern Mexico, foreigners expressed little interest in Oaxaca. One Frenchman, two Spaniards, and two English speakers, all residents of the area, were the only foreigners to invest. Of 742 purchases, one-third of the new owners came from the middle and upper classes of professionals, merchants, and bureaucrats and one-third were individuals of unknown social origin. Most surprising, roughly one-third were Indians. This diversity contrasts dramatically with the concentration of land and wealth occasioned by the Reform in other parts of Mexico.[13]

In summary, for the first three-quarters of the nineteenth century, Oaxaca was embroiled in nearly constant turmoil. Isolated from the

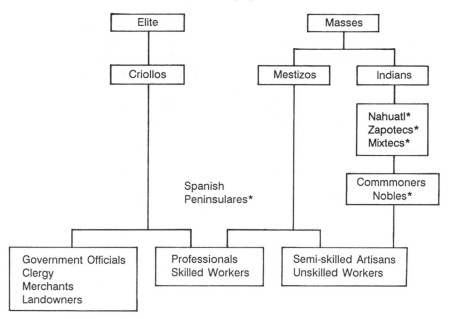

*These indicate social positions that existed in a previous epoch, but not in the present one.

Figure 2.6
Oaxaca's Post-Independence Social Structure

broader economic system in which it once had a preeminent position, only superficially transformed by the fundamental changes of the Reform, it had relatively little population growth and lost an entire elite class replaced by an unstable local upper class. With no elite possessing the necessary resources to dispossess significant rural populations, socioeconomic inequality was reduced as a result of the Reform.

The Porfiriato, 1876–1909

Sustained calm and renewed economic activity did not return to Oaxaca until 1876 when its native son, Porfirio Díaz, commenced thirty years of what has been called the most efficient despotism ever seen in the western hemisphere (Simpson 1966: 288). Díaz was a liberal who believed in progress and development. He intended to transform Mexico into a modern nation distinguished by its material growth and well-being. Because of the weaknesses of private institutions, he believed the state had to direct the transformation, maintaining order and imposing stability. If in this process the masses did not share the prosperity engendered by progress, so be it. Progress was measured by overall material growth, not by its distribution or the social well-being of the general population; it did not matter who had the material goods, only that they existed and were increasing. The Mexican lower classes provided the labor, foreigners the funds, and the government the peace to make it all possible. As some have said, Díaz held Mexico while the foreigner raped her.[14]

Díaz did have an impact on his native state. Infrastructure, foreign investment, and economic activity all increased. A rail link from Mexico City to Oaxaca City in 1892 encouraged foreign investment in agriculture and mining.[15] The railroad link to Mexico City also eased access for nonlocal goods into the area.[16] Prices of such goods were generally high, and they were mainly consumed by local and resident foreign elites. Cash crops increased, and haciendas expanded. The state began to export maize, beans, and beef to other parts of Mexico. Mining attracted both English and U.S. investment, as the state had more than one hundred mines and the city had a metal foundry ready to open just as the Revolution broke out. Foreign investment in breweries, cigarette manufacture, and factories producing glassware, soap, hats, shoes, and matches contributed to a minor resurgence of industry in the city. The American and English presence was sufficient to support an English-language newspaper published in Oaxaca during the first decade of the twentieth century.

Nevertheless, in comparison to central and northern Mexico, the Díaz regime had little effect in Oaxaca. Monterrey in northern Mexico, for example, benefited by a rail connection to the United States that laid the basis for its role as a regional industrial center.[17] The state of Morelos, on the other hand, became the focus of large-scale agricultural enterprises that displaced thousands of peasants. In contrast, Oaxacan indigenous communities still maintained control of most of their lands. Haciendas remained relatively few and none was bigger than five hundred hectares (about twelve hundred acres). Agriculture remained primarily subsistence and focused on the local indigenous market economy. Mining and industry, although significant, were still small in scale. Moreover, mining began to dwindle in 1907. An economic crisis hit in 1909 and the Revolution of 1910 brought mining activities to a complete halt.

The one significant exception to this generalization was the state's southern coastal and mountain areas, a region that had a smaller number of indigenous communities and poor communication with the capital city. Under the direction of this region's non-indigenous elite, commercial agriculture became increasingly important. Coffee was introduced into the southern mountains in 1885 when the government offered rebates to anyone who planted more than two thousand trees. It soon came to be the most important regional product.[18] It was not, however, shipped through the capital or controlled in any way by interests in the city. Rather, it left directly from the region's seaports or over primitive roads through the northern part of the state to either Mexico City or Veracruz on the Gulf coast. Throughout Díaz's tenure, and for a good part of the twentieth century, the coffee producers remained isolated from economic and political life in Oaxaca city. But, as we shall see in Chapter 5, by the mid twentieth century they would mount a challenge for control of the state government.

With the enforced calm of the Porfiriato the city began to grow again at about 2 percent a year, more than doubling during Díaz's nearly thirty-five-year reign (see Figure 2.5). Díaz had an even greater effect on the city's infrastructure. The last fifteen years of the century saw the beginnings of modern public education, the installation of electricity, and the construction of a theater, a slaughterhouse, and a branch of the national bank. The last decade of Díaz's rule, the first decade of the twentieth century, saw even further expansion of the city's public infrastructure: a market, a park, a new building for the Institute of Arts and Sciences, and a sewer system, the most concentrated growth in infrastructure in the more than two thousand years of Oaxacan urban civilization.

While all of these were public facilities, in effect they reflected the city's newly increased socioeconomic inequality. The city's majority did not have adequate resources to utilize these new facilities, but the foreign elite and locally prominent citizens (formerly the local elite and now slightly less than elite) all appreciated and benefited from these amenities. Their children attended the institute and they could deposit their money and obtain loans from the local bank. (The majority had to put their children to work, rather than send them to school, and they had no extra cash to deposit nor could they qualify for loans.) The houses of the elite got electric and sewer connections. (The majority lived in neighborhoods without electricity or sewerage; those who lived in the central city in reach of the new services, could not afford the costs of connection or service.) The servants in the elite's homes bought meat at the local market for their employers to eat at the midday meal after which the family might frequent a performance at the new theater. (The majority could afford meat only on special occasions and then they would butcher it themselves—they could never afford to attend the theater.) All these public facilities were to benefit the elite and were beyond the means of most Oaxacan urban residents, the semi- and unskilled middle and lower classes.

The Porfiriato was more successful at creating a new elite (a significant portion of whom were foreign entrepreneurs) than the Reform era had been. Most of the nearly one hundred working mines in the state were owned and operated by North Americans. English capital established two important textile plants in the state, one in the Oaxaca Valley and the other in the Sierra de Juarez. Moreover, many of the important commercial establishments were owned by foreigners: Spaniards, Frenchmen, North Americans, and Germans. Many had overlapping interests in the principal economic areas. One Englishman was both a large landowner and a mine owner. Another had mining and manufacturing interests

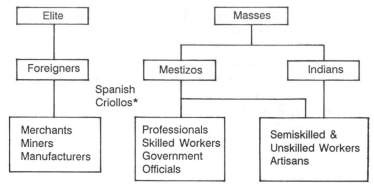

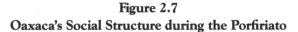

*This category no longer existed during the Porfiriato.

Figure 2.7
Oaxaca's Social Structure during the Porfiriato

while he also served as the English consul. The foreigners constituted an important part of the local elite, which consisted of these prosperous merchants, the mining owners (who maintained homes in the city, although their mines were in rural areas), the few large landowners, and owners of manufacturing plants. At the turn of the century, there were at most three hundred foreigners, less than 0.1 percent of the city's population.

The rise of the foreign elite displaced prominent Oaxacans from the position they had had one hundred years earlier during the cochineal era. The Oaxacans continued to be professionals, merchants, and, increasingly, bureaucrats. The lower classes similarly continued in the traditional skilled and unskilled trades (Figure 2.7).

The Revolution, 1910–1925

The Porfiriato did not create in Oaxaca a large mass of landless peasants, such as existed in Morelos—the home state of Emiliano Zapata, a revolutionary leader. Therefore, the Revolution's beginnings were almost invisible in its countryside. The federal government sent only a single infantry battalion to Oaxaca to assist in putting down the first reported revolutionary outburst in 1910. After arriving, the battalion found no rebels and returned to Mexico City a few days later.

The beginning of the revolution did convulse the local elite, however, as supporters of the Porfirio Díaz regime and those supporting the new contender, Francisco Madero, fought with each other much as the liberals and conservatives had done a century earlier. Minor military battles plagued the state virtually continuously from 1910 to 1925, with the same economic effects the War for Independence had had a century earlier. Foreign investors, primarily in mining and transport, left in 1910 and never returned. Trade and communication routes were controlled by various fighting factions, and goods were often confiscated. Hunger again stalked the land. The Oaxacan struggles differed from those in northern and central Mexico in one critical respect. There were no revolutionary leaders in Oaxaca, only old line Porfiristas and moderate liberals who valued proper legal procedure. No one championed land reform and radical social and economic restructuring. The Oaxaca elite was either truly conservative, advocating no change, or reformist, promoting a return to Benito Juárez's legal liberalism. The lack of revolutionary leaders who could become part of the national political class cost Oaxaca dearly for fifty years after the fighting stopped.

In 1915, early in the revolutionary movement of Venustiano Carranza, Oaxacan conservatives betrayed and murdered his brother, Jésus Carranza, and seceded from the nation. The Oaxaca Sovereignty Movement (Garner 1988), as it called itself, claimed that since the Revolution began in 1910, Oaxaca had remained at peace, that Oaxaca could carry out its own reforms without outside pressure, that it was the only state that respected law and order and the Constitution of 1857, that the bloodshed caused by the internecine battles among Zapata, Francisco Villa, and Carranza was abhorrent, that Carranza was a dictator who had plunged the country into war without the people's permission, and that henceforth all of these outsiders were ordered to stay out of the state (Waterbury 1975: 433).

Oaxaca was so unimportant that Carranza ignored the Sovereignty Movement's reputed secession for a few months. In early 1916, the Carranza forces rode into the state and quickly and soundly defeated the Oaxacans. Many of Oaxaca's elite, mainly in fear of and some in response to reprisals, moved from the capital of the state to the capital of the republic, Mexico City. The same insecurity forced rural upper class members to relocate within the city, occupying the recently vacated upper class positions in the local social hierarchy. The secessionists withdrew into the mountains from which they continued a guerrilla war until 1919.

This era spawned the first clear political activities by non-elite urban residents. At the turn of the century, socialists began organizing in the textile mills, the most important of which were located outside the city of Oaxaca. There is no record of the socialists having organized strikes or gaining any concessions from the mill owners. The Catholic Church, nevertheless, reacted strongly by organizing a Círculo Católico de Obreros (Catholic Workers Circle), which according to the Church had two thousand members, most of whom were artisans in the city. The Catholic Workers Circle was clearly an effort to deter and combat more radical workers' organizations. There is no evidence that it ever raised its voice on behalf of workers against their employers.

Effective worker organization in Oaxaca did not arrive until the Revolution. In the midst of struggle and a severely depressed economy, urban workers in Oaxaca fought for and obtained a few significant advances. The work week was officially reduced to six days in 1912, but it remained at six-and-a-half days for many (shop owners argued that even this half-day of rest would result in vice, vagrancy, and prostitution in the city). The first labor union was formed in 1916. Its members demonstrated against price rises on basic goods and against the owners of haciendas, factories, and shops who were paying workers in script not backed by the national government. But the demonstrations had little effect in the severely depressed economy.

The election of García Vigil as governor in 1920 resulted in a brief respite from open political struggle in the state, much like that in the Juárez governorship of 1848 to 1852. Although Oaxaca was not completely pacified, García Vigil attempted a number of reforms. Most important, he wrote the state constitution, which is still in force. He also redistributed land and attempted a tax reform. The land reform was small and successful, but the tax reform, the burden of which was to fall primarily on landholders, was rejected because of opposition from the northern caudillos (landed political leaders) who led the secessionist movement. (The conflict between the Oaxaca City–based elite and the rural elite reemerged thirty years later in 1950 in a similar fashion. See Chapter 5.) García Vigil's aggressive reforms earned him enemies within the state; disgusted by corruption in the central government, he withdrew recognition of it. Having cut off nearly all his political base, García Vigil was murdered in 1924, marking the end of this short period of calm and reform. Not until 1925, when the federal government itself consolidated power, did civilian authorities in Oaxaca assume full control.

As had occurred one hundred years before, the violence associated with the Revolution diminished the city's population from thirty-eight thousand in 1910 to some twenty-eight thousand in 1921 (see Figure 2.5). The first group to leave was the foreign elite. As the revolutionary period ended, foreigners had again abandoned Oaxaca, leaving it a smaller city. This time some of the infrastructural improvements of the Porfiriato remained: the central enclosed market, the theater, the park, the Institute of Sciences and Arts building, and the sewer system. All the industry, however, disappeared as quickly as had weaving following the demise of cochineal.[19]

The "Institutionalized" Revolution, 1926–1950

When García Vigil was murdered, Oaxaca had experienced nearly fifteen years of constant political turmoil and economic activity. This was not so lengthy as the sixty-five years of virtually continuous instability in the nineteenth century, but it was surely sufficient to disengage the region from the larger political and economic system of the nation. The city's economic activity again returned to the familiar, limited foundation as a commerce and service center to the surrounding agricultural communities. The consolidation of the federal government in the late 1920s reduced Oaxaca's political autonomy and its national importance.

The focal point of the local economy was the rotating market system that linked the city, various smaller marketing centers, and the rural hinterlands. Oaxaca hosted the largest of these weekly markets near a market built during the Porfiriato on a site that had served as an open-air market since the Spaniards razed the Aztec garrison. D. H. Lawrence describes this market as it existed in the mid 1920s in his essay "Market Day":

> The market is a huge roofed-in place. Most extraordinary is the noise that comes out, as you pass along the adjacent street. . . . To buy and to sell, but above all, to commingle. . . . The stalls go off in straight lines, to the right, brilliant vegetables, to the left, bread and sweet buns. Away at the one end, cheese, butter, eggs, chicken, turkeys, meat. At the other, the native-woven blankets and rebozos, skirts, shirts, handkerchiefs. Down the far-side, sandals and leather things (1982: 47–48).[20]

This vivid depiction remained fairly accurate until the market moved fifty years later (see Chapters 4 and 5). The market served primarily as a means of redistribution of locally produced items, most of which were produced outside the city in surrounding villages. A small number of externally produced goods moved through the market, primarily clothing materials such as thread, satins, and other notions.

Surrounding the market were large commercial establishments, owned primarily by Spanish immigrants,[21] which sold imported items almost exclusively: white sugar, lamps, musical instruments, hardware, medicinal drugs, and nonlocally produced clothing. Some goods were also exported from the region. The black pottery of Coyotepec traveled to the United States, while other pottery was shipped to Mexico City and Puebla. National and international demand for castor oil provided a significant income to the peasants who raised castor bean plants.

The small amount of industry that did exist in Oaxaca was devoted to the regional market. Clothing was produced by local tailors who imported textiles from other parts of the republic, sewed in their own homes, and sold to middlemen. Electricity and internal combustion allowed production of ice, carbonated water, and lemonade, and powered imported motor-driven mills for the grinding of corn and wheat.

While economics disengaged from the broader system, politics ceded control to the federal government. In the late 1920s, national political authorities finally consolidated control over the state through the establishment of a de facto one-party system. In 1929, President Plutarco Calles formed the Partido Revolucionario Institucional, the Institutionalized Revolutionary Party, generally known by its acronym, PRI. The PRI formally incorporates three major groups: the peasantry through the Confederación Nacional Campesina (National Peasant Confederation) (CNC); the workers, through the Confederación de Trabajadores Mejicanos (Confederation of Mexican Workers) (CTM); and the "popular sector," originally the middle classes and more recently the urban poor, through the Confederación Nacional de Organizaciones Populares (National Confederation of Popular Organizations) (CNOP).

The PRI has ruled Mexican politics ever since its founding. From its formation until the late 1980s, it had never lost a presidential, gubernatorial, or senatorial election, thus effectively controlling the federal and state governments. Moreover, because of Mexico's extreme centralization of government, it has indirectly controlled most local governments. In the city of Oaxaca, no one other than a PRI candidate has held political office since 1929. Even when an official is extraordinarily unpopular, the federal government replaces him with another PRI candidate.[22]

The most important effect of Oaxaca's quiescence through most of the Revolution and of its brief period of sovereignty was not immediately evident. Oaxaca's resistance to the Revolution isolated it from national political currents. When the Revolution became institutionalized through the PRI, Oaxaca could be and was easily and consistently ignored. The region could generate few revenues of its own and the central government consistently underfunded it (González Casanova [1965] 1970). Financial crises plagued both the city and the state for nearly fifty years, until political disruptions described in Chapter 5 forced massive state intervention. In the early years, the most Oaxaca received from the federal government was a road linking the city of Oaxaca with Monte Albán, which stimulated archaeological investigation in the valley. Even its representatives to the national House of Deputies were selected in Mexico City. The state governor, while a Oaxacan native, was virtually always a Mexico City resident before assuming the governorship.

Oaxaca did create some political alternatives. For example, independent workers' parties in Oaxaca were organized in the 1930s, and, over the protests of shop owners, an eight-hour work day was established. Meanwhile, in northern and central Mexico, which contained most of the nation's industry, the force of organized labor became increasingly important. But in Oaxaca, since industry was so small, the labor presence was largely symbolic.

With the decline of violence in the early 1920s, the city's population began to increase again, rising throughout the 1920s at a rate of about 2 percent per year (see Figure 2.5). A natural disaster, however, most dramatically affected the city's population. An enormous earthquake struck in 1931. As the city shook and trembled, walls not only cracked, but split and crumbled. Roofs toppled to the ground, and buildings collapsed. When the residents rose from the ruins, they saw a city in shambles—20 percent of its buildings destroyed and another 50 percent severely damaged. The earthquake also completely devastated the confidence of the city's resident economic elite. According to survivors, the prospects of more tremors prompted many of means to abandon the city for the national capital. Property was virtually worthless, and a handful of families accumulated the majority of urban landholdings, thus establishing an economic foundation that would last for at least fifty years.

Apart from a few immigrants from Republican Spain, Oaxaca had few foreigners in 1940. In the decades of the 1930s and 1940s the elite consisted primarily of local manufacturers and wholesale merchants, plus one or two foreigners, high government officials, and a few mine owners. Although a few pretenders to descendants of the colonial aristocracy were around, Malinowski and de la Fuente believed none was left at that time (1982). A neighboring rural village, Zaachila, had one Indian family who claimed to be a direct descendent of the prehispanic Indian aristocracy.

The consumption patterns of the elite, however, had changed in a hundred and fifty years. The improved infrastructure of the Porfiriato brought in from outside goods and services consumed primarily by the local elite. Electricity was only used by the elite, as was the opera house. Few outside the elite ate meat from the slaughterhouse. By the 1930s, the elite's style and standard of living reflected both Latin and North American influences. They had large houses with indoor plumbing and used many items imported from Mexico City and abroad. Many had cars, sewing machines, radios, and books produced abroad, although food and other domestic items, such as kitchenware, were primarily locally produced. Although the city's production was still largely isolated from the broader world, in terms of goods used and consumed by the elite, Oaxaca was being reintegrated into the broader world economy.

Just below the elite was an urban mestizo middle class of professionals and skilled workers very similar to that which existed at the end of the colonial era. In the 1930s it consisted of teachers, shopkeepers, wealthier artisans, and government and commercial employees. Better-off middle-class households could afford to take part in some elite activities. Some had electricity and attended the opera house occasionally. The better-off could afford to eat meat slaughtered in the city slaughterhouse and probably possessed some imported goods.

At the bottom of the social hierarchy remained the urban poor, the small artisans, wage laborers, and urban-based cultivators. Consumption for the lowest class had changed the least in one hundred fifty years. None had electricity, attended the opera house, or consumed much in the way of imported goods (other than satin ribbons). The only infrastructural improvement of the past century and a half readily available to them was the permanent market. They could also attend the movie houses. More important, they were free of the forced conscription common in the first three-quarters of the nineteenth century and for fifteen years during the Revolution. The primary difference, however, was the completion of the shift from hereditary to an economic class basis. By the time of the Revolution, the ethnic divisions that marked society below the elite throughout most of the colonial period had virtually disappeared. Upon arriving in the city, Indians were recognized as Mexicans or mestizos. There were no longer Indian quarters nor were Indian languages or dress much used by those who lived in the city.

In the one hundred fifty years between Independence and the beginning of the contemporary era at the mid twentieth century, Oaxaca had experienced two turns of the cycle of engagement and disengagement. Although the region never recovered the preeminent role it had in the cochineal era, the Porfiriato did deliver infrastructure, manufacturing, population growth, a foreign elite, and increased inequality reflected in public facilities that only a few could afford to patronize. The wake of the Revolution, however, washed out both the foreigners and the economic links to the broader national economy. Devastating earthquakes cracked the social foundations of the local elite, prodding many to seek security in Mexico City and demonstrating a fragility among the local elite similar to that observed during the colonial and nineteenth-century Reform periods. The social structure remained remarkably similar to that previous to the Porfiriato: at the top was a local merchant elite, primarily mestizo with a few Spaniards, that was slightly better off (at least compared to socioeconomic differences at other times in Oaxaca or in other parts of Mexico after the Revolution). The professionals and skilled workers below the elite were almost exclusively mestizo, had a relatively fragile economic base that depended on an indifferent central government and a relatively poor local population. The bulk of the population, as always, was semi- and unskilled. It had now lost its unique Indian ethnic identities completely and become a relatively undifferentiated urban working class (Figure 2.8).

Conclusions

Our brief review of more than two millennia of Oaxacan urban history reveals both constants and cycles. Constant have been the pres-

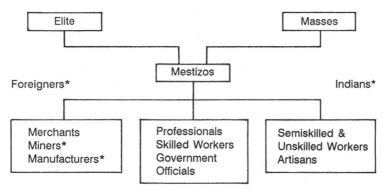

*These categories no longer exist.

Figure 2.8
Oaxaca's Postrevolutionary Social Structure

ence of urban sites and continuous marked stratification. Overlaying these have been cycles of engagement and disengagement with a broader system. During periods of engagement economic production and social inequality both have increased. During these periods, the central state usually strove to reduce the political autonomy of Oaxaca's local elite.

The city of Oaxaca, and before it Monte Albán (for purposes of this discussion we will treat them as singular, that is, the one dominant city in the region), has exhibited a remarkable constancy in its economic base and in social inequality. The extensive and fertile valley has produced surpluses that, combined with village craft specialization, have permitted the creation and maintenance of urban centers and elites. Those centers and elites have always fundamentally depended upon the surrounding agricultural areas, and with few exceptions the region has constituted a social and economic system unto itself, isolated from broader areas. The primary economic function of the urban center has been to provide a service and commerce center for the peasant villages. In the prehispanic era, the services of administration seemed to dominate over commerce, while the reverse has been true since the arrival of the Spaniards. But throughout, both functions have been essential to Oaxaca's urban areas.

While population has waxed and waned and the degree of stratification has changed over time, there has never been a period without marked social differences. During the prehispanic era stratification appears to have been related to the size of the major urban area and associated population density. The larger the major urban area and the more dense the population, the more marked were the inequalities. The cochineal and Porfiriato eras provided further apparent confirmation of the relationship, supporting this hypothesis for Mexico in general during the latter

half of the nineteenth century. In both cases increased economic activity
produced urban population growth and the foreign elite benefited significantly more than the rest of the population.

During both the prehispanic and early colonial periods, there appear
to have been at least three class levels determined largely by heredity. For
the prehispanic Indians, birth determined whether one was a noble or a
commoner. At the beginning of the colonial era, white Spaniards headed
the social system with all Indians subordinate to them. Within the Indian
population nobles maintained some privileges beyond that of commoners.
Differences among groups of Indians, for example, Zapotecs and Mixtecs,
were maintained through language and residential segregation in the city.
In short, in the early colonial period, ethnicity clearly and rigidly determined social position.

During the last two hundred fifty years of the colonial period, the
growth of a mestizo population and the incorporation of Indians into a
money economy gradually altered the basis of social inequality. Social
classification schemes became increasingly complex, although an individual's racial classification depended mainly on what he or she could get
away with. Society gradually accepted mestizos and frequently granted
them legal parity with whites. Meanwhile, differences among Indian
groups steadily eroded in the city. By the end of the colonial period the
class system was based almost solely on economic wealth rather than on
inherited traits. Moreover, while social stratification was marked, Spaniards in Oaxaca were never capable of accumulating great wealth and
establishing incontestable social differences between themselves and the
mestizo and Indian population.

After Independence and for the following one hundred fifty years,
social inequality remained basically unaltered. During the Porfiriato a very
small class of elite foreigners emerged, but they were dispatched with the
Revolution, as the peninsulares had been with the War for Independence.
The elite was an urban elite based on landholding, commercial interests, and the professions. Land shifted constantly among the urban elite
throughout the colonial era, the nineteenth century, and the first half of
the twentieth century. Low-level professionals and skilled artisans constituted the middle class and semiskilled and unskilled workers composed
the lower class. Indian ethnic identity within the city had disappeared.
Social inequality in Oaxaca at the beginning of the 1940s had more in
common with the end of its own colonial period than with the rest of
Mexico in the 1940s.

During the prehispanic era, Oaxaca apparently was never entirely
submissive to external authorities. The Aztecs established a trading post,
but had no military presence. The arrival of the Spaniards ostensibly
eliminated Oaxaca's political independence, drawing the region, at least
nominally, into a much larger system that stretched from the tip of South

America north through Mexico and east to Europe. Ultimate political decisions were now made far from Oaxaca—in Mexico City or even Spain. For much of the period, however, Oaxaca was a colonial backwater and its integration was more formal than real. Its geographic isolation and the ability of the indigenous population to resist Spanish exploitation deterred its incorporation into the larger colonial system. In the colonial and postcolonial periods, the central state endeavored to establish control over Oaxaca's locally resident elite. Cortez sought to dislocate the first Spanish settlers; nearly three hundred years later colonial authorities attempted to limit the power of the locally resident alcaldes who profited handsomely from the cochineal trade. Throughout the nineteenth century and the first part of the twentieth, central authorities sought to enlist Oaxaca into the national battles for state control.

The resident elites in Oaxaca repeatedly resisted control from Mexico and beyond. The first settlers ignored the wishes of Cortez to have them settle elsewhere and established the city itself. The colonial alcaldes disregarded Spain's reform mandates, and the local elite continued exploiting the local population for its own, rather than the Crown's, benefit. Throughout the nineteenth century and during the revolutionary struggle, while competing armies marched through the region, Oaxacans frequently formed battalions to maintain their independence from either side and to defend their isolation.

Oaxaca's isolation from national political currents proved harmful following the revolutionary period and the consolidation of the postrevolutionary government through the formation of the PRI. In this time, Oaxaca received few benefits from the central government. The highest political officials were more representative of Mexico City than Oaxaca, and the region was again left primarily to tend to its own affairs. Unlike most parts of Mexico in the 1940s, Oaxaca had no large landed class, no large numbers of dispossessed peasants, no revolutionary heroes, no beneficiaries of the Revolution, and no seeds for industrialization.

All these themes have reemerged since the mid twentieth century. In subsequent chapters, we detail the persistence of Oaxaca's monumental architecture, although now supplemented by numerous squatter settlements, the continuation of stratification based upon economics, the changes in stratification following Oaxaca's reintegration with the national and international systems, and continued efforts by local elites to resist control from Mexico City.

3

People and Places:
Oaxaca's Social Geography

Oaxaca's colonial wealth and historical isolation are reflected in its charming contemporary image. Original colonial buildings and replicas reconstructed in the wake of the 1931 earthquake offer a rustic allure complementing the cool, relaxing ambience. Picturesque Indians in colorful and traditional costumes from Oaxaca's rural regions float through the city's center murmuring among themselves in indigenous languages. While the city bustles with people going to and fro, the crowds seldom press and overwhelm. The plights of most third-world cities seem absent in Oaxaca. One can easily believe Oaxaca has been spared the disruptions and devastation of recent urban population growth, overcrowding, traffic, unfulfilled demands for services, and the growth of squatter settlements and shantytowns.

But appearances are seductively deceiving. The city has experienced significant population growth and the allied consequences of development. Oaxaca's beguiling patina may obscure these effects from the casual observer, but they are assuredly present. This chapter goes beyond the city's charming surface to describe Oaxaca's social geography—who lives in Oaxaca and the conditions they live in. We focus particularly on the alterations in Oaxaca's demography and physical environment since 1950. We begin with a discussion of and reflections on two sources of these changes, the city's recent population growth and its resultant demographic structure. In the following section, we describe the general living conditions in Oaxaca, specifically the low overall level of services the city offers and how most Oaxacans can meet no more than their minimal needs. The final section examines the structure of Oaxaca's neighborhoods, emphasizing differences in their history, structure, and services. More concretely, we find a partial cycle and two trends:

45

The Partial Cycle

Oaxaca's population declined early in this century, grew rapidly at midcentury, and then saw a decline in the growth rate, although population itself has continued to increase.

The Trends

1. In response to a housing crisis, squatter settlements mushroomed and gradually evolved into stable neighborhoods indistinguishable from settlements with legal origins.
2. The central state, in the form of the federal government, has assumed an increasingly important role in determining Oaxaca's social geography.

Population Structure

Beginning in the 1940s, the nation of Mexico exhibited two population trends. First, it had high overall population growth, among the highest in the world, averaging over 3 percent a year. The second trend was increased rural-to-urban migration that resulted in heightened urban growth rates. Mexico City has been Mexico's preeminent city since the Aztec era; for all of the twentieth century it has contained more than 50 percent of the entire nation's urban population and in the 1980s became the largest urban center in the world. Other cities in Mexico have also exhibited high urban growth rates since the 1940s, particularly Guadalajara and Monterrey, two industrial centers in central and northern Mexico, and the cities along the U.S.–Mexican border.

The population growth rates and total population of Oaxaca City are relatively small compared to these other Mexican cities. Nevertheless, Oaxaca has experienced growth since the 1940s sufficiently rapid to produce urban problems. Between 1940 and 1985, the city averaged just over 4 percent annual growth compared to 7 to 10 percent in Mexico's most rapidly growing cities (Figure 3.1). Even 4 percent, however, is an unprecedented rate for Oaxaca. The city, whose physical arrangement had changed only slightly since the demise of cochineal and the end of colonialism, has burgeoned on all sides in the past four decades, enveloping the formerly separate Indian agricultural communities on its periphery and moving up the hillsides toward Monte Albán.

Migrants to Oaxaca City are overwhelmingly rural Oaxacans (Rees

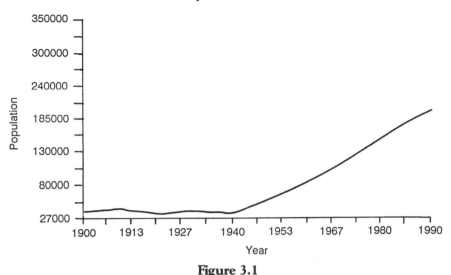

Figure 3.1
Oaxaca City's Contemporary Population Growth

et al. 1991) who have not previously lived in urban locations (Table 3.1). Nearly 70 percent of the migrants moved directly from their birthplace to the city. The largest proportion of the population comes from the valley's Zapotec regions, for which the city is the closest and most familiar urban center. For many individuals and households a move to the city does not represent a major break with their past. One could argue that the valley is one large metropolitan region centered on the city of Oaxaca. Buses make daily trips from most valley villages, which use the city as a market, educational, and cultural center. Students and workers may live with relatives in the city, but a pattern of daily bus commuting is becoming more and more common (Uzzell 1976). Each Friday and Saturday, the buses and trains in and out of the city are full of men, women, and children who have come to the city to market their goods and purchase the week's necessities (Waterbury 1970).

Apart from residents of the valley itself, migrants come from all of the district capitals in the state. Near-empty villages barely able to sustain their permanent populations spring to life on days devoted to patron saints, when relatives from the city return to participate in the festivities. These expensive festivals, often sponsored by migrants living in Oaxaca or Mexico City, include basketball competitions with teams from nearby villages, dances, and much social drinking. Relatives from the city will wax eloquent on the virtues of village life and how they are going to help improve it. A few hours later they pile into their cars or buses and return to the city to await next year's party.

Fewer than 10 percent of the city's residents come from areas outside

Table 3.1
Migrant and Native Household Heads in Oaxaca

	Migrants	Natives	Total
Percentage of population	66%	34%	100%
Birthplace in State of Oaxaca	87%	100%	91%
Age	40	39	39
Married	83%	82%	83%
Completed secondary school or more	16%	21%	18%
OCCUPATIONS			
Construction	18%	11%	16%
White-collar private-sector employee	18%	20%	17%
Government employee	23%	23%	23%
Held present job for over one year	70%	76%	72%
Work in the informal sector	50%	43%	47%
Monthly income (U.S. dollars)	$91	$110	$90
Number	977	493	1470

the state, and most (two-thirds) of these come from other Mexican urban centers. However, with each successive group of migrants there are relatively fewer who were born in rural areas and fewer whose last place of residence was rural. The 1970s witnessed the most significant increase in migrant households from urban areas outside the state, as the federal government expanded rapidly in Oaxaca, bringing with it technocrats and other bureaucrats.

Oaxaca is being transformed into a city with a young native urban-centered majority and an older generation of migrants. Oaxaca's in-migration peaked in the decade of the 1950s when the city grew by nearly 60 percent for the decade, close to 5 percent per year. Since then the rate of growth has declined to slightly under 50 percent for the decade of the 1960s and approximately the same for the 1970s, when it was just under 4.5 percent growth per year. In the 1980s, it has been approximately 6 percent per year. Only one-third of household heads are native to the city, but among the economically active population the percentage of native born rises to 45, and among the entire population it reaches 60 percent. Furthermore, over one-third of the households in the city have owned land for more than ten years, and 85 percent of the household heads have been in the city for ten or more years.

Oaxaca is an increasingly stable urban society, and family structures reflect this trend. Eighty-three percent of the adults are married, leaving small minorities as either widowed or single. As anyone who has lived in or visited Oaxaca can attest, children are an important part of life for all levels of Oaxacan society. Almost three-quarters of Oaxaca's households

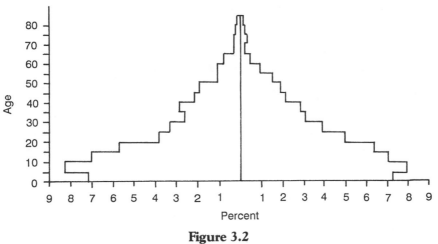

Figure 3.2
Oaxaca's Population Pyramid

have between three and seven members; the 1987 average of 5.6 (Murphy 1991) is above the Mexican average of five.

While 50 percent of the population is under seventeen, as the population pyramid demonstrates (Figure 3.2), there is some indication that household size in Oaxaca had begun to decrease by the mid 1970s. As discussed in Chapter 6, birth control is becoming increasingly accepted and the preschool population has begun to diminish relatively, a demographic transition that began in Mexico's three major cities (Mexico City, Monterrey, and Guadalajara) a decade earlier. Nevertheless, with most households still in their childbearing stage and one-half the city's population under the age of seventeen, the city's population will continue to grow for some time.

Through most of the first half of the twentieth century, Oaxaca was a quiet provincial town with urban services shared fairly equally by all segments of the population. The population growth that began in the 1940s, however, has strained all available urban services and created a situation in which class and residential location play an important part in determining one's well-being. In the remainder of this chapter we describe the nature of Oaxaca's urban services and how the city is segmented into various neighborhoods, each supporting a different standard of living for its inhabitants.

Living Conditions

Water and Sewage

When population grows rapidly, finding enough water, and especially finding enough clean water, can be an immense urban problem. The situation of Oaxaca epitomizes this challenge. Stories abound concerning Mexico's *turista* blues. Mexicans are rightly sensitive concerning the subject, and President Jimmy Carter created an international incident when he referred to it during an official heads of state gathering in Mexico. Some Mexican cities, such as Mexico City, heavily chlorinate their water, and water-borne intestinal infections are relatively rare. Nevertheless, water everywhere is different, and individuals can react severely to non-pathogenic organisms in different types of water. These reactions are as likely to occur for Mexicans in foreign countries as for foreigners in Mexico.

In most parts of Mexico, however, water-treatment facilities remain inadequate, and in Oaxaca population growth has overburdened its treatment plant. Over one-third of Oaxaca's households do not have water in their house or on their lot. Among those who do, the pipes may only deliver water a few hours each day or a few days each week. The municipal water system was designed in the late 1930s for a city of twenty-five thousand (Aceves 1944). In spite of a population nearly ten times beyond the system's capacity, the government has done little to expand or improve the water-treatment facilities. New sources of water have been tapped, but much of it is not treated before reaching residential households. The growing use of irrigation in the valley further complicates the city's water problems; the water table has fallen considerably since the 1970s and even the city's fanciest neighborhoods and ritziest hotels ration water during the dry season.

The supply of water is a future problem; the security of the present system is an immediate one. In the rainy season, water overflows the overburdened treatment facilities, mixing contaminated and treated water. And in both rainy and dry seasons, ancient, leaky pipes permit contaminants to enter the city's water supply, thoroughly polluting it.

In 1972 one of the authors took a sample of water from a squatter settlement to the city's health department for analysis. The director of the department indicated that all water in the city was clean and drinkable. There was no need, he claimed, to analyze it. After the director left for more important business, one of the laboratory technicians indicated her willingness to perform the analysis anyway. The following day, the lab technician discreetly handed him a slip of paper, which declared that the water was replete with E. coli bacteria and unfit for human consumption by U.S. standards.[1]

Middle-class Oaxacans—and visiting anthropologists—stay healthy by buying bottled water, available by delivery in gigantic forty-liter glass jugs, from one of two bottlers. In 1990 each bottle cost about 60 cents (U.S.). Ten years earlier, it cost half that. Most Oaxacans cannot afford bottled water and must make do with what is available. It is not surprising then that many in Oaxaca suffer from chronic intestinal infections. Mexico has one of the highest rates of amoebic infection in the world, and dysentery and its common consequence, dehydration, remain the main cause of death throughout Mexico, and in Oaxaca as well, for children from birth to six years of age.

Sewage disposal poses an even greater problem than water. Underground sewage pipes serve only the central city and the immediately adjacent middle-class areas, fewer than one-third of the city's households. Even for the area served by the system, Oaxaca has no sewage-treatment plant. The sewage collected is dumped directly into the Atoyac River completely untreated. In the dry season it remains there, collecting in large pools. In the rainy season it floats on to the villages downstream. The two-thirds of the households not connected to the system generally use an open latrine or, more likely, *aire libre*, that is, the open air somewhere behind the house.

Electricity

Electricity is far more widely available than either piped water or sewage. The city has had it since the end of the nineteenth century, but until recently service did not extend beyond the central city. All of the areas that have grown in the past forty years, and which now contain the majority of the population, had no electrical service until the 1960s. Even then, only the low-lying areas, not those stretching up the steep hillsides, were served. Not until the 1970s did communities on the hills overlooking Oaxaca receive electricity. Presently, virtually every area of the city has electric lines and over 70 percent of Oaxaca's households officially have electricity. Another 15 percent clandestinely tap into the system.[2]

While middle-class residents and those in the central city have had electricity for more than sixty years, it is a new service for most Oaxacans. Generally, they put their kerosene lanterns away on a shelf and installed a bare light bulb hanging from the ceiling. Many left the light bulb burning all night long. Soon they began staying up later. Women frequently were anxious to buy an electric blender, a wonderful improvement over a stone mortar and pestle for grinding chilis and tomatoes. Most already had battery radios, but they soon replaced them with electric ones. Not until the late 1970s could most Oaxacans afford a television set. Until the mid 1970s there was only one channel to watch, and it broadcast less than a full schedule. To this day, most inhabitants cannot afford a refrigerator and there is no perceived need for heaters or air conditioners.

Having electricity also forces repeated contact with the Mexican federal bureaucracy. When one of the authors was doing his dissertation field work, he lived in a government project. The house he rented was wired for electricity, but he had to arrange to have it connected. The federal electrical commission provided him with a meter, which he carried home and plugged into its slot on the outside of the house. He received no bill for more than two months. One evening upon returning home, he flicked the switch and no lights came on. After investigating with a flash light, he discovered that the whole meter had been removed. The follow-ing day he told one of his neighbors that the electric commission had apparently taken his meter for not paying for his service, even though he had never received a bill. His friend informed him that the electric commission does not send bills; one just goes downtown to the office every month or so and pays whatever they say you owe them. But, the friend added, it was easier not to mess with them anyway. All one had to do was jump the wires where the meter plugged in. Then, one could have electricity for free. The friend proceeded to get a couple of pieces of copper wire and demonstrate. Sure enough, it worked.

Nevertheless, the anthropologist felt a little guilty and after a couple of weeks arranged to have his meter reinstalled. The electric commission indicated that sometime in the next two or three weeks someone would come to reinstall the meter. In the meantime, the anthropologist jump wired the house after dark and disconnected the wires during the day in case the meter man showed up.

Health Care

Oaxaca City, with its medical school, is well supplied with doctors, hospitals, and clinics. Many of the doctors are trained at Mexico's finest medical schools and a significant proportion went on for postgraduate training in the United States or Europe. By U.S. standards, health care is also inexpensive. The most expensive specialist charges no more than $5.00 (U.S.) for an office visit and the entire cost of delivering a baby, including prenatal care and hospital expenses, is barely over $100 (U.S.). Several anthropologists, including Murphy, have had children delivered in Oaxaca clinics. Not one has had a serious problem and all saved a considerable amount of money.

Mexican health care delivery is largely socialized, at least in theory. One organization, the Instituto Mexicano de Seguro Social (IMSS), takes care of salaried employees in the private sector; another, salaried em-ployees in the government (ISSSTE); and, still another, petroleum workers. Essentially, these all serve workers with steady jobs in large firms, that is, workers in the formal sector (which we discuss in the following chapter). For the rest, 50 percent of Oaxaca's work force, there are the private practitioners, clinics, and one hospital provided by the national secre-tariat of health.

While health care costs in the private sector are low by U.S. standards, they remain far beyond the reach of the poor of Oaxaca (Graedon 1976; C. Stepick 1979). Five dollars per visit equals more than a day's wages for many—and that does not include the cost of medicines. Few find the clinics satisfactory alternatives either. They are usually staffed by recently trained personnel, reluctantly fulfilling their year-long social service duty, an obligation for all professionals in Mexico to be completed immediately after their schooling.

The squatter settlement in which one of the authors worked provides an example of the public health care provided to the poor. The community had a clinic for about two years in the 1970s. During that time it had two doctors. The first had grown up in the squatter settlement immediately adjacent. He was kind and sensitive to those who came for treatment. He was correspondingly well respected and had a good number of patients, most with intestinal disorders, colds, and the flu. One patient, Juana, however, had severe stomach pains, so painful that she could not climb the hill to her house. The doctor tried a few different medicines, but nothing seemed to provide permanent relief. Finally, an attack struck that doubled her over and would not cease. The doctor ran down the hill to the nearest telephone—about a quarter of a mile away—and called an ambulance, which immediately rushed over and took Juana to the city hospital where they operated and removed her gall bladder.

The anthropologist followed on his own. He found the admitting nurse and was informed of the problem and its treatment. He explained Juana's economic circumstances. Her husband was an unskilled laborer with a drinking problem. He worked only about half the time and would disappear for days, even weeks. Juana made tortillas by hand in order to survive during his absences. Her income from tortilla making was probably less than a dollar a day. The nurse referred the anthropologist to a social worker, who politely listened to the story. She indicated that Juana would have to pay only a nominal fee. A week later Juana was released in good health and paid the equivalent of $2.00 (U.S.) for all her care.

The community's experiences with the second doctor were less heartwarming. He came from a middle-class family and medicine was for him a way to make money. He had no interest in performing social service and even less interest in a community of poor squatters who could not afford private care. He showed up on less than half the days he was scheduled for. When he was present, he was distant, condescending, and even insulting. People came less and less often and he kept shorter hours. Soon the clinic was closed; as a result, the people had fewer health options.

Cristina, also discussed in Chapter 6, provides an example of private health care available to the very poor. As a widow of a government employee she qualified for free health care from IMSS and usually took advantage of it. But she was not entirely satisfied. One always had to wait a long time and the doctors were noticeably unfriendly. They delivered most babies by caesarean operation and tried to talk poor women into having tubal ligations. Cristina wanted neither a tubal ligation nor a caesarean delivery. Most important, though, the father of the child was not her deceased husband. Because of this, Cristina could not utilize IMSS for her pregnancy and delivery. Instead, she had to seek private-sector health care. Cristina was the cook for one of the authors and his wife during their first field visit in Oaxaca. One day when they went to eat they found her oldest boy, who was about twelve, struggling to prepare a meal. When asked where his mother was, he simply indicated that she had left for a while. "Where did she go?" "Oh, downtown." "When will she be back?" "Maybe in a little while. I'm not sure." "What did she go downtown for?" "I think it had something to do with her being pregnant." "Did she go to have the baby delivered?" "Yes, I think so."

After breakfast, the family went down to the midwife's house where Cristina had delivered her son the night before. She was lying on a wooden bench covered with newspapers stained with dried blood. The afterbirth had not been cleaned nor had Cristina been given anything to eat or drink. But the baby was delivered and at a price Cristina could afford, $4.00 (U.S.). Not all midwives offer such sickening care; some provide care superior to clinics and hospitals, but at a correspondingly higher cost.

Because of the high cost of private health care, many self-diagnose and self-treat their illnesses. Prescription drugs are universally available in Mexico without a prescription. Indeed, one simply has to describe one's symptoms to whomever is working at the pharmacy and they will provide you with something, usually some kind of antibiotic. Perhaps in response to this reality, Mexican law requires that all pharmacies have a medical doctor officially associated with them. In Oaxaca, virtually all the pharmacies are owned by doctors, many of whom claim that the pharmacies really make their living for them. Seldom though are they physically present in the pharmacy to provide sound consultation (Higgins 1975).

Transportation

Cristina made her late-night rush to the midwife using Oaxaca's most common form of transportation, feet. The city remains physically manageable, at least in an emergency, to all those except on the most distant edges. A circle six kilometers (less than four miles) in diameter would enclose 80 percent of the population, and one can walk almost anywhere in less than an hour. It is, of course, better to ride if one can. Buses serve most Oaxacans' transportation needs and make a lasting impression on every tourist. The bus is Oaxaca's greatest tourist bargain.

Both tourists and locals look forward to bus rides with anticipation of exhilaration and dread. During the morning, noon, and evening rush hours the buses overflow with passengers and packages, even though there is seldom more than a five-minute wait. Unless one lives at the end of the bus line, when the bus arrives at the stop it is inevitably already full. Men and women in their working best hang out the doors as the driver attempts to collect his fare from riders who do not dare release their grip on a railing. Those passengers outside are fortunate; inside the bus is an oven of closely packed, sweating bodies. While city buses are not supposed to allow animals on board, sometimes one can sneak a chicken or turkey on by hiding it in a wicker basket with a cloth over the top. Hot and tired children keep their mothers at wit's end; they are compelled to try to balance numerous bags of food on their heads while shushing their children. Amazingly, one almost never hears an argument. People politely move aside at each stop as other people push on and off. As the bus gets more crowded, passengers squeeze more tightly against the windows and lean farther out the doors, their eyes focusing in the distance to remove themselves from their immediate circumstances. Since Oaxaca remains geographically compact, such trips average about twenty minutes and seldom exceed thirty.

Nearly everyone would prefer the convenience and status of their own car, but few can afford one. Until the mid 1970s traffic jams were unknown in Oaxaca; one rarely saw more than two cars at any of the city's traffic lights. Traffic and cars were so unimportant that one well-educated Oaxacan born in the city did not even know what the traffic lights were for until a North American anthropologist told her.

Since the late 1970s, however, traffic has increased noticeably. The influx of government bureaucrats brought unprecedented numbers of automobiles onto Oaxaca's streets. Significant numbers of villagers in the more prosperous valley communities now own vehicles as well, which they frequently drive to the city on the network of paved roads expanded by the federal government in the late 1970s and early 1980s. Now even tranquil, old-fashioned Oaxaca has something resembling traffic jams. Most downtown streets are one-way and have only one lane. Frequently, traffic will be backed up to a depth of three and four vehicles, and on rare occasions even beyond the next block. Parking has also become a problem and some of the decaying colonial buildings have been demolished and turned into parking lots. Oaxacans often blame the traffic problems on tourists, but a recent (1990) count shows that even in the summer tourist season almost all vehicles are local. The thick, high colonial walls remain, muffling much of the traffic noise for the tourists in search of colonial Oaxaca.

Recreation and Other Amenities

When tourists visit cathedrals, museums, and archaeological ruins, they encounter few Oaxacans. When Oaxacans have free time, they prefer to enjoy—not culturally enrich—themselves at movie theaters, in bars, at sporting events, or visiting relatives. The elite may go to the country club, a friend's ranch for riding horses, or one of the city's good restaurants. Before Mexico's 1980s economic crisis, the elite also traveled extensively throughout Mexico and the United States.

Those below the elite are likely to find their recreation within the city, although the middle-income groups as well traveled within Mexico before the crisis. Even the poorest try to go to their home village for patron saint's day festivals. In the city, there are many more activities available than in a village. Oaxaca has six movie theaters, which are jam packed on weekends. They offer varied fare, about one-half Mexican and one-half foreign, the vast majority of which is from the United States. Violent films clearly predominate, but there are also Sunday morning matinees for children and infrequent art films, the prints of which usually appear to be the distributor's discards. One of the authors saw *2001: A Space Odyssey* in Oaxaca. It took ten minutes for him to realize that the film was not shot through a wire screen.

The authors' favorite movie theater no longer exists. It had to make way for progress. It was in the chapel of a sixteenth-century monastery that had gone through numerous transformations since its disentailment during the nineteenth-century Reform period. It had successively served as a city hall, storage and staging area for numerous armies, and as the municipal jail. Converting the chapel to a theater proved simple: long and wide, resembling many full cathedrals, it had a high arched ceiling with some faint, peeling frescoes. The choir's balcony had already collapsed under some previous usage. The huge wooden double doors were removed and replaced by thin metal and a ticket box. Rough-hewn wooden benches served as seats, and the projector was placed on a platform at the rear. The theater specialized in Tarzan films of the 1930s and 1940s and had a devoted, youthful clientele.

In the early 1970s the government-owned national hotel chain, El Presidente, gained control of the former convent and refurbished it, making it one of Oaxaca's premier, and certainly most picturesque, hotels.[3] Instead of serving as a movie house for Oaxaca's youth, the renovated chapel serves as art gallery and auditorium for banquets and classical music concerts.

The most popular family activities are private fiestas. The size and guest list of the fiesta depends upon the importance of the event. They usually mark transitions, particularly religious ones, in family members' life cycles: baptism, confirmation, saint's day celebrations, and marriage. Immediate family members may be the only guests, but more likely the extended family at least will attend. In the colonias populares, the fiestas are sometimes open to all neighbors. Live or recorded music plays all day, and everyone dances, eats food appropriate to the fiesta, drinks mescal, beer, and soft drinks, and visits.

While families attend fiestas, many amusements attract primarily men. In the late 1970s Oaxaca obtained a minor league professional soccer team, but it has not yet captured the city's imagination; games of *pelota mixteca*, descended from prehispanic ball games, draw crowds nearly as large.[4] There are also weekly professional wrestling bouts, as obviously phoney and choreographed, and with crowds as rabid, as anywhere in the world; boxing matches are more realistic and produce even more excited crowds. But outdrawing all other male activities are the bars and corner stores that sell beer and mescal. The bars cluster in the city center and are busiest on Saturday nights, the evening after the weekly market and the only evening when men do not have to go to work the following day.

Even more people, however, simply go for a walk. They may not frequent the museums, but they do appreciate and enjoy the loveliness of Oaxaca, its tranquil charm and beauty. The amenities available in Oaxaca are far different from those of cosmopolitan centers such as Mexico City. Oaxaca, however, still has more to offer than the villages, and it is much quieter, more relaxed, and more manageable than the nation's capital.

Housing and Neighborhoods

Oaxaca presents a housing paradox. The private real estate market barely exists—few houses or lots are ever advertised for sale. Yet, the city's housing stock has grown dramatically since the 1940s and few families perceive a housing shortage in Oaxaca. The growth of housing stock has been primarily through extralegal means, through squatter settlements, the colonias populares. In this section, we examine the growth of colonias populares and three other less significant, but still important, types of neighborhoods: government-sponsored housing, *pueblos conurbados*, and middle-class neighborhoods. Table 3.2 presents summary data for each neighborhood type and Map 3.1 indicates the geographical location of neighborhood types.

City Center

The central city remains distinct from the rest of Oaxaca. Despite the effects of earthquakes and impoverished economic conditions, Oaxaca's central city presents a charming image to the casual visitor and symbolizes the heart of the city for permanent residents. Colonial buildings offer a facade of rustic charm to the tourist, visiting dignitary, or upper-class Oaxacan who does not wish to look too closely at the com-

Table 3.2
Housing and Neighborhood Conditions

	City Center	Colonias Populares	Government-Sponsored	Pueblos Conurbados	Middle Class	Overall
Percentage of population	14.7	51.4	16.8	8.9	8.2	NA
SERVICES						
Electricity (%)	87.2	57.7	77.8	82.7	94.0	71.6
Water in home (%)	52.6	10.5	56.1	23.1	44.4	29.1
Sewage (%)	66.7	7.4	66.5	11.5	65.8	32.2
HOUSING CONDITIONS						
Shacks (%)	5.7	38.2	10.9	21.7	13.6	22.2
No. of rooms (mean)	3.0	1.9	3.1	2.6	2.7	2.6
Desire neighborhood changes (%)	11.5	49.0	41.0	21.2	13.6	36.6
Participate in community association (%)	8.0	4.1	14.0	8.7	8.4	8.2

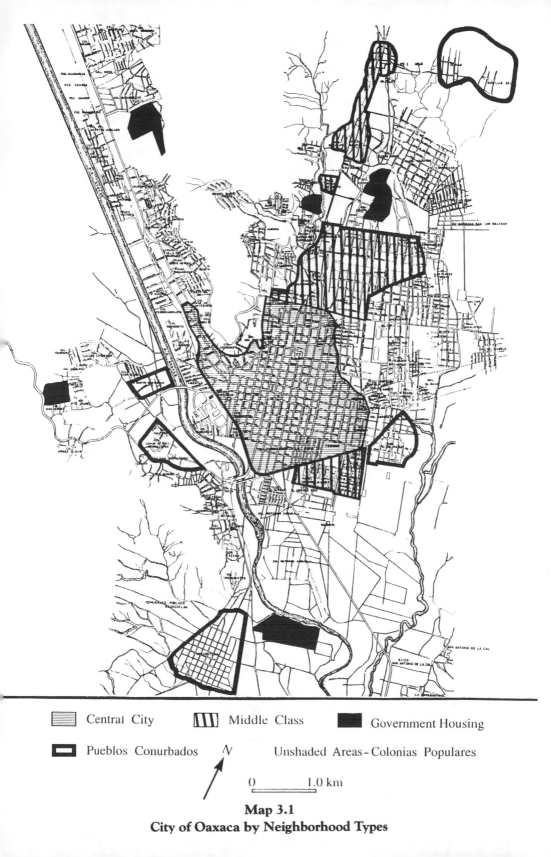

Map 3.1
City of Oaxaca by Neighborhood Types

Central City   Middle Class   Government Housing

Pueblos Conurbados   *N*   Unshaded Areas = Colonias Populares

0 _____ 1.0 km

bined effects of rapid population growth and slow economic development. The *zócalo*, (town square) remains the city's focal point, as it has since the city's founding. It is charming and tranquil, filled with towering shade trees and tropical plants surrounding a bandstand and flanked by the state government office, cathedral, and sidewalk cafés. Since the government banned motor traffic from the zócalo and the adjoining alameda, the area is filled with quiet and peace. At least three nights a week the bandstand provides music, performed either by a marimba band or by the state's military band, which plays excellent arrangements of marches and modern pop tunes.

Through the 1950s, Oaxaca maintained the weekend evening tradition of a parade around the zócalo in which chaperoned young ladies marched in one direction and young men in the opposite. Today tourists, natives, roving vendors, and shoeshine boys all commingle, heading in no particular direction. While there are beggars in Oaxaca, they are relatively few and infrequently disturb the idyllic setting. Indians from all Oaxaca's regions can be identified by their language group and village's distinctive dress: all white with a single gold cordon for Yalalag, intricate multicolored weaves for Trique, elaborate floral patterns set off by gold jewelry for Tehuantepec, and numerous others.

The architecture is colonial, although many buildings have been reconstructed in the wake of this century's earthquakes and a more recent self-conscious effort of preservation. The INAH is engaged in a constant struggle with developers and local architects to retain the city's architectural heritage. Their success in protecting the zócalo has made the center city the pride of Oaxaca. It is the locus of elaborate festivals, particularly at Easter and Christmas, when there are parades, sculptures of lights, fireworks, and many stands selling *buñuelos*, a special fried pastry dough served with thick cane syrup in small pottery bowls. When finished with the *buñuelo* one smashes the bowl in the street for good luck, leaving pottery shards that will surely confound future archaeologists.

Oaxaca is particularly noted for one Christmas custom: the *Noche de Rábanos*, (Night of the Radishes). Small booths are constructed in front of the government palace to display the works of competing radish carvers. Long Chinese-style and small, round red radishes are carved into incredible and delightful shapes, usually associated with Christmas, Christianity, and death, with which Mexicans have a peculiar fascination. Manger scenes feature figures of Mary, Jesus, Joseph, the Wise Men and their camels—all fashioned from radishes. And, inevitably, there will be long radish skeletons on crosses, with every rib meticulously sculpted.

On nights such as these the zócalo is packed with people from every segment of the city. The Christmas and Easter seasons consist of a constant series of such colorful and entertaining spectacles, giving the impression that Oaxacans are deeply religious. Most homes contain an altar and many women attend mass at least once a week. Moreover, everyday speech is filled with expressions such as "If God is willing" and "Go with God." We should not, however, overestimate the influence of the Church. Most men attend only on ceremonial occasions, such as baptisms, weddings, and funerals. Churches are packed for Christmas and Easter, yet the majority of Oaxacans remain in their homes even during these holidays. Urban neighborhoods do not sponsor saint's day festivities as villages do and they have no religious-based cargo system as most Oaxacan villages have.[5] The popular Christmas and Easter festivities are primarily secular events providing free entertainment for residents and a curious delight to tourists. Walking through the area, one can hear English, French, German, Zapotec, and several other Indian languages, as well as the distinctive Spanish of visitors from other parts of Mexico.

For all its charm, the zócalo is not solely a scene of tranquility and periodic exuberant celebration. It is the symbolic locus of Oaxaca's social tensions, the place where groups congregate to confront the government with their underlying discontent with the state's economy and social structure. Dramatic demonstrations in the center of the city have forced the resignation of three governors since 1947 (all of which we discuss in Chapter 5).

As one moves out from the zócalo, Oaxaca assumes the appearance of many other middle-sized Mexican cities, with modern buildings, indistinguishable from those in northern border towns, more and more evident. Yet, even here Oaxaca has more impressive colonial buildings than many other Latin American cities. Oaxaca's mineral and cochineal wealth underwrote lavish expenditures by the Church in the colonial period, and in spite of the anticlericalism of the post-Independence Reform era, Oaxaca still has more than 287 cathedrals, convents, seminaries, and chapels. Most were built of native stone by Indian labor in the sixteenth century. The most impressive and well known is the Santo Domingo basilica, begun by the Dominicans in 1575 (G. Hernández Díaz 1988:9) and called one of the world's great examples of baroque architecture (Mullen 1975:27). The choir section over the main entrance contains a huge stained-glass window about seven meters (twenty-two feet) in diameter; when the afternoon sun catches the window, it brilliantly illuminates the gold leaf cupola ceiling above the choir. The massive main altar and one of the side altars are resplendent with gold leaf that dazzles and reminds the onlooker of Oaxaca's colonial wealth.

The typical colonial secular building, of which numerous examples still remain, is one-story high with meter-thick walls of either stone or adobe covered with plaster and fronting the sidewalk. Windows are decorated and protected by ironwork, while the main entrance is a heavy wooden door wide enough for a carriage, but with a smaller cutaway door for people, to pass through. The entrance opens onto an inner courtyard, which may retain a fountain that in an earlier period served as the water source for the household. The rooms of the house open onto the court-yard, which connects with another courtyard or two further away from the street. The thick walls absorb much of the heat and street noise, leaving the interior of the house cool and quiet. It is over the future of these secular buildings that INAH and the local elite are battling. After the earthquakes early in this century, a few families bought large numbers of destroyed or abandoned buildings. The strict enforcement of the federal law governing building in areas declared colonial zones is seen by these families as a hindrance to their attempts to convert sections of the center city to commercial use. One of the major complaints against INAH is the time it takes for permits to be processed. In one case an investor waited for over a year for a decision concerning the conversion of an abandoned building near the center market. In the final two months of negotiation the contractor who was to make the conversion visited INAH offices two to three times per week before going directly to the governor's office for assistance. As the investor explained to one of the authors, this kind of action slows development in the city because investors must tie their funds up for indefinite periods of time. During the course of these negotia-tions, this investor could have earned a return of over 60 percent through simple bank investments. Rooms fronting the street in traditional build-ings are converted into retail establishments serving either tourists or residents, while inner rooms become restaurants, hotels, offices, or apart-ments. In some areas owners who do not wish to invest in the redevelop-ment of their property have converted colonial dwellings into crowded apartments known as *vecindades*, in a move reminiscent of the activities of slum landlords north of the border.

However, despite the cries of harassment leveled against INAH by the commercial and landowning elites of the city, a growing number of business establishments are to be found in the city center. Situated within the eight blocks surrounding the zócalo are an average of 9.38 commercial establishments per block, and this figure drops by only three if we expand the area to include the forty-seven blocks surrounding the central square (Nolasco 1981).

In recent years some commercial construction has occurred outside the center city: a new government office building has been opened on the eastern side of town; a new bus station and market are situated on the south; and two new shopping centers have been built to the north. This dispersal can be attributed more to Oaxaca's growth in the last decade than to INAH's policies, since the size of some of the new construction, notably the market and bus station, would likely have precluded their being located downtown in any case.

The heavy concentration of commercial activity in the city's center obscures from the casual observer its residential role. To Oaxacans, the city center is one of the most desirable places to live. It is close to nearly everything, and, to a greater extent than in other sections of the city, it has all the services and facilities of a modern city—water and sewage, garbage pick-up, paved streets and sidewalks, convenient public transportation, nearby shops and markets, and police protection. It also has the city's main public markets, including the large weekly peasant market.

The city center is also the residential bargain of Oaxaca. Most of the residents in this area are able to live in well-constructed houses. While those houses are not so large as those in the upper-income sections of the city, they are more than Oaxacans can expect to have in middle-income neighborhoods on the city's fringe. Center-city residents are not, as in many North American cities, trapped in a decaying urban core; instead, Oaxaca's center contains many of its middle-class citizens and those right below, what we label the aspiring class (see Chapter 4, "Income Groupings"). Eleven percent of the center-city residents are either professionals or the owners of one of the commercial establishments in the area, and another 46 percent of the household heads are employed in these same commercial establishments. Incomes for households here are equal to the median income of households in the moderate-income colonias of the city: the equivalent of $150.00 (U.S.) per month.

The settled, economically secure nature of these households is reflected in their demographics. Household heads in the center city are not young recent migrants looking for work, who would be found in the cores of other Latin American cities. Rather, household heads are older than in other sections of the city (their mean age is 43), and their households are smaller (the mean size is 4.7 versus 5.2 members). They have owned their homes longer than people in any other part of the city, and they are better educated than the average urban Oaxacan.

Perhaps because of their location in the center, their manageable family size, their stable income, and their relatively good housing, the residents of the center city are the most content in Oaxaca. Nearly two-thirds see no need to improve the building in which they live. In short, they are firmly established residents of an urban center who lead prosaic and comfortable lives largely out of sight of tourists and the other residents of the city.

Beyond the Center City

As one moves away from the city center, architecture becomes increasingly diverse. Within any particular neighborhood there is an obvious and extensive class mixture. Large expensive houses staffed with gardeners and maids may adjoin houses constructed of tar paper and bamboo. Zoning is almost nonexistent, and the landscape strikes North American observers as chaotic and confusing.

As the city's population has grown, it has spread out from its original boundaries and absorbed formerly distinct barrios, villages, squatter settlements, private subdivisions, and public housing projects (Map 3.2). As in many urban areas of developing countries, population expansion and economic growth have made urban land an effective hedge against inflation. In some areas the inflation in urban real estate has been astronomical. In Mexico City, for example, urban land values increased over 6,000 percent between 1960 and 1980 (Vélez-Ibañez 1983). In Oaxaca it is difficult to measure the change, since so little land is for sale as residential lots. As owners wait for commercial developers or the government to offer them an acceptable price, tracts sit empty with high walls placed around them to keep out squatters.

Another aspect of the lack of a land market is that a number of villages, either now incorporated into the city or lying at the outskirts of the city, control *ejidos* (communal lands) that cannot be sold. That a house is built on ejido land, however, does not mean it is not marketable. Ownership of buildings and other improvements is distinguished from land ownership. Individuals are able to pass their homes along to their children or to sell the house to a third party if they have the approval of the village council or ejido commission. Thus, for village and villager alike the existence of communal holdings is no impediment to the acquisition of land upon which to build a home. Urban housing on communal village lands is only one example of the irregular or squatter settlements generally referred to in Oaxaca as colonias populares.[6]

Colonias Populares

In the 1950s, a land shortage was emerging in the city, and squatter settlements had just begun (Yescas Peralta 1958). In the 1960s, with the increasing pressure on land caused by the city's growth and the absence of a land market accessible to ordinary people, land invasions became a more common occurrence (Butterworth 1973). Chapter 5 provides a detailed description of a land invasion and the formation of two colonias populares. Here we focus on a more general overview of colonias populares and the living conditions within them.

By the mid 1970s, over 60 percent of the metropolitan area of Oaxaca was covered with housing that had its origin in some type of irregular land occupancy. Most such occupations occurred on land owned by the state or land for which there existed a contested claim. Landowners with shaky or false title to property may attempt to head off invasion by selling plots to poor families who do not have the resources to determine the legal status of the land being offered. Low prices and easy terms are offered because the seller, having little capital to invest and possessing

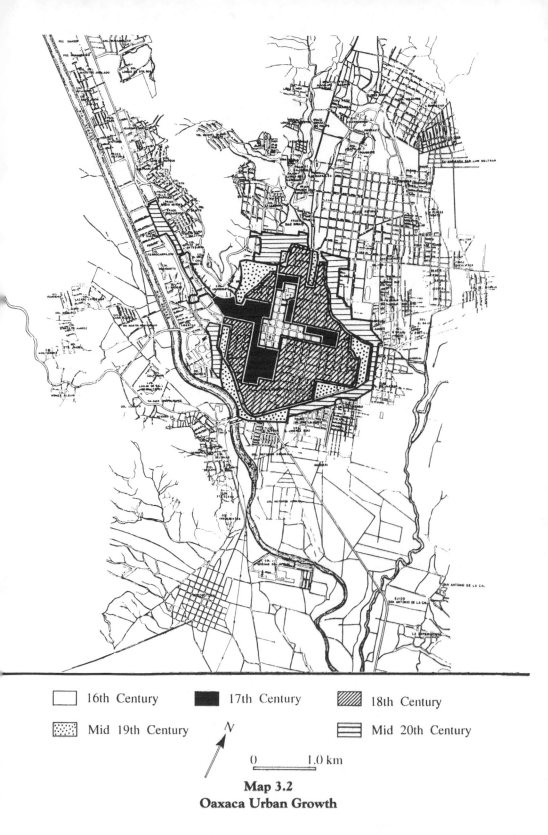

Legend:

- 16th Century
- 17th Century
- 18th Century
- Mid 19th Century
- Mid 20th Century

N

0   1.0 km

Map 3.2
Oaxaca Urban Growth

only dubious title to the land, usually provides no services or infrastructure such as water or streets.

Some state governors have proven prone to evict squatters, but most have been lenient. By not evicting irregular occupants, the state, in effect, provides an indirect housing subsidy to people who would otherwise have no place to live. By giving them land of little value, the government allows squatters to fulfill a basic need for housing and at the same time demonstrates the benevolence of the existing political system.

While much attention is paid in the press to the more dramatic, larger-scale invasions (one of which is covered in detail in Chapter 5), in many areas of Oaxaca takeovers by squatters have occurred through slow accretion. Members of one or a few families unobtrusively occupy a piece of land in the hope that they will not be removed by the owners. Once a lot is occupied, the legal system may eventually legitimize their holding. Beside those who obtain title by buying land and receiving a registered title in Oaxaca, there are those who have legal squatters' rights. In most cases, Mexican law confers possession rights on people who have occupied a plot for ten or more years. [7] In Oaxaca, this constitutes approximately 15 percent of the households. Another 26 percent of them occupy land to which they do not hold any recognizable title, but of which they consider themselves the owners and which they effectively control. The occupiers would like to and do proceed as if they have full rights, excepting only the formally stamped documents.

Some government officials, however, maintain the same ideology nineteenth-century liberals used over one hundred years ago to disentail Oaxaca's church property. They see the rights of urban squatters as irregular and thus an impediment to the market for land and real estate development. With the hope of promoting further private urban housing development, the National Commission for the Regularization of Land Tenure (CORETT) was established. For a fee, CORETT confers legal title on a lot's current residents. Most squatters, however, see few if any problems with the current state of affairs. They claim, quite justifiably, that after ten years they will have de jure legal rights without paying and that presently they have de facto rights. Moreover, as soon as they do register, they will become vulnerable to government taxing, which they now avoid since the government cannot tax someone who is not the legal owner of the property. The relationship between squatters and CORETT is not always peaceful; at the time of the political disturbances mentioned in Chapter 5, several CORETT survey teams were the victims of gunfire.

Having effective ownership of a housing site is, of course, not itself sufficient—some sort of house must be on that site. Vacant land is worthless land for most Oaxacans, excepting some of the elite who engage in urban land speculation. When land is acquired, whether legally, extra-legally, or illegally, housing springs up almost immediately. The struggle to improve it then begins.

Families usually build with their own labor (the elite being the exception) at the pace money and effort allow. Progress for many is slow, disrupted by economic difficulties and uncertainty. Like land acquisition and services, the building of houses is accomplished largely outside a regular market for residential construction. Materials are purchased by households (and in rare instances donated or subsidized by the government) as funds become available. Most home and site improvements are carried out by the members of the family, with some hired labor for the completion of specialized tasks, such as plumbing or electrical work.

Frequently, households begin their stay in a colonia popular in a single room made of bamboo or wattle and daub. With time they collect the materials for the construction of a wall or perhaps an entire room. Once the materials are in hand, the family will begin the addition, moving into the new structure as soon as some semblance of a roof is in place. In about fifteen years, if the head of the household has held a steady job and medical or other emergencies have not drained the family's savings, the family will be living in a house constructed of permanent materials (such as concrete blocks) with two or three bedrooms and an attached kitchen. If the family has been fortunate enough to win the lottery (an extraordinarily unlikely event) or be admitted into one of the government housing programs (more likely for those with steady work in a large firm), the time of construction may be cut in half.

It is possible in the colonias populares to discern a fine gradation in the standard of living from neighborhood to neighborhood, beginning with the poorest, least serviced, and most inhospitable dwellings, to slightly better but very poor areas, poor communities, and finally to moderate-income neighborhoods. These last neighborhoods contain the homes of stable families: most of the heads of household are in their forties and have adolescent children in school or working to help support the family. In all cases, the choice of invasion for housing and the condition of their home is a reflection not of the absence of moral character, but of their (lack of) material well-being. Median household income for invasion families is 11 percent below the established federal minimum wage in the city.

The major component in the development of a colonia popular is time: the older the settlement, the better it looks. As in other parts of Latin America, such areas have passed through a series of changes over time, taking them from flimsy, hastily constructed shantytowns to self-built, aesthetically inoffensive, and even pleasing neighborhoods indistinguishable from all but the wealthiest.[8] In Oaxaca nearly half the colonias populares have completed this process.

Nevertheless, to the outsider, most of these "self-constructed" communities are uninviting neighborhoods with substandard housing, and some may imagine them filled with thieves and prostitutes—certainly not safe at night or even, one fears, at midday. The reality is much less threatening and, indeed, ordinary. It is also much more developmental and dynamic than is generally suspected by those in charge of the city's future. The communities are usually quiet both day and night, except for a blaring record player somewhere or for the occasional saint's day festival or weekend party. Throughout the day activity pervades the community: children are seen running errands for their parents, who because of the births and baptisms of these children have been able to establish compadrazgo relationships with other adults in the community. Women visit over fences and on buses and paths as they travel to and from market or to the ubiquitous *tienditas* (small neighborhood stores). These microenterprises sprout on the lots or in the front rooms of numerous homes in the colonia and form the focus of much of its social life. They specialize in soda pop, candy, bread, cooking lard and oil, soap, toilet paper, perhaps chilis, a little fruit, and, if there is a refrigerator, cheese and meat. They are staffed by unpaid family labor, their goods are bought in the center city at no discount, and they barely turn a profit. To neighborhood residents they offer convenience, credit, and almost around-the-clock availability of goods. In addition, some offer beer, mescal, and regional short-order food for the late-night supper. Often these *tienditas* serve as the centers of social activity for many of the men in the colonia, who no longer need to travel to the city center to fraternize and drink with their friends.

There is virtually no other economic activity in the community. Contrary to some descriptions of Latin American squatter settlements (for example, Portes 1985), Oaxacan squatter settlements do not contain a significant amount of informal production, that is, economic activities uncontrolled by the state (discussed further in Chapter 4). Some women may take in laundry or make handmade tortillas to sell either to neighbors or in the market. But most people now buy machine-made tortillas, which renders the market for the handmade variety too small to support many households. In addition, some women and men make handcrafted piecework products to be sold wholesale to merchants in the market. This work, however, is a supplement to the household's income and seldom results in more than a few pesos a day for the family. Like a store in the home, it enables a household to make use of the labor of individuals who would otherwise contribute little or nothing to the group's well-being and provides a steady, if small, source of income during times when a household member is without a more regular job.

Oaxacan colonias populares are not loci of informal activities primarily because the city's geographic compactness also means business, whether formal or informal, can locate wherever it pleases. The city center has significantly better infrastructure than most squatter settlements (for example, telephone service, potable water, and transportation links) and access to the broader current of goods that flows through it. Thus, colonias populares, lacking this infrastructure, present important disadvantages while offering no significant advantages.

Neither do colonias populares contain important subsistence production. Many households have a small vegetable or herb garden, and many have chickens or even a pig. The vegetables provide a meager supplement to the family's diet, and the animals are usually viewed as a form of savings. Poultry is kept for fiestas, for which the standard Oaxaca *mole* with chicken or turkey is mandatory. Pigs are sold primarily in the event of an emergency requiring a large sum of money. The income generated and the proportion of subsistence produced is minimal compared to that gained through wages and work.

In summary, encompassing over 60 percent of the city's area, colonias populares are clearly Oaxaca's most pervasive neighborhood type. They present a diversified appearance from shantytown to established community, and while their roots are at best extralegal, they contain decent families struggling to improve themselves, usually against the wishes of government authorities.[9] In this last dimension, they contrast with the next neighborhood type to be discussed, government-sponsored housing.

Government-Sponsored Housing

In the early 1970s the Mexican government increasingly inserted itself into the housing market by creating agencies to build subsidized housing. The most massive of these organizations is INFONAVIT, which has constructed housing for workers covered by the IMSS. Parallel to INFONAVIT, ISSSTE provides for the housing needs of workers in the public sector. The Instituto Nacional para el Desarrollo de la Comunidad y de la Vivienda Popular (INDECO) was given the task of devising a plan for providing housing, first to formal sector workers who did not earn enough to meet the mortgage payments demanded by INFONAVIT and ISSSTE and, second, to informal sector workers not eligible for those programs.[10]

In Oaxaca the efforts of INFONAVIT and ISSSTE are concentrated in the northern area of the city, an area that used to form the boundary between the middle-class neighborhood of Colonia Reforma and the ancient village of San Felipe del Agua, where a major portion of upper-income Oaxacans reside. Here, beginning in the 1970s, INFONAVIT constructed a series of condominiums and duplexes that today number more than fifteen hundred households.

The location of these units has caused some difficulty for Oaxaca's municipal authorities. It broke the de facto social segregation of the city, which had reserved the area north of the city for elite single-family dwellings. People who had built substantial homes in San Felipe and Colonia Reforma were quite displeased. Moreover, the government projects strained the city's sewer and water systems. Municipal authorities did not have the resources to expand those systems, and the state and the federal government also proved unwilling to help. The result is that rather than being connected to the city's sewer system, sewage from these units is dumped into the adjacent Jalatlaco River, which runs open through half the city and in a covered culvert through the remainder. In the case of water, because of the communities' location closest to the city's primary source in a spring above San Felipe, these units take precedence over much of the rest of the city. Since their opening, water shortages in the city center have been more frequent and severe. In the early 1980s, the city delayed the opening of an INFONAVIT development by refusing, temporarily, to supply it with water.

Residence in these units is determined by lottery. All formal sector workers who do not own a home already and whose employers contribute to the INFONAVIT wage tax are eligible. When a group of houses is finished, a lottery is held to determine who will be offered a unit, to be purchased through a payroll deduction plan. Theoretically, families must live in the unit they purchase; in reality, many individuals continue to live in their old home, often located in one of the city's colonia populares, and rent the INFONAVIT or ISSSTE unit to friends or other family members.

Owners frequently complain that housing in these communities is expensive and of poor quality. They feel they could have gotten more for their money if they had been able to use the payroll tax funds to construct a house of their own design with the contractor of their choosing. For example, Alfonso, whose life history is presented in Chapter 7, had been chosen in the lottery. His home in one of the city's colonia populares is a wattle and daub structure with a leaky tar-paper roof, concrete floor, latrine, and no piped water. He saw clearly the advantages of the modern conveniences of the new homes, but he also saw numerous disadvantages. Both house and lot were much smaller than he currently had: while his current house was really one large room, it could be effectively divided by curtains, and his lot is large enough to support a small garden. Moreover, he has no payments on his current house, having squatted on it over ten years ago and therefore owning it. He would have to make monthly payments on the new house. In the end, he decided to turn down the government house and remain in the squatters' settlement.

There is also discontent over the restrictions on ownership placed on residents by INFONAVIT and ISSSTE. If an individual wishes to sell his or her property, the only legal purchaser is the government, which sets the price and then resells the unit to another member of the pool. Residents feel this is an infringement on their rights as property owners and that IN-

FONAVIT often sets a purchase price below the market value of the property. INFONAVIT argues that the restrictions on rental and resale of the units are designed to prevent speculation with publicly financed housing. To get around the restriction, an irregular market has developed in which holders rent and sell their property through extralegal arrangements, much as villagers do with their communal land.

As in the case of the irregular nature of holdings in many of the city's colonias populares, the extralegal nature of landholding does not seem to have diminished people's belief in their rights as property owners. Demand for INFONAVIT and ISSSTE housing is high because housing is at a premium in Oaxaca, and despite unhappiness over construction quality and size of the units they represent a step toward "modernity" for many young people in the city. The "condominiums" are small, with from one to three bedrooms. They have, however, all the modern conveniences of water, sewers, electricity, and bottled gas, and the prestige of living in a modern development. For some young members of the formal sector, moving into the ISSSTE or INFONAVIT complex represents the only alternative to living with parents, and it is not uncommon for young couples to delay their wedding until a home has become available to one or the other party. In such a case the wedding reception is often held at the new home, with family and friends crowded into the small living–dining room, and with a band and dancing in the small backyard (if the family is lucky enough to have drawn a ground-floor residence).

In Oaxaca, federal government efforts to provide housing for informal sector workers have resulted in only two relatively small housing projects: one created in response to a 1975 squatter invasion and another created for individuals of slightly greater means, both of which are detailed in Chapter 5. In the wake of citywide turmoil in 1975, the state governor asked INDECO to sponsor a site-and-services housing project. INDECO purchased a plot of land on the city's northern periphery, adjacent to the Pan-American Highway. The lots were distributed by a lottery and INDECO arranged for electricity and water connections. After pressure from the community, INDECO further provided a community center and a building for a primary school. Today, the community is indistinguishable from spontaneous squatter communities that waited somewhat longer to obtain services.

For those slightly better off, in the mid 1970s INDECO purchased sixteen hectares (about forty acres) of flat corn-farming land on the bank of the Atoyac River across from the city. The land was cleared, surveyed, subdivided, and advertised as available to individuals who were of moderate means, were not covered by one of the other government housing programs, and did not own a home. Over one thousand applied for the five hundred lots. To decide who would receive lots, a lottery was held to pick winners and their lots.

The agency then arranged for the provision to the lots of electricity, water and sewer connections, and a primary school. The new residents paid for these services with time payments and were advised that they could add more services to the colonia if they organized their own financing. The government provided advice on both private and public projects and subsidized materials for construction to lot owners, but it did not make decisions for the colonia or implement projects. The agency viewed itself only as the initiator of the housing project. It had obtained the land, subdivided it, and financed the first services. From then on the colonia was to proceed on its own, as squatter communities do, with initiative and momentum from within carrying it forward. INDECO planners were relying on a community-based political organization to arise and carry the colonia forward to completion.

Today the site-and-services communities' appearance is not unlike that of the established squatter communities in the city. Houses are in varying stages of construction using a variety of materials. There are a large number of houses made of concrete or brick, but bamboo and wattle-and-daub houses also exist, as do the ubiquitous walls surrounding lots.

Socially as well, the residents are virtually identical to those in the uncontrolled settlements. Incomes of heads of households are slightly higher, but as would be expected fewer of these are employed in the formal sector of the economy and therefore face more irregular incomes. Education is low: most heads of households have not completed primary education. Demographically, they are identical to other residents of the city: marital status, the number of children in the household, and the number of nonworking dependent individuals in the household is the same as residents of colonias populares in the city. The only significant difference is that they are in a government-sponsored site-and-services project, which has made it possible for them to secure title to their land with less difficulty than their neighbors and has facilitated the introduction of some basic services (Prince 1988; Stepick and Murphy 1980; Prince and Murphy 1990).

Pueblos Conurbados

In colonial times when transport was slow, independent communities were often no more than a few kilometers apart. Communities were also separated along ethnic lines, with paired villages for Spaniards and Indians in close proximity, allowing the Indians to serve the Spaniards' daily needs. As described in Chapter 2, Oaxaca was originally surrounded by several separate Indian communities. The Indian barrios of Jalatlaco and Xochimilco were physically absorbed into the city by the end of the colonial era and lost all autonomy in the nineteenth century. As Oaxaca has grown in the past thirty years, it has surrounded physically and absorbed politically a number of other autonomous village communities.

There is seldom any mistaking these pueblos conurbados even in Oaxaca's increasing urban sprawl: they retain a rural flavor and their plazas, although by no means as elaborate as Oaxaca's central zócalo, are still centers of community activity. Often the local government offices are on one side and masses are held in a church on the other. The adjacent basketball court serves as the social focus for the community team, and elaborate saint's day festivals are more traditional than in Oaxaca City. Their rural flavor makes the pueblo conurbado one of the most desired places to live in the city and has resulted in a dramatic population growth in these communities, threatening to bury all their existing communal lands under housing.

More than in the rest of the city, the houses in these communities are of adobe on large lots with trees and room for animals. Roofs are of red tiles, floors of earth, and rooms large. Unlike their counterpart, villages in the distant rural parts of the state, utilities in these urban villages are common: 83 percent of the homes have electricity and 43 percent have water on the lot (many in the form of private wells). But like the villages, sewage and toilet facilities are almost nonexistent.

Commercial activity in the pueblo conurbado is well established. Besides numerous *tienditas,* there are larger stores with more diversified stock, including clothing and basic housewares. One may also find mechanics, doctors, a bus depot, restaurants, and bars. Although almost no one does, it would be possible to provide most of the household's daily needs from within one of these communities.

Economically and demographically, these areas present a mixed picture of urban and rural styles and values. Households are larger than in the city (averaging 6.1 members), and more heads of households work in agriculture (19 percent). Yet most workers are in some type of blue-collar (31 percent) or service (25 percent) job that generally takes them to the city every day. Incomes are low. Half the households must survive on the equivalent of less than $120.00 (U.S.) per month. What is not found in these urban villages is the rural pattern of extended households. Nuclear families predominate, as they do for the entire city.

The most notable difference between the pueblos conurbados and the rest of the city is in community social relationships. There is a spirit of community independence and self-reliance not typically found in colonias populares. It is easier to get communal work parties organized, easier to find neighbors willing to help. Materially and economically it may differ little from the rest of the city, but socially the difference is marked.

Middle-Class Neighborhoods

In Oaxaca, middle-class areas exist adjacent to the INFONAVIT and ISSSTE housing projects, near the medical school north of the center city, and on the southern edge of the city. As would be expected in the most affluent sections of the city, the streets are paved and, in the older parts, lined with shade trees. Most homes have the traditional wall surrounding them, but more and more are imitating the North American style of open front lawns. As befits the modern middle class of Mexico, virtually all homes have a car and a servant who helps with the domestic chores. Inside, homes in these areas of the city are furnished in a manner remarkably similar to homes of the middle class in the United States, although the colors may be bright for North American tastes. The rooms also tend to be smaller than those of the North American middle class or even their counterparts in the pueblos conurbados. Houses usually have two to four bedrooms, a living room, den, kitchen, and one, two, or even three baths. All have piped water and sewer service, except for the relatively few poor households scattered about the neighborhoods. Not surprisingly, household incomes in these areas are the highest in the city. Most heads of these households are employed in the white-collar sector of the economy (64 percent).

The middle-class community's social life is also most like North American middle-class communities. Communal work parties are unheard of. Street life is usually quiescent, except for children playing, servants going to the market and to and from work, or women shopping at the local minimall, which houses a grocery store, clothing stores, several candy shops, and a theater. In general, one may know one's immediate neighbors, but social networks revolve around work and relatives.

Conclusions

The goals of this chapter have been to describe the people who live in Oaxaca and their living conditions. We have seen both continuity and change from the historical trends observed in previous chapters. Like Monte Albán over a thousand years ago and Antequera de Oaxaca during the colonial epoch, contemporary Oaxaca presents a picturesque, charming surface to the casual observer, with impressive architecture reflecting its spiritual importance through the numerous churches and its political position at the zócalo and in other government buildings. Behind this, however, lie complex events and forces.

Oaxaca has experienced a demographic cycle in this century similar to those in previous centuries. The earthquake in the early part of the century devastated and depopulated the city. Increased links to the outside world in the contemporary era produced significant population growth, just as they did during the colonial cochineal era. The city's population-growth rate peaked in the decade of the 1960s, but even then the growth rate was considerably less than it was in Mexico's more industrialized northern cities. It appears as if the city's demography is becoming increasingly responsive to external forces. Federally funded improvements in public health, especially vaccinations, but also correction of the inefficient, less than adequate water and sewer systems, mean that epidemics no longer decimate the population as they did a few hundred years ago. It must be stated, nevertheless, that diseases do still kill infants, especially among the poor.

During the contemporary era of the past forty years, the city grew far more than it had since the Spaniards founded it four hundred fifty years ago. It has mushroomed far beyond the boundaries of the Atoyac and Jalatlaco rivers, which defined it from its founding by the Aztecs over five hundred years ago until the early 1950s. The result of immigration has been squatter settlements and colonias populares, most of which lack basic urban services. Many households still draw their water from common spigots and most lack sewer connections. Houses usually have few rooms with small uncovered windows. The city remains largely undeveloped, especially in comparison to the larger cities of northern Mexico, which have experienced higher population growth rates, a somewhat more developed infrastructure, and frequently a greater degree of socioeconomic inequality.

The Oaxacan colonias populares, however, apparently differ from those in other Latin American cities. They are neither the loci of important informal economic activities nor of significant subsistence production. In that sense, they do not reduce the "social wage" of labor that capitalists provide. Goods, services, and particularly food are no cheaper in colonias populares than in any other parts of the city. Nevertheless, Oaxaca squatter settlements do partially decrease the social wage assumed by employers or the state by making affordable housing available. The primary social function of Oaxaca's colonias populares can be depicted as reducing the costs and increasing the availability of housing by forcing households and families to use their own labor to construct and develop their dwellings. If it were not for squatter settlements, either wages or the state's investment in public housing would have to be higher to provide housing for the majority of the population.

Our review of Oaxaca's social geography further reveals important diversity and an evolution of neighborhoods. While the colonias populares now compose the greater part of the city, they offer the widest range of living conditions and reflect different stages of community evolution. The oldest parts of many are indistinguishable from other sections of the city, while some of the newest seem to be nothing but shacks and slums. The oldest area, the city center, also has an extensive range of services and contains the attractive zócalo and colonial-style buildings. The nicest areas, the middle-class zones, have a broad range of services, but have been buffeted on their fringes by the government's imposition of housing projects for formal-sector employees. The government's housing projects have services, but are cramped both physically and by rules and regulations. Former villages retain some political autonomy and a bit of a village ambience, yet they are largely incorporated into the city.

The most important change in recent years is the increased role of the federal government in housing issues. The state was indirectly responsible for the city's population growth, both by promoting migration through the extension of a transportation infrastructure of rural roads and through public health measures that diminished mortality. It has directly attempted to solicit and incorporate support for its policies from the urban population—tolerating squatters' invasions and legitimizing their land tenure. It has similarly extended itself to those with steady jobs by constructing subsidized housing and through other activities described in Chapters 4 and 5.

Collectively, these factors produce a city comparable to but clearly distinct from both its historical roots and other Mexican cities. In the past forty years, it has outgrown its infrastructure, but still not to disastrous proportions. It has little of the crowding, noise, or pollution of Mexico's major urban centers. There are no people sleeping on the streets nor even enough visible beggars to taint the city's quiet charm for the tourists or local upper classes. The poor are largely invisible, living on the city's outskirts in self-constructed housing that they have gradually improved.

4

Contemporary Economics

The flight from Mexico City to Oaxaca is scarcely half an hour, but the cultural distance is great. After leaving Mexico City's urban chaos, the plane passes over rugged mountains with innumerable small villages. It soon descends into the Oaxaca Valley, passing in between Monte Albán and Oaxaca City. The pyramids are the highest structures on Monte Albán, while down in the city the church bell towers are the highest points. There are no modern skyscrapers, no traffic jams, and no smog to be seen. Cows and goats graze just off the ends of the runways, and small villages flank the airport.

If one comes on the day's first flight from Mexico City and heads directly for the zócalo, one may see the early morning shape-up where the city's construction day workers wait hopefully for crew bosses. A little later, the stores will open. Most carry modern, industrially produced goods, yet the tourists' eyes are caught by stores carrying Indian handicrafts: hand-loomed rugs, carved onyx, embroidered dresses, blouses, and shirts. The main market on the city's edge is just six blocks away from the city center. There market vendors, primarily women dressed in the conventional Zapotec print dress with apron, put out their wares on tables and on the ground under their bamboo and cotton-cloth sun umbrellas. Across the street, at the second-class bus station and on the adjacent peripheral road unmuffled buses and trucks shatter the bucolic tranquility. The buses carry peasants going to and from market or to jobs in the city, or their sons and daughters who commute into the city for their secondary education. The trucks bring in agricultural goods from the countryside and industrial goods from Mexico City.

Quickly and easily, one sees nearly all of Oaxaca's contemporary economy. The historical continuities are striking. Oaxaca City's primary economic function is still as a marketing and service center tied to the surrounding rural hinterland. Industry continues to be virtually absent, as

77

it has been since the demise over one hundred fifty years ago of cochineal and the associated weaving industry. Nor does the city exhibit the social ravages and gross inequalities of third-world development. Slums and beggars are hidden and few, as are sumptuous mansions and millionaires.

Yet these obvious observations are not entirely accurate. The city is not the same as it was fifty years ago when Malinowski and de la Fuente conducted their landmark study of the Oaxaca market, and it is certainly not the same city the Spanish Peninsulares fled over one hundred fifty years ago. Today, the economy is more complex and important links have been reestablished between it and the outside world. The completion of the Pan American Highway in the 1940s literally paved the way for Oaxaca's reintegration with the national economy. The most influential transformation has been in the visible, central role in the economy assumed by the federal government.

This chapter explores the economic contrasts between Oaxaca's old-fashioned past and its increased links with the modern world. We focus on three aspects: (1) Oaxaca's primary economic activities; (2) the emerging differences between the formal and informal sectors; and (3) Oaxaca's income groups. We find one constant and one trend that has a number of significant consequences:

The Constant

Oaxaca's economic base remains firmly rooted as an administrative and service center to the surrounding hinterland, as it has for over two thousand years.

The Trend

The central state, that is, the federal government, has increased its economic role, just as it has augmented its importance in the social geography described in the previous chapter. This has had several important consequences including:

Increased employment in the public sector and in construction;

An emerging, but not fully developed, distinction between the formal and informal sectors;

A distinction at the bottom of the socioeconomic hierarchy between those whom we label the very poor and the minimum-wage income groups;

An increase in the size of the income group we call aspiring, which falls between the minimum-wage and middle/elite income groups and is directly dependent upon the federal government's increased presence.

We conclude the chapter by discussing the implications of these conditions for Oaxaca's social class structure.

Oaxaca's Primary Economic Activities

From the 1940s through the beginning of the 1980s, Mexico experienced what many have called an economic miracle, embodied in high rates of industrialization and economic growth. In 1982 the miracle came to a screeching halt as Mexico fell into a debt crisis. Economic growth stalled and inflation severely eroded earning power; as a consequence, the federal government drastically curtailed its expenditures.[1] As of the early 1990s, the national economy had still not recovered. An in-depth discussion of the recent history of Mexico's national economy is beyond the scope of our work; nevertheless, an overview provides a context for understanding Oaxaca. The region remained largely isolated from the economic miracle, as it had been isolated previously from the Reform and the Revolution. The 1980s crisis, however, did not spare it: inflation, eroded earning power, and curtailed government spending are all evident.

Aggregate economic statistics reveal that Oaxaca's productivity lags far behind that of the rest of the nation. The state's per capita production ranks next to last and it produces only 1 percent of the nation's total industrial goods. The statewide illiteracy rate is more than 40 percent, and indicators of malnutrition, infant mortality, and disease point to a generally poor, underprivileged population. In short, the state of Oaxaca is among the least developed in Mexico. The basis of Oaxaca's regional economy has remarkable continuity: a market-oriented agricultural economy whose three most important productive activities are agriculture, artisanry, and commerce. While there is some overlap in geographic location among them, agriculture and artisanry are primarily based in rural areas, while commerce revolves around the city of Oaxaca.

The city's economy reflects its reliance upon the surrounding region. It has virtually no industry and its economy is one of the most service-oriented of any city in Mexico. Table 4.1 reveals that in spite of the significant population growth discussed in the previous chapter, the character of the city's economy has not significantly changed since 1940. Indeed, the most notable change is a decline in the proportion of the work force in industry. The most significant increase has been in construction, an expected increase given population growth and the physical expansion of the city. The proportion of workers in the remaining categories held remarkably constant for nearly four decades. The number of agricultural

Table 4.1
Oaxaca's Occupational Distribution

	1940	1950	1960	1970	1977
Services	32.8	34.4	42.3	34.0	31.5
Commerce	14.3	18.3	19.5	18.2	17.3
Construction	4.5	6.2	6.2	6.4	13.1
Industry	33.9	30.0	22.0	19.6	11.4
Public sector*				9.7	21.9
Agriculture	9.2	9.2	3.1	6.4	4.9

*The category Public sector was not distinguished from the Service sector before 1970.

workers on the city's periphery has declined as the city's expansion has eliminated most of the agricultural land. Commerce increased in the 1940s (14.3 to 18.3 percent of all workers) and has not varied by more than 1 percent per decade since 1950.

The number of workers in the service sector jumped 8 percent in the decade of the 1950s and then apparently declined again. The decline, however, actually reflected a reclassification. In 1970, for the first time, government employees were distinguished from the rest of service-sector employees. Adding them back in for 1970 and 1977 indicates that, proportionately, the service sector, too, remained remarkably constant. There is a notable change, nevertheless, in the growth of government employment between 1970 and 1977, from 9.7 to 21.9 percent. Both later in this chapter and in Chapter 5, we shall discuss the source of this rapid growth. The principal conclusion is that the city's economy maintains the same base it has had for centuries—providing commerce and services to itself and the surrounding region.

As Chapter 2 demonstrated, the valley has been characterized for millennia by an agricultural economy. It has also been market-oriented for nearly as long, although the local Indians' persistent control of the land has helped them resist the incursions of outsiders and the consolidation of large landholdings. For the local region, then, small-scale, market-oriented subsistence agriculture continues to predominate,[2] although artisan handicraft production assumes greater importance than agriculture in some villages.[3] Until the opening in 1948 of the Pan American Highway, access to markets outside the region remained limited because of poor transportation.[4] While some rural producers have become successful distributors (blanket weavers, in particular), most distribution is controlled by Oaxaca City wholesalers, who export much of the production to other areas of Mexico and abroad, and by small- and medium-sized establishments that cater locally to tourists.

Commerce has traditionally been central to Oaxaca's economy. The region has a long-standing, probably prehispanic, rotating market system with weekly markets in different large villages on different days. The weekly Saturday market remains Mexico's largest peasant market. It also serves as a distribution point for goods flowing in and out of the region. Malinowski and de la Fuente noted the presence of a few mass-produced goods in the Oaxaca market, such as satin ribbon and cotton thread. The vast majority of goods consumed then were locally produced. The inauguration of the Pan American Highway generated a far-reaching change (Hayner 1948); by linking Oaxaca with Mexico City to the north and southern Mexico and Central America to the south, it reconstructed the commercial links (described in Chapter 2) early Antequera de Oaxaca had with the outside world via the port of Santa Cruz Huatulco. Commercial activity expanded as agricultural products and artisan handicraft goods flowed out, while mass-produced industrial goods and some agricultural produce flowed in from Mexico City and beyond. Residents of the city now wear ready-made dresses, pants, and shirts complemented by manufactured shoes. The "traditional" Zapotec woman's garment is now a mass-manufactured plaid-print dress. Most Oaxacans presently eat off plastic or porcelain plates using metal cutlery and cook on kerosene or gas stoves. Even the food they eat is likely to be produced outside the region, as the valley has been a net importer of corn since the late 1960s. Although goods may be produced outside the city, many of the market's merchants are city residents. The same is true for those who are involved in the transportation, stocking, and wholesaling of goods.

Until the mid 1970s, Oaxaca's market filled the streets surrounding the city's central market just one block from the zócalo. Every Saturday city streets came alive with traditional costumes and Indian dialects as vendors from throughout the valley, state, and nation gathered to distribute their products to tourists, wholesalers, and fellow Oaxacans. Vendors began arriving on Friday evening and worked long into the night to set up booths and arrange their wares. By early Saturday morning the market was teeming with sights and sounds, flooding the senses of tourists who wandered about looking for a bargain (difficult to arrange with Zapotec traders whose ancestors have been merchants for millennia) or a piece of local color to take home. One literally waded through the narrow aisles, buffeted by the masses of buyers and sellers squeezing, jostling, and pushing to their destination. Streets closed to traffic as vendors filled them with two or three narrow aisles of stalls. To the tourist, the scene was one of overwhelming confusion, but exciting and seemingly full of exotic adventure.

In reality, the market was highly organized. Each half block or block specialized in a particular product. In one area, stall after stall was filled with fruits of the season. In another, fresh vegetables and flowers greeted the eye with a compact garden of colors. Farther down were the stalls of the dairy vendors who sold the famous local cheeses and chocolate. Then came stalls of chilis, where huge baskets overflowed with ten, fifteen, even twenty different varieties, each with a unique aroma and flavor. For the tourists, there were blankets and other wall hangings from valley villages and urban weavers, and embroidered shirts and blouses from almost every region of the state. For villagers, the Saturday market was an opportunity to come to town to earn cash and to enjoy being in the city, visiting friends whom one might not see otherwise, going to a movie, or seeing the talent show regularly sponsored by a local radio station.

The market was moved a few blocks to the edge of the city in the mid 1970s (see Chapter 5), but it still retains the same flavor. Many of the sellers, today as previously, are peasant producers who come to the city to sell part of their surplus, but the majority are full-time merchants who buy their goods from wholesalers or peasants and resell them in smaller quantities. Some work only the Saturday Oaxaca market, while others travel the weekly circuit of markets throughout the valley.

Since the 1950s, the presence of modern commerce and mass-produced goods has increased in the peasant market and has penetrated more deeply into the countryside on an ever-expanding network of roads. Because of the state's general poverty, the number of large commercial outlets has not expanded as much as small stores with mass-produced manufactured goods. One small shopping center has recently been built in a middle-class neighborhood, but it contains only local businesses. Beyond a modest Sears Roebuck store and a large national food store chain, little outside investment in retailing is evident. Automobile distributors are all locally owned, as is the one retail store that approximates a department store. In the mid 1980s two multinational tire companies established automobile service centers in the area. Both are franchises, but they are operated by non-Oaxacans. Most retailers are local residents. Some, primarily those with stores immediately surrounding the zócalo, are descended from the Spanish merchants described by Malinowski and de la Fuente (1982) in the 1930s.

The most important part of Oaxaca's service sector, and that most affected by increased links to the outside, is the tourist industry. Several daily flights link Oaxaca with Mexico City. The tourist industry is based on Oaxaca's reputation for serenity and charm, on its handicrafts, on the wealth of monumental architecture left by the Zapotec and Mixtec civilizations and the Spanish colonialists, and on the access provided first by the rail link at the beginning of the twentieth century, later by the completion of the Pan American Highway, and then the establishment of daily air service in the late 1960s.

The ruins of Monte Albán gaze down upon the city from their majestic perch. Numerous other sites in the valley are within a half-hour's drive. Mitla, at the end of the valley toward the Isthmus of Tehuantepec, is the second most famous and popular site. It was a major religious center at the time of the Conquest, and the Spaniards built a Catholic church on the ruins of the former ceremonial center. Many of the buildings remain intact and are elaborately decorated with *grecos,* intricately carved geometric designs. On an archway behind the church one can still see the remnants of an original prehispanic fresco.

The more adventurous tourists visit not only the archaeological sites, but also the villages producing handicrafts. In addition to Teotitlán del Valle, where rugs are woven, there is San Bartolo Coyotepec, just a short drive from the city, which specializes in black pottery. Tourists can see the forming of pots and other ware on simple wheels consisting of the tops of two gourds placed peak to peak, turned by one hand while the other shapes the clay into delicate forms. The pots are fired in the most basic of ovens, a cavelike pit in the earth covered with brush and wood burned overnight.

There is much for the tourist to enjoy within the city as well. Many of the old colonial buildings in the downtown area have been transformed into hotels and handicraft shops. All the churches and colonial buildings are within walking distance of the zócalo. Attached to the baroque Santo Domingo Church is the Museo Regional de Antropologiá e Historia, which has an extensive collection of jewelry, metalwork, and other artifacts recovered from Monte Albán and elsewhere in the valley. Oaxaca's most famous modern artist, Rufino Tamayo, whose work has been exhibited in New York and other international art centers, has established a museum in another old colonial structure to display his fine collection of prehispanic artifacts.

The sidewalk cafés bordering the city's central plaza are apt to serve more tourists than locals, though this may not be immediately apparent to a North American observer. Despite the popularity of Oaxaca as a vacation spot among North Americans and Europeans, most of Oaxaca's tourists are Mexicans. The tourist industry has expanded continually since the opening of the Pan American Highway, but in the 1970s growth in the industry was particularly dynamic. The number of daily flights from Mexico City increased from two to five in just four years. A new, less mountainous highway between Oaxaca and Mexico City opened, saving at least an hour's driving time. Hotel accommodations increased in availability as the two best hotels expanded and a sixteenth-century convent was converted into a luxury hotel.

For two weeks every July, Oaxaca teems with tourists in town for the *Lunes del Cerro* fiesta, which brings together colorfully dressed traditional folk dancers representing indigenous groups throughout the state. The festival is supposedly modeled on the prehispanic *guelaguetza,* the yearly presentation of tribute required of dominated groups by their overlords. Today the state governor performs this role, accepting symbolic offerings after each group has danced in a grand open-air amphitheater, built with the valley's green granite on Fortín Hill, overlooking the city and directly opposite Monte Albán.

Over 80 percent of Oaxaca's tourists have always been Mexicans, but through the 1960s and 1970s Oaxaca was favored by many young travelers from the United States and Europe. Not only was the valley inexpensive, authentically exotic, and far from the artificiality of modern society, but it was also distinguished for its high-quality marijuana and hallucinogenic mushrooms. The locals, however, tended to view this class of tourists with suspicion and even active dislike, as the values of the two groups frequently clashed (see Esparza 1979; and Esparza and Holderman 1975).

The peak of the "hippie invasion" in the late 1960s corresponded with the common Oaxacan's acceptance of and efforts to emulate North American fashion—at least as filtered through Mexico City. Young women were no longer content to wear simple cotton-print dresses. Slacks became popular, as did modern hairstyles. For the men, bell-bottom pants predominated, along with carefully coiffed hair. While class and income frequently limited their success in emulating this style, the goal of young Mexicans was clearly a well-groomed look. Young foreigners, who were obviously wealthier than the locals but nevertheless disregarded their own personal appearance, offended and mystified many Oaxacans, who thought the foreigners were mocking those who of necessity patched their clothes or went barefoot. Clearly, there was something abnormal about these people: only the poorest Indian would go barefoot in Oaxaca, not those who had money to travel around in cars and stay in hotels. And the only cultural equivalent of women who wore skimpy, revealing clothes were prostitutes or the mentally disturbed.

The hippies congregated in the zócalo, where natives and tourists alike enjoyed the slow pace of life where people can sit for hours just watching people. Those who could afford it sat at one of the sidewalk cafés sipping a beer or coffee, while others sat for free in the central plaza. Hippies, however, would frequently sit at a café table and refuse to order anything. Soon crude hand-lettered signs appeared: "WE DO NOT SERVE JIPIS."

Tourism today focuses primarily on the Mexican, North American, and European middle classes. New hotels have been built, new restaurants opened, and a special bus service to Monte Albán established. Long-haired, unkempt young tourists still arrive, but they are perceived as neither a problem nor a threat. Instead, the immediate problem is the decline in tourism occasioned by the economic crisis of the 1980s.

Since the 1940s, the federal government has assumed an increasingly important economic role, a role that escalated in the wake of the 1968 nationwide student movement and the late 1970s oil discoveries. From a national perspective, Oaxaca has been an inconsequential player.

The state receives one of the lowest federal subsidies, despite having the ninth-largest population of the thirty-two states and districts (INEGI 1985). In spite of this, the federal government constructed new infrastructure and improved transportation links to the outside. Increased federal funds in the late 1970s and 1980s created a multiplier effect on the local economy significantly stimulating, most notably, the local construction industry.

Oaxaca, as a state capital, was affected by increased government expenditures in three ways. First, the expanded government sector placed more individuals on the public payroll at all income levels. Second, the expanding middle-level bureaucracy increased the demand for housing and services (both commercial and domestic) in Oaxaca, thereby opening opportunities for local entrepreneurs as well as for the steady stream of migrants flowing into the city from the countryside. Finally, demand for real estate and construction materials greatly constrained the housing market for the poor.

While government employment leaped from 10 percent to 22 percent of total city employment between 1970 and 1977, the middle- and upper-level jobs went largely to bureaucrats from outside the state. Agencies such as the federal electric commission, the departments of public works, tourism, and internal affairs, all of whose roles at the local level expanded during this period, needed trained individuals immediately and could not wait for Oaxaca's educational system to catch up with the new employment demands.[5]

The federal government, however, did expand local educational opportunities. In the late 1970s, through the construction and upgrading of a wide assortment of technical and professional, as well as primary, secondary, preparatory, and university-level schools, Oaxaca became an educational center for Mexico's entire southeastern region. As in the case of the bureaucracy, many of the educators for these new and expanded institutions are immigrants. While outsiders obtained the best new government jobs, Oaxacans did fill most of the new lower-level posts as construction workers, truck drivers, and street sweepers. Regardless of the job, government employment is much desired at any level because it is secure and generally offers the best fringe benefits.

The construction industry is important any place where population is growing. Oaxaca's construction industry, however, showed no significant relative growth until the interval between 1970 and 1977, when its share of the occupational distribution more than doubled. From the mid 1970s through the late 1980s construction boomed in Oaxaca, primarily because of increased government investment in public construction projects for infrastructure, housing, and hotels. The state and federal governments' investment in construction rose from just over $3 million (U.S.) in 1970 to almost $22 million (U.S.) in 1980 (Oaxaca 1982, vol.

3). INFONAVIT, designed to provide affordable housing for formal-sector workers, constructed more than one thousand new housing units in this period. Meanwhile INDECO, the federal agency aimed at those with more modest incomes than most formal-sector workers, promoted site-and-services projects that resulted in the construction of close to one thousand working-class and several hundred middle-class houses.

Notably absent from this discussion of Oaxaca's principal economic sectors is industry. While government employment is booming and is highly desired by workers, industrial employment in Oaxaca is wanting. Only 10 percent of the state's and 11.4 percent of the city's workers are employed by industry, compared to 20 percent nationwide and 50 percent in Mexico City. In 1970 the city had 405 industrial operations with a total production of $73,600 (U.S.) (Oaxaca 1982: 816). The only major industry in the metropolitan area is a plywood factory owned by Papelera Tuxtepec, the state-owned wood products firm based in Oaxaca state's northwest region. It alone employs nearly 50 percent of Oaxaca's industrial workers. Small food-processing plants, such as the municipal slaughterhouse and North American–licensed soft-drink bottlers, employ 10 percent of the workers in the industrial sector, while textile factories serving the tourist trade employ 5 percent. The remaining industrial enterprises are minuscule—a small limestone extraction plant is located in the northwest quadrant of the city and another in the nearby *municipio* of San Antonio de la Cal. A small plastic-container plant has located in El Tule, some fifteen kilometers (nine miles) east of Oaxaca City.[6] Just before the 1980s economic crash, a factory producing commercial truck trailers opened. It, too, is somewhat outside the city, but most of its nearly two hundred workers are city residents.

Oaxaca's geographical isolation remains one of the greatest deterrents to industrial development. In spite of rail, highway, and air links to Mexico City, transportation remains slow and dangerous because of the rugged mountainous terrain. For industry, connections with Mexico City are critical, as it provides most inputs and the largest market. The valley has few inputs itself: neither water nor electricity is abundant, there is no large agricultural surplus, and little mineral production. Nor is the local market large. Instead, it is dispersed and mainly poor. The city does offer inexpensive labor, but that exists at only a slightly higher cost in even greater abundance in Mexico City.

Access to liquid capital is another barrier to industrial growth in Oaxaca. Money that comes into the region from the outside is, ironically, attracted by Oaxaca's very underdevelopment. Tourists seek the quaint and bucolic while government projects endeavor to ameliorate material deprivation. Foreign investment does not extend much beyond the soft-drink manufacturers, Sears, and some tourist services. Non-Oaxacan Mexicans control most of the region's capital. Until the late 1970s only one bank in the city was owned by Oaxacans. By the mid 1980s, all banks were owned by outsiders. Bank investment in the area is low and actually declined from $3,280 (U.S.) per capita in 1960 to $1,840 (U.S.) in 1970. Even in the 1980s, bank deposits consistently outpaced investments (INEGI 1985: 371–375).

In summary, this section has detailed Oaxaca's continued primary economic role as the service and administrative center for the surrounding agricultural hinterland. Commerce and even tourism are spin-offs of this continuity. The expanded federal government presence boosted the construction industry in the late 1970s. It also created a distinction between the formal and informal labor markets, the subject of the next section.

Formal and Informal Labor Markets

In attempting to explain conditions of underemployment associated with developing countries and regions, social scientists have constructed an analytical distinction between formal and informal labor markets. The formal sector is generally defined as those economic activities regulated in some way by the government. It consists of large firms engaged in "modern" industries, government bureaucracies, and professionals. Workers in this sector are skilled and relatively well paid, while the primary labor concern of employers is the stability of the labor force.

In contrast, the informal sector may be defined as noncontractual and not legally regulated employment. It includes direct subsistence production (home gardens and animal husbandry), noncontractual wage employment (domestic servants and others), small independent business ventures in industry (for example, piece work), services, and commerce (street vendors and independent merchants). Firms in this sector are highly competitive, with lower-than-average profit margins and an intensive use of labor. Jobs require little or no prior formal training (though some, as in artisan handicraft production, become highly skilled) and cluster at the low end of the wage scale.

Virtually no one disputes the existence of these two sectors throughout urban areas of the developing world. There is controversy, however, over the function and importance of the informal sector and its relationship to the formal. One group of voices maintains that informal activities are largely survival strategies created apart from the formal sector and in response to the dearth of employment opportunities there. Another holds that the informal sector is integrated with the formal sector by providing goods and services at a lower cost.[7]

Here we examine Oaxaca City's economy in terms of these labor markets. After presenting an operational definition of the distinction between the two, we describe briefly the main informal and formal economic activities within the city, and then contrast the two sectors in terms of type of economic activity and background characteristics of those employed in each.

Data from less-developed countries have always been difficult to classify into sectors on the basis of occupational class or income. The distinction between the informal and formal sectors of the economy is not a function of income level or job class. One historical indicator of membership in the formal sector in Latin America is whether or not the employee or household has access to social security (Dotson 1953; Eckstein 1976; Schnore 1967; Whiteford 1964). We operationalize the distinction between formal and informal sector in just this way: workers covered by the Mexican social security system (IMSS or ISSSTE) or receiving similar benefits from their employers are considered part of the formal sector along with self-employed professionals and owners of large commercial establishments.[8] All others belong to the informal sector.

The development of Oaxaca's formal sector has proceeded fitfully through the twentieth century. As discussed in Chapter 2, in 1912 the official work week was reduced to 6½ days and in 1916 the first labor union was established. No further advances for workers' rights were made until the 1930s, when the eight-hour work day was instituted. The most momentous advance occurred in the early 1950s, when the national social security system was created to provide health benefits to employees in all firms with ten or more workers. The range of benefits available has gradually increased and can now include subsidized loans for housing or subsidized housing itself, government-guaranteed loans for emergencies, pensions, subsidized and sometimes free health care, and many of the fringe benefits, like paid vacations, which workers in developed countries take for granted. Perhaps more important than the benefits themselves is the economic security and stability they bring. Workers in the formal sector seldom are laid off, either temporarily or permanently, a factor of great importance at any time, but especially so during Mexico's recent economic crisis.

By the late 1970s, the formal sector included one-half of Oaxaca's workers, including 54 percent of the heads of households and 40 percent of households' other workers. If the law were strictly enforced, the proportion of formal-sector workers would be higher and the distribution more even, but enforcement of labor laws has never been universal and their application has been seen primarily in response to the pressures of local organized labor more than from the positive efforts of the federal government (in Chapter 5, we examine some of Oaxacan labor's struggles for benefits). Today, almost all government jobs in Oaxaca carry with them automatic fringe benefits. Employees in many areas of private business and industry also receive a standard array of benefits.

The vast majority (74.8 percent) of workers in the formal sector are

Table 4.2
Formal- and Informal-Sector Occupational Distribution*

	Informal	Formal	All Workers
Agriculture	8.3%	1.3%	4.9%
Merchants	19.2	1.7	10.5
Artisans	8.0	2.7	5.4
Services	28.1	8.9	18.6
Construction	20.0	5.9	13.0
Industry	8.9	2.9	5.9
Private employees	5.8	32.3	18.9
Public sector	1.8	42.5	21.9
Professionals		1.3	.7
Entrepreneurs		.6	.3

*We intentionally combined occupational and industrial classifications to distinguish between those who worked for others in the informal sector and those who were self-employed. As the discussion will indicate, the only entirely self-employed are the professionals and entrepreneurs.

employees of either private concerns, most engaged in commerce (32.3 percent), or the public sector (42.5 percent). (See Table 4.2.) Public-sector employment is generally the most highly esteemed. Beyond the numerous fringe benefits government employees receive, they also have the highest job stability. While particular agencies may rise and fall with changes in presidents and governors, public-sector workers almost always land on their feet again, usually in the same or a renamed agency, doing just what they had been doing before. Employees in the private formal sector work generally for large retail firms concentrated in the city center. Virtually all belong to government-affiliated unions.

In light of their fringe benefits, job security, and wage levels, formal-sector workers are the elite of the labor force in Oaxaca and throughout Mexico. Unlike organized workers in Europe, the United States, or Canada, they are not, however, an independent economic and political force in the city or nation. Government-affiliated unions with limited membership control organized labor and formal-sector employees. The unions assure that workers' demands remain consistent with the government's definition of the national interest. They have not successfully or even forcefully defended workers' interests in the face of the 1980s economic crisis, and workers' purchasing power has declined since the onset of high inflation in the mid 1970s.

Union leaders exercise considerable power in the workplace. In many respects they, rather than employers, control access to formal-sector employment, determining who can join a union, and thus who can work in the formal sector. For example, some workers claim that it is a "union" rule that one must have a secondary education to be a driver for the government or that only men can perform certain tasks.

The largest component of the informal sector, service work, reflects both continuities and changes in Oaxaca's economy. That sector remains the largest and the conditions of work have changed little in the past forty years. However the sector has increased in absolute size because of population growth and tourism. The largest proportion (28 percent) of informal-sector workers are in service industries, often engaged in domestic work in homes and in the smaller hotels and restaurants of the city. While many of these individuals legally would qualify for some type of fringe benefits, the realities of Oaxaca's labor market are such that if any maid or cook in a private home, or chambermaid, busboy, or waitress in a restaurant or hotel agitated for benefits, he or she would be replaced by someone from the city's pool of underemployed workers.

When waiters at one of the fancy restaurants on the zócalo formed an independent union and demanded higher wages and fringe benefits, the restaurant owner simply closed the establishment. It remained closed for several months, although its associated hotel remained open, until the owner opened a "new" restaurant on the same premises, with new waiters and, held over from the previous restaurant, cooks who had not joined the strike. If a union is not sanctioned by the government and if management has its tacit compliance, workers can bring little effective pressure to bear in their quest for better and more secure working conditions.

While tourism provides the major impetus for the city's large service sector, home and domestic service is one of the fastest-growing parts of the labor market. With the increasing commercial and governmental activity in the city, more and more middle-class families are settling in Oaxaca. The result has been an increased demand for maids and gardeners. According to several middle-class government employees, one of the reasons they agreed to move to Oaxaca was that the availability of cheap domestic labor would enable them to live in a style no longer affordable in Mexico City. On the other hand, Oaxacan middle-class families have been heard to complain about the "servant problem" caused by the influx of outsiders who, rather than depending on the traditional patron–client relationship between maid and employer, compete for domestic help through wages, causing a shortage of cheap, reliable, long-term help.

The lives of live-in and daily maids are not easy. They are expected to rise early and prepare breakfast for the family. They then wash dishes, make beds, clean house, hand wash piles of laundry, often do daily food shopping, and other household chores as needed. For less than minimum wage they work six or seven days a week, and may be on call twenty-four hours a day. Vacations are rare, and maids must generally ask permission to leave the house to visit family or friends or even to see a movie. Gardeners receive slightly better treatment: while pay remains low, they are given more free time and can go home to family in the evenings and on Sundays.

For informal service workers in the hotel and restaurant business (which is also expanding in response to increasing numbers of middle-class families who eat out for business and pleasure), conditions are only marginally better. In contrast to domestic servants, hotel and restaurant employees are not on call day and night; their jobs, however, are insecure. Moreover, waiters and waitresses depend for a good portion of their income on tips, which fluctuate with the state of the national and local economy.

Construction workers form the second greatest component of the informal sector, making up about 20 percent. As mentioned in the previous section, construction has expanded because of the increased presence of the federal government. Its presence, however, has not transformed construction into primarily a formal-sector activity. Although a PRI-affiliated union of construction workers does exist, most workers do not belong to it. Employers prefer to hire nonunion laborers, who will accept lower wages without social security benefits. For construction workers who do not have a job, the day begins early. Every morning between six and seven o'clock, long before tourists and merchants appear, men gather in the northeast corner of the zócalo. They clump in groups of three to five, talking among themselves, perhaps smoking a cigarette, and shivering in the early-morning cold. Around 7:00 A.M., pickup trucks begin to arrive. A few drivers want ten or fifteen laborers, but most want one, two, or three for a day's work. They try to hire workers they know. Newcomers must make friends with the regulars so they will be recommended and taken along. Trucks do not come after 7:30, but those left behind continue talking and waiting as the tourists and merchants arrive. They talk about other jobs they have heard of in Oaxaca, the Isthmus of Tehuantepec, Mexico City, or even the United States. Slowly they drift away, most of them back to their homes. Some go from construction site to construction site looking for work.

The construction industry in Oaxaca is informally but trenchantly hierarchical. An individual who wants a job done contracts with a *contratista* (contractor), who assumes the overall responsibility for the project. He delegates tasks to *maestros* (subcontractors), with whom he has worked in the past and who have demonstrated a capability to perform the job on time and at a low rate. The contractor may or may not have a written agreement with the various *maestros* working below him. Most likely, they will establish the price, design, materials, and timetable by verbal agreement. The relationship is based on *confianza*—trust. If one party fails to keep his part of the agreement, neither is likely to resort to the formal legal system. Instead, the aggrieved party will apply moral pressure; references will be made to the long-standing relationship and its past accomplishments and the responsibility each party has to the other. If agreement is still not achieved, the relationship will simply be broken, leaving the job in whatever state it has reached.[9]

The *maestro*'s relationship with his workers mirrors his own to the contractor. Workers are hired on a personal basis. If the *maestro* needs more workers, they, too, are found through personal networks of *confianza*. Workers on a job tend to know one another, and they have usually worked together before. Yet they have no formal assurances of wages and working conditions. They are employed at the discretion of the *maestro*, and he, at the discretion of the contractor. If pay is withheld or one is arbitrarily dismissed, there is no formal recourse for either being rehired or receiving some form of compensation. Construction workers all have stories of unscrupulous contractors and *maestros* who tell the person above them that workers are receiving a higher salary than they actually are and then pocket the difference. Employers frequently deduct the contribution for social security from a worker's wage, but never deposit it with the IMSS.

Workers learn which *maestros* and which contractors are trustworthy and try to establish stable relationships with them. They thus tend to establish relationships with more than one *maestro*, switching among them as the opportunity or need arises. They may not have steady permanent employment because construction work itself is unsteady and each job stage requires a different number of workers. Those with some skills and experience can have virtually continuous work, although it may be at four or five different jobs in a year. Those without skills, new arrivals in the city, or unreliable workers may go months before finding work, and then only on a day-to-day basis.

The expansion of government construction projects in the late 1970s greatly increased the demand for workers. While government projects did not require workers to be covered by the social security system, they did indirectly raise construction workers' wages. For the first time, skilled construction workers could earn more than the minimum wage. Even those without well-developed skills or personal networks could usually find employment.

Nearly as many informal-sector workers are merchants (19 percent) as are in construction. This, again, reflects a continuity with the past, as informal merchants form an integral component of the regional economy. For the most part these are owners of the small shops that dot every neighborhood in the city. When a household has accumulated some excess capital, especially if the home is located at an intersection or on a well-traveled street, it is a common practice to open a little neighborhood store to sell small quantities of both perishable and nonperishable goods to neighbors. These stores usually employ unpaid family labor. They may have no more than a dozen or so customers in a day, but their rewards may be more social than economic. For the owners of these shops (often women), the store represents a degree of independence and gives them a break from the drudgery and monotony of keeping a household in the bleak environment of a poor urban colonia.

The other merchants in the informal sector are the small-scale market vendors. They are most plentiful at the weekly Saturday market mentioned above. Many of these vendors come to the market from rural areas for just one day. Most, however, are city residents who may sell only on Saturday or who maintain permanent, small stalls. There are also the vendors who walk the streets of Oaxaca with merchandise acquired, generally on credit, from a local merchant. These individuals can be seen on almost every street corner in the central part of town, selling small items such as razor blades, pencils, combs, and sheets of plastic that serve as inexpensive raincoats. Their existence depends on their relationship with a retail merchant, who sells them goods at a smaller markup than seen in the store, on the assumption that roving vendors touch a clientele the store will not reach.

The other type of roving vendor, the traveling sales agent who visits some or all of the various periodic markets in the valley and its surrounding mountains, similarly depends on a merchant. At every market, these vendors set up a stall displaying the cheapest variety of industrial products: flashlights, scissors, mirrors, safety pins, knives, spoons, plastic ware, and the like, all acquired from a retail merchant using these traveling salesmen and women to extend his market. In some cases, generally where clothing is involved, vendors may have a truck to transport merchandise from one market to another. These trucks open from the rear to create a traveling store complete with a loudspeaker, allowing the salesman to announce to everyone in town the arrival of the most spectacular bargains imaginable. Large-scale merchants, who are in the formal sector, perceive all these informal merchants as undesirable competition. In the next chapter, we discuss how struggles between the large- and small-scale merchants formed a vital part of Oaxaca's political activities in the 1970s.

In the city of Oaxaca production of textiles and pottery is dominated by a few firms, which may employ as many as fifty to a hundred workers, usually men, as well as numerous women who embroider in their spare time at home. These workers, who never sell directly to consumers, are unmistakably wage laborers. Production is organized and controlled by a wholesaler, and wages are usually piece rate. The fastest workers can earn more than the minimum wage, but most only approximate it. The largest firms provide social security and fringe benefits to those who work within their walls, but employees of smaller firms and those who work at home receive neither.

In the tourist handicraft industry, where authenticity, or its image, is prized, mechanization has been minimal. Instead, sweatshops and the *maquila* ("putting out") system have expanded in size rather than changed in form. Many poor urban women make extra money by embroidering peasant blouses and dresses using materials provided them by a middleman or representative of a retail firm. As demand increases, more products are put out, and the producer is paid for his or her product. If demand declines, artisans will find they cannot sell their blouse or serape. Employers are thus saved the trouble of hiring and laying off workers and providing for overhead in work space and other facilities. Given Oaxaca's reputation as a handicraft center, it is surprising that only 8 percent of informal-sector workers are involved in artisanry. Most artisan handicraft production is performed by families based in villages, and it has not yet been transformed into urban wage labor.

As Table 4.3 reflects, there are significant differences in individual background characteristics between workers in the formal and informal sectors. Females are more likely than males to be involved in informal activities. Informal workers are also more likely to be young or old and not in the prime earning years of 25 to 44. Informal workers are also likely to have substantially less formal education. On the other hand, migrants to the city and natives are equally likely to be informal-sector workers. In short, to be male, educated, and in one's prime earning years correlates with a greater likelihood of gaining access to the formal sector and its more stable work, fringe benefits, and higher income.

By definition, formal-sector workers have more fringe benefits than informal-sector workers. As Table 4.3 indicates, they also tend to earn more. Just over 10 percent of informal-sector workers earn more than the official minimum wage, compared to nearly one-third of formal-sector workers. Moreover, the highest incomes, those more than five times the minimum wage, are concentrated solely in the formal sector. Nevertheless, not everyone in the formal sector earns a decent income. Indeed, over two-thirds of Oaxaca's formal-sector workers earn less than the minimum wage, a particularly surprising finding since membership in the formal sector should at least provide the minimum wage. The most dramatic difference between workers in the two sectors is in job stability. Nearly 98 percent of formal-sector workers have held their current job for a year or longer, compared to only 45.6 percent of informal-sector workers.

In the period from 1977 to 1987, a period of crisis in the Mexican economy, patterns of employment changed radically in Oaxaca. These ten years saw a dramatic rise in the percentage of households drawing income from the informal sector of the economy. The rise in the percentage of households with no worker in the formal economy (from 40 percent in 1977 to 60 percent in 1987) indicates that new workers are not finding stable employment and that established heads of households, who represented the largest single group in the formal sector in 1977, have been

Table 4.3
Informal- and Formal-Sector Comparisons

	Informal	Formal
INCOME AND EMPLOYMENT		
Over minimum wage	8.8%	68.6%
Top .6 percent of distribution	0.2	0.9
Stable jobs in past year	45.6	97.7
SEX		
Male	44.0	56.0
Female	53.0	47.0
MIGRATION		
Nonmigrant	39.8	39.8
Within last 5 years	32.6	35.2
AGE		
Less than 24	12.7	5.6
25–44	48.6	62.9
EDUCATION		
Illiterate	19.9	4.4
Beyond secondary	3.8	31.0

displaced from the formal into the informal sector. This change is even more dramatic for women. We would argue that this pattern suggests a fundamental restructuring of Oaxaca's service economy. With households falling out of the formal and into the informal sectors, the differences that existed between them (for example, in household income) are being reduced or eliminated (Murphy et al. 1990; Murphy 1991; Selby 1991).

Income Groupings

So far we have examined the types of jobs and the conditions of work available in Oaxaca's economy. Now we concentrate on the primary benefit of work, income, its importance in determining social position, and how it is distributed within the city.

As Chapter 2 indicated, when Spanish colonists first arrived in Oaxaca, and for some time afterwards, income was not the prime determinant of an individual's social position or of the region's overall pattern of stratification. Hereditary considerations were paramount. Spaniards and their descendants topped the social hierarchy with Indians ranking below them. Within the Indian community the hereditary aristocracy still maintained certain privileges. The penetration of a money-based market econ-

omy, however, slowly transformed the foundations of stratification. Today, descent from Spanish forebears may contribute to prestige, but income is the basis of a person's place in the local social hierarchy and
consumption patterns.

In Oaxaca, as in other modern urban settings, individuals and
households depend for their survival and reproduction on wage labor
(Eames and Goode 1973; Schmink 1984:89). In short, income fundamentally determines the degree to which a household is able to provide for its
members in the modern economy. As such it provides a ready and reasonably accurate measure of socioeconomic standing. As demonstrated
in Table 4.4, Oaxaca's income levels are dismally low. For heads of
household the median income in 1977 was 2,150 pesos (about $100 U.S.)
per month, slightly above the city's minimum salary equivalent to $90
(U.S.). When we consider total household income, the median rises by
17 percent to 2,522 pesos (nearly $110 U.S.). Comparing Oaxaca with
other secondary Mexican cities reveals that even by Mexican standards,
Oaxacans are poor. Of ten secondary cities surveyed by INDECO,[10] Oaxaca
has the lowest income levels. The median income of heads of household is
less than one-half of all but two of the other nine cities (Villahermosa and
Venustiano Carranza) and is barely over 20 percent of that in Tampico,
the secondary city with the highest median income (Selby et al. 1990).
The other surveyed cities, with the exception of Mérida, are either all in
more-developed northern Mexico or boom cities linked to Mexico's oil
development. Thus, Oaxaca's economic isolation clearly has depressed
income levels (although it may be argued that Mérida is as isolated as
Oaxaca).

Between 1977 and 1987, mean household income for the city fell by
more than half in both the formal and informal sectors. Median household income stayed more or less the same in both sectors, indicating a
reduction in salaries at the upper end. Informal-sector income maintained
its position at about 74 percent of formal-sector income, but formal-sector
incomes were the hardest hit by the crisis, with a 56 percent reduction,
while informal-sector workers suffered a 51 percent reduction in this
period. While the gap between the two sectors has been decreasing,
households in each sector have maintained their median incomes by
increasing the number of workers, adding an average of half a worker each
over the ten-year period. Stated another way, the worker-dependency
ratio has decreased, as each worker can support fewer dependents (Murphy et al. 1990; Murphy 1991).

While the comparative figures on median income reveal that overall
Oaxaca is very poor, not everyone is equally so. Most Oaxacans, especially
the poorest, divide society into two economic classes: the humble people,
that is, the poor, and the "decent people," that is, the rich. The distinguishing characteristics are not always clear, however. The poor believe

Table 4.4
Median Income Levels (Pesos) in Oaxaca
and Other Secondary Mexican Cities

City	Household Head	Total Household
Oaxaca	2,150	2,522
Mexicali	5,044	7,023
Venustiano Carranza	4,025	5,825
Querétaro	4,982	6,016
San Luis Potosí	4,979	7,006
Mazatlán	5,986	6,350
Villahermosa	2,956	3,875
Reynosa	3,605	4,047
Tampico	9,989	12,744
Mérida	4,027	4,983

that decent, rich people do not have to struggle. They are born into their position, have easier jobs, which return more money, and their children have no difficulty obtaining access to the best schools. The best schools and the decent people's social contacts, in turn, give them and their children the easy jobs. Our analysis of the family and household (Chapter 6) and the presentation of four life histories (Chapter 7) confirms this perception. A simple social dichotomy also is useful in examining political movements in Oaxaca, which, as Chapter 5 demonstrates, have frequently grouped the dispossessed masses against the elite aligned with the federal government. Nevertheless, we feel that a dichotomy may be misleading when examining income in Oaxaca, hiding important differentiation, particularly levels of poverty and the recent growth of an *aspiring* class.

Thirty percent of Oaxacans, whom we might label as *very poor,* earn less than the minimum wage (Table 4.5). As a group they receive just over ten percent of the city's total income. The remaining 70 percent earn more than the official minimum wage. Conditions, however, may actually be worse than this first glance indicates. The regional minimum salary is established by the Comisión Nacional de los Salarios Mínimos (minimum wage commission) for each of the regions of Mexico. Everyone in Oaxaca, from worker to government official, states that a family cannot live comfortably on the minimum wage. Instead of accurately reflecting objective needs, the official minimum salary serves as a relative scale of value, an instrument of political policy against which social progress is measured. The political goal is to increase the number of workers earning more than the minimum salary, even if they still do not earn enough to live comfortably.

The Fondo de Vivienda (FOVI), a bank-sponsored and government-regulated fund responsible for providing housing loans to low-income workers, provides a more ethnographically realistic figure. It calculates that a household must earn 1.8 times the local minimum salary to have sufficient earning power to cover a subsidized loan. Mexican government agencies are generally willing only to risk assisting those who surpass this "real" minimum wage. By this standard, Oaxacans fare poorly. Thirty-five percent, a group we label *minimum wage*, fall between the low official minimum wage and the "real" minimum wage, although they earn 24 percent of the city's total income (Table 4.5). Combining the very poor and the minimum wage groups, we find over 65 percent of Oaxaca's population is not earning a sufficient income as defined by FOVI. A final distinction can be drawn between those who earn more than the real minimum wage, that is, 1.8 times the official minimum wage, and those who are capable of surviving without any direct government assistance. The government-regulated bank fund draws this last distinction at 4.8 times the minimum wage. We label those above the real minimum wage but still deemed worthy of government assistance the *aspiring* group. They constitute nearly 28 percent of the population and earn a surprising 40 percent of the city's total income. The highest-income group, the only one FOVI considers completely self-sufficient, constitutes only 7 percent of the city's population. We label this group, which earns a total of 25 percent of the city's income, the *middle/elite*.

The groups correspond roughly to the different social classes described in the chapter on Oaxaca's history; here, because of the availability of more complete data, we have identified them with greater precision. This differentiation reveals a continuation of the socioeconomic inequality that has characterized Oaxacan society for millennia. In this study, however, we describe four classes whereas others, such as Chance and Malinowski and de la Fuente, delineate only three. In addition to one more class than described for earlier eras, we also distinguish the classes differently in two ways: (1) our distinction between the very poor and the minimum wage groups is not found in earlier analyses, and (2) we include more people in our highest-income group, the middle/elite.

Before the contemporary era, unskilled and semiskilled workers and artisans all clustered at the bottom of the socioeconomic hierarchy. We find in the contemporary era, however, a significant distinction between the very poor, which tends to be unskilled, works in the informal sector, and has an income less than the official minimum wage, and the minimum wage group, which is more likely to be semiskilled or artisan, works in the formal sector, and has an income greater than the official yet still less than the real minimum wage. The axis on which this divergence turns is the increased role of the state, particularly the federal government, in the local economy. The differences between the two groups have been created by the existence of an official minimum wage and the development of a

Table 4.5
Median Income of Household Heads and
Total Households by Income Group (Pesos)

	Household Head	Total Household	% of City's Income	% of City's Population
Very poor	1,230	1,427	11	30.2
Minimum wage	2,096	2,437	24	35.1
Aspiring	3,994	4,982	40	27.7
Middle/elite	6,044	11,000	25	7.1
Citywide	2,150	2,500	100	100

distinction between the formal and informal sectors. As argued above, while the minimum wage falls short of providing a genuine minimal standard of living, it does reflect the federal government's efforts to establish a floor on earnings. Moreover, as the previous section revealed, not everyone in Oaxaca's formal sector is doing particularly well nor is everyone in Oaxaca's informal sector doing poorly. But again, the expansion of the formal sector by the federal government (through the provision of fringe benefits) is another effort to establish and extend a minimal standard of living. Our distinction between the two groups reflects the differences between those workers who have been reached by the state's endeavors to ensure a minimal standard of living (even if that level is not truly sufficient) and those who lie beyond the state's efforts.

The relationship between income and sector, however, is not perfect. There are some professionals and large-scale merchants who do not have fringe benefits, yet have relatively high incomes. More subtly, there are some who receive fringe benefits, yet still have wages below the official minimum wage. For these reasons, we have based our distinction primarily on income and secondarily on informal- versus formal-sector positioning.

The very poor account for considerably more households in which every worker is in the informal sector than does the minimum wage group. Heads of households among the very poor also are more likely to be working in occupations that have traditionally been located in Oaxaca's informal sector. The proportion of the city's population distributed between the very poor and the minimum wage groups is also different from earlier estimates. Chance judged that about 75 percent of the city's population at the end of the colonial era was semiskilled or unskilled. The 1977 survey found 65 percent in what most closely corresponds to these categories. The difference could be accounted for by the greater precision of our measurement, but we suspect it reflects a growth in the next more prosperous group, the aspiring income group.

While the minimum wage group contains those whom the state has tried to help, the aspiring group embraces those who have indeed been helped by the increasing federal presence. Not only do households in the aspiring group, by definition, have an income above the real minimum wage (as estimated by FOVI), but they also have a significantly lower percentage of workers in the informal sector and are likely to be working for firms that are either a direct or indirect result of the increased presence of the state. They are likely to have formal-sector jobs, either working in middle-sized, private firms or for the government. Moreover, and perhaps most important, as a group the aspiring class has the highest proportion of the city's income, 40 percent. Chance estimated that 20 percent of Oaxaca's population at the end of the colonial era was either professionals or skilled workers. Our aspiring group is probably somewhat more narrowly defined than his group, since some of Oaxaca's professionals will make it into the middle/elite, yet we still found nearly 28 percent belonged in the category of aspiring.

This would seem to argue for a growing middle class in Oaxaca. In a minimal sense this is true, since the aspiring group does lie between the extremes. But we think it would be misleading to label them as *middle class,* with the implications of a secure and comfortable existence and political support for the status quo. First, FOVI judges the earnings of members of this class to be above the true minimum wage, but not sufficiently high that they can exist without some form of government support. The high proportion with government jobs reflects their intimate ties to the increased presence of the state. Moreover, as Chapters 6 and 7 will reveal, the comforts of their lives are dramatic only in comparison to those below them and fall far short of what anyone in a developed nation would label comfortable. Finally, as Chapter 5 will show, many have engaged in intense political struggles to obtain this middle-range status.

Our highest income category, the middle/elite lumps together what others may have distinguished. It includes the professionals and owners of medium-sized establishments that both Chance, for the colonial period, and Malinowski and de la Fuente, for the early 1940s, labeled as middle class. It also includes Oaxaca's traditional, commercial elite and the newer, government-based elite. We have decided to combine these groups to emphasize not only their economic similarities, but also the vast gap that exists between Oaxaca's elite, the elite of a poor, isolated secondary city, and the national elite wealthier than anyone in Oaxaca. We wish to underline how even Oaxaca's elite are more middle class by national standards than upper class.

While the middle/elite does exhibit a particular income profile, we do not want to lose sight of its internal social differences. The first group constituting the middle/elite is the traditional city-based commercial elite. Since the city's founding, its elite has been engaged in commerce. During two periods, the first years of colonial rule and the cochineal boom era, the commerce included international trade, but local trade within the city and with its surrounding hinterland has usually predominated. Correspondingly, the city's elite has been insular. During the Porfiriato, little changed for the city of Oaxaca. Although there were some foreign miners and owners of small industry, virtually all of them left with the onset of the Revolution.

The second group included within the middle/elite consists of agro-exporters. In contrast to its effect on the region surrounding Oaxaca City, the Porfiriato initiated a significant economic and social change in the state's southern coastal and mountain region. Commercial export agriculture, particularly of coffee, began to dominate. Through the first half of the twentieth century, the agroexporters were oriented more toward the outside world of Mexico City and the United States than toward Oaxaca. They had little influence or presence in the city. In the second half of the twentieth century, increasing numbers established residences in the city, which they saw as the stronghold of the state's political power. The increased links with the external economy through new roads and air service have buttressed the agroindustrial elite, who have often established homes in the city and who, as we shall see in the next chapter, sometimes seek political power.

The last group within the category is the most recently developed, the national elite composed primarily of individuals who have migrated to Oaxaca to assume positions in the federal government. The increased transportation links to Mexico City and the overall growth in the federal bureaucracy contributed to the local growth of this class, but far more immediately important were the political disturbances of the 1970s, described in Chapter 5, which swelled tremendously the number of federal-government workers in Oaxaca.

The old commercial elite trusts neither of these groups of outsiders. Members of the old local elite are still slightly suspicious of the new arrivals, in spite of the latter's power, learning, and prestige. One manager, for example, moved to Oaxaca over forty years ago to head a major public works project in the city. Trained at major universities in Mexico and Europe, he joined the faculty of Oaxaca's Institute of Sciences and Arts. His children, all born in Oaxaca, hold positions of power in the city and state government. He, however, is still considered an outsider, that is, a non-Oaxacan, by members of the old elite.

In short, we describe Oaxaca's class structure as: (1) a middle/elite consisting of three subcomponents, the bureaucrats and technocrats, the merchant capitalists and traditional professionals, and the agricultural exporters, (2) a formal-sector proletariat consisting of two subcomponents, aspiring and low-level professionals and skilled workers, and mini-

wage semiskilled and unskilled workers, and (3) the informal sector proletariat of the very poor, consisting of unskilled workers and the self-employed (Figure 4.1).

We are left at this point with the question of the implications of these classes and associated income groups in terms of material inequality. The literature generally argues that income inequality throughout Latin America has increased since 1950, the beginning of our contemporary era. Between 1950 and 1975 in Mexico, the lowest 20 percent saw their incomes decline both relatively and absolutely, while those between the 20th and 80th percentiles exhibited a relative loss but an absolute increase in income. Those between the 80th and 95th percentiles gained the most. Their incomes increased both relatively and absolutely, while the top 5 percent fell slightly in relative terms (Felix 1983).

For Oaxaca, unfortunately, we do not have precise longitudinal data, but we can attempt an indirect assessment of the recent evolution of relative and absolute income inequality. First, the overall level of infrastructure, the level of collective consumption, has improved since 1950. Virtually everyone now has electricity and many streets, for example, have streetlights. The expansion of paved roads has eased access to areas outside of Oaxaca most importantly back to residents' home villages and north to Mexico City. At the individual and household level, the widespread increase in the use of modern manufactured goods has generally meant a greater increase of goods for virtually everyone. Luxury items, previously available only to a few, are now more generally available. In the early 1960s few poor families had radios; by the early 1970s virtually all families in Oaxaca had a radio. By the end of the 1970s, many even had television sets. A similar trend occurred in kitchen conveniences—virtually all have blenders and many have a bottled-gas or, at least, a kerosene stove.

On the other hand, as reflected in the predominance of squatter settlements as a neighborhood type, the housing shortage affects all three lower-income groups equally. Many households among the very poor, the minimum wage, and the aspiring income groups cannot find adequate housing in the private sector. Members of each participate in the phenomenon of squatter settlements. Similarly, many among these three income groups most likely lack piped water, indoor plumbing, and sewer service. This lack of services considered basic in the developed world reminds us that Oaxaca is still in a developing nation. It is important to remember that our income categories, such as very poor and minimum wage, refer specifically to conditions in Oaxaca. By standards of the developed world, the very poor are destitute and barely distinguishable from the minimum wage group. The aspiring, meanwhile, would be poor in the developed countries and the middle/elite far from elite by either Mexican or international standards. Their living standards only approach that of the devel-

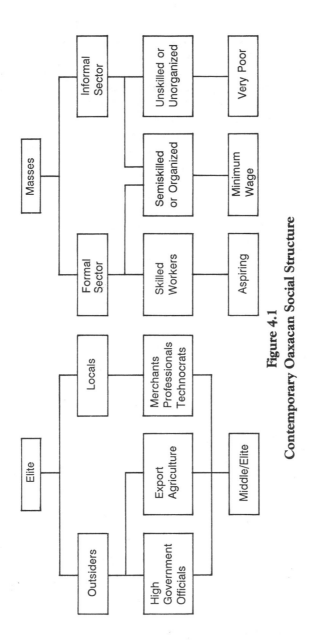

Figure 4.1
Contemporary Oaxacan Social Structure

oped world's middle classes. Thus, while all in Oaxaca have apparently improved in absolute terms since 1950, all still lag behind the developed world and the top echelons of Mexican society.

A question remains concerning the recent evolution of Oaxaca's inequality, of an increasing or decreasing gap between the rich and the poor. Are the very poor farther from the middle/elite than previously? How about the minimum wage and aspiring groups? Are they approaching the middle/elite or simply further distinguishing themselves from both the very poor and the middle/elite? And, more specifically, how have they been affected, either equally or differentially, by the 1980s economic crisis that severely eroded workers' incomes nationwide?

Trends in relative inequality, even with our imperfect data, are not uniform. Changes in diet, education, and self-constructed housing respond more quickly to changing economic conditions. The 1976–77 recession and the 1980s crisis have affected all in Oaxaca, but they did not affect everyone equally. The diet of the very poor has declined dramatically. The very poor are also more likely to withdraw their children from school and to see their housing conditions decline. The development of the formal sector and the increased number in the aspiring class have mediated some of the harshness of economic downturns and, as indicated earlier in this chapter, state efforts have created a distinction within the masses between the very poor and the minimum wage groups. Moreover, Oaxaca's reintegration into the larger economy and the efforts of the state (most visible in an increased need for education and corresponding demand for teachers) have apparently expanded the size of the aspiring income group. While this group has existed at least since colonial times, it is now proportionately larger than at any time in the past. These two groups, the minimum wage and the aspiring, fared better in absolute terms during the crisis: they had higher wages, although these suffered a dramatic decline; they enjoyed greater job stability; and, most important, during the crisis, they benefited from free health care. The very poor, in contrast, not having the fringe benefit of social security and being unable to afford private medical care, commonly endured illness without proper treatment during difficult economic times.

During the boom years of the late 1970s, consumption styles of the middle/elite significantly and conspicuously distinguished themselves from those of the lower-income groups. Members of this group traveled frequently to Mexico City and the United States for vacations and shopping sprees. They bought modern consumer convenience goods such as washing machines and dishwashers even though they still had domestic servants working daily. Virtually all of them could afford an automobile and many had two. While the quantity and value of the consumer goods obtained by the three lower-income groups also increased during this period, they did not improve so dramatically and visibly. Yet, the above listing of the improvements for the middle/elite reflect again its national and international position. Its members' living conditions improved dramatically during this period, and yet they obtained no greater luxury than what would be a middle-class life-style in the developed world. This group was the hardest hit by the economic crisis of the 1980s, reversing its past progress. Few of its members can now afford to go to the United States and few are making new purchases of washing machines or automobiles. In 1987, only 21.5 percent had automobiles and, as shown above, household incomes have stayed stable through the crisis only by increasing the number of workers contributing to them.

In short, data analyzed for Oaxaca appears to confirm data for Mexico as a whole that demonstrate a general overall rise in living standards since 1950 with the middle aspiring group achieving the highest relative gains. The data apparently do not confirm, however, a long-term absolute decline for the least-prosperous 20 percent, whose standard of living has varied more widely and who have maintained some material improvements. One possible explanation is that the least-prosperous 20 percent of Mexico's population does not live in cities and that the very poor in Oaxaca, while destitute, are perhaps materially better off than corresponding residents of rural areas.

Conclusions

This chapter has explored the economic contrasts between Oaxaca's old-fashioned past and its increased links with the modern world. We looked particularly at Oaxaca's economic structure from three different perspectives: (1) Oaxaca's primary economic activities, (2) the formal and informal sectors, and (3) income groupings. We found an economy that has been more stable than transformed, continuing a two-millennium tradition of providing services to the surrounding agricultural hinterland. We also found support for the same trend of an important increase in the presence of the state that we described in the previous chapter. The federal government has created an emerging distinction between formal and informal sectors that appears less marked than in other Latin American cities. In terms of income groups, overall consumption levels have risen since the mid 1950s, although the middle/elite have prospered the most, while the two middle-income groups have apparently grown in size. The consumption levels of all income groups respond visibly to short-term changes in the economy, but, not surprisingly, the very poor suffer the most.

Virtually all the city's economic discontinuities with its past result from the increased role of the state. The state has been responsible for increased links to the outside and consequent expanding consumption of mass-produced manufactured goods, an emerging distinction between informal and formal economic sectors, a reinforced distinction between locally and nationally based elites, and a distinction between the very poor and minimum wage groups and a growing income group, which we label aspiring, dependent upon the state's role in the local economy.

Both the very poor and the minimum wage income groups are poor by absolute and relative standards. They earn less than a real minimum wage and they earn less than people in other Mexican cities. Nevertheless, the very poor are distinguishably worse off than the minimum wage group—to which the state has responded and which it has made noticeable efforts to incorporate. The state has also significantly increased the number of residents included in the group we label aspiring. This income group and class have been with Oaxaca since at least the end of the colonial era, but with increased state presence it has assumed a larger role both in relative numbers and in income within the city. In light of these effects and other political influences described in Chapter 5, we believe the state now shares the stage with the family as one of Oaxaca's most important social institutions.

Nevertheless, these state-induced transformations have been less completely developed in Oaxaca than in larger Latin American cities. For example, Oaxaca's informal sector does not provide low-cost inputs to manufacturing nor is it linked to multinational enterprises. Because the formal sector is so new, linkages between it and the informal sector are obvious and inevitable. The informal sector is critical in the construction industry, an industry that boomed during the early and mid 1970s largely in response to government initiatives in expanding the bureaucracy in the city and in constructing new schools. The growth and nature of Oaxaca's neighborhoods, which we addressed in the previous chapter, are also related to Oaxaca's informal sector. Both the private sector's middle-class home construction and the public sector's housing projects have exploited the broad availability of informal construction labor. While construction workers have benefited from the building boom, their labor is still not cheap enough for the majority of the population to afford it for their own houses. As outlined in the preceding chapter, for the majority to obtain housing, they must participate in the irregular land market and build their own home with their own labor. Oaxaca's economic conditions, combined with its demographic growth, thus produce the squatter settlements that now occupy more than half the city's area.

A recent analysis of Latin America's contemporary class structure described five classes: (1) the dominant class of owners of modern capitalist enterprises (a numerically insignificant class in most Latin American countries), (2) the professional–bureaucratic class who lack control of the means of production but exercise some direct control over the working class, (3) the formal-sector working class protected by government regulations and provided with fringe benefits such as social security, (4) the petty bourgeoisie of the informal sector, and (5) the working class of the informal sector (Portes 1985).

Our analysis reveals that in Oaxaca these distinctions are sometimes absent and frequently blurred. First, as would be expected in a secondary city, the dominant class is entirely absent in Oaxaca. Oaxaca has no industrial capitalists, few large landowners, and even fewer landlords. The professional–bureaucratic class does exist, but its interests overlap significantly with two other components of the local elite: the traditional merchant capitalists and the rural-based, but city-resident agricultural exporters. The three together form the locally dominant class. Combining bureaucrats with professional technicians captures the reality of many individuals' careers moving in and out of government positions; it misstates, however, the peculiar social relations in Oaxaca, where those of the traditional professions, for example, lawyers and medical doctors, have been closely linked with the merchant capitalists. Moreover, the tension between locals and outsiders vitiates much of the potential solidarity of this class in Oaxaca.

The importance of the petty bourgeoisie informal sector is difficult to ascertain in Oaxaca, primarily because the distinctions between formal and informal sectors are not so starkly evident as they are in larger cities. Most enterprises in Oaxaca are small and unmechanized. There are hardly any that can be labeled "modern." All pay low wages. One, of course, could label all Oaxaca owners as informal petty bourgeoisie, but that would, we believe, distort the reality, first because it would obscure the links between Oaxaca's merchant capitalists and the local traditional professionals, and second because it would include the employers who do indeed pay minimum wage and offer fringe benefits. While this class is, of the five offered by Portes, most like the informal petty bourgeoisie, we believe it is better labeled merchant capitalist–traditional professional.

The last two groups, the formal- and informal-sector workers, are somewhat easier to distinguish in Oaxaca. They correspond closely, although not perfectly, to our distinction between the very poor and minimum wage income groups, but again the distinction is probably less marked in Oaxaca than in larger Latin American cities. Also, the formal–informal dichotomy obscures an important social division between low-level professionals, such as teachers, and skilled workers and the semi-skilled and unskilled formal-sector workers, a distinction we capture by distinguishing between the aspiring and minimum wage income groups. We believe that the aspiring group has not only a higher income, but also a closer identification with the government policies that have benefited it, including high public expenditures on collective consumption such as education and electricity.

Our review of Oaxaca's economy has revealed an "in-between" city:

isolated from but linked to the broader national and international econo-mies, fundamentally constant yet notably altered. Overall consumption levels have risen, yet lag behind the rest of urban Mexico: Oaxaca's middle/elite barely achieve the middle-class standards of the developed world. Absolute inequality appears to have decreased in the contemporary era, especially with the relative rise of the two middle-income groups, the minimum wage and the aspiring. Yet, relative inequality is constantly in flux as it responds to upswings and downturns in the national economy. The second half of this study addresses how Oaxacans have adapted to the "in-betweenness" of their constant and changing city.

5

Community-Level Adaptation

At 3 A.M. the distorted screeching of a battery-powered megaphone shattered the peaceful night. "Everyone up. Everyone must leave. File peacefully into the buses. Everyone must leave immediately!" The army swept through the flimsy dwellings of the new colonia popular, pulling people from their slumber and roughly shoving them onto waiting buses. As the buses filled, their unmuffled engines roared, adding to the disturbingly dark cacophony. The buses lumbered off to imprison the newly displaced squatters.

After emptying a group of dwellings, the soldiers splashed kerosene and set them aflame. Orange-red, crackling bonfires soon spotted the hillside, illuminating the soldiers at their work and a few figures escaping to older, better-established, squatter colonias across the adjacent highway. The megaphone and the soldiers continued. A long line of buses left one after the other. More bonfires appeared until the entire hillside was speckled with flames. An hour before dawn the operation was complete. No squatters or squatter dwellings remained, just smoldering ashes and the dim, burnt, formerly chalked outlines of lots assigned by the squatters' leaders.

The army's forcible eviction of the squatters in mid July 1975 was the most dramatic event in a tense conflict that racked Oaxaca's tranquility for weeks. It initiated a series of demonstrations and counterdemonstrations, sometimes with the same individuals marching one day in favor of the squatters' actions and the next marching in protest against them. The actions deeply divided the city as the government-affiliated unions demanded that their members support the army's repressive tactics while many of the city's inhabitants filled the streets in protest of the government's policies. National attention converged on Oaxaca as state officials were called to Mexico City for consultation and advice.

Oaxaca is far from being the charming and quaint traditional city it seems. Since the completion of the Pan-American Highway, recurring, episodic clashes between the old and new elite and between the elite and the masses have repeatedly shattered local tranquility. Such clashes represent Oaxacans' most spectacular endeavors to confront and alter their condition. They are not, however, their only efforts; Oaxacans also adapt in other less dramatic, less visible ways. In those lulls between confrontational politics, Oaxacans quietly accommodate and vigorously respond to conditions of socioeconomic inequality.

This chapter addresses these contemporary responses to Oaxaca's economic and social inequalities by concentrating on class-based political activities and voluntary organizations. First, among Oaxaca's class-based political activities, the most striking form of adaptation, we find two distinct types: intraclass responses, particularly local elite efforts to resist the central state's incursions, and interclass conflict focusing on working conditions. Next we address voluntary organizations, concentrating on a less sensational, but for Oaxaca's masses a more broadly important form, neighborhood political organizations. These organizations incorporate members of all of Oaxaca's income groups, although they are most important in the three least prosperous groups. Their goal generally is access to the means of subsistence and collective consumption, that is, land, housing, and associated services.

Throughout our discussion we emphasize four themes: cycles of core–periphery conflict, first between the local elite and the central state, then between the masses and the central state; cycles of regime tolerance followed by repression of challenges to the structure of inequality; the trend toward the increasingly important role of the state in managing conflict and in attempting to address some of its causes; and the constant pragmatic instrumentality of the participants in political activities, that is, how their activities take into account the structural realities of local inequality. This awareness of structural realities includes, as most important, assessing the real power of the central state and its tolerance of challenges. The prime mover behind all these activities is inequality, whether seen in struggles by the conservative elite to maintain Oaxaca's isolation and their own local domination or in more radical attempts to redirect benefits to the masses.

Class-Based Political Action

Two types of class-based conflict have characterized Oaxaca in the years since 1950: clashes within the elite between the traditional, commercial, local forces and the newer, nonlocal elites drawing their power from either the state's agroindustry or Mexico's national politics and economics; and popular movements striving primarily for improved working conditions and land. As the following narrative depicts, alliances constantly shift and the two types of strife often overlap.

Dominating the conflicts of the 1950s was intra-elite confrontation as the established, locally oriented commercial elite resisted efforts to integrate Oaxaca's rural agricultural sector further into the national and international economies (Tamayo 1956). In the late 1960s and through the 1970s, popular movements dominated when small-scale merchants countered efforts by large-scale merchants to displace them. In addition, the masses struggled to obtain land for housing and participation in the formal sector with its associated fringe benefits. We shall see that a key catalyst in both was student organization, until it was targeted by the state in the 1970s for repression and dissolution.

The first conflict of the contemporary period, and the most obvious intra-elite contest, occurred between 1950 and 1952 when agroexporters, based within the state but outside the city, succeeded in placing Manuel Mayoral Heredia in the state governorship. As mentioned in Chapters 2 and 4, commercial export agriculture, particularly of coffee, began to dominate the southern coastal and mountain regions of the state during the nineteenth-century reign of President Porfirio Díaz. For more than fifty years, however, these coffee interests exercised no political power within the state. The geographic barriers between them and the state's capital oriented them economically directly to the outside world through the ports or through roads to Mexico City. Their political ties were correspondingly directed more to Mexico City than to the city of Oaxaca. Finally in 1950, they moved to assume political control within the state of Oaxaca. Through ties of fictive kinship (compadrazgo) with the then president of Mexico, Miguel Alemán, Mayoral Heredia, a coffee producer, became the 1950 PRI candidate for the governorship of Oaxaca.

Upon assuming office in December 1950, Mayoral Heredia installed his own coterie of bureaucrats connected to Mexico City, displacing the local Oaxaca City politicos. Soon thereafter, Mayoral announced his intentions to modernize Oaxaca's agriculture, particularly the export-producing sectors. He proposed a new paved road linking Pinotepa Nacional and Huajuapan de Léon, both in the western part of the state, to provide coffee growers access to the Gulf of Mexico ports and increased North American and European markets. He also introduced legislation to provide ten-year subsidies for new industry and tax laws to finance agricultural infrastructure improvements, including the procurement of tractors, through state-backed bonds. Current taxes, Mayoral argued, were barely sufficient to meet the state's most immediate necessities. Growth could only be financed through deficit spending.

The city's elite viewed these proposals and the political change they represented with extreme disfavor. The issue was not simply the direction of Oaxaca's economic future—whether or not it should become more closely integrated with the nation and the world. Also implicated was a resurrection of the political question of who should control the state, whether local or Mexico City interests.

The Oaxaca elite was based on commerce, as it had been since the city's founding. The elite's commerce was not national or international, but local, directed toward the immediate market of the city and its surrounding hinterlands. They could see little benefit for them or anyone in the city from the growth of agricultural exports, particularly from the state's southern region. They argued that the proposed road, which bypassed Oaxaca City, would benefit the state of Puebla, through which the goods would pass, rather than Oaxaca. They further believed the burden of the tax and revenue proposals to finance these ventures would fall on them. To their ears, it sounded as if they were being directed to pay for the economic gain of outsiders—agroexporters who had never had a role in the city's economics or politics. The merchants protested loudly and gained the instant support of the local politicos whom the new governor had displaced. Not only had these politicos lost their bureaucratic positions, but they also had strong professional and personal ties to the city's commercial sector. Primarily law professors from Oaxaca's Institute of Arts and Sciences, they had been and were teachers to most of the city's elite. Further, many were the legal representatives of the city's businesses. A significant number were related to the local commercial elite through ties of marriage or compadrazgo.

This ready coalition of the city's commercial and political representatives easily garnered support at the local university, since many of the students were of the local elite and had the local politicos for professors. Through their political experience and ties, the city-based coalition gained support from national organizations including other universities and the private sector's National Chamber of Transformation Industries, the National Chamber of Commerce, and the State Federation of National Chambers of Commerce. Ironically, these organizations, ostensibly sharing a national orientation in favor of economic progress, supported Oaxaca's local forces in attempting to maintain its isolation. After two demonstrating students were shot by state police, the students organized parallel support from schools throughout Mexico culminating in a one-day national student strike. Meanwhile, the governor who had sought national economic integration had constructed no national political alliances. His only support came from the armed forces. In response to nearly daily demonstrations and a citywide general strike, an army regiment occupied the city.

By the time order had been restored, the governor had lost political legitimacy. He dismissed his cabinet and replaced them with local Oaxacans. He also named a local merchant, Harloc Hamilton, as the new state coordinator of agricultural affairs. Hamilton announced a new plan for Oaxaca's agricultural sector. He further stated that studies would need to be made before the introduction of any changes, though no studies were scheduled or subsequently undertaken. He judged the dirt roads constructed for oxen adequate for the state, and found no need for more irrigation, although he did indicate expansion might occur at some indefinite time in the future. In short, the state government would do nothing to help the agricultural sector modernize. Soon thereafter, Governor Mayoral Heredia resigned.

The city's commercial elite had apparently won a complete victory over the agroexporters. In spite of its economic success, the south had not been able to transform economic power into state-level political power. As with previous battles between national and city elites, the local elite emerged victorious. More than four centuries earlier, a similar group had defeated Cortez in his efforts to control the valley. Nearly two centuries ago, another had defeated the Spanish king's efforts to reform the alcalde mayor system during the cochineal boom. The dramatic changes brought by Juárez, Díaz, and the Revolution largely washed over this elite, after each of which it emerged again dominant. At that moment in 1950, the local elite thought it could keep the state of Oaxaca from being drawn further into the national and international economic system.

Throughout the 1950s, the local elite successfully maintained its position and there was little overt political resistance in Oaxaca. Political activities began to increase in the 1960s, however. First there were disputes about housing. Three factors created and determined the outcome of these disputes: increased migration into the city in the 1960s without corresponding increases in either the supply of affordable housing or formal-sector employment (Chapters 3 and 4); the regime's tolerance for challenges to the structure of inequality; and a politicized student left galvanized by the national 1968 student movement.

As mentioned in Chapter 3, squatter invasions, usually on the city's periphery, began in Oaxaca in the late 1950s (Butterworth 1973). Most of these early sorties were autonomous and on a small scale, and authorities usually dislodged those who took part, often only to see them return a few weeks or months later. Until 1968, the local power structure was intolerant, removing squatters as soon as they invaded. After 1968, state governors Bravo Ahuja (1968–70) and Gómez Sandoval (1970–74) were more tolerant, as was President Luis Echeverría (1970–76)—if the invaders selected federal land and appeared reasonably well organized. Throughout the 1960s, disputes (albeit nonviolent ones) were also growing between the large merchants in the city's center and the small merchants and roving vendors who participated in the weekly Saturday market. Finally, in the early 1970s workers not covered by the benefits of the formal sector began to organize independent unions, which struggled for improved working conditions, particularly coverage by fringe benefits such as the *seguro social* (social security).

These local pressures became much more acute in the wake of the 1968 student revolts in Mexico City.[1] In Oaxaca, students stepped into the vanguard of organizing the emerging discontent. Whereas, in the dispute of the early 1950s students had supported the local established elite (Martínez Lopez 1982), in the new era they entered the political arena against this group. The first organized response came from the Federacíon Estudiantil de Oaxaca (Oaxaca Student Federation) (FEO). Through most of the 1960s, FEO's primary activities were social, organizing dances and the like, but after 1968 and into the early 1970s it assumed a forceful political role. The Coalición de Obreros, Campesinos, y Estudiantes de Oaxaca (Coalition of Workers, Peasants, and Students) (COCEO) was founded in 1972 and led the student political movement until 1977. Both groups actively reached out beyond the university to politically dissatisfied rural and urban groups.

In 1969 and 1970, FEO organized a successful resistance to increases in city bus fares, an issue that recurred numerous times throughout the 1970s and 1980s (González Pacheco 1984). By commandeering buses and obtaining the support of bus drivers, service was halted and after a few days the price rise was rescinded. FEO also helped organize resistance by small merchants to large merchants' efforts to relocate the central and Saturday markets from downtown Oaxaca to the city's periphery. As indicated in the previous chapter, Oaxaca's Saturday market remains Mexico's largest peasant market. As the city's population grew, the market became even more important to the local economy. The organization representing large-scale, permanently located merchants, the Federación de Mercados (Market Federation), argued that the smaller vendors were unhygienic, the old market was too crowded and too Indian, and that tourists were repelled by all these features. The argument had little substance. While the smaller vendors had unhygienic practices and the market was crowded and "Indian," these features were as likely to endear as to repulse tourists. The Market Federation's real goal was to capture a larger share of the expanding retail market by minimizing competition from small vendors. The federation merchants believed they could accomplish their ends by banning the temporary and roving vendors from the city-center market and relocating the Saturday market to new, more controllable facilities on the city's edge.

As in 1952, the wishes of the city's commercial establishment eventually prevailed, but only after a protracted struggle and not with the intended results. Plans for the new market were drawn in the early 1970s, and by the fall of 1974 construction was completed. The new structure, however, lay empty for four years as the smaller merchants, organized by student leaders, resisted the move. The government stalled, not taking a definitive stand, by claiming the market did not meet minimum building standards. The Market Federation continued to press its case and in 1978 soldiers and police forcibly relocated street vendors to the new building. The move, however, was not total: the old central market building was not razed as planned, a few roving vendors still displayed their wares downtown on Saturdays, and a number of merchants who had long held stalls in the old market simply refused to relocate.

Nevertheless, the resistors fought a losing battle. By the early 1980s the change was dramatically complete. Business at the new market, a ten- to twenty-minute walk from the old one, was back to the volume of the old, and tourists and locals no longer hesitated to bypass the merchants in the city center. The large merchants had won the battle, but the small merchants had won the war. The latter's victory can be attributed less to their organization, and more to the weekly peasant market's being crucial to the regional economy and Oaxaca's still being small enough that relocation of the market to the city's periphery presented no impediment to shoppers' access to it.

The permanently located merchants achieved greater success against roving vendors in the city center, particularly blanket sellers who approached tourists in sidewalk cafés and on park benches. In the mid 1980s, roving vendors were outlawed and their number visibly decreased as many had their wares confiscated, although some trying to maintain their market engaged in cat-and-mouse games with the police.

In the early 1970s student-led political activities were riven by factionalism exacerbated by government repression. The university administration banned the FEO and arrested some of its leaders. A portion of the student movement went underground and irregularly exploded bombs. The guerrillas chose as targets the offices of the Confederación de Trabajadores Mexicanos (Mexican Workers Confederation) (CTM, the PRI-affiliated association of labor unions), a private North American library, and the site of Oaxaca's major summer festival, the *Lunes del Cerro*, which was being remodeled. This last location, as a focus for tourism, foreigners, and top government officials, was an appropriate symbol for the bomb's blast. The explosion, however, was no more than a symbol itself and did not cause any delay in construction.

The aboveground student-led opposition movement ultimately had a far more significant impact. From 1972 to 1976, the movement led efforts to bring more workers into the formal sector and to protect and provide land for the poor. COCEO supported and helped organize two rural land invasions by villages seeking to regain control of land taken from them by large landholders[2] and involved itself in two urban land invasions in colonias on the outskirts of the city, San Martín Mexicapan and Santo Tomás Xochimilco (see Map 2.3). In San Martín Mexicapan, the state director of CNOP,[3] the city's municipal president, and the state attorney general organized the eviction of villagers from communal lands so that they could be subdivided and sold. With the help of COCEO, the villagers won the legal battle but were unable to evict the new settlers, who had quickly built housing. In the second case of COCEO's involvement in urban land disputes, in Santo Tomás Xochimilco, the government of the city of Oaxaca illegally bought communal land for the construction of a municipal slaughterhouse. After protest and negotiation, COCEO obtained indemnification for the colonia from the city.

COCEO's efforts peaked in 1974 when it spearheaded an effort to increase Oaxaca's formal sector by organizing independent unions of bus drivers, auto mechanics, university workers, municipal workers, bakers, social workers of the Instituto Nacional Indigenista (National Institute for the Indigenous) (INI), and workers in the city slaughterhouse. In late 1973 the bus drivers of one urban bus company went on strike over low wages, a seven-day work week, up to seventeen-hour days, lack of job security, and the absence of medical benefits. The company responded by firing the strikers. The COCEO-formed union rejoined by commandeering the buses. For a few days the government took no position in the dispute, but then ordered the strikers to return the buses. Demonstrations and counter-demonstrations followed until the union accepted a government proposal to create a new independent cooperative bus line.

In March 1974, the municipal workers organized an independent union that included street sweepers, gardeners, garbage collectors, and night watchmen at the public city markets. The government-appointed conciliation and arbitration board recognized, in spite of the government's opposition, the union's right to exist. The union struck, demanding a 45 percent wage increase, the benefits due government workers, such as inclusion in the health insurance program of the social security administration, and gloves and masks for the garbage collectors. In effect, the union was demanding that all city employees become part of the formal sector, that is, eligible for fringe benefits. After a week of garbage accumulation throughout the city, the government offered and the workers accepted a 20 percent wage increase and other benefits. In September 1974, an independent union of the state's public works department struck and won a 6 percent increase in wages, a forty-hour week, and enrollment in IMSS, the government-sponsored health and social security program. The following month the workers in the municipal slaughterhouse struck and won a 22 percent wage increase and enrollment in the same health and social security program. The gains made by the independent unions in 1974 were substantial—every strike was at least partially successful, and most of them won virtually all the benefits demanded. Despite these advances, as of 1987 many municipal workers were still earning below the legal minimum wage. In 1990, the city formed a new company to collect its garbage; the workers were paid more than those in the original company (which still operated) but they had no benefits and worked split shifts.

Toleration of these independent unions ended in December 1974 with the inauguration of a new governor, Manuel Zárate Aquino. Soon after Zárate Aquino's inauguration, bombs exploded in different parts of the city. The new governor blamed COCEO, which he claimed was creating a climate of insecurity through its "subversive" activities. The government subsequently stepped up its pursuit and persecution of the non-COCEO underground movement but, most important, it began to move against the independent trade unions. It successfully decertified and destroyed the bus drivers and auto mechanics unions. When COCEO attempted to protest a rise in bus fares in the nearby town of Zimatlán, the governor threatened army retaliation.

The biggest confrontation occurred in the city itself, when a group of city residents invaded some vacant urban lands—an event leading to the eviction and burning with which we began this chapter. The movement was not initiated by or aligned with COCEO. The state director of the federal public works agency had masterminded the invasion in order to increase his political power by recruiting support among the urban masses. The director's plan had been to convince the owner of a large tract of land to the north of the city to relinquish a portion of it in exchange for the introduction of streets and water on the remainder of his extensive holdings. Reportedly, the bureaucrat would then offer the land to the urban poor. The agency's director used university students with ties to the Communist Youth Party as intermediaries to implement this plan. The students, in a move reminiscent of Oaxaca's earliest colonial history, communicated with the urban poor through neighborhood politicians, the caciques.

A cacique from an established colonia popular, adjacent to the land in question, acted prematurely, organizing twenty families and invading the land. When no government response materialized, invasion fever spread. Within a matter of days, more than twenty-five hundred people had occupied the vacant land straddling the Pan American Highway on the northern edge of the city.

Those seeking land were a mixed group. Although the urban poor, and particularly those in the informal sector, were well represented, other squatters came from the formal sector and still others were not even city residents. The urban poor who participated in the invasion generally were families with adolescent or preadolescent children who already had, or soon would have, a great need to establish a household for themselves. These families fit the archetype of squatters—highly desirous of housing but lacking requisite resources to obtain it because land was priced beyond their means. Generally they were not from the same colonias as the organizing caciques. The poor from the same colonias as the organizers spurned the affair because they felt the caciques were more interested in extending their personal power than in the welfare of the squatters.

Many, perhaps most, participants were opportunists. Among them were urban blue-collar and middle-class workers employed in more productive, formal sector occupations in the city and with access to other government housing programs, including INFONAVIT and ISSSTE. In addition, small-time rural speculators from villages surrounding the city saw this as an opportunity to acquire valuable urban real estate and joined the invasion. In general, both these categories of participants were investing only a small part of their time and little or no capital, risking governmental repression in hopes of reaping significant economic benefits by later selling their lots.

Reaction followed quickly. Since Oaxaca is the state capital, the landowners did not waste time appealing to municipal officials but proceeded directly to the governor, the most visible and important official in the city. They argued that the invasion was a threat to private property rights and the free-enterprise system. Following this meeting, the governor issued a proclamation giving the squatters seventy-two hours to vacate the land. Newspapers duly printed the proclamation with accompanying editorials and articles condemning the invasion.

The squatters reacted with ambivalence. Some left immediately; some claimed they would stay to the end; others waited indecisively to see what would happen. They did not need to wait long. At 3 A.M., only thirty-six hours after the proclamation had been issued, the army advanced. The squatters were forcibly evicted, herded into buses, and imprisoned overnight while what remained behind was burned. The eviction was well-organized and nonviolent, although the military did burn the homes of a few legal residents who had the misfortune to live nearby.

The following morning the students organized a sit-in in front of the government palace on the zócalo. At first it was small, varying from twenty-five to seventy-five individuals throughout the day. Two days later those supporting the squatters regrouped and held mass demonstrations drawing fifteen hundred and then twenty-five hundred people. Those attending held banners demanding the government fulfill what it claimed was a constitutional obligation to provide land for the poor.[4]

After two weeks of demonstrations, the governor appointed Jorge Antonio, the state director of INDECO, to formulate a response ameliorating the situation. Viewing himself as a technocrat, Antonio was not interested in ideological matters concerning the rights of the urban poor, nor in their potential political power. Rather, he concerned himself with the pragmatic issue of finding land for those who needed it, at least those with need as he and his organization defined it. He forged a solution similar to the plan that had set off the original invasion. This time, however, the governor approved the plan and specifically excluded any participation by the alleged initiator of the invasion or his agency.

Antonio received no assistance at either the municipal, state, or federal level in implementing his plan. Once an arrangement to trade land for infrastructure had been made, he had to find capital to finance it. The most he could obtain was a loan from his own agency for the infrastructure on the donated land's two hundred fifty lots. The director devised a bureaucratic sieve whereby two thousand five hundred families could be reduced to the two hundred fifty most needy who were also able to pay for the lot in small monthly installments. Construction began in colonia Santa Rosa, and today it is one of the most developed poor areas of the city.

This last was the most recent significant victory of the student-led movement in Oaxaca. Beginning at the end of 1975, the state took the initiative in repressing it, and the demolition was completed in early 1977, when, as in 1952, federal troops occupied the city and the governor resigned.

Although political activity and government repression took place throughout the state, the main focus was the university. The difficulties began with university elections for the rector, equivalent to a university president in the United States. Beginning in December of 1975, Universidad Autónoma Benito Juárez de Oaxaca (UABJO) students struck for two months to protest the appointment of unpopular directors in some of the university's schools. The selection process produced two rectors, one chosen by majority vote and the other imposed by the state government. The two factions forcibly occupied different buildings within the university and snipings and killings occurred. In response to the confusion and not wishing to take sides, the federal government withheld its subsidy to the university.

Through the next year, disputes within the university and between the state and federal governments and the university convulsed first the campus, then the city, and ultimately a significant part of the state. The original impetus for the disputes was soon forgotten as each side responded to the other's actions. Students and their allies reacted against government repression, while the government and its allies attempted to restore the public order disturbed by increasingly frequent strikes and demonstrations.

Meanwhile, other disturbances cropped up throughout the state, many of them organized by COCEO. Villages and towns claimed that the government and PRI had refused to recognize the election of non-PRI candidates to municipal office, most notably in Juchitán in southern Oaxaca. During a demonstration protesting the state's imposition of PRI candidates, the state police sprayed the crowd with machine-gun fire, killing three and wounding over fifty. In the capital, a strike against city bus fare hikes and separately against fare increases for bus trips to the coast resulted in the arrest and detention of more than fifty strikers at one demonstration.[5]

In the midst of this turmoil merchants, landowners, service clubs, and the PRI formed the Fusión Cívica de Organizaciones Productivas de Oaxaca (Oaxaca Civic Coalition of Productive Organizations) (FUCOPO) to reestablish civil peace and to promote, as it stated, "social stability [and] economic progress, and to combat subversive agitation." FUCOPO announced a shutdown of all businesses for three days and asked for the arrest of all "delinquents disguised as students, workers, and peasants" who had taken part in recent disturbances and of the intellectuals planning these events. On the second day of the shutdown, pro- and antigovernment supporters clashed in the city's public markets. University students claimed that state police beat up fruit and vegetable vendors who dared to break the business shutdown.

The day after the citywide shutdown, a demonstration against the government by more than one thousand participants massed at the university's school of medicine. They began to march on the city plaza, but when they got within two blocks the state police attacked the marchers, wounding at least twenty-five and killing one. The marchers ran in panic, carrying the wounded to shelter. That night federal army troops took control, occupying all the city's major streets. The following day, Governor Zárate Aquino asked for a leave of absence and that evening Oaxaca had a new governor, General Elisco Jiménez Ruíz, who maintained order with the aid of federal troops who occupied the city for the next nine months.

With this swift, violent blow public demonstrations ceased and COCEO was broken. Henceforth, university disturbances, which did continue although in lesser force, did not spread to other nonuniversity groups in the state.[6] Moreover, organized political activity on behalf of the masses virtually disappeared.

Equally important, in the wake of the army's occupation the federal government's presence dramatically increased in Oaxaca. Federal expenditures increased substantially, as did federal employment, reflected in the 1977 data reported in the previous chapter. All federal agencies in the state had their staffs increased,[7] a move the government hoped would partially mollify the local population. Most visibly, INFONAVIT undertook a massive building project and new schools were started. Non-Oaxacan bureaucrats, with little local knowledge or experience, flowed into the city, and Oaxacans who had left the city for advanced education also returned. Even their new political positions, however, oriented them away from Oaxaca and toward the center of Mexico's power, Mexico City. As a result, the old commercial elite, without the resources to overcome external influences, no longer battled external elites directly as they had done in the 1950s and before the Revolution. As the old elite's control slipped away, its members complained that the outsiders were condescending, insensitive, and prone to misjudge local needs.

The political activities we have examined here arose in response to the effects of Oaxaca's national reintegration and associated patterns of inequality. The local elite sought to maintain dominance over the rural agricultural exporters. Small merchants resisted the large merchants' efforts to dominate local commerce. And the masses sought solutions to housing problems and access to the benefits of the formal sector. In retrospect the student-led efforts to establish worker–peasant–student coalitions had minimal success. Some urban poor obtained housing sites and services, small merchants delayed relocation from the city center, and many lower-level government and some private-sector workers were given benefits and brought into the formal sector. At the same time, these struggles revealed the force of government repression. Many protestors were jailed and beaten, some were wounded and even killed, and, most important, the national government, aligned with the united elite, broke the opposition political organization and deeply inserted themselves into the local economy.

Voluntary Organizations

Mexico is not a nation of voluntary organizations and few Mexicans join organizations simply for social or recreational activities. Oaxacans, however, do commonly find voluntary organizations instrumentally valuable in their confrontations with local conditions of social inequality. The masses tend to participate in vertically structured voluntary organizations, those that articulate with the socially or politically powerful, with access to resources they cannot get on their own. The elite, on the other hand, tend to join voluntary organizations that reinforce horizontal social relationships, that is, associations with other members of the elite.

Most important for the masses are neighborhood political organizations. With over 60 percent of Oaxaca's housing rooted in some form of irregular possession, political activity surrounding land and housing is important. As we indicated in Chapter 3, the existence of such a high percentage of extralegal housing reveals that the state has tolerated and used irregular settlement as a major policy tool for addressing urban housing shortages. The impetus for action lies with the squatters themselves, who struggle with the state to achieve recognition of their communities and for the provision of services. These neighborhood-based political activities are far more frequent and common than strikes, public demonstrations, or the mass land invasions just described. They have, as well, a more enduring effect than other activities in uniting people in political activity.

Santa Rosa, the colonia that arose from the 1975 squatters' invasion, exemplifies the process of unity building. Once the two hundred fifty families were selected, colonia formation began. Poverty, lack of housing, and the army's early-morning forcible dislocation and repression forged an extraordinarily steadfast body politic. The student organizers of the invasion resolved to obtain services as quickly as possible for those who qualified for the government site-and-services projects. Even as the government agency administering the colonia, INDECO, was still assigning lots, the students began organizing the colonia's future residents. They advised them to keep constant pressure on the agency for the provision of basic services: roads, water, electricity, a primary-school building, and a community center. Delegations met daily with the government agency, though the bureaucrats contacted responded accurately that they had no budget to find such services.

For the first year, the colonia held meetings nearly every week and attendance was virtually universal. Debate was lively and impassioned, and the members vowed to fulfill the left's slogan, *El pueblo unido, jamás será vencido* (The people united will never be defeated). The members of the colonia refused to accept the bureaucrats' excuses and continued their daily demands. In just over a year, the government agency had bulldozed roads, provided electricity, piped water to every house, and built a school and community center. Colonia Santa Rosa had as many services as any colonia popular in Oaxaca, and its residents had received them in a shorter period of time. The residents' slogan appeared to be confirmed: the people had not been defeated.

Not every colonia popular, however, is so united or so successful. A counterexample is provided by Colonia Benito Juarez, which lies above the Pan American Highway as it enters Oaxaca from Mexico City and climbs the Cerro del Fortín to overlook and skirt the city's center. Colonia Benito Juarez began as an extension of the colonia immediately below it and on the other side of the highway, Colonia Santa María. Santa María was legally developed in 1960 and 1961. At the same time there were two attempted invasions of the land above the highway. Both times, lawyers who claimed legal ownership of the land persuaded authorities to expel the invaders. A little over a year later, an official from a local market organized another invasion, declaring the land was free land. A new state governor proved reluctant to remove the squatters, and the lawyers claiming ownership arrived to collect installment fees for the occupied lots. Most began to pay. The legal colonia below the highway extended an offer to the new residents to join with them, which they did nominally for a few years. In the late 1960s more residents began arriving above the highway, and a movement challenging the lawyers' ownership of the land began.

One faction refused to pay the lawyers any installments. The lawyers could not muster enough political support to evict the nonpayers and gradually all who had not yet paid for their land stopped making payments.

Meanwhile, Santa María, the colonia below the highway, was progressing at a faster rate than that above. It was larger and its residents had more money. Their streets were broader and more extensive than in Benito Juarez. They had electricity and were discussing plans to obtain piped water. They sought the participation of those above the highway but got little response, as the residents of Benito Juarez mistrusted those of Santa María, believing they would unfairly benefit from joint cooperation. The residents of Benito Juarez refused to recognize Santa María's elected officials, its *mesa directiva* (neighborhood council), and when plans to obtain water materialized they refused to participate. Settlers in Benito Juarez formed their own ad hoc mesa directiva and formally split from Santa María.

The newly organized residents in Benito Juarez instituted weekly tequios (communal work projects), which concentrated on building streets in the steep hillside. Because the mountain was steep and rocky and the colonia small, work progressed slowly. The residents began collecting funds for their own water project, but the funds disappeared. The responsible officials were dismissed and the colonia elected a new mesa directiva.

Benito Juarez's new mesa directiva began again, although in an environment of suspicion. Up until then residents had carried water from Santa María by hand, across the highway and up the hill—time-consuming and backbreaking work—in two twenty-liter cans suspended from a pole balanced on their shoulders. In the dry season the trip is hot and dusty; in the rainy season, with seventy pounds of water suspended on the back, the chore is slippery and treacherous. The mesa directiva approached the city government for access to city water, but the official with whom the representatives had an audience curtly dismissed them, stating with justification that the city did not have enough water to go around. Moreover, he said, the residents were illegally occupying the land on the hill; they had no official status as a colonia. At best, they were a part of Colonia Santa María below them and should cooperate with its residents to obtain services. Further, the waterline did not have enough pressure make it up the hill; the incline was too steep. Rather, he advised, the squatters should come down off the hill into the flat part of the city, occupy legal lots, and then he might favorably review their request.

Benito Juarez's leaders humbly offered their gratitude for the important official's time and turned to leave. Just as they were about to pass through the office door, one of them turned back to the official. He stated that the colonia was not asking for much, they were a small colonia of humble people who had to climb a steep hill with heavy buckets of water and cross the busy Pan American Highway. Children and mothers daily risked their lives. All they were asking was for the right to tap into the city's water supply. The colonia would supply all the materials, all the pipe, and the labor to dig the trench, lay the pipe, and build a storage tank on the other side of the highway in their own colonia.

The official hesitated briefly. A broad smile came to his face and he replied that in that case he and the city's government would be delighted to assist the colonia. He would order the papers drafted immediately. The papers were drawn up and Benito Juarez did buy and lay the pipe and construct a holding tank. Meanwhile, members of the mesa directiva made at least one journey a week to city and federal offices seeking official recognition of the Colonia Benito Juarez as an independent, legitimate colonia. Because of the residents' mistrust of the political system, only a few individuals accompanied the community's delegations downtown and nearly as few donated to the water fund.[8] As a result, the colonia could afford only a ¾-inch pipe to extend up the hill from the main pipe and could not afford a pump to supplement the low pressure. The holding tank is consequently more often empty than full and water is rationed by locking the tank's gates from midmorning until afternoon and then again in the early evening. Another problem persists: the city official had neglected to mention that the water to which he had so generously given them rights was untreated, entering the colonia before it reached the city's water treatment facility.

Benito Juarez was not the only colonia receiving untreated water. The main sources of water for the city are San Felipe and wells along the Atoyac River. Along the main pipes connecting these sources to the purification plant lie many of the new squatter settlements. In order to save costs, the government has simply allowed these communities to tap into the untreated source rather than spend the funds necessary to bring water back from the treatment facility to the colonias. Moreover, the people of the colonias populares must pay more for this untreated water than households in the more affluent areas of the city that receive piped, treated water into their homes. As in the case of Benito Juarez, the communities get permission from the municipal government, and only permission, to tap into the city's water supply. They themselves must pay for or provide all the materials and labor to lay the pipe and build the collecting tank, at which they queue up (usually every day, though it may be every second or third day if they live high on an especially steep hillside) to get their family's water allotment.

Colonias populares usually have their greatest success in obtaining electricity. The formation of the Comisión Federal de la Electricidad (Federal Electric Commission) (CFE) centralized efforts to provide electricity to every portion of the city and state. This is not entirely an apolitical act: as one government functionary put it, "Electricity is generally available to people in large part because it is visible." On the other hand, sewers, which are underground, cannot serve the important function of reminding people of the goodness of the government and the PRI.

Many of Colonia Benito Juarez's experiences are typical of Oaxaca's colonias. Organized politically by a mesa directiva with a president, secretary, treasurer, and perhaps other officials, their first task is to obtain basic services and official recognition of the community. Official recognition usually requires continuous lobbying of city and state officials, as it did with Benito Juarez. The provision of services demands the mobilization of colonia capital and labor, since the government seldom finances or assists in their construction. To buy materials each household is assessed equally, and for labor each household must contribute one laborer to the weekly tequios or pay the equivalent of an unskilled laborer's daily wage. Every Sunday most of the newer colonias have work crews laying pipe or bricks, chipping roads from the hillside, or involved in some other communal project.[9]

Unlike Benito Juarez, most colonias retain solidarity and do not disintegrate into factionalism until they have reasonably secure land tenure and basic services (Higgins 1972; 1979). Once basic services are obtained, most colonia organizations do become like Benito Juarez, dissolving into factions among the leaders and apathy among the majority. At this point, the colonia's political organization often becomes a tool in some resident's efforts to establish a local political fiefdom for his own advancement. Charges of corruption and malfeasance abound, and residents frequently refuse to pay levies or participate in communal projects. A large number of families simply ignore their community's political organization. While all colonias have a political organization, the 1977 survey revealed that for all the city's colonias only between 40 and 60 percent in each colonia say they are aware of any organization in their neighborhoods. In reality, most popular neighborhoods have athletic teams and other voluntary organizations for males and females of all ages, but only about 10 percent of the survey's respondents stated that they actively participated in some type of organized colonia group, whether tequios or soccer teams.

Citywide, residents evince little interest in neighborhood modification, with almost two-thirds claiming they want no changes in their neighborhood. This apparent satisfaction may reflect an underlying cynicism and a suspicion of attempts by the government, whether local or federal, to improve their living standards. Experience also teaches that expanding basic services may easily cost more than is at first evident. An INDECO-sponsored site-and-services project for middle-income groups, which we briefly discussed in Chapter 3, provides an apt illustration.

In this case, INDECO's director and his social workers attempted to organize the new colonia's residents into a mesa directiva, a set of committees, and, potentially, a tequio. INDECO sought the colonia's active participation in the installation of its sewer lines, the colonia residents, however, saw no reason for their participation. From their point of view, the government agency developed the colonia and, under Mexican law, colonia developers, not the residents, are responsible for providing all basic services. The director and social workers responded that the law specifically exempted government agencies from these requirements, their agency did not have the resources to provide sewer lines, and the only way the colonia would get them would be through the residents' own vigorous participation. The colonia residents angrily responded that IN-DECO had misled them; moreover, they contended, even if they were to participate the burden would be unfair. Over one-third of the lots had been purchased by speculators who paid for the land but had not occupied it. These owners clearly would not participate as much in a tequio as residents, thus saddling the residents with an even greater load. Not only would the speculators not participate in the tequio, but they would reap its benefits, since the sewer system would increase the value of their lots as much as those of the residents who gave their labor to the project.

INDECO, also piqued at the uninvited and unforeseen attempts at speculation, pressured absentee owners to construct some type of housing on their lots or face possible dispossession, since eligibility for a lot was contingent upon a need for housing. Failure to build, from the agency's viewpoint, constituted prima facie evidence that the purchaser did not really need the lot. Ironically, while INDECO was bemoaning the colonia's apparent apathy, the residents themselves organized two projects. First, without any outside assistance, they constructed a church. Their next project was a kindergarten and primary school. Having organized an ad hoc committee, within two years they had constructed two rooms and had teachers holding classes for grades one through six. The school directress requested and then received six additional classrooms within four years of the completion of the original two. The colonia successfully and quickly accomplished these projects because its residents wanted them and they believed that the colonia had the responsibility for initiating and completing them (Prince 1988, Prince and Murphy 1990).

Residents of the center city and the middle-class neighborhoods participate in colonia organizations even less than do the rest of Oaxacans. Both types of neighborhoods already have all services and there exists little need to organize mesas directivas and committees. The city center had services installed over a half-century ago, and the builders of middle-class houses know they cannot sell a house without services. In these areas, families remain isolated behind thick adobe and concrete-block walls and are more likely to ignore each other than to be on either good or bad terms.

In one exceptional case, a middle-class colonia organized itself to oppose INFONAVIT's intentions to build a working-class housing project within the boundaries of its neighborhood. Meeting at a local sports club, members of the colonia selected an ad hoc mesa directiva and began organizing their response. Using the telephone, they mobilized their political contacts and resources literally overnight. Individuals who had previously conducted bitter, public feuds through the local press united against the housing project. Within a week, INFONAVIT quietly scuttled its proposal and neighborhood solidarity vanished even more quickly than it had materialized.

As with the poorer neighborhoods, this middle-class neighborhood organized only for pragmatic, immediate goals that no one else could or would achieve for them, protection of their colonia from the intrusion of working-class housing. Because the less-developed colonias have so much less and frequently because no one else can provide them with basic services, they need to organize to construct their colonias. Once they accomplish this and provide themselves with basic services, colonia organization simply dissipates or devolves into factionalized bickering with some individuals attempting to subvert the organization for personal gain. The majority of the colonias' residents reserve their energies and wealth for the household domain, our subject in the next chapter.

One distinctive feature of the Mexican political system is the PRI's efforts to incorporate the majority of the population through voluntary organizations. In the urban areas the most relevant are CNOP and the PRI-controlled unions affiliated with the CTM. Many Oaxacans distrust both and join them only if forced to or if it appears certain they or their community will receive some material benefits.

From most workers' perspective, the unions are an extension of the government and not the voice of the workers' interest. Most formal-sector jobs require union membership and virtually all unions are affiliated with the PRI. Inasmuch as the fundamental allegiance of the unions is to the maintenance of the PRI's political control, their politics include no serious confrontation with the government and they seldom actively oppose local elites. In short, they practice politics of cooperation rather than conflict. For example, many union workers participated in or were at least sympathetic to the 1975 land invasion discussed in the previous section. Their unions, however, sided with the government and the local elite demanding the protection of property rights against those who lack housing or a means to obtain it. In the demonstrations occasioned by the squatters' invasions, Oaxaca's PRI-affiliated unions commanded that members demonstrate in favor of the government or risk losing their jobs. Many unionized workers, therefore, marched for both sides, in one to maintain their job and in the other to demonstrate their true political feelings.

In spite of this cynicism about unions, there are times when participation in a political voluntary organization is willfully chosen. Community organizations forge ties with external organizations if they believe such a relationship will provide material benefits to the community for a minimal cost. Colonia Benito Juarez first had relations with INDECO, which had provided materials and labor to construct a stone retaining wall and a few steps in the eroded gully that served as one of the colonia's perpendicular footpaths. Ostensibly INDECO is not a political organization. Rather, it is a federal agency with a mandate to provide materials, services, and technical assistance. Benito Juarez leaders therefore had no second thoughts about receiving materials from INDECO: at worst they would have to attend a public ritual where they would thank the INDECO director for his attention to their community. [10]

In the late 1970s the PRI-affiliated CNOP attempted to broaden its political base throughout Mexico by reaching out to the urban colonias populares. Benito Juarez's leaders earnestly debated whether they should cooperate with CNOP. There was no doubt the colonia needed help. After ten years, it had few services: electricity, a sometimes-filled tank of polluted water, a few narrow, steep, and eroded footpaths, and the INDECO-supported retaining wall. CNOP promised to help, but the colonia's leaders were not sure they should believe the promises. They knew as well that CNOP would demand something in return, at a minimum permission for posters advertising PRI election candidates to be plastered throughout the colonia. Members would also probably have to appear at various public events, such as the May Day parade, on behalf of CNOP. After much debate, dissension, and finally consensus they decided to cooperate with CNOP. The CNOP affiliation did provide the colonia with materials for new stone steps up the hill at the colonia's main entrance, a welcome gift since the colonia is built on an incline that averages twenty degrees and reaches thirty degrees in some parts. There are about twenty-five steps, each twelve feet wide, from the colonia's entrance beside the Pan American Highway to the first cross street up the hill.

In return, as expected, PRI election workers plastered campaign posters throughout the colonia and hosted a few candidate tours there. CNOP also requested residents' presence at demonstrations, but the colonia leadership found greater difficulty in fulfilling this obligation. Some were already committed to participate on behalf of their union and most simply refused. Usually only the president and treasurer would go to demonstrations at CNOP's request. While the affiliation still formally exists, the colonia has not received any material benefits since the construction of steps over seven years ago.

Ethnic organizations and village groups are surprisingly absent in Oaxaca. The state of Oaxaca has more indigenous peoples still speaking native languages than any other Mexican state and the ethnicity of language and village identification permeates Oaxaca's rural regions. [11] City-based organizations of individuals from the same rural villages are common in many Latin American cities and some Oaxacans have established such organizations in Mexico City and even in Los Angeles,[12] but the city of Oaxaca is different. Oaxaca's migrants quickly abandon their ethnic identities and enter the daily life of the city as members of the working class (see Higgins, Camp, and Payne 1982). On market day tourists see traditional dress and hear numerous Indian languages, but it is virtually certain that none of these Indians are permanent city residents. They, like the tourist, are sojourners, whereas rural migrants to the city quickly adopt city dress and language, becoming Mexicans and no longer Zapotecs, Mixtecs, or whatever. They speak Spanish and wear shoes, even if only inexpensive plastic ones, manufactured cotton clothing, print dresses, pants, and shirts.[13]

One of the authors vividly remembers the embarrassment he caused during his first field trip to Oaxaca as he attempted to give a friend, a pair of Italian sandals resembling huaraches, common Indian shoes. The friend, embarrassed by the implication that he was an Indian, made it clear to the novice field worker he would not wear the gift even if it were forced upon him. Spanish, even if it is only rudimentary and full of grammatical errors and slang, is taken up as quickly as possible and becomes the language of the home. Migrants want to be certain their children learn the city language, and their ethnic identity is saved for the trips back to the village. There they can speak their native tongue and enjoy their Indian heritage without suffering the condescension of urban Mexicans.

Oaxaca supports no football teams based upon rural village affiliation, as is so common in other Latin American cities. The city does have amateur football, baseball, and even *pelota mixteca* teams that incorporate a good number of Oaxaca's youth, but membership is based on either extended family, colonia residence, or work place, not on ethnicity or village roots. A possible exception to this denial of ethnic heritage is in Sunday drinking sessions, where a group of men from different villages and language groups get together with their resident anthropologist for a few beers and perhaps mescal, the locally produced and popular distilled liquor. It is then likely that a multilingual language lesson will emerge, with each asking the other how to say some important word or phrase in their language—words like *beer, mescal, cigarette,* and others a bit more profane. Everyone seems to express the most interest in English, but they all listen intently to each other, noting similarities with their own language and struggling not to slur the new words. This knowledge is forgotten as soon as the drinking stops, if not sooner.

If these men have any identity other than Mexican, it is first with the village they come from and secondly with the language they speak— not as Indians. Migrants from the same rural village have very little contact with each other in the city, unless they are part of the same extended family. Individuals are more likely to interact socially when they return to the village for the saint's day festival than they are in the city.

The absence of ethnic solidarity or even ethnic consciousness in the city is curious. Immediately surrounding the city, villages maintain their individual identity. Moreover, as mentioned above, at least some villages have established village organizations in Mexico City. Yet, when individuals from those same villages move permanently into Oaxaca City, they adopt an identity as Mexicans.

The transformation, we believe, is both structural and strategic. While indigenous groups have largely maintained control of their lands since the entrance of Europeans more than four centuries ago, they have never dominated politically. At best, they conserve a partial political isolation in their villages; outside of them, non-Indians—first Spaniards and then Mexicans—have exercised economic and political control. Those who have control may have been based in Oaxaca City, rather than in Mexico City, but are still of a different culture from the inhabitants of indigenous villages. The control may have been less complete and therefore less rapacious than that in other parts of Mexico, but the indigenous people still face condescension and deprecation. One is far more likely to succeed in the city, economically, politically, in school, or however, if one adopts a Mexican identity, rather than maintaining visible indigenous roots, and reinforcing horizontal social relationships is unlikely to be economically rewarding. Moreover, there is little need to reinforce ethnic identity through formal organizations, when the social basis of that identity is so easily maintained by contact within the city and easy access to one's village. Most migrants from indigenous villages are only a short distance away on well-served bus routes. Finally, Oaxaca City does not overwhelm one as does Mexico City; social ties and individual identity are more easily maintained when one's friends and former village companions within the city are no more than a few minutes away by bus.

Voluntary organizations for the elite appear to be more social than the vertical, instrumental voluntary organizations of the masses. These appearances, however, are deceiving. The elite frequent the two sports clubs, organize a sports league in the private schools, and participate in service organizations such as the Rotary club and the chamber of commerce. The last is, of course, explicitly for business purposes. All of these organizations provide some recreation and social enjoyment, but also have their instrumental benefits, serving an economic as well as a social function by reinforcing networks and by providing contacts and information on business or job opportunities for the emerging group of government bureaucrats and local and outside entrepreneurs. The linking of members of the same class rather than those of hierarchically different classes is what most distinguishes them from the voluntary organizations of the masses.

Establishing and reinforcing horizontal ties is most important for the newest faction of the city's elite, the nationally oriented elite based primarily in the federal bureaucracy. The old commercial elite and the newer agroexporters both have a relatively firm economic base and have been establishing ties with each other, since birth, through informal social mechanisms. Members of the new elite, however, frequently come to Oaxaca with few or no local ties. Arturo, for example, frequently takes his children to one of the sports clubs on weekends; while the children play and swim with their friends he plays tennis or golf with his. For Arturo this is an important means of contact with the business and governmental power structure in the city. Not from Oaxaca, he first came to the city when sent there by the government agency for which he worked. As far as the old locally oriented elite of the city are concerned he is and always will be an outsider representing the interests of Mexico City. Despite his position as the state director of a major federal agency, a position with important implications for the city and state's future, he and his wife have never been invited to join one of the elite clubs or to visit the home of one of the elite families in the city. For Arturo, then, a weekend visit to the country club is when he must make the informal contacts and strike deals that enable him to carry out successfully his private tasks and official duties. Indeed, when a change in administration at the national level made it difficult for Arturo to remain at his post, a golf partner, not a family member, helped him find a post within the state bureaucracy. Arturo's case illustrates one of the major divisions in Oaxaca's elite, that is, between those who see themselves as Oaxacans first and those who feel primary loyalty to the national government and culture.

An important auxiliary effect of the private voluntary organization has been to change the way in which Oaxacan families entertain. In the past, families of all levels either entertained their fictive and nonfictive kinfolk at home or at a restaurant rented for the occasion. Today, as the sports club example illustrates, entire families go to public places on the chance they will meet individuals with whom they share business or other interests. In addition, some of the clubs, the Rotary and the Optimists for example, require the members to entertain club members even if they are not from the same informal social circle within the city. Club cookouts bring together men and their families who in the past would not have socialized because they or their wives came from different camps among the city's elite. In one case a club required all the members to place their names in a box; each individual drew the names of five couples whom they were then required to entertain in their home some time in the next year.

Eduardo's wife, Gloria, complained about having to entertain in her home couples she did not know, and especially about two couples whom she thought below her social stature. She went along with the activity, however, because her husband asked her to. Perhaps because of the generous *cubas libres* served to loosen things up, the evening went well. Eduardo found he had much in common with a young engineer who had moved to the city with the CFE. The guest became a potentially important liaison since Eduardo's business has many technical dealings with the electric commission. Gloria found that one of the women was from San Luis Potosí, a city in northern Mexico where some of her father's family lived, and that Gloria's uncle had been the woman's teacher in *preparatoria*, high school. Since Gloria had often visited San Luis Potosí, they had much to talk about and by the evening's end were planning an outing for their children at one of Oaxaca's sports clubs. In short, for the newer members of the city's elite, voluntary organizations provide social contacts they need to work effectively in the city and help them discover social networks spread throughout the country.

Oaxaca's locally oriented elite has the least need to create new or to discover old social contacts. Men and women are born into a status that automatically determines the clubs they will belong to and schools they will attend. Their social relations outside the immediate family focus on ritual occasions in the domestic cycle such as baptism, confirmation, and marriage ceremonies. Those attending are their social peers, the ones whom the new elite must meet through the country clubs and arranged dinners. The old elite do belong to a Lions and a Rotary club, but membership is limited to the old elite and the relationships complement their already well-developed informal relationships.

Conclusions

This chapter has described Oaxacans' contemporary class-based political movements and voluntary organizations, and demonstrated some of the ways Oaxacans have employed them in reaction to the structure of inequality described in the first half of the study. We have delineated four themes: (1) cycles of core–periphery conflict, first between the local elite and the central state and then between the masses and the central state, (2) cycles of regime tolerance and repression of challenges to the structure of inequality, (3) the trend toward the increasingly important role of the state in managing conflict and in attempting to address its causes, and (4) the constant pragmatic instrumentality of the participants in political activities. The prime mover behind all these activities is inequality, either conservative elite struggles to maintain Oaxaca's isolation and their local domination or radical battles to redirect more benefits to the masses.

These struggles are hardly new to Oaxaca. Core–periphery, intra-elite contests began at least with the conflicts between the conqueror Cortez and Oaxaca's first Spanish settlers. Such struggles likely predate even this, stretching back to battles between Zapotecs and occupying

Mixtecs. Yet, we cannot assert that history is simply repeating itself, for Oaxaca and the political struggles it encompasses have undeniably changed. Before this century, because the state could not effectively assert control, local authorities prevailed in any center–periphery conflict, and for most of this century, until the 1970s, local authorities continued to have de facto independence. The central state for much of this time was not interested in Oaxaca, since the city had not participated much in the Revolution and did not possess attractive resources for development. Its interest was roused only when violent conflict occurred that local authorities could not dominate. In the mid 1970s, however, local authorities yielded their effective power to the federal government.

Contemporary alliances have also shifted. In the first dispute discussed in this chapter, between the city's established commercial elite and the emerging agroexporters, students sided with the commercial elite. In more recent political movements, students, profoundly influenced by the 1968 student revolts, have sided with the masses. Moreover, the issues have changed: no longer a question of isolation versus integration, it is more likely to be a problem of conflicts initiated by the masses, members of the three lower-income groups, over the distribution of resources.

Organized populist movements predate the contemporary era, arising during the revolutionary period of the early twentieth century, when Oaxacan workers formed their first labor union, demonstrated against price rises, and achieved an official reduction in the work week from seven to six and a half days. The increase in the frequency and importance of popular protest, however, beginning in the 1970s, reflects the contemporary structure of inequality, including population growth, a shortage of affordable housing, expansion at the national level of the formal sector of the economy, which offers substantial fringe benefits, and the need to struggle to attain those benefits. These conditions, along with the impetus provided by politicized students and tolerance from two state governors and one president, forcefully mixed to create an active local political movement and nearly ceaseless political activity in the years from 1970 to 1977.

The movement's demise originated with a change in the state's governor. Governor Zárate Aquino, who entered office at the end of 1974, proved intolerant of challenges to the status quo, such as those contained in the creation of unions independent of the PRI. His initial repression in the years from 1974 to 1976 sharpened the strife. The movement's denouement arrived when it convulsed the university and occasioned the imposition of federal troops on the city and an army general as governor. Calm did return to Oaxaca, as the federal government asserted its dominance and vanquished the underground, violent opposition. The opposition political organization was fundamentally broken, demonstrating that the success of class-based responses to inequality depended directly and fundamentally on the central state's tolerance of such activities.

While we have said squatter invasions and the political activity of the early 1970s was class-based, reality is somewhat more complex. The political movements undoubtedly gave the appearance of being class-based, of incorporating the working masses too poor to afford private housing and excluded from the benefits of the formal sector. Certainly this group formed the bulk of the movement and benefited the most. We must, however, add some important qualifications: the political activities of the 1970s were not purely for and by the masses. Opportunists abounded; in particular, the 1975 squatters' invasion was instigated by the local director of a federal agency hoping to expand his political base. He was certainly not a representative of the urban poor himself and benefiting them was of only limited, instrumental importance to him. Moreover, many of the invaders were professionals or from the middle classes with no objective need for land, hoping to benefit from the actions of the federal bureaucrat and the urban poor. As a more general example, when neighborhood political organizations devolve into factionalism, opportunistic individuals frequently attempt to use them for their own benefit. In short, the seemingly class-based political movement was primarily but not entirely class-based and succeeded only in addressing some of the more egregious inequalities involving housing and the availability of fringe benefits.

These class-based political activities also clearly demonstrate the trend toward the state as both the initiator and the object of responses to inequality. While the urban poor frequently talk in terms of "we the poor" or "the humble people," as opposed to "the rich, the decent people," the objects of their political activity are not the individuals frequently claiming ownership of the invaded or sold lots but the state, which they perceive as having the resources to fulfill their requests. Similarly, those in the informal sector who attempt to organize independent unions perceive the state as assuring the provision of fringe benefits, even though their employer may be in the private sector.

The evolution from local to central-state domination can be seen in the response of the state to these challenges. During the 1950–52 dispute, national political authorities stood on the sidelines until order was significantly threatened. The national political elite then supported the strongest local forces, Oaxaca's local commercial elite, who ironically stood for maintaining Oaxaca's isolation from the national system. Here, as in all of the most serious disputes, the central state acted as an arbiter, and did not intervene until local authorities appeared unable to control violence. The central state still appears to be an arbiter of local disputes, but its power is now more fundamentally important in its expanded day-to-day presence.

In the mid 1970s, the state did not simply repress those challenging the status quo. Instead, close on the heels of the army occupation and the reestablishment of order in 1977, the federal government sent bureaucrats and money into the city to placate the masses after having crushed their organization. Repression, it may be said, is now the initial stage of central state involvement in a crisis; the second phase of its involvement reflects its efforts to integrate or coopt the dissidents. New resources accruing to the area allowed a tremendous increase in government services and government-funded construction, which buoyed the local economy until the national economic crisis that began in 1982. Moreover, this second stage fundamentally transformed the local political structure, bringing non-Oaxacan bureaucrats, with little local knowledge or experience, into the city and ending the direct conflict between commercial elite and the external elites, as had occurred in the 1950s and before the Revolution. Instead, the old elite stuck to themselves and grumbled about the new intruders, some of whom had been in Oaxaca for more than forty years. They steadfastly excluded the newcomers from their intimate, informal social circles, perhaps accelerating and ensuring their loss of power. In response, the new elite created their own voluntary organizations, service organizations, and country clubs.

While the importance of the federal government has increased, Oaxacans themselves continue to relate to the state and political activities in much the same way, engaging in political activities for limited, recognizable ends. When the state is more tolerant of challenges, Oaxacans are more likely to engage in explicitly political activities, but when their limited ends are achieved or there is clearly no chance of attaining them, they abandon them. Patterns of political participation in neighborhoods exemplify this political pragmatism, as when residents of a colonia band together, exhibiting impressive solidarity, as they seek secure land tenure and basic services only to see the solidarity dissolve into competing factions once services are obtained. In general, whenever the issue is of immediate, concrete importance (such as housing, wages and fringe benefits, or the cost of transportation), when an organizing vehicle emerges to lead (such as the student-led groups), and when the chances for success appear likely (as when the governor and government positively respond to popular pressure), then a class-based political movement emerges and even flourishes. The worker–peasant–student coalitions led by COCEO and others achieved some successes, including instances when urban poor have obtained housing sites and services, small merchants delayed relocation from the city center, and the Saturday market reemerged as Mexico's largest peasant market. In addition, transportation price hikes have, at times, been rescinded and, usually, delayed, and many lower-level government and some private-sector workers have obtained fringe benefits, incorporating these workers into the formal sector. The students' goals were far more ambitious than those of the typical Oaxacans, and after a number of important successes the state crushed the students' organizations.

Dramatic political movements reallocated state resources to influential groups of people, while voluntary organizations have, on occasion, accomplished the same for poor neighborhoods. These events, however, are both episodic and quite limited in their scope, assisting with housing and improving at times the working conditions of some workers. They do not find or create jobs for individuals, nor do they provide assistance in the day-to-day, or more substantial family and household activities. To address their more persistent, enduring needs, Oaxacans have found they must maintain social stability in their personal relationships amid the turmoil of grand political events. We have described how voluntary organizations, such as unions and social clubs, are instrumentally employed for these ends. The primary arena for maintaining stability, however, is the family and household, the subjects of the next chapter.

6

Family and Household: Oaxaca's Social Firmament

David was born in Oaxaca City in 1955, but his father was a migrant from a village in the valley who had come to the city about ten years before David's birth. A few years after David's father came to the city, he returned to his village to marry his sweetheart. A couple of years later, David was born, followed by three other children. When David was about four, the family moved to their present house in a squatter settlement. The land is very steep, lying right above the Pan American Highway as it climbs the Cerro del Fortín overlooking the city. When David's family first moved to the community it had no streets, no water, and no electricity. It was nothing but lots marked by white chalk and scattered shacks that had been hastily constructed. Now, nearly twenty-five years later, it is difficult to distinguish the community from any other in Oaxaca. The streets down next to the highway are paved. Roads crisscross the mountainside and are lined with high arching streetlights. Electricity and water are both available and there is an elementary school at the bottom of the hill.

David attended that school, where he was a good student, good enough to gain admittance to the federal secondary schools (the equivalent of junior high schools in the United States). His father and mother constantly emphasized the importance of education and how it would allow him and, through him, them to move away from that steep hillside to a more convenient, less dusty, more attractive community. David listened and learned. After successfully completing secondary school, he enrolled in Oaxaca's new technological institute for a career as an architect. He again was a good student, although he was somewhat disappointed with the low standards of the school. Professors frequently were late for class, came unprepared, or sometimes did not show up at all. His progress was also frequently arrested by the student strikes of the 1970s. Although the movement was centered at the university and not the technological institute, students from all schools participated. David

137

fervently believed in their cause: eradicating the exploitation of the poor by the rich and the biases of the upper educational system in favor of the better-off, and addressing the poor's needs for housing, services, and better wages and working conditions.

David was equally committed to finishing his education and fulfilling his commitment to his parents. He did indeed complete his education and found a job working for the national oil company, Pemex. He has not yet earned enough money to move his parents down off the hill into a better neighborhood, nor has he forgotten his goal even though now married with a child of his own. He has established a separate household but plans to move into a new one with his parents as soon as he can afford it.

David's story is typical in many ways of Oaxaca's younger generation. City-born, of migrant parents, they live in communities that began as squatter settlements with few, if any, services. The communities and their conditions improved, but they remain desirous of moving into still better circumstances. They have more education than their elders and have found jobs in the formal sector. The political movements of the 1970s attracted and involved them, yet did not deflect them from their personal and family goals. For them the community level actions described in the previous chapter were episodic, important but limited in scope and time. Foremost and constant is their commitment to their family and the household in which they grew up.

This chapter explores the nature of that commitment among Oaxacans. It first seeks to establish that the household and family, not the individual, form the cornerstone of Oaxacan social life. It then addresses the dynamic nature of Oaxacan households, how they change as children are born, grow up, and leave, as extended family members come and go, and as those who retire from work are cared for by younger family members. We also discuss the varying forms of gender roles in Oaxaca, especially the manifold evolution of traditional machismo, and examine the role of compadrazgo in incorporating others into the family and household through a web of reciprocal rights and obligations. The final section analyzes the similarities and differences among households in each of Oaxaca's four income groups. The analysis intends to demonstrate how households in these four groups adapt to the social, economic, and political conditions we have described in the foregoing chapters.

Household Structure and Organization

The Primary Role of Households and Families

Broad political and economic forces have determined the level of resources available in Oaxaca, its underdevelopment, its demographic growth, urban problems, and social movements. Various social groups have responded to and attempted to alter these conditions. Individuals also respond, adapt, and try to change these conditions. But neither social groups nor individuals are the most important, basic social units in Oaxaca; rather, households and families form the foundation of Oaxacan society. The resources an individual acquires in order to confront the world, to succeed or merely to survive in it, derive primarily from a collective household and family effort.

The household and family play a direct and crucial role in most decisions affecting individual development. They determine how much education children receive—whether or not the children continue through secondary school and on to the university—and whether or not one migrates to Mexico City or the United States. In short, households and families fulfill the functions "concerned with day-to-day necessities of living" (Bender 1967: 499). The household and family are the smallest functional group, but fulfill the maximum corporate function (Netting, Wilk, and Arnould, 1984), making household decisions within the confines of limiting structural constraints (Balán and Jelin 1980: 15), such as those described in the preceding chapters. We therefore conceive of households as having "relative autonomy" (Humphries 1982).

We use both the words *household* and *family*, because they overlap considerably. To Oaxacans, as we shall see in the examples below, family is the more important culturally. The family is expected to fulfill all of the functions delineated above, and is, under ideal circumstances, also coincident with the household. All family members should live within the household, yet, for numerous reasons, some imposed and others from individual choice, family members often do not live together. The realities of the family and household diverge, families may not match the ideal, and, instead, households fulfill these functions. Households are more constant and concrete than families, which may become dispersed, move apart, and then later reunite. For these reasons, most of the subsequent discussion refers to households rather than families. Regardless of whether we use household or family, the crucial distinction is between these two social units and the individual. In Oaxaca, it is clear that the individual cannot be understood apart from his or her family and household. We cannot meaningfully refer to an individual's achievement, class standing, or socioeconomic status except by describing those of families and households.

For defining household and family Elizabeth Jelin suggests beginning with a provisional definition of the unit, which is then disaggregated and analyzed in relation to specific activities and finally reconstituted analytically (1982: 14). This critique, like the life-course approach, emphasizes the fluid interaction of individual time, family time, and historical time (see, for example, Carter 1984; Foster 1984; Haraven 1978). As the examples presented in this chapter indicate, Oaxacan families and households are flexible and dynamic, so much so that we find it of little use to attempt an operational definition of family. It is simply too slippery: which individuals are considered "family" depends on particular and highly varied family and household histories within the context of the broader forces described in previous chapters. A child who leaves home at an early age may disappear for decades and no longer be considered a family member. Cousins, uncles, and aunts are even more likely to drift away from the family. Yet, second and third cousins and similarly distant relatives can sometimes remain or even become part of a family. The key relationship, we find, is reciprocity: if potential family members construct and maintain reciprocal social relationships with each other, then they are considered real family members. Those who live in the same household ipso facto have reciprocal social relations, although those living in distinct households may or may not. If they visit (or, less likely, write or phone), supply money, goods, or information (such as employment possibilities), then they are considered part of the family.

We are, however, going to operationally define household as a social group living in a single dwelling area, such as a house lot or, as Mexicans refer to it, *solar*. We do not limit household to a single unit or structure because in Oaxaca, as in other places, there may be more than one occupied house or structure on a lot, all under the control of a single head of household (Eames and Goode 1977; Lomnitz 1977; and Singer 1968).

Households, not individuals, are also the budgeting units. Households calculate their budgets on the income of all wage earners regardless of how small the income. Children, for example, do not dispose of their income from such activities as shining shoes in isolation from the rest of the household. The money earned by a child or other relative as a third or even fourth worker in the household is often critical to the household's well-being. Everyone commits his or her share to the collective and the collective determines how it will be expended. The decisions about how to spend it may be made by a patriarchal autocrat or by democratic consensus; regardless, the household collective forms the basic unit, not the individuals who compose and contribute to it. Neighborhood organizing committees recognize this fundamental ethnographic reality by levying labor requirements on the basis of the household. Each household, not each adult, is required to provide an able-bodied male for the Sunday morning tequios.

Individuals can and do make up their own minds and ignore the wishes of the rest of the household. They do so, however, at great risk. They may find themselves entirely on their own, with no resources to carry out their decisions, no place to sleep, no food to eat, no money to borrow, and few friends upon whom they can rely. Accordingly, few Oaxacans live alone: only 8 percent of Oaxaca's residents are single, 5 percent widowed, and 3 percent divorced.

Household Structure

While households form the firmament of Oaxaca's social structure, their composition is neither simple nor static. Individual households have an internal dynamic of their own, a domestic cycle, that begins for purposes of analysis when individuals form a separate household, and continues through the birth of children, their growth, and ultimately the formation of new households. The process ends, analytically, when the children leave the originators of the household again on their own. These changes affect a household's needs—a household with younger, nonworking children, especially children in school, has the greatest economic needs. Children must be clothed and fed, and school itself requires certain expenditures. Once children leave school and begin working, needs are reduced and resources may increase if the child remains within the household.

These changes are continuous and even reversible with children being born at different times, attaining different amounts of schooling, getting jobs, and leaving to form their own households. Nevertheless, we can distinguish five types:

1. Young households with no children (9 percent of Oaxacan households)
2. Households in which at least one child is under five years old (46 percent)
3. Households where all children are at least five years old (29 percent)
4. Households in which all children are fifteen years old or more (11 percent)
5. Married couples or single householders at least forty-five years of age living without children at home (5 percent)

The above statistics reveal that most Oaxacan households have small children. In general, Oaxacans are family oriented and they cherish children. Only 14 percent of Oaxaca's households are without children, 9 percent of which are young families that have not yet had children and 5 percent older couples whose children have grown and left home to establish their own, independent households. Nearly one-half of Oaxaca's households have a child under five, while nearly 30 percent have all their children under fifteen. Households average just under three children, although there are a few with ten or more.

For an outsider, such as an anthropologist, the easiest and quickest access to Oaxacan social life is through children. If a couple has no children, Oaxacans extend their regrets and wish the couple the best of luck. They are even reluctant to address a married woman as *señora*, instead of *señorita*, until she has had a child. To Oaxacans, a family without children is clearly a family without happiness and joy. Children offer a household both immediate pleasure and hope for the future. Even in the midst of the most dire poverty and unfortunate circumstances, children provide warmth and comfort to a family. There is also the possibility they will obtain a good education, a good job, and take care of their parents in the future. For all except the highest income group, one's own children remain the primary social security institution.

There are two reasons we find few Oaxacan households at the end of the domestic cycle, where the household head is forty-five or older and no children live at home: first, Oaxaca is a town of the young and middle-aged. It simply has proportionally fewer people above forty-five years of age (see Figure 3.2). Second, many older heads of households gradually turn the household over to an adult child, who assumes the duties and responsibilities of the head of the household as the family grows and as the parents' ability to earn declines. The case of José demonstrates this household dynamic.

José was born in the Mixteca Alta, a region plagued by long droughts and extensive soil erosion. The region is the greatest source of Oaxaca's rural-to-urban migration. José's mother and father were extremely poor. A priest who served the region recognized José as an exceptional boy and arranged, with the permission of his parents, to place him in a regional boarding school. He performed well, but the school proved too harsh. While a young teenager, José escaped and ran away to Oaxaca where he lived with an uncle and aunt. In spite of his intelligence, quick wit, and verbal ways, he could only find work as a construction helper. While the pay was low, he worked hard and steadily, and within a couple of years he returned to his village and found a wife, a traditional Mixtec girl who, unlike most migrants, after twenty-five years in Oaxaca City barely speaks Spanish. José proceeded to have four children, two boys and two girls.

José was born with a club foot and has never been able to advance significantly as a construction worker. His house is of plain adobe, neither plastered nor whitewashed. The floor is dirt and the roof of tar paper. The household cooks over a kerosene stove, except for the homemade tortillas José's wife prepares on a traditional *comal* over a wood fire. The household has no television set or other modern conveniences except a radio. José has struggled to support his family and he knows he cannot support them much longer. Already, the number of days per month he can find and push himself to work has dropped considerably. He has placed all his hopes in his children and has sacrificed considerably so they may continue in school. He self-consciously does this not only for the children's sake, but also with the expectation that at least one of them will support him and his wife in their old age.

His eldest, Onésimo, finished elementary school (grades 1 to 6) fifteen years ago and decided to work rather than attend secondary school.

Finding no suitable job in Oaxaca he went to Mexico City, where he lived with José's brother. When he couldn't find satisfactory work, he began looking around for another alternative and chose a career in the military. [1] Onésimo is based in Mexico City, where he has a rather easy desk job, almost assuredly better than he would have found if he had not remained in the military. More important to him and his family, he has been able to continue his education, finishing both secondary and vocational studies in accounting. He does not really like Mexico City much—too much noise and smog, and too many people. Whenever he is given free time he visits Oaxaca and stays with his family. He still contributes to the household income by supporting the studies of his younger siblings.

The second eldest, Alfonso, chose a career as a lawyer and attended Benito Juárez University in Oaxaca. He is keenly aware of both the support received from his older brother and his father's expectations. The 1970s student movement repeatedly stalled his career. He did not, however, regret these interruptions; to the contrary, like Davíd, Alfonso supported the goals of the movement and actively participated in the events mentioned in the previous chapter. Throughout, his family commitment endured, and upon graduation he found employment, although not at a particularly high salary since law is the most popular career at the university. He then married and brought his bride to his father's household, where José had constructed a small one-room adobe house for them in the household compound. While the house is modest for a lawyer, Alfonso cannot afford anything else as long as he maintains his commitment to repay his father and brother. Instead of moving out and establishing a new household, he lives on the same lot with his father and plans to build a bigger house for the entire family once he has paid his debt to his brother.

The youngest two children are daughters. Both consistently graduated at the top of their classes through elementary and secondary school. The elder of the two, however, dropped out of secondary school one year short of completion in order to get married. Her father was terribly disappointed, but he maintains good relations with her and there is constant visiting between the families even though the daughter lives on the other side of the city. José has also maintained his hopes for his youngest daughter, who is still in school and still receiving excellent marks.

José's household history demonstrates how the dynamics of Oaxacan household structure affect education, income, housing, and retirement. He began in Oaxaca by moving in with his childless aunt and uncle, thus forming an extended household and transforming it from a type 5 (older residents with no children present) into type 3 (a household with all children at least five years old) and then, when he turned fifteen, type 4 (household with all children fifteen or older). Later, he established his own household in Oaxaca. It began as a type 1, that is, with no children, and progressed through types 2 (at least one child under five), 3, and 4, as he and his wife had children that grew within the household. It appears, however, that it will not become a type 5 household, one with older adults and no children living at home. Rather, the second son is assuming responsibility for his parents and becoming the head of household, transforming it directly from a type 4 household to an extended type 2 household.

José's household also typifies the burden for the lower-income groups of type 3 households, that is, those with all their children of school age. The household's material deprivation stems not from an absolute lack of resources, but from a devotion of those resources to the education of the children. Households with children over the age of five have the greatest economic burdens: not only do children above five eat more but, more important, they go to school. Even families who send their children to public schools still must provide them with pencils and pens, notebooks, uniforms, and other incidental expenses. In other words, these households have many dependent, nonworking members. In over one-third of all households, each worker must support two or more dependents. In over one-third of the households, each worker must meet the needs of at least three people.

While most households have many dependents, a minority are actually extended households containing more than parents and their own children. Only 25 percent of Oaxacan households had a live-in, nonnuclear family relative at the time of the 1977 survey. This figure masks, however, the dynamics of household membership and the considerable informal interaction among family members who do not live together. For example, migrants, such as José, frequently first move in with relatives upon arriving in the city. As soon as they find a steady job and an appropriate alternative, they commonly form their own household. Kin from the countryside may send a son or daughter to live in the households and attend the better Oaxaca schools. When they finish school they, too, leave to return to the village or, more likely, to remain in Oaxaca or move on to another city. José's case provides some insight, but that of Virginia and Abel is even more illustrative.

Virginia and Abel moved to Oaxaca in the 1950s and set up a *union libre* (common-law) household. They maintained close ties with their respective villages, returning at least three times a year, on the village's saint's day and whenever there was a birth or death of someone in the extended family. Virginia's brother remained in the village to tend to the family lands. The brother's son, their nephew Raúl, liked school and did well in the elementary grades. The village had no secondary school, so Virginia's brother asked if she would take care of Raúl while he attended school in Oaxaca. The brother would pay for food and Raúl would help with household tasks, as Virginia and Abel were getting older and needed some help in the home. Raúl came to live in Oaxaca and did well in secondary school. Later Abel's son (by a previous marriage) asked if his two oldest children could come to live in Oaxaca under an arrangement similar to Raúl's (who was now in *preparatoria*). Raúl had always liked his younger cousins and it was agreed that he would introduce them to the ways of the city and city schools. A couple of years later, Virginia's youngest son moved to the city and lived in the home. As a master baker, he makes a fair wage and is able to take care of his parents as well as his own young family.

This household started with only adults and later became an extended type 4 with the incorporation first of a nephew and then grandchildren. With the arrival of Virginia's son it then underwent another transformation, becoming an extended type 2 household.

The example of rural children staying with extended family for education reveals how extended households play important roles in current Oaxacan regional society. Even if one does not presently live in an extended household, one's closest, longest-lasting social relationships are usually within the extended family. Family members frequently rely upon each other for resources in a system of delayed, indirect reciprocity, sharing information about jobs or about life in the city or the United States. Extended family are always invited to the most important life-cycle ceremonies—baptism, first communion, graduation, marriage, saint's day celebrations, and funerals.

If extended family members live close enough to each other, own a car, or study or work in the same area, informal interaction is frequent. A son or cousin may eat his *comida,* the midday meal, at a relative's house or come over after a meal for conversation. Many families have also maintained the custom of an extended family gathering once a week for a joint meal at a grandparents' or one of the children's houses. Extended families are also likely to take their vacations together.

Gender Roles

Forty years ago, when Oaxaca was still largely isolated, gender roles closely fit the traditional stereotypes of macho males and submissive females. While machismo is variously and often vaguely defined, macho males are generally considered dominant, aggressive, and sexually promiscuous. In their ideal they maintain a mistress and frequently claim a desire to father as many children as possible. Females, in contrast, are to be domestically oriented and remain faithful to one man, directing their energies and attentions solely to him and the family he has provided.

Through the 1940s, the upper class manifested one aspect of these relationships in a weekly promenade. Women and young ladies were not allowed to meet with the opposite sex unless closely chaperoned. Every Sunday night there was the promenade around the central plaza, the zócalo. Everyone dressed in their Sunday best; women walked in one direction, usually in groups of three or four plus a chaperon, and the men walked in the opposite direction. Automobiles, discotheques, and country clubs have now replaced this tradition.

The lower classes, of course, never had the finery to parade on Sunday nights nor can they now afford automobiles, discotheques, or country clubs. For them, adolescent intersexual behavior is more likely to occur on their neighborhood streets, frequently concealed by the evening shadows. Not uncommonly, such liaisons end in pregnancy and marriage, although in the past decade unintentional pregnancies have declined in Oaxaca. In the mid 1970s, after consistently supporting the Catholic Church's position that birth control is immoral, the Mexican government and its president at the time, Luís Echeverría, endorsed birth control. They commenced substantial birth-control education programs that have affected all of Mexico's larger cities. The upper- and middle-class families and women first changed their attitudes; because Oaxaca's upper and middle class are small, the overall effect in Oaxaca is diluted.

In the poor neighborhoods, women frequently express interest and desire to practice birth control, although they also voice concern about possible harmful effects, particularly those following their husband's discovery of their use of it. In one case, a poor woman began birth control without her husband's permission or knowledge. When he discovered it, he beat her and proclaimed that he would abandon her if she did not stop. In spite of this example, we have heard more anecdotes of mutually agreed upon birth control and limiting of family size than of wife beating because of it. Among the middle and upper classes, the desire to have at least one child of each sex affects fertility more than anything else. For example, Ernesto and his wife have three children with no intention of having another. They say that two children would have been ideal, but the first two were girls. They tried a third time and were lucky: they had a son, Gilberto. They admit that even though it would have been difficult economically, they probably would have tried another time if the third had been a girl.

Not all couples, however, achieve this modern equality of the sexes with a limited number of children. Some men still retain the traditional macho view. Alejandro is a fifty-five-year-old master construction worker. He migrated to Oaxaca from a nearby village nearly forty years ago. In the intervening years, he has acquired the numerous skills of the local construction industry and the network of friends needed to keep him continually employed. He lives in one of Oaxaca's older squatter settlements, where he maintains a two-room adobe house with concrete floor. He married his wife, who is from the same village, soon after he arrived in

Oaxaca. She has provided him with four children, two married adults and two still in school and living at home. Alejandro proudly refers to himself as macho. One of his life's most important goals is to leave as many descendants as possible. He strives for this by pursuing his *libertad*, his freedom to have as many women as possible. He claims he has had up to four lovers at once. Presently, he has one full-time mistress, Cristina, with whom he has had a relationship for nearly twenty years.

Cristina was previously married to a schoolteacher who died in a car accident. After her husband's death, she was left with five children, all boys, and a pension of the equivalent of $16 (U.S.) a month. She obtained a job as a cook in a local tourist hotel and sent one of her children to live with her family near Veracruz. But she did not earn enough to support her children adequately and she felt that by working ten hours a day she was neglecting her children, one of whom was still an infant. After hot grease severely burned her hands and forearms while she was working, she dropped out of the labor market. She met Alejandro at a neighborhood party; he danced with her and relieved her loneliness. They soon started an affair and Alejandro provided her with a small sum of money each week.

In the 1970s, Cristina had four more boys before a girl by Alejandro came. Alejandro, however, did not want to stop. By the mid 1980s, Cristina had thirteen children, five from her former husband and eight more by Alejandro. Alejandro claims he has a responsibility to provide for the children he has fathered. His support, Cristina retorts, is insufficient. Cristina's house, for example, for the first ten years of her affair had seen virtually no improvements. It was a two-room adobe building with a dirt floor and one bare electric light bulb. Her three eldest sons are now working and they contribute to the family, although two are married and maintain separate households. Through their contributions, Cristina has purchased a few amenities: some new dishes, a radio, and most recently a gas stove. One son had bought a television set, but he took it with him when he got married. Cristina would like to go back to work; her sister has moved to the city and could care for her children. But Alejandro refuses to let her work. He says she must take care of his children.

Both Cristina and Alejandro's legal wife are caught in a cultural and economic bind. As a master builder, Alejandro earns enough to provide them with a greater income than either is likely to earn on her own. Although the amount Cristina receives from Alejandro is not great, it provides a steady income, as long as she does Alejandro's bidding. If she were to leave Alejandro, she would enter the unstable world of unskilled domestic work, where an abundance of workers lowers both wages and job stability. Alejandro's wife is similarly caught. She must accept the role of the suffering wife with a macho husband. If either woman attempted to strike out on their own, they could find themselves in Juana's position.

Juana is about the same age as Alejandro and also was born in a village near the city. Her parents died while she was still an infant; her grandmother raised her and, according to Juana, treated her as a slave. She was forced to herd sheep all day long and not allowed to go to school. She stole away to enroll in school anyway, but when her grandmother found out she severely beat her. When she was fourteen, Juana married. Unfortunately her husband, who was fifteen years older than she, treated her just as her grandmother had. For three years, she suffered his beatings and bore two children before she ran away and took up living in the city, where she found work as a washerwoman.

She has met other men and has had off and on liaisons with some, bearing another two children. But she has steadfastly refused to establish a permanent relationship. To her, *libertad* means the freedom to avoid all entanglements with men. Her home is not so nice as either Cristina's or Alejandro's wife, nor has she been able to educate any of her children beyond elementary school. But she bears her suffering with pride and dignity and has raised her children to adulthood. They work as laborers and construction hands, as do many children from these neighborhoods, and their support has enabled Juana to enter semiretirement.

For many working-class families, the wife's ability to work and the willingness of the husband to have her work allow economic advancement and security. For example, Pedro and Fermina live in a modern house in one of the government's self-constructed communities. Pedro moved to Oaxaca from the village of Ejutla in order to attend secondary and preparatory school. His wife-to-be, Fermina, was studying nursing at the time. After they both finished their studies, they married and have worked ever since. Pedro is the owner of a radio and television repair shop which, like most such businesses, is subject to up-and-down cycles. For him, everyone else's hard times are his good times, since people repair broken radios rather than buy new ones. Conversely, when the general economy is good, business is bad for Pedro. During these times, the household relies on Fermina's income as a nurse in one of the city's large government hospitals.

Fermina loves her work and has no intention of giving it up. Pedro gladly accepts this and even assumes child-care duties when Fermina's more rigid schedule prevents her from being at home. Pedro and Fermina have raised six children in this manner, five girls and a boy. They are all doing well in school with the oldest having finished medical school and the next in line currently completing training as a nurse. Each of the daughters has commented on her desire to continue her career and her own unwillingness to marry a man who would stand in the way of her professional advancement, although several are married or pregnant.

The willingness of parents to educate both male and female children, if financially possible, further reveals the changing gender roles in

Oaxaca. Parents are pragmatic; given equal capabilities and limited resources, male children have priority, since the local economy has more good jobs for males than females. If a daughter, however, demonstrates exceptional ability or determination, parents support her, recognizing that her special qualities can overcome the biases of the labor market.

Working wives are also found among the upper-income levels. The wife of a department manager of Papelera Tuxtepec worked as a schoolteacher. Similarly, the spouse of the state director of an important federal agency works several days a week as a clerk in the building-supply shop owned by her parents. The motivations in both cases are both personal and economic. The cost of a middle-class life-style has risen so dramatically since the onset of the 1980s Mexican economic crisis that two incomes have become necessary to maintain what one income provided during the boom years of the late 1970s. Secondly, many of these women have lived outside the city of Oaxaca and have enjoyed a much more cosmopolitan life-style. They view themselves as part of a national culture, which ideologically and constitutionally promotes the participation of women in the construction of modern Mexico.

Compadrazgo

Compadrazgo, cogodparenthood, is one of Mexico's most important social institutions. It spans the gap between formal, instrumental social relations, such as the voluntary organizations discussed in Chapter 5, and the intimate, family and household ties discussed in this chapter. On a day-to-day basis, for the less significant and some more momentous occasions, one must rely upon more intimate relationships. Compadrazgo characterizes the most significant of these relationships outside the family and the household, permeating all levels of society and with no less importance for the elite, both old and new, than for the masses. It also intertwines with the other forms of social organization and activities described in this chapter. Individuals related by compadrazgo are likely to participate in political demonstrations together, to live near each other in the same or similar colonias, to belong to the same union or the same soccer club. Ties of compadrazgo also provide social resources for individuals to use in their efforts to adapt to Oaxaca's socioeconomic inequality.

Ostensibly, compadrazgo rests on the relationship between godparents (*padrino* and *madrina*) and a godchild (*ahijado/a*). Frequently, strong ties develop between godparents and a godchild, especially for baptismal godparents. Godparents may become lifelong counselors and even assume responsibility for their godchild if the child's parents cannot for any reason continue care. Juana, for example, comes from Oaxaca's lowest income group and is a single parent with five children. Her primary occupation has been domestic work in various private homes in Oaxaca.

Each of her children has a godparent in one of these homes. Because of this godparent relationship, Juana was able to place her youngest son in the home of the child's godparent, who offered to house, feed, and care for the child while he attended school. In return, the child was expected to do small chores around the house. To Juana, this was not a case of exploiting her child's labor. She felt that because of the godparent relationship, her son would be better fed, have finer clothes, and be able to get more education than if he had stayed at home. She also trusted that the family would not mistreat its own godson.

The example of Juana and her son, however, are atypical compadrazgo examples. In the vast majority of cases the relationship between the two sets of parents, rather than between the godparents and godchild, constitutes the essence of compadrazgo. Compadrazgo may confirm an existing relationship, such as that between neighbors or coworkers. Or, it may formalize and neutralize social distance that could otherwise degenerate into conflict, such as among politicians. *Compadre* relations are formal. Compadres always refer to each other, not by name, but as "compadre," and normally use only the formal *usted*. In all cases, rather than forging new social relationships, compadrazgo strengthens and amplifies preexisting ones. Among the poor, compadrazgo relations frequently serve to respond to recurring economic emergencies. Among the better off, the relationships reinforce social networks important to career building.

Most compadrazgo relationships are between people of the same economic class. In the colonias populares, compadres are most likely to live in the immediate area. For example, in the Colonia Benito Juarez, Faustina, the wife of the former president who served for fifteen years, and the daughter of the former vice-president, Rosa, live opposite each other and are comadres. The two women maintain cordial relationships, talking and trading with each other more than either does with any other household in the colonia. If one needs a few extra beans or some short-term child care, the other provides it. They look to the other first if they want their house watched while they are out. If they can, they help each other through temporary economic crises. In short, they depend upon each other to smooth out the vicissitudes of their lives. The compadrazgo relationship also reinforces the solidarity between the two households in the face of political turmoil in their neighborhood. When Faustina's husband was president of the colonia and Rosa's father vice-president, Benito Juarez's fractionalized feuding, discussed in the previous chapter, subjected both families to allegations of corruption. The women use their relationship to withstand the conflict with the rest of the colonia.

Relatives and coworkers, even though they may not live close by, may also be compadres. Alejandro has a compadre who lives in a village just outside Oaxaca. Both Alejandro and his compadre think they are somehow relatives, although they are not quite sure how. They are old working buddies. They do not always work together, but have frequently in the past. If one of them is out of work and cannot easily find a job, he goes to his compadre. The other is likely to have work and in most situations can provide a job, even if only temporarily, for his compadre. Alejandro will also use his compadre for purely social purposes. When he feels like taking Cristina, his lover, and her kids for a day to the country, they go to his compadre's for a Sunday afternoon visit. If the resident anthropologist is available, everyone will pile into his car. Otherwise, they use the municipal bus system.

For the elite, social relations, and especially compadrazgo, are likely to be geographically dispersed. Spread throughout the middle-class sections of the city, compadres often include some families living in the city center. Those new elite families who have migrated to Oaxaca from out of the state, such as those in the recently expanded government bureaucracy, are likely to maintain compadrazgo relationships in Mexico City and other major Mexican cities, which may not be important on a day-to-day basis but can play a crucial role in an individual's career advancement.

Juan, for example, is a young, recently graduated architect from the city of Querétaro. He currently lives and works in Oaxaca. He got his first job with a federal agency in Oaxaca because his father and the local director of the agency had been classmates in law school and had subsequently become compadres when Juan's father had baptized the other man's first son. When Juan graduated from school, his father called his compadre and asked if there was a position in Oaxaca for Juan. He was assured that Juan could get a job as soon as he arrived. After a trial period in which he carried out private tasks for his father's compadre, Juan became one of his boss's personal aids. Juan has reinforced the ties with his father's compadre by asking him to baptize his own first child, and thus become a compadre to Juan as well. These ties have made Juan an important member of his father's and his compadre's circle of associates. Juan's career is now tied to that of his compadre; the overlapping relationships of compadrazgo assure that his compadre will pull him along whenever he receives a promotion. Juan has also become a compadre to several other young engineers and architects within the government bureaucracy. These other fictive kinship ties guarantee that even with changes of administration and a potential downfall of his compadre and boss, Juan will be able to attain a post in the government.

Some compadrazgo relationships are between individuals of different classes. Workers of the lower-income group, especially those in the informal sector, commonly request one of their patrons to become a compadre, thereby hoping to obtain more leverage for future job openings. For example, Raimundo owns and drives a dump truck. His work continuity rests upon contacts with the owners of construction firms who contract with him when they need hauling. To strengthen these ties, Raimundo has asked several of the city's contractors to become his compadres. Many refused, fearing the responsibility of ensuring that Raimundo had steady work, which would provide their potential godchild with necessary food and clothing. Three city contractors, however, did accept, and from those Raimundo can count on a contract whenever there is work to be done. While the contractors may have increased responsibility towards Raimundo's family, it is at least partially counterbalanced by Raimundo's reciprocal obligations. Although unstated, these obligations include Raimundo's responsibility to serve his compadre contractor first when work must be done. Moreover, if a compadre contractor claims he cannot pay the normal rate, Raimundo will accept a lower fee without complaint.

Oaxacans may also seek to establish compadrazgo relationships with outsiders. One rural village in the valley, Santa María, where an anthropologist has worked for more than two decades, is particularly noted for latching onto anthropologists. On one occasion, a young anthropology graduate student was venturing to the village for a brief, first visit. After the bus had pulled out of the last village before Santa María, there were still no seats for the young lady. While standing, one arm hanging from the cross bar running along the bus's ceiling, she felt a consistent nudging in her armpit. A squat, stocky woman at least a foot shorter in height finally caught the anthropologist's attention. The woman asked where the young lady was going, although the bus could only be going to Santa María, the remaining stop on the run. After the woman discovered the young lady was going to see the local anthropologist, she quickly asked if the graduate student would become her comadre.

In the city, people are somewhat less abrupt. They ask anthropologists to become compadres only after a longstanding, well-developed relationship has been established. Relationships with outsiders such as anthropologists convey a social intimacy and respect that Mexicans do not allow other, nonfamily members. The relationships still are likely to be instrumental, regardless of one's class position. The poor may use it to acquire financial support for their children's education or, when times are particularly dire, loans and gifts of money. They recognize that outsiders have more money, but they also view it as more shameful to make a request of an outsider than a Oaxacan compadre.

For the middle and upper classes compadrazgo ties with individuals living outside the city of Oaxaca are most frequently used for access to resources and goods not available in Oaxaca. The compadre who is an anthropologist may be asked to bring articles of clothing or adornment that his comadre wishes to give to a daughter who is having her fifteenth birthday celebration. A more important role for the North American compadre is the access it gives his Mexican counterpart's children to North American culture. It is not uncommon for a child from Oaxaca to visit his father or mother's compadre in the United States or Canada for a few months in the summer or even for an entire school year. Many of these Oaxacan families recognize the growing integration of Oaxaca with the national economy and Mexico's economy with that of the United States and hope to use their relationship of compadrazgo to expose their children to the English language and North American culture.

Households and Oaxaca's Income Groups

Measuring Available Resources: Per-Adult Equivalent Income

This section examines the differences by income group among Oaxaca's households. We analyze each of the income groups separately because they constitute distinct social groups that have access to different resources and different opportunities. Clearly, some households have few resources, while others have many. This section examines the nature of those differences among the four income groups that we delineated in Chapter 4.

As the first section of this chapter indicated, a household's resources vary through time as household members come and go, are born, grow, become educated, and work. Each of the five stages of the domestic cycle outlined above corresponds to different economic expenditures within a household. To capture this dynamic, we adjust household size according to the age of its members. We could adjust for each of the five stages or create a simple dichotomy distinguishing between children's age above or below fifteen. The simpler approach in our experiences yields results substantially similar to the more complicated one. We, therefore, count each individual under the age of fifteen as one-half an adult.[2] Thus, a household of two adults and two children, both under fifteen, would be counted as a family of three. We call this, three per-adult equivalents (PAES). The more people a household contains, the more PAEs it has and, we argue, the more it costs to maintain itself. We thus feel a more accurate measure of a household's real income is given by adjusting income for a household's PAES. To obtain a household's PAE income, we divide its PAE into the total household income (including that earned by spouses, children, or anyone else belonging to the household).

We use age fifteen as our cut-off point for adulthood because it forms a critical point in the lives of the majority of Mexico's young people. For women, a ritual, the *quince años* party, also commonly marks this transition. Traditionally, the *quince años* indicated that a girl was ready for marriage and was the occasion on which her parents formally presented

Table 6.1
Income Groupings by Total Household
and Per-Adult Equivalent Median Income

	Total Household Income*	Per-Adult Equivalent Income
Very poor	1,427	399
Minimum wage	2,437	666
Aspiring	4,982	1,143
Middle/elite	11,000	3,489
Citywide	2,500	667

*In 1977 pesos per month.

her to the community. Today, it reaffirms the family and household's real and fictive kin relationships and, via the level of the party's lavishness and style, the social status of the parents. For young men the event is more modest, often consisting of a formal *comida* with the child's godparents. Age fifteen also frequently coincides with the termination of the first stage of schooling, a time when the household must make a major decision on the child's future: work or higher education.

Table 6.1 presents the total household and per-adult equivalent (PAE) incomes of the city's four basic income groups first described in Chapter 4. Column one, total household income, presents the untransformed data, that is, not adjusting for per-adult equivalencies. Column two, per-adult equivalent income, displays the transformed data, in which a child under fifteen is counted as one-half an adult. The adjustment has a notable effect. The difference in median income between the two lowest-income groups' total household and PAE incomes remains of about the same magnitude and is the smallest difference of any of the adjacent pairs of income groups. It thus makes little difference to the very poor if one adjusts for the number of children and adults in the household. The gap, however, between the next two income groups, the minimum wage and the aspiring, is reduced from just over a 100 percent difference to slightly more than 70 percent. Thus, we can say that once we take household size into account, the aspiring income group is not so well-off relative to the next-highest income group as it seemed at first. Moreover, the distance between the two most prosperous groups, the aspiring and the middle/elite, increases substantially from 120 percent for the untransformed data to over 200 percent for the transformed data. Thus, the city's top income group is relatively better off than it might appear at first glance.

What social and economic factors might distinguish these income groups? There are, of course, numerous possibilities, from attitudes and values to material possessions and human capital. Based on our ethnographic experience, combined with analysis of the survey data, we

Table 6.2
Household Characteristics by Income Group

	Very Poor	Minimum Wage	Aspiring	Middle/ Elite
HOUSEHOLD STRUCTURE				
Age, mean of household heads	39	38	39	42
Percentage female-headed households	20.0	9.0	11	16
Per-adult equivalent units, mean	3.6	4.0	4.6	4.4
Dependent-to-worker ratio, mean	3.0	3.3	3.3	2.0
Household configuration, percentage nuclear	83.0	80.0	76.0	72.0
EDUCATION				
Household head, mean years	1.5	2.1	3.8	5.4
Household's total education, mean years	2.1	2.4	3.6	4.6
OCCUPATIONAL PRESTIGE[*]				
Of household head, mean	4.7	5.3	5.9	5.9
Of secondary worker, mean	4.4	4.8	5.8	6.3
Economic sector, percentage of workers in informal sector	61.3	38.3	22.8	22.0
Job stability, percentage household heads with stable employment	49.6	74.4	87.9	78.0

[*]Occupational prestige was determined by asking a group of Mexican nationals to rank the occupational categories on the INDECO survey with respect to prestige.

focus on the five general factors and eleven specific variables, which are displayed in Table 6.2.

This selection of variables is hardly surprising. They would appear in virtually any contemporary analysis of socioeconomic class. Some are characteristics of the head of the household, while others are household measures. Some attempt to control for the household's demographic load and its position in the domestic cycle. Some of the variables are structural or exogenous to the household, that is, the households have little or no control over them, such as age and sex. Others reflect manipulations by individuals and households in their struggles to survive, such as a household's total education and number of children. Regardless of whether the variable is exogenous or endogenous, each is potentially important in determining a household's income group and explaining the differences among Oaxaca's income groups.

The Very Poor

Oaxaca's poorest residents enjoy few of the amenities of modern society. Just over one-half had electricity in 1977. Only one-third have water on their house site, and the residents of one community spend up to 20 percent of their meager incomes on water alone. Only 20 percent have sewer hookups. Moreover, they pay dearly to live in such miserable conditions, spending the highest proportion of any income group (18 percent) on shelter and services. Another 70 percent of their income is spent on food, leaving just over 10 percent for anything besides food and shelter.

These dispiriting conditions spring primarily from this group's educational and occupational characteristics. Households in this group are the least educated, have the least prestigious jobs, the most job instability, and are by far the most likely to have all their workers employed in the informal sector. This combination of factors severely restricts a household's ability to earn a stable, let alone sufficient, income. For example, in Cristina's household, discussed in the section on gender roles, all workers are in the informal sector. To compensate for the lack of a steady income, her household must rely on numerous income earners. Her lover, Alejandro, has been a construction worker for over thirty years. He trained his two eldest stepsons, Pepe and Cachi, when they became old enough to learn, each beginning at about twelve years old. At first, they worked only with their stepfather. After about five or six years of this apprentice work, each had acquired enough skill and contacts to obtain work independently. Pepe felt sufficiently secure to get married, while Cachi still lives at home. Now, all three often work at different construction sites. As a result, neither household is tied to the instability of a single job. In times of need, they can rely upon each other. They may have to tighten their belts for short periods between jobs, but they do get by.

In Chapter 4, we demonstrated that informal-sector work is both less stable and less remunerative than formal-sector jobs. For this group, the very poor, however, all work has low remuneration. Formal-sector work in this income group actually pays no more than informal work.

Similarly, stable jobs pay slightly less than unstable jobs. Thus, having a formal-sector job does not necessarily imply having a well-paid job, or even a job that affords a minimally sufficient income.

The very poor's most significant adaptation to their wretched material conditions is demographic. They have the smallest households in the city, both in absolute size and number of PAE units. They also have the lowest percentage of extended family households. Despite having the smallest average number of workers per household, they still have fewer nonproductive members than any other group except the most prosperous class. In short, contrary to common stereotypes of large, poor families, the very poor in Oaxaca have adapted to their extraordinarily low incomes by maintaining small households.

The very poor also have the highest percentage of female-headed households, indicating that the combination of low education and being female is a nearly insurmountable handicap in Oaxaca's labor market. Female-headed households among the very poor, however, have smaller families than male-headed households among that group (and even compared to any group of households within the city). Female-headed households among the very poor have a lower dependent-to-worker ratio and a slightly higher PAE income than male-headed households in that group.

Cristina has a larger than average family, but fluctuations in household size reflect a common pattern among the very poor. Her eldest, Pepe, worked and contributed to the household from the time he was thirteen until at nineteen he married and established an independent household. He now lives less than 150 yards from his mother's house and maintains daily contact.

The second eldest began working when he was about twelve. He is now over twenty and still not married. His job as a construction worker frequently takes him outside Oaxaca for months at a time, but he always returns home when the job finishes and frequently visits on weekends. When he is working in Oaxaca and sleeping at home every night, his mother considers him a member of the household. When he is working out of town and comes home infrequently, his mother may or may not consider him part of the household, depending perhaps on the last time she saw him and if he contributed money to its support.

The next eldest went to school longer than the first two, neither of whom completed elementary school. This third son not only finished elementary, but also got one year of secondary schooling. But he then fell in love, got married, and moved out at the age of seventeen. This example indicates how households among the very poor reduce the pressure of household size and dependents by going to work and establishing independent households at an early age. If they cannot make it through higher levels of schooling, it is the only effective response to their woeful material conditions.

In short, this group's primary mode of adaptation to their difficult economic conditions is social, rather than economic. As our examples indicate, they actively adjust household size, keeping the number within the household to relatively low numbers, thus spreading the low income among fewer individuals. At the same time that they lower household size, they maintain strong family ties. While family members may be dispersed, members still maintain close contact and cooperation, thus demonstrating the close complementarity between household and family.

Despite, or perhaps because of, having the lowest education levels in the city, the poorest view education as the best path to advancement for their children. The very poor, however, encounter difficulty in persuading their newly educated children to remain in Oaxaca when jobs in Mexico City or the United States are more plentiful and higher paying. Pedro, for example, has failed at keeping even one of his educated children at home. He, his wife, and the children still in school live in a two-room house with no services, no electricity, no running water, and no sewer hookup. Of his older children, one barely finished elementary school, while the other completed secondary school. Compared to their father, who had virtually no formal education, both had advanced considerably. And, in the process, while attending school they received some vocational training through apprenticeships, one as a welder and the other as a mechanic. Yet, this level of education and skills was worth little in Oaxaca. Both felt they needed to resettle in Mexico's more industrial cities, where a shortage of skilled laborers would compensate for their lack of a high school level education. Both left Oaxaca as soon as they found promise of employment somewhere else. They love their parents, but as one of them said, "There is nothing for us here. If we are to succeed, we must move away from the city. Even if we stay in Oaxaca, it is much better to find our own place to live where we are not a burden to our parents."

Perhaps they would not be a burden, but they nevertheless experience a frustration and contradiction between their responsibilities to their parents and the opportunities available in Oaxaca. They could never earn enough in Oaxaca both to bring their parents out of their poverty and to take care of their own families' aspirations, which include a university education for their children. It is better, from their point of view, to use one's own meager resources for the next generation and visit the grandparents occasionally rather than engage in daily conflicts over the disposition of the collective income. From Pedro's perspective, now a grandfather, he has lost what was for him a considerable investment in the education of these two boys. They remain a beloved part of his family, but do not contribute materially to his household. He hopes that even though he has few assets to pass along, one of the younger children who remains at home will stay there to take care of him and his wife in their old age.

The Minimum Wage

With a household income above the official minimum wage, the minimum wage group has slightly better housing conditions than those of the very poor. Instead of shacks, most have sturdy, permanent houses of solid adobe or concrete-block walls and concrete floors. Their houses are also slightly larger and better serviced. Nearly 70 percent have electricity, although less than half have water on their property and almost three-quarters do not have sewer hookups. They do have, however, a firmer hold on their homes. Almost half claim a recognizable title to their property and another 20 percent legally rent housing.

These improvements stem from this group's educational and occupational characteristics. Close to half of the heads of household have completed all six years of elementary school, an accomplishment that can mean the difference between being a hotel bellboy and a government development project chauffeur. Yet the household's total education is only slightly improved over the very poor (an index mean of 2.4 versus 2.1 for the very poor). This is reflected in notable occupational improvements for the household head, but only minor improvements over the very poor for secondary workers.

This group has one-third fewer households with all their workers in the informal sector than the very poor, and the household head's job stability is 50 percent higher. For example, Marcos obtained four years of elementary schooling in his village in the Mixteca Alta. When he moved to Oaxaca City in the 1950s his ability to read and write earned him a job as a store clerk in one of the larger retail firms in the city center. He has held that job ever since. His wages are still barely above the minimum, but the job does provide the fringe benefits of the *seguro social.* His extraordinary job stability also allowed him to keep all six of his children in school at least through the elementary level. He found it more difficult, however, to support them much beyond that. He concentrated on one, his oldest daughter, whom he supported until she finished school and became a nurse. Nurses still do not earn much in Oaxaca, but they do have relatively high occupational prestige and job stability.

The increased income and job stability of these households makes it easier for the household heads to maintain larger families. Compared to the very poor, households in the minimum wage group have more children, a higher dependent-to-worker ratio, and more extended families. Whereas Cristina's children set up independent households as soon as they were married, households in the minimum wage group can afford to keep their families together. José's household, discussed earlier in this chapter, which has one son in the military and another who became a lawyer, falls into this income group because of the earnings of his son,

Alfonso, the lawyer. Although Alfonso is married, José built him a house on the family lot and thus kept him within the household. José's earnings as an unskilled construction worker are insufficient to support everyone, but Alfonso's contribution allows the family to stay together.

The Aspiring

The houses of the aspiring group households are distinguished from the lower-income groups primarily by their size. They are twice as large as those of the minimum wage group and are most likely to have five rooms. The services they have, however, are much closer to the minimum wage and very poor groups than to the income group above them. Just over 40 percent have water in their house, the remaining 60 percent still have to carry it, most likely from a communal faucet, onto their lot. Less than one-half have sewer hookups available. The best serviced homes are likely to be among the high proportion who live in one of the government projects, ISSSTE or INFONAVIT, designed for formal-sector workers. Although space in these housing projects is more restricted, they do come with complete services of electricity, water, and sewer hookups.

Educational and occupational characteristics reflect the same upward trend observed in comparing the minimum wage and very poor groups. Among the aspiring group, both household heads and entire households have significantly more education than in the minimum wage or very poor groups below them. Close to 70 percent have completed at least elementary school, and another 25 percent have finished either technical or professional training.

Occupational characteristics reflect this educational advantage. Household heads' occupational prestige is as high as the city's highest income group. This group has the most job stability and nearly as few households with all workers in the informal sector (22.8 percent) as does the middle/elite income group (22.0 percent). Their education has allowed them to occupy the skilled technical and professional positions that opened up in the wake of Oaxaca's reintegration with the national economy. Workers in this income group are store clerks, bank tellers, technicians, and low-level professionals. These jobs may pay only slightly above the minimum wage, but include full benefits. In the case of Javier, for example, advanced education enabled him to become a technician for the national telegraph company. It provided him with a good income, benefits, and the security of working for the government. For Javier's neighbor, Pedro, technical training in electronics allowed him to open an electronic repair shop at a time when a scarcity of radios and phonographs made repairing used equipment a relatively lucrative profession.

A considerable proportion (42 percent) of these households has a second worker. The second worker's income most frequently falls below that of the head of the household, but his or her occupational prestige matches the other's. There are two ways in which this can occur: first, the household head's spouse may have similar education and skills. For example, Juan is a teacher at the local technical school. His wife, Victoria, teaches at an elementary school. While teachers are not well paid in Mexico, they do enjoy considerable job security and prestige. The second way is that increased occupational characteristics of the head pave the way for the completion of the children's education, which is reflected in this income group's household educational index (3.6 versus 2.4 for the minimum wage group). This represents a continuation of a trend noted in the minimum wage group: whereas the minimum wage household of Marcos was able to continue the education of only one child beyond elementary school, households in the aspiring group are likely to be able to continue supporting more of their children. And, as in the minimum wage group, at least some of these are likely to remain in the household after finishing their education and beginning their careers. Thus, the aspiring group also has larger households (in terms of the number of PAEs) and is more likely to maintain an extended household (24 percent versus 20 percent for the minimum wage group), while maintaining the same dependent-to-worker ratio as the minimum wage group.

Perhaps the most important factor for this group is one we could not measure: their informal social networks among the city's powerful and influential. Those with this income group's high occupational prestige find themselves in a position to make and use inside contacts. As in any complex social structure, individuals in the right place have friends who pass on information about such things as job opportunities, a favorable land transaction, or a good deal on construction materials. Or, they may know someone who can assist in placing children in a good school where the children can further develop social contacts that may later prove instrumental. These contacts may involve participation in Mexico's traditional and corrupt *mordida* (bribe) system. But corruption is not the core. Rather, informal social networks are the essence of such wheeling and dealing. The households of this income group simply have greater access to a social network of other relatively highly placed individuals and households.

Ramón had moved away from Oaxaca in order to finish school in Mexico City. When he returned he found the school to which he wished to send his children had closed its enrollment. Graduates of this school have virtually automatic admittance to the city's most prestigious preparatory school, attended by most of the children of the city's professionals and entrepreneurs. Rather than send his children to an inferior school, Ramón talked to a coworker and compadre who was also an officer in the prestigious school's parents' association. The coworker then met with the school's director, informing him that if Ramón's children were admitted

Ramón would help support the school and the parents' association, and besides, Ramón was the coworker's compadre and thus deserved a favor. The school director subsequently enrolled Ramón's children.

Ramón's neighbor, Lázaro, used his connections for more immediate financial benefit. Lázaro works as an accountant in one of the local building supply houses and in his work interacts extensively with Oaxaca's biggest construction contractors. Lázaro became aware of a piece of urban property coming up for sale at a good price. He concocted a partnership with one of the city's contractors wherein they would buy the lot together; Lázaro would arrange for credit for the building material and the contractor would supply the machinery and labor. The rental on the newly constructed house provides a nice supplemental income for both of them. Neither Ramón nor Lázaro holds a high position in his organization. Their web of personal relations, however, enabled them to use their positions to the benefit of their households.

In a very real material sense, modern Oaxaca benefits most the households of the aspiring income group. The economic boom of the 1970s increased the worth of formal education. The heads of these households already had considerably more education than those of the two classes below them. They and many of their spouses were first in line, ready and qualified, for the new semiskilled and skilled positions requiring basic education that opened up. Once in these positions, social networks provided them with further openings. They often had opportunities for advanced technical training. For example, after completing elementary schooling in the 1960s, an individual may have begun as a clerk and advanced to accountant with on-the-job training. Or, an individual who first worked as a truck driver could rise to midlevel management as a firm expanded and needed people who knew the organization. The increased informal social contacts these higher-prestige jobs offer also present further opportunities—for getting their children into the right school, finding a good deal on land, obtaining professional expertise at a reduced rate, and other similar benefits. This group's high job stability, increased number of second workers with good jobs, and their informal social contacts all combine to lessen the burden of educating other members of their household.

The Middle/Elite

Oaxaca's highest-income group enjoys a relatively comfortable life, but not quite so comfortable as one might expect. Over 10 percent still do not have electricity and over 50 percent do not have piped water or sewer hookups in their houses, but they can afford septic tanks and most likely have servants to carry water to the sinks. Members of Oaxaca's middle/elite, at least as we have defined it, are not rich and living in luxury;

they do not typically live in extravagant mansions with tennis and jai alai courts and swimming pools. The few houses that sport these amenities are atypical. It is not unusual for two or more children in this income group to share a bedroom and for the woman of the house to engage in domestic chores, such as cooking and cleaning. The houses are indeed likely to be larger with separate living and dining rooms, a kitchen, and more than one bathroom. Most have a gas stove with an oven and a refrigerator, although it may only be a small, apartment-size one. Very few are likely to have a washing machine and dryer or a dishwasher. Taxes on these luxury items are extraordinarily high and servants are relatively inexpensive.

The middle/elite group partially reconfirms the trend of increasing education and occupational characteristics. This group is on average the best educated in Oaxaca. Over 50 percent have finished secondary school and 30 percent have professional training. Yet a significant minority, nearly 40 percent, have no more than an elementary education. This reflects the mixed composition of this group. As we discussed in Chapter 4, Oaxaca's current elite consists of the old commercial elite, the agroindustrialists, and the new bureaucrats. Those who have little education are either from Oaxaca's old commerce-based elite or the agroindustrialists. For them, education has not been necessary to maintain their current socioeconomic position.

The three different components of this class also complicate the income group's occupational profile. The household head's occupational prestige is, on average, no higher than for the next less prosperous group, the aspiring. The middle/elite have proportionately only slightly fewer households with all workers in the informal sector and they actually have more unstable jobs than the aspiring group. Among the middle/elite, however, job instability is likely to reflect upward career mobility. Professionals above the middle level of the bureaucracy move in and out of the public sector as opportunities in the private and government spheres open and close with changing administrations. They have the contacts and opportunities to move into the most advantageous and lucrative positions in either the private or the public sector.

Alonso, for example, was an economic analyst for the governor of Oaxaca. His position was a political appointment of *confianza*, that is, he was a member of the governor's personal team. While the governor was in office, Alonso was paid by the state to develop its long-term economic plan. When the team leader, the governor, left office, Alonso moved with him to an important position in the local branch of a national bank. When the banks were nationalized, Alonso's previous government experience and his ties to the former governor elevated him considerably within the bank. Throughout his occupational ascent, training and skills were important, but social networks were paramount.

A household's second workers in the middle/elite group have the

highest occupational prestige of anybody in Oaxaca, higher than that of
the heads of household. This reflects a trend observed, but incompletely
realized, in the lower classes. Increased income and occupational characteristics allow a household to provide more education for its children and
to come closer to the cultural ideal of an extended family living in one
household. Although households in this group have fewer dependents
than those in the aspiring and minimum wage groups, the dependent-to-
worker ratio is the lowest because adult members are more likely to be
working. Children in this group commonly live with their parents while
they are attending the university and even for their first few years of
employment. When still in school, they often begin working in the office
of a friend of the household as a semiskilled professional, much like an
apprentice, such as a helper to an architect or engineer, a draftsman, or an
accountant. This work not only contributes to the household income,
but, more important, it also establishes the child in the web of informal
social contacts of the city's establishment. For example, Isác, the son of a
prominent physician in Oaxaca, was studying public administration at the
national university in Mexico City. His father arranged for him to aid
Manuel, the director of the Oaxaca office of one of Mexico's major public
works agencies, while he worked on his degree. Isác spent his vacation
time in the Oaxaca office helping with personnel and administrative
matters. When he had to be in Mexico City attending classes, he would
serve as the liaison between the local office and the national bureaucracy.
When Isác graduated, he moved directly into the national administration
of this same government agency.[3]

This group also has the second-highest percentage of female-headed
households. Because of this group's greater access to medical services,
women in this group simply live longer, on average, than in any other
income group. If a woman is widowed, divorced, or separated, the income
level provided by the husband's estate and perhaps supplemented by the
widow's family will still support her. Women in the middle/elite group can
readily afford, much more so than women of the three income classes
below them, to avoid permanent relationships with men. Thus, if the
male head of household dies or abandons his middle/elite wife, she more
often than not will simply remain single, living with her children and
raising them using her own funds or those of her extended family to
maintain them.

Conclusions

David, whose story began this chapter, achieved his job with Pemex,
and his associated socioeconomic mobility, because of his tenacity in
pursuing his education and because of the new job possibilities created in
the 1970s by the national government, of which both the technology

school that educated him and Pemex that employs him are parts. Both the higher education opportunities and the subsequent job position exist, as we attempted to demonstrate in Chapter 4, because of Oaxaca's reintegration into the national economic and political system. Davíd's story also reflects the most significant characteristic of Oaxaca society, an individual's foundation in and commitment to family and household. Without the support of his family, he never would have been able to continue his schooling. In return, he remains committed to supporting his father, mother, and siblings, despite his marriage. Davíd thus exemplifies the underlying connections between the layers of analysis in this book. Broad social, political, and economic forces, discussed in the first half of the book, create openings that families, not individuals, attempt to exploit.

This chapter has attempted to establish that in Oaxaca, family and household are the most fundamental social units and that structure, processes, and adaptation to socioeconomic inequality can only be understood from the perspective of families and households. We use the concepts of both family and household because they complement each other. The family is a more cultural unit, an abstract concept that exists in peoples' minds. As a cultural category, family is constant, an abstract set of social relations and interpersonal commitments. The household, on the other hand, is more social, a material and objective unit.

While families and households constitute the basis of Oaxaca society, they nevertheless exhibit considerable variation. We have discussed four sources of variation: household structure, gender roles, compadrazgo, and income groups. A household can be conceived as proceeding unilinearly, beginning with the creation of a new domestic group through marriage, proceeding through the birth and growth of children, and finally being reduced again to the original domestic pair. This conceptual framework corresponds well to the stereotypical pattern of the life cycle of North American households. Social realities in Oaxaca, however, are at once simpler and considerably more complex. Oaxacans' commitment to family produces much more continuity than the unilinear development of the household more often seen in North America. Children frequently marry and establish themselves within the context of their natal family and household, having a room or small house on the same lot as one of their sets of parents. Similarly, elderly Oaxacans are incorporated into the households of their children. Moreover, few Oaxacans wait long to have children and few households exist without school-age and younger children. As a result, few households are found in the beginning or ending stages. In addition, households are likely to incorporate, unincorporate, and perhaps then reincorporate extended, nonnuclear family members. Thus, particular Oaxacan households seldom follow a defined cycle. Individuals, of course, do progress more or less unilinearly from childhood to married adults and on into retirement. But household structure does not reliably reflect those changes. Families and households remain much more consistent: there are always children and there are always adults. Sometimes the children are all young and sometimes they are all old. Usually there is some mixture of young and old children.

While households commonly and frequently vary their structure, the variation reflects not an independent, or in some sense "natural" household life-cycle evolution. Rather, it reveals social responses to political and economic conditions. Individuals migrate in search of better educational or employment possibilities and then frequently integrate themselves into a relative's home. Raúl and Virginia, for example, helped their nephew from the village by incorporating him into their household. He, in return, assisted them in household chores. Married children live on their parents' *solar*, such as José's son, Alfonso, both because of a commitment to their parents and because of a housing shortage. When they find better housing, they move. If they can afford it, however, they frequently move their parents with them.

Compadrazgo allows the family and household to extend its resources and incorporate others in a web of reciprocal rights and obligations. Elites and masses alike are linked in ways that both reinforce the various forms of social organization and adaptation mentioned above and cut across them. Individuals in the same neighborhood or who work at similar levels in an organization are frequently linked by compadrazgo, thus reinforcing preexisting social relations. These social relations may also cut across class lines to cement a relationship, for example, between employer and employee. The needs addressed by compadrazgo are much more focused than those of political movements, and are usually limited to the individual and family. Compadrazgo provides a means for a family to reach out beyond itself to benefit itself; such a relationship with one's boss, for example, does not benefit one's neighbors, let alone others of one's social class or income group. It is intermediate between the broad social movements discussed in Chapter 5 and the more narrow, private family and household struggles to adapt discussed in this and the following chapter.

Income group, however, is probably the most important source of variation among families and households. The very poor are the least able to support large households. They are, therefore, the most likely to break up the family by having children leave at an early age. At the other end of the income scale, members of the middle class/elite also have relatively small households, although not so small as members of the very poor group. While their children may leave home to attend a university in Mexico City or even the United States, they are also more likely to have fewer children, and the children they do have can more easily afford to establish an independent household when they marry.

Gender roles also influence household composition and reflect political and economic conditions. The cultural role of the macho male still exists and remains important, but its manifestation is influenced by other factors. Some women in the very poor group, for example, regretfully submit to the tyranny of macho males because they see no other alternative. Cristina, Alejandro's lover, and Alejandro's legal wife are both caught by the juncture of his macho beliefs and Oaxaca's political economy. The two women believe, with good reason, that they cannot work and support their children, both materially and spiritually, without the assistance of a man. The few jobs Oaxaca has for relatively uneducated and unskilled women pay very low wages, offer few benefits, and possess little job stability. Nevertheless neither macho males nor submissive, domestically oriented females are universal in Oaxaca, either as cultural ideals or as social realities. Even among women who do maintain stable marital relationships the material exigencies of poverty force many into the workplace.

Yet, poverty is not the only force altering traditional gender roles. The economic crisis of the 1980s, and even before that event, simply the ambitions of many, induced women of the higher-income groups to join the work force. Moreover, the highest proportions of female-headed households are not only among the very poor but also the middle/elite. The very poor female-headed households reflect women such as Cristina, who would rather not maintain a household without a man present (although as indicated by the example of Juana a few very poor women self-consciously choose to live without men). On the other hand, middle/elite female-headed households reflect not so much necessity as freedom. They are likely to be widows (and not unmarried lovers) who have the material resources, and the social resources through their families, to maintain themselves without remarrying.

With respect to the relationship between households and families and Oaxaca's four income groups at least one consistent trend has emerged: higher levels of education of the head of household produce an occupational advantage, including increased prestige, a position in the formal sector with associated benefits, and job stability. All of these advantages allow for: more educational opportunities for children, larger families, and more extended households. Graphically, this can be presented as:

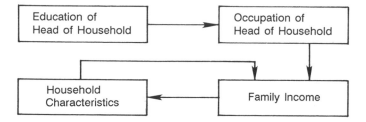

We believe, however, that the situation is somewhat more complicated. First, this depiction does not address the issues of how the head of the household obtains his or her education, nor the determinants of the distribution of occupations and associated incomes. As we attempted to establish in earlier chapters, both the availability and the importance of education reflect Oaxaca's reintegration with the national system. The federal government has been responsible for expanding Oaxaca's educational system and the job opportunities that require higher education. Secondly, families and households significantly govern educational opportunities, both within the immediate family and for more distant members who may come from a village to attend school in the city. Thirdly, an individual's access to education also significantly depends upon one's income group. The very poor commonly cannot afford the school expenses and foregone income education entails for their children. Income group in combination with other social factors can be even more limiting. A female head of household among the very poor group will find tremendous difficulty in advancing the education of her children. Subsequently, the children will have little chance for socioeconomic mobility. On the other hand, at the opposite end of the economic spectrum female-headed households in the middle/elite income group are common and they and their offspring have high levels of education and are likely to remain in the middle/elite group.

As these examples indicate, the relationships between income group and other variables are not entirely linear. Two of the three household-structure variables, PAE units and dependent-to-worker ratio, increase as PAE income rises through the three lowest-income groups. But then, for the highest-income group, the middle/elite, PAE units and the dependent-to-worker ratio declines again. A similar pattern is found in two of the four occupational variables, economic sector and job stability. Again, the middle/elite have fewer formal-sector workers and less job stability than the class immediately below them, the aspiring.

We argued in Chapter 4 that the aspiring class is Oaxaca's newest income group, the one most directly created by Oaxaca's reintegration in the national system and most dependent upon the federal government. The trend of these occupational variables, we believe, further confirms that argument. It is the presence of the federal government that has created and expanded the formal sector, and it is in the formal sector that one finds the most stable jobs. Yet, these jobs do not necessarily have prestige or income equal to that provided by some of the more elite activities, such as business and the law.

The trends across income groups in household structure appear to indicate that members of the aspiring group, and to a lesser extent of the minimum wage group, are utilizing their incomes to strive toward the traditional Mexican family type. A primary goal and benefit of increased economic well-being to Oaxacan households is the ability to maintain the family together within a single household. Households in the aspiring group are able to maintain larger households, as measured in PAE units, while still having the highest dependent-to-worker ratios. In contrast, the very poor must maintain both relatively low household size and low dependent-to-worker ratios. The middle/elite could support larger households and higher dependent-to-worker ratios, but instead more of the people who live in the house work, households are slightly smaller, females are more likely (than in either the minimum wage or aspiring groups) to be household heads, and newlyweds are the most likely to establish their own households. The only way in which the middle/elite come the closest to the traditional Mexican ideal is in having the highest percentage of households that are extended.

In previous chapters, we have attempted to convince the reader that broader forces beyond individuals, families, and households determine the range of opportunities available. In this chapter, we have initiated an argument that the availability and improvement of human capital is not simply a reflection of individuals' and households' desires, drive, and willingness to sacrifice and take advantage of opportunities. Families and households from all income levels share desires, drive, and a willingness to sacrifice. The rewards for their efforts, however, are largely determined by forces beyond their control, including the socioeconomic position of their natal household and luck. This argument, we believe, can best be advanced by examining in detail the life histories of households in each of the four income groups, the subject of our next chapter.

7

Four Households

In the previous chapter we described the differences among Oaxaca's four income groups. In this chapter our intention is to add depth to those descriptions by presenting the life history of a household in each group. These life histories typify the dynamic strategies Oaxacans employ to cope with their changing environment. While these life histories serve as the culmination of our description of the city, in our personal experience they provided the inspiration and final reference for our work. As anthropologists, fundamental social reality lies for us in the concrete struggles and joys of individuals and families. María Teresa and her daughter Elodia, Alfonso, Javier and Margarita, and Abel, as well as others, have been our teachers in the field. In many ways watching them over time helped us develop the ideas we present here. Their range of incomes is great, and they are unlikely to meet on an informal social level, but these four families exemplify the common bond among all households in an intermediate Mexican city: one must struggle to survive. The interviews for these life histories were conducted in the late 1970s, after Oaxaca had begun to suffer the economic shocks from the 1976 devaluations. In a few cases we added information to update them to the 1980s economic jolt. Each life history begins with a description of the family's house and then discusses migration, employment, the dynamics of family and household structure, gender relations, and political involvement.

María Teresa and Elodia: A Very Poor Household

María Teresa and her daughter Elodia are residents of one of the mid-1960s squatter settlements. Our focus on them admittedly violates our definition of households as cohabiting individuals. Although María Teresa lived for an extended period with her daughter, Elodia, she has since moved to the house of one of her other daughters, Eustolia. We

171

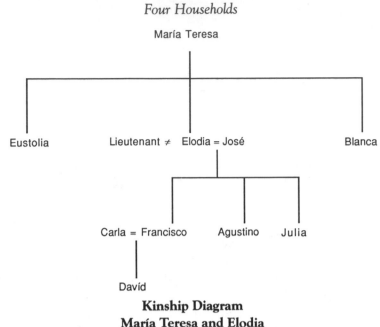

Kinship Diagram
María Teresa and Elodia

nevertheless consider them together because they illustrate the struggles of a female-headed household and the daughter's transition to a traditional nuclear-family household. As in the three other cases presented in this chapter, mother and daughter are migrants to the city. Theirs is a clear example of the "push factor" in migration: the death of a parent early in María Teresa's life left her in the care of grandparents. While she claims life was not hard in the village, her grandmother clearly felt it necessary to push María Teresa into an early marriage rather than invest time in education, which in the grandmother's eyes could only have a negative payoff.

This story also demonstrates the link between urban wages and rural villages. Although María Teresa insists life was easier when she was a young woman, she was forced to send her two daughters to work in Oaxaca City to help support the family back in the village. This decision is a version of a strategy common to many Mexican households and reflected in the second life history, that of Samuel: sending family members to the United States in hope of receiving remittances sufficient to enable the rest of the family to remain intact in their present location (Roberts 1973; Selby and Murphy 1982). Throughout María Teresa's and Elodia's story, one is struck by the strength of character and will in these two women who, despite tremendous hardship and obstacles, continue to struggle for the future of their children.

María Teresa's and Elodia's family participated in the massive squatter invasion mentioned in Chapter 5 that produced Colonia Santa Rosa.

Elodia's son, Francisco, was part of the first wave of invaders. While Elodia and her mother continued living above the invasion in Colonia Benito Juarez, also discussed in Chapter 5, they did travel down the hill to the invasion site to attend the organizational meetings with the invaders. The rhetoric and arguments of the student organizers convinced them of the justice of the invasion and their right to land and services. Later, when the government decided to build a site-and-services project in response to the invasion, both mother and daughter were selected in the lottery for new lots. María Teresa has now moved to that project, where she lives with her other daughter, Eustolia. Elodia and her family remain in Colonia Benito Juarez, not because they prefer it to the site-and-services project, but because they have not been able to purchase materials to begin building there.

Elodia's lot in Colonia Benito Juarez has a couple of trees that provide some shade from the usually hot afternoon sun. Typically the family keeps a few chickens, which run freely through the lot and frequently out into other parts of the neighborhood. The house, a single room about three by five meters (about ten by sixteen feet), is of adobe bricks with a fiberglass roof, the latter donated by INDECO after one particularly harsh rainy season. The door, made from scraps of discarded wood and metal, hangs somewhat loosely from the hinges and has no lock. A small opening in the adobe about half a meter square and covered by a particle-board shutter hinged on the inside constitutes the only window.

Inside, darkness prevails even at midday, because the one bare electric light bulb is used only in the evenings. The floor is packed dirt. Furniture consists of one bed with an old metal frame and planks supporting a thin, sagging mattress, and a kitchen table with three chairs of rough-hewn wood. On one wall is a portable metal cupboard with two sliding glass doors on the top and an open shelf in the middle. Behind the glass doors is the family's best ware, opaque glass dishes, bowls, and dinner plates. On the shelf is a plastic flower arrangement and miscellaneous important papers, such as birth certificates and school report cards. The small family altar sits atop a small table in the corner. It consists of several religious pictures of saints, some candles, a cross, and an inexpensive glass vase filled with now-dried flowers that are replaced by fresh ones on special occasions.

This is María Teresa and Elodia's story—how they explain and interpret their lives when given an opportunity to reminisce freely. María Teresa speaks first:

MARÍA TERESA: I was born in 1914 in Santa Marta Chichihualtepec, a village a little below Ejutla. When I was eight days old my mother died. My father had died a few days before. They both were killed by what was called the fever.

My grandmother raised me. Now I don't even want to remember those things. Everything was cheap; and as people from a village, we had much to eat. Whatever was in season we could eat—vegetables, nopales. We didn't have to buy things, and what we did buy was cheap. Then a peso was a lot! When we wanted to buy a piece of cloth to make a dress, with a peso we could do it—twenty-five centavos a meter, a whole dress for a peso.

We had goats, nearly a hundred. My grandmother sent me to herd the goats in the mountains. There I ate nopales, herbs, whatever there was, because when I got back to the house at night it was always very late. I just wanted to grab my blanket, lie down, and sleep.

I wanted to go to school, but my grandmother wouldn't let me. There were things to do, work to be done, and school would teach me to be lazy. I wouldn't want to do what needed to be done. But one day when the teacher came to the house to enroll students, my grandmother wasn't there, and I signed up. When the first day of class came, I said I was going to school. Oh, she was angry. She wouldn't let me go. The whole first week, she wouldn't let me go. But after a week the teacher came to find out why I hadn't come.

My grandmother said that she had not wanted me to sign up for school, but the teacher responded that I was on the list. My grandmother got angry with me and said, "Why did you put yourself on the list? Do you always do things on your own?" "No," I said, "I wanted to go to study. If I just stay with you I won't be able to learn anything. Who knows what would happen to my head?" So, I went to school for a year. I could only go for a year and study the first book. But I learned how to read and write.

Then everything in school was free. It didn't cost us anything because the government gave us the notebooks, paper, pencils, pens, ink. Everything they gave us. The teacher just said, "Here, take this and tell me when you need more." The children then were very careful. They didn't draw monkeys and things like that in their books. If you didn't do your lesson, you couldn't leave for the midday meal. You just had to stand there, quiet, with your stomach growling.

After a year in school, I left to get married. My grandmother gave me what I needed. I didn't want to leave school, but my grandmother said I should get married. On the twenty-first of June I turned thirteen, and on the twenty-second of July I got married. I barely knew my husband. He had asked my grandmother for my hand. I knew who he was, but I had never talked with him.

My husband was an orphan, too. He had been raised by his aunt and uncle, and they gave him his herd of goats. Whenever we were hungry, we could kill a goat and have a barbecue and eat cheese, too. Then goats were cheap, three pesos each. Now [the late 1970s] they're worth five hundred or six hundred pesos. Cheese was cheap, too, fifty centavos each. Now they're fifty or sixty pesos each. Things were O.K. then.

But when Eustolia was seven years old and Elodia four, and the youngest just eighteen months, my husband was killed. He had gone to a fiesta in a neighboring village. He liked to drink and got in an argument there, and they beat him. I wanted the police to do something, but we didn't have any money. My uncle advised me that if I tried to do anything, I would just make enemies and would have to leave the village to live somewhere else. "Why fight more?" he said. "You can't bring him back to life."

After my husband died, there was nothing we could do. We were all women, myself and three young daughters. We couldn't do all the work. I had to sell the land and animals in order to survive. The land we had was ejido land. It wasn't private property, but communal. We only got five hundred pesos for all of it.[1] My daughters were in school, but they had to leave to earn money. The two oldest went to Oaxaca to become domestics. There they stayed, living and working in the houses of rich people, while I stayed in the village and made tortillas for people who didn't want to make their own.

Eventually, after my daughters were grown and had families of their own, I moved to Oaxaca, too. I've lived with both Elodia and Eustolia, whichever one has more room for me. I can't work any more, but I can help out around the house. I can still wash clothes, cook, take care of the kids, and go look for firewood. Finding firewood is more difficult here in the city than it is back in the village. You have to walk sometimes for miles and miles to find abandoned wood. But I prefer tortillas made over a wood fire and *comal* to those machine-made ones.

Now I sit back and watch my grandchildren. I'm glad their life is not as difficult as mine or even their mothers'. They can go to school and at least finish elementary school. Of course, one needs more education now, but at least they have a chance. They'll never be rich. They'll never live in a fancy house nor will they ever have servants. But they have a chance, if they can finish their schooling, to suffer a little less than we have.

ELODIA: I was ten years old when my mother sent me and my sister to Oaxaca to work. I had been in school for only a year. I worked in a house here in Oaxaca. I swept, mopped, washed, and things like that. They paid me three pesos fifty centavos a month. My sister was in another house. They paid her seven pesos a month. They treated me very badly. They were always admonishing us for not working hard enough, but they never gave us any time off. Even on Sundays we couldn't leave the house. Seven days a week we had to work. We couldn't even go to the corner store. While the family ate meat and other things, we were given only beans and tortillas. After three months both of us changed to another house where they paid us a bit more. They paid me fifteen pesos and thirty to my sister.

All this time my mother and other sister stayed back in the village. One month our money would go to them, and another month we would keep it. We worked like that for three years. Then, my sister, who was fifteen years old, said she was going to visit our mother and she would come for me on Sunday. "I'm going to see my mother, too," I said to myself. And there I was, waiting and waiting for my sister. But she didn't come. And there I was worrying about her. She said she was going to come on Sunday, but she didn't come. So I said to the woman I worked for, "I need permission to leave to go to my village because my sister said she was going to come and she hasn't come. I'm afraid something has happened to her." The señora said, "No, you can't go. She'll get here." But I wanted to go. I wanted to see my mother, too. So I left, and when I got to my village, my mother told me that my sister had left with a man. She had gone with her boyfriend. I said to myself, "Who's going to go with me to Oaxaca?" My mother said to me, "Your sister has left Oaxaca. You shouldn't go back, either. You're still young, and you shouldn't go by yourself. I worry about you a lot because you're still small. It would be better if you don't go."

So I stayed in the village with my mother and my other sister. My mother made the tortillas, and we carried the firewood and the water so she could make the tortillas. But life was hard in the village. We couldn't survive. Eustolia and her husband had moved to Ocotlán, and her husband said all of us could come and live with them. So we moved to Ocotlán (thirty minutes south of Oaxaca City by car), and we lived there eight years. There we made *empanadas* to sell at the Estrella del Valle bus station. Times were pretty good then. Although we sold the *empanadas* for only twenty centavos each, we sold a lot of them, and everything was cheap. Life was better in Ocotlán than back in the village. Sometimes we would drink milk and have meat for breakfast.

There was a lieutenant there who wanted to marry me. I was only thirteen years old, and he was about thirty. But he wanted to marry me, and he spoke to my mother and my mother said to me, "Why don't you want to get married?" And I replied that I was too young. I hadn't thought about marriage. Later the lieutenant died. I never wanted to marry. But when I was twenty-one, I met the father of my children, José. We lived together. But then I was older, twenty-one.

He took me to the lowlands, to the coffee *fincas* where we worked for a while. He and others picked coffee, and I helped them. Things were pretty good there. It's sort of like being in a village. One doesn't have to buy wood for cooking. If you want to have a little coffee, you don't have to buy coffee. It's just lying there on the ground, and the bosses said we could just pick it up if we wanted to use it. There was no mill, so we ground it ourselves with a hand grinder. I used to get up at five in the morning to grind four or five kilos each day.

We didn't really suffer there. Not like back in my village. They gave a little piece of land to us to grow things on, and it was very productive. The corn ripened in August, and there was enough to sell.

A while later the cotton harvesting began, and the same *patrón* took us to where the cotton plantations were. He took us in a truck, and we didn't have to pay. Where the cotton was, there was a lot of fruit, too—avocados, bananas. We didn't suffer. Whenever we were short of anything, we just made a list and gave it to the *patrón*, and he would bring it to us. We were never able to save anything. We had to spend everything we had, but we always had something to eat. Food was very cheap. Whenever we had to buy meals, it was only five pesos for all three meals.

But eventually, we came back to Oaxaca. The *patrón* told us there was no more work and took the little piece of land away from us. We came to where my mother lives in Oaxaca City.

When I got here, I said to my mother I was going to work. My husband had not worked in Oaxaca before, and it's hard to find work without having *conocidos* to help. He does somewhat better now, but still there are times when he can't find work. Even when he does work, the pay of a peon is not enough for a family. So I had to work, and I went to look up a comadre I have over in the Colonia Alemán, and I went to work for her. And my husband began working as a construction worker. After some months my comadre said she was going to Mexico [City] and, if I wanted to continue working, I could go with her to Mexico. But I had my children here in Oaxaca. I have three, two boys and a girl, Francisco, Agustino, and Julia. I couldn't go to Mexico. So I went to another comadre. These others were good people. I didn't suffer because I didn't have to work that hard. I just had one room and the kitchen to clean, and I had to go to the market and buy things and make the food. The woman didn't have much to do, and she treated me well.

But my daughter, Julia, was getting older, and my mother didn't want to take care of her all the time. So I had to leave that job and begin doing day work so I could take my daughter with me. That was harder, because lots of people don't like you to bring your children along.

Finally, I decided to try something else. I decided to look for clothes I could sell. I knew someone who did that, and I asked her if she could give me some of her clothes and I would sell them. So I went door to door selling clothes—usually here in the valley, or even in this colonia. But some times I would go way out into the country, like back to my village and other villages. But I didn't like traveling that far in those places, and they like to barter. Rather than giving you money, they give avocados, beans, squash, or peas—something like that. Many times I would trade for those things and bring them here and sell them and keep some to eat for my family.

But then as the kids started growing, I couldn't afford to leave the house so much. I had to stay here to take care of them. I have to worry about what's going to happen to them now. I want them to get as much education as possible. It's only by way of education that one can get ahead.

We still don't have enough really to save and get ahead. We don't have any skill or training that will allow us to get ahead, to get a steady job. When there's work, my husband works; but when there's not, he doesn't. Then we have to ask for a loan from someone. Then when there's work, we're working to pay back the loan.

That's why I want my children to go to school. Here in the city there are schools. Back in the village there aren't any schools, and the children suffer. They don't have much chance of preparing themselves. Here, even the poorest can go to secondary school. I would like them to learn a business or at least be teachers so they won't suffer. I don't want them to have to move all over like I had to do in search of work. I don't want them to have to work for others like I did, work for rich people who mistreat you and then fire you when you speak up for your rights. I wish I could go back to school, be young again, so I could learn a trade that would make me rich. I wonder what kind of work I would have been able to get if I had kept on going to school. I think I could have become a teacher.

I have one child, Agustino, who is like I was. He's very restless, but he doesn't forget things. The others are more forgetful. Francisco, the oldest, dropped out after finishing elementary school. I wish he could have continued, but he wanted to work, to earn some money. Now he's a construction worker like his father. His father helps him find work; so it's not as difficult for Francisco as it was for my husband when he first started working in Oaxaca. He's got his own wife, Carla, already started a family, one son, Davíd. So, I'm a grandmother.

They lived with us for awhile, but that didn't work out very well. We have only one room and it was a bit crowded, so he found a place to rent in another neighborhood. But it doesn't look like he's going to be any better off than we are. Even though he finished elementary school, it's not enough anymore. You need secondary or even preparatory nowadays, and the poor can't afford to send all their kids to school forever.

My daughter, Julia, she's in the secondary school studying to be a secretary and working, too. She works as a clerk in a store downtown. She works hard because the señora doesn't have any other employees. But she still has a lot to learn. They are only paying her two hundred pesos [$10 U.S. in 1977] a week. When she gets enough experience, she can look for work somewhere else. I just hope she can finish school and learn a trade. But it's hard now. Every time you turn around the schools are asking for money—money for this, money for that. Who knows what for? And there goes the money. There's not enough to go around, and it's hard to keep the children in school, especially the girls—they almost never finish. I don't know if Julia will make it or not.

But I have hopes for Agustino. I think he may not have to suffer as much as we have. But he will have to work. The poor always have to struggle for everything. No one gives us anything. Look at our housing problems. In the village, everyone has a place to live, but here in the city there aren't any places. You have to pay for everything, and they don't pay you enough to afford it. That's why we have to fight for our housing. We took part in the squatters' invasion in 1975, the one where thousands invaded and the army came and pushed us out. The government was against us all the way, but the students helped. They organized us and kept the pressure on the government. The capitalists were against us and forced the government to kick us off the land. But we workers have to stick together and fight them. With the students' help we were able to do that. We got this new colonia, Santa Rosa, because we stuck together and didn't give in. Once the government said they would build the colonia, they still dragged their feet and didn't deliver. But we kept up the pressure and finally got our colonia. But even then we couldn't stop. We had to keep up the pressure to get our services, to get the water, electricity, and school that had been promised. If we stick together, then we can get something out of the government. Otherwise they don't give the poor anything. They just ignore us.

María Teresa and Elodia have battled continuously against the ravages of poverty. The tragic death of María Teresa's husband dissolved her economic base, producing and reinforcing poverty while revealing the absence of economic opportunities for female-headed households in rural Oaxaca. María Teresa's husband's land was communal land, which is legally controlled by the community, but she was able to sell the rights to use it, although at lower than normal market price. The push from rural roots initiated a persistent family and household dynamic structure as individual members migrated to and from the city, between various rural locations, and in and out of particular households. For both generations, María Teresa and Elodia, working conditions have been harsh and remuneration minimal. The conditions of domestic child labor confronted by Elodia can only be described as superexploitation. While she made no mention of the sexual abuse or beatings frequently mentioned by others, she clearly suffered.

Oaxaca's contemporary reintegration with the nation has brought little noticeable improvements for this family. Their gender and lack of skills have excluded them from the emerging formal sector. They must rely solely upon their family and informal social networks. When in need of work, they look first to comadres and friends.

In spite of this domestic flux and struggle, firm family ties have endured. María Teresa's and Elodia's family has been and remains the primary institution in their lives. As indicated in Chapter 6, one of the primary adaptive responses of the very poor is to maintain small households. María Teresa and Elodia each had only three children and everyone moved in and out of households in search of employment and to keep expenses as low as possible. Reintegration has materially affected them first in a way they only indirectly realize. María Teresa fondly recalls her youth as a time when everything was cheap and she did not need to struggle so strenuously and ceaselessly. Nevertheless, she is materially somewhat better off now than she or her grandparents were. The number of consumer items in her life has increased: María Teresa's housing is somewhat better in the government site-and-services project, which has more readily available water and electricity. The family has a radio. Others in their class have television sets and, a few, a gas stove. Yet, as we shall see from the other life histories, María Teresa's and Elodia's material well-being has not improved as much as others in Oaxaca. A refrigerator is unlikely for anyone in this income group; a car, impossible.

The most obvious impact of reintegration upon this family is in politics and housing. The 1975 squatter invasion permeated their lives and consciousness. They not only participated in the invasion and subsequently received lots from the federal agency involved, but they henceforth articulated a radical critique of their own conditions and society. This vision, however, is limited by structural realities. They did obtain a lot with services much more quickly than other colonias populares, but the government's violent suppression of the student movement deterred them from expanding their political battles into, for example, the area of employment. The other consequence of reintegration is ideological but less radical. The hopes of these women for a better life reside primarily in their children, and their faith in education is impressively strong. The descriptions of the very poor in the previous chapter, however, reveal the limits of that hope. Elodia's children have already confronted rising credentialism. They have more schooling than their mother, but her eldest is only an unskilled construction worker and her daughter is a store clerk. The poor recognize that despite a strong will to succeed, they and their children have a limited future. We have witnessed many others who begin working while still completing their studies. Despite the ideals expressed concerning education, for many young people among the poor, work and family become greater commitments than finishing school.

Alfonso: A Minimum-Wage Household

Alfonso lives in the same squatter community as Elodia, Colonia Benito Juarez. Farther down the hill, closer to the Pan American Highway, his house is built in the same way they build houses back in his village—one long rectangular room with wattle-and-daub walls; the roof is tarpaper. He has incorporated but two modern features, a concrete floor and, not so long ago, a composting outhouse built by INDECO as part of a pilot sanitation project for squatter communities. Inside, the house is as dark as Elodia's house. Alfonso has two bare light bulbs, but again they are used only in the evenings. The room, about eight meters by three (twenty-

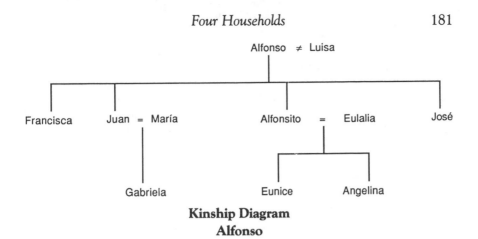

Kinship Diagram
Alfonso

six by nine feet), is partially divided by particle board in the middle that stretches halfway across the house's width. The house has three beds, each with a metal frame and mattress. Wires stretch above the beds from which curtains can be hung for nighttime privacy.

Alfonso has more furniture than does Elodia. The kitchen table is still rough-hewn but larger and covered with a plastic tablecloth. Another large table against one of the long walls is covered with various "modern" items: a radio, a television set that no longer works and costs too much to repair, and piles of schoolbooks. Against another wall is a wooden wardrobe with a built-in mirror. On top and beside it sit numerous cardboard boxes filled with old clothes, books, and other family belongings. Against another wall, still encased in the clear plastic covering them when they arrived from the factory, are two small sofas Alfonso earned by being the top worker at a local weaving factory. Kitchen cookery consists of one aluminum frying pan and some pottery vessels that hang from nails in the side of the table. Beside the stove is yet another table with the remainder of the kitchen ware—locally produced ceramic pots, metal plates and cups, plastic glasses, and spoons. (Most Oaxacans of this class do not eat with forks, but prefer to use tortillas. When a tortilla is inappropriate, which is seldom, they use a spoon.)

Alfonso's story illustrates what may happen to households in this income group. Alfonso displays the ambiguity toward education found among many individuals in this social class. He himself always wanted an education, but his father was opposed, forcing Alfonso to learn to read and write on the sly and eventually receive his elementary school certificate when he was forty years old. This experience has led Alfonso to value education for his children, but he also displays the concern that time and money spent on education may be wasted if his children are forced to return to the work place before completing their degrees.

ALFONSO: I was born on the twenty-fifth of August in 1925 in Santa Ana Chiquihuitlán, a Mazatec village way back in the mountains. My parents were poor, but we did have a fair amount of land. We had coffee, fruit, oranges, *maguey, zapote,* all kinds of fruit. What we didn't have was money. There wasn't any money in my village, only bartering and farming. Three or four villagers had cattle, fifteen or twenty head. They were the rich people of the village, and sometimes they got into conflicts with other villages over rights to grazing land. Our village also got into fights with a neighboring village over land boundaries, but that village, too, was an Indian village. There was only one Spanish speaker in the whole area. There weren't any haciendas or outsiders. Not until today. Now, Germans are buying up land all around the village and planting sugar. But in those days it was purely Indians, no Spanish or any other outsiders.

When I was little, I was like all the other kids. I played a lot and helped with chores somewhat. We played with stilts, and sometimes we would suck all the juice out of a lemon and use it for a ball. When I was fourteen or fifteen, I realized that I needed schooling, but my father said I couldn't go. But I had a friend who was a teacher, and I asked him how to write my name. I used to go down to the river during the midday meal and cut down a banana leaf, and with thorns from an orange tree I would practice writing my name on the back of the banana leaf where there was a little white powder. I would write letters, draw birds, bulls, goats, write my name. One time when I was doing this the teacher came by, saw what I was doing, and offered to teach me at night. I used to go with a candle to the teacher's house. We didn't have any other kind of light in the village, and he taught me the twenty-nine letters in the alphabet. Then he said we had to stop because I would hurt my eyes. But with those letters I taught myself to read. My friends had some books in their houses, and I took the books and asked them how they pronounced the letters together, and little by little in the end I learned to read. I learned to read perfectly well, but without knowing commas, periods, and things like that.

When I was seventeen I decided I wanted to leave the village to explore, to learn something about other places. Three of us left together. We didn't have any money. We took some tacos, some tortillas. I took my guitar, which I had just got a month before. So we left. And we walked and walked and walked for two days until we found a place where we could work—a place where they were harvesting bananas. Others cut them, and we were hired to carry them to the cart. We worked for two days and earned three pesos each, and then we went on to another place where they were harvesting sugarcane. And there they paid us one peso fifty centavos for each ton of cane. It took us from six in the morning until six at night to earn one and a half pesos.

But that was better than working back in my village. The first time I worked as a day laborer in my village, they paid me one centavo for working from dawn to dusk. Later, they raised it to one-half real, or six centavos. That was grueling, barbarous misery. Working in the sugarcane was better. We worked in the cane for three months and then went back to the village.

I stayed in the village about three months, just long enough to plant some cane and bananas and make some adobes. Then I got the idea I should come to Oaxaca. My brother was already here. He worked in a huarache factory making really nice huaraches; so I came to stay with him and worked in the factory, too. Then he went as a bracero to the United States in 1944, and I stayed in Oaxaca to take care of our mother, who had also come to the city.

Working in the factory was interesting. I learned how they cut the skins, tanned them, and dyed them, how to work with mountain lion skins, deer, goat, and others. But I didn't really like it. It smelled—it really stank. So I got another job in a textile factory. I tried to work as a construction laborer, but there wasn't any work. So I went to the textile plant.

A friend of mine introduced me to the owner of the textile plant, and I asked him if there was any chance for me to learn to weave. He said sure, but first I would have to learn how to spindle thread like the five or six young women were doing. I was afraid I would fail, but in five minutes I was able to spin the spindles. Later, the owner arrived and said I was doing a very good job and promoted me to weaving on the big wooden looms. I worked for two or three months there. Then the owner had some problems with his wife, and they came and put him in jail, and the factory closed, leaving me without work.

I was without work for about six months. My mother made tortillas to support us while my brother was still in the United States. I asked my brother to send me two or three hundred pesos so I could buy a loom from some Spaniards who lived a few blocks away from us. They had a whole bunch from another business that had gone under. He sent me the money, and I bought the loom and began my own business. I produced a whole stack of weavings, and my friend from the huarache factory offered to display my wares in his showroom and act as a middleman.

But in those days, about 1945 or 1946, there weren't many tourists in Oaxaca. The highway wasn't finished and no airplanes came, so there wasn't much of a market. Three or four months later my friend came back and said he hadn't sold a single one. So he gave them back to me. I might have done better if I had connections in Oaxaca's hotels where there were a few tourists, and certainly better if I had connections in Mexico City and the United States like weavers do today. But back then, none of that existed here. Then there was no one to sell to here in Oaxaca. I then decided to go out and try to sell them myself. I gathered up a whole bunch and took off for the mountains, for the land where I come from. I went to Tuxtepec, but I couldn't sell any there, either. From there I went on to my village, where I planted coffee and bananas on some land I had.

That's when I got married. I married the woman I had promised my father I would marry. I had known a number of women in all my traveling, but it was this one my father liked. Before he died, he told me, "This is the one I want to be your wife, my daughter-in-law. I don't want any other, only this one," he said. Well, I said, "Good. If that's the way he wants it, that's the way it will be." So I went up to her and said, "I've decided. Do you want to go with me? If you do, well let's go." A few days later, I talked with her family and we were married. By the Church, not by the state. Then I came back to Oaxaca.

In 1947 I began to work in Casa Brena. Casa Brena now is a big, strong business, but then it was difficult. I asked if I could be a traveling merchant for them. But the boss said only if I had five thousand pesos to put up front. If I knew how to weave, however, he said I could work for him; only it would be piecework and only if there was a request for something. If there weren't any requests, there wouldn't be any work. It was really difficult, and I already had my first child, a daughter, Francisca.

One day in the zócalo I met a friend, and he asked if I wanted to help out with a vaccination project with an American company vaccinating cattle up in the mountains. We got paid according to how many cattle we vaccinated, but we always earned something. So I did it for about eight months, and then I came back to Casa Brena.

There was more work, but still we didn't earn much. The best weaver would earn no more than five pesos a day, six days at five pesos—thirty pesos a week. And that was for the best weaver. So there were good weeks and many bad, bad weeks. There were weeks of twelve, eighteen, twenty pesos.

I returned to the tanning factory for a little while. The factory had changed by then. They had a new technology. It was all chemicals, machines, and motors. My job there was to iron with an electric iron. I worked for three years there, and I liked it. But then the owner had an argument with one of his partners, and the factory closed. So I returned to Casa Brena. By that time I had four kids and couldn't afford to take any risks, and Casa Brena had become established. They didn't pay much, but there was steady work.

I stuck with Casa Brena until I retired with my bursitis a few years ago. I couldn't work anymore—my shoulder hurt too much—and I couldn't run the looms. But all the time I worked for Casa Brena I was the best weaver they had, and I worked hard. Because I work fast I could usually earn somewhat above the minimum wage doing piecework. But that is just enough to get along, to pay the rent, feed and clothe the kids. Casa Brena also gave us *seguro social*; so we didn't have to worry about doctors' bills. Whenever there was an illness, we could get it treated. That was one good thing.

We used to rent a room in the center of the city down near Casa

Brena. We paid seventy or eighty pesos a month. But one day the landlady said, "I'm going to need this room you're living in. I'll give you three months free rent, but then you have to move out." That is when we found out about this colonia. I began to buy this lot where we are now. I told the lady, "O.K., I have a lot and I'll begin to build a house on it." But it was the rainy season, and I couldn't make adobes for the house. When the three months were up, I still hadn't built a house. The landlady said we had to leave. I pleaded for an extension, and even my boss from Casa Brena pleaded with her, but it did no good. She said we had to leave, even if our new house wasn't finished. So I came up here and just threw up a little wattle and daub house like they have back in my village. That's the house we still have today. I still haven't been able to make a better house—first, because there's no money; second, because all the materials are very expensive; and third, because the builders these days want to make money but they don't want to work. They want to spend a year making a house. Finally, this place isn't all that great for making a new house. It's real high and steep here. What will happen if there's an earthquake? The pipe that brings water from Santa María [a colonia down the hill and across the Pan American Highway] will break, and then where are we going to get water? The government certainly won't give us any. They have hardly ever helped us with anything. So why should I build a place here?

When that big land invasion happened a few years ago I was all for it. The students must be on the side of the workers and the poor people. The government is just trying to screw us, and we must stand up for our rights. After the invasion, I marched in the demonstration with the invaders. I also marched in the other demonstration against the invaders, but that was because my boss told me I had to. The union said everyone at Casa Brena had to march even if we didn't believe in it. So I marched in both demonstrations, but my heart was with the invaders.

Just when we moved to this colonia, Colonia Benito Juarez, my wife left us. We had been having difficulties for quite awhile. She kept nagging me all the time, that I didn't earn enough money, that she couldn't buy all the things she wanted, all the things the children needed. She wanted all kinds of things. Back in the village people are satisfied with very little. There's not much there and people learn to adjust themselves to what's available. At certain times of the year, pineapples are ready and everyone eats and eats pineapples. Then there are no more pineapples and you eat something else. You have to learn to take advantage of what there is and not wish for something that can't be.

But here in the city things are different. There are more things and a lot of stuff is always available; so lots of people want things all the time. For rich people that's all right because they have the money to buy whatever they want. But for us, for the *gente humilde* [the humble people], we can't afford to buy whatever we want. We have to adapt ourselves to what we can afford. But my wife didn't want to do that. She wanted everything. I, too, wanted everything, but we couldn't afford it. I worked as hard as I could, twelve hours a day, six days a week. It was the best job I could find, but it just didn't pay enough for everything she wanted. So she finally left. I had to take care of the family myself. Fortunately, we had raised good kids. They didn't misbehave, and they cared for each other. We had to just keep on going, keep on struggling.

When my wife left there was no woman in the house, no one to wash the dishes and clothes, clean up, cook, and do all those kinds of things. We all chipped in. Everyone in the family helped. But my daughter, Francisca, helped the most. She was the oldest, thirteen, and she became the mother to her younger brothers. She washed and ironed, cooked and cleaned up, and, most important, looked after them, made sure they behaved while I was off working.

She unfortunately had to drop out of school. She was an excellent student, nothing but top grades, and she was in secondary school at the time—the only child in the whole colonia in secondary school. But the littlest was only six years old then, and we needed someone to be at home to take care of the little ones. So Francisca had to drop out of school and become a mother.

She did that for six years straight, and she did an excellent job. But then the anthropologists offered her an opportunity to go to school in the United States. She had worked with them on their research as an assistant. She helped them with their Spanish, and they helped her with her English. As a way to pay her back, they arranged for her to go to high school in the United States. I wasn't sure she should go. The other kids were still young, and I wasn't sure they could take care of themselves. But she wanted to go, and they said they could take care of themselves. So she went, and she was gone two years. In two years she learned English really well and graduated from high school. She was all ready to go on to college there, but when she came back to visit she decided she had to stay here.

Her oldest brother, Juan, had left the house. He went to live in Mexico City, where he found a job and began working with the Jehovah's Witnesses. But the younger ones, Alfonsito and José, were having more trouble. When I was off at work they would get into trouble and they wouldn't obey me like they did their older sister. They began to get into fights and drink and smoke marijuana. I was really worried about them. I would try to discipline them, but they just talked back. When Francisca returned and saw how they were behaving, she decided she couldn't go back to the United States. She stayed here and took care of her brothers.

Because of her English she was able to get a job in a tourist hotel. She started out as a telephone operator at the big Marqués del Valle on the zócalo. Although that's a big hotel, they don't treat their workers very well. They didn't pay her more than the minimum wage, even though she spoke English better than anyone else there. Sometimes they didn't pay their workers for weeks and weeks. So she finally quit and found another job at the new Presidente Hotel in Oaxaca, the one that used to be a convent. She started as a telephone operator there, but soon worked herself up to the head of the front desk. They treated her well there, raising her salary, sending her on trips to Mexico City. It was a good job, and she got to make use of her English. After being there for four years and seeing her brothers straighten themselves out and grow up, she finally decided she could go back to the United States and school in hotel management. That's where she is now.

Meanwhile, my eldest son, Juan, the one who went to Mexico City, has moved to the Isthmus [of Tehuantepec]. Last year he finally got married, at the age of twenty-eight. He's learning to be a jeweler, but his main work is for the Jehovah's Witnesses. He doesn't make much money and frequently he has to ask us for some help.

The middle son, Alfonsito, got married three years ago. He married the girl who lived across the street, Eulalia, and they now have a daughter, Eunice. So I'm a grandfather. They live here in the house, and Alfonsito works as a carpenter at a little factory down the hill toward town.

The youngest, José, is still in school. He's in medical school here in Oaxaca. He's a good student like his sister was, and I have great hopes for him. I have to use the few pesos I have to pay for his schooling. The only way they can progress is through schooling. The only ambition I have is for them to complete their schooling. It's for their schooling that I make sacrifices. If I had not supported their schooling, this place could be filled with rooms. I could have built a lot more, well-built rooms of concrete with floors and everything. But what for? What good would it do if my kids didn't have the schooling to support and advance themselves?

I don't want them to have to work like that. Sure, they'll work, but not the same kind of work. Not hard physical labor. For example, now a kid who has completed secondary school, wherever he goes they'll give him some kind of work, and he won't have to grab a pick and shovel. He just presents his diploma, and yes, they'll give him some kind of work. If God lets me live, I'll not lose my hopes that my kids must finish their schooling, and with time, they'll be all right.

Still, you can never tell with kids. You hope they have the constitution to stick it out, and to work hard, to finish school, and then to find a job and work and earn. But you can never tell. Two of my kids, the youngest, José, and the oldest, Francisca, are making something of themselves through education, but the other two didn't do much of anything. They're not going to end up any better than I.

The youngest brother, José, the one in medical school now, has always been an outstanding student. His older sister bought all these books for him: encyclopedias, dictionaries. Books I can't even read. When José was in secondary school and the *preparatoria,* he taught classes for his professors. His teachers had him tutor other students and teach whenever they couldn't be there. He still tutors and makes some extra money that way. Soon he'll be done with school, finish his social service for the government, and then begin earning money. It's taking him awhile to finish because of all the problems and strikes at the university. But he says they're important.

If the poor want to get ahead, they have to work hard—work, work, work continually, and not have any vices. The rich can inherit their wealth, but the poor have to work. The poor can work and work and still not become rich. They don't earn much, and they have to limit themselves just to break even. They have to find a way to live with only the minimum necessary and nothing more. Sometimes, we have to live on beans alone. Beans are the basis of our life. They're still the best, cheapest food. A small amount will be sufficient for the whole family, for breakfast, the midday meal, and dinner. One has to know how to manage money and manage life. You can't earn 250 pesos and spend 300. If some emergency comes up, they won't have the money to pay for it, and they become even poorer. You have to learn to manage even when you're earning, because the day will come when you can't earn, when you're sick, or there's no work, or some emergency comes up. It's hard for the poor to get ahead. We can't, but maybe our children can, if they just have a little more luck than us.

But I can't say I've had a cruel life. No I can't say that. A cruel life would be, for example, if today I wake up and my kids don't have anything to eat, not a piece of tortilla or even a piece of bread. Then I would have to go see who would loan me five or ten pesos so I could get something to eat. And if no one would loan me the money, my children would have to go all day without anything to eat. That would be a cruel life, a truly suffering life. No, I've always had a life that's been more or less normal. I've had enough to eat and to enjoy myself. I've known poverty, but not infinite, cruel poverty. Now, I'm retired. I spend most of my time back in my village where I still have some land. I plant coffee, bananas, and other crops. I also work to improve my village. I helped bring in the road and electricity to the village. Trucks and buses can now come in all the way to the plaza. We used to have to walk in or go by horse to get to the village. Now we can get our produce out and sell it.

While María Teresa's husband's death forced her to abandon her village, Alfonso left in search of adventure. His subsequent escapades demonstrate the effects of isolation and integration upon individuals in the minimum wage group. Before Oaxaca's reintegration, his sojourns brought him many experiences, but relatively little income. As with

María Teresa and Elodia, he, too, found himself subject to forces beyond his control. He lost two jobs because the factories were suddenly closed and he repeatedly had to rely upon informal social networks to find work and make a living. As a weaver, he could earn a piece rate in a factory, but even then only when there was a demand for his goods. His entrepreneurial efforts at weaving failed because they were far ahead of their time. Although Alfonso is a man and he had more skills than María Teresa, he could not improve his lot and distinguish himself from the very poor while Oaxaca remained isolated.

Oaxaca's subsequent reintegration finally provided a context that rewarded Alfonso's skills. Oaxaca's linkage to the national and international economy first provided him with a relatively well-paid job vaccinating cattle. More importantly for Alfonso, reintegration provided the basis for Casa Brena, Alfonso's employer for the longest period, to expand its production and to enter the formal sector. Despite the low wages they offered, Alfonso eventually returned to work there for the security it presented. And, being in the formal sector has played an important role in his life. It has provided him and his family with free health care. While Oaxacans frequently complain about the quality of service available at *seguro social* health centers, those in Alfonso's class cannot afford to ignore it. *Seguro social* doctors diagnosed his bursitis and arranged for him to receive disability payments, which, while only a third his former salary, have been welcome. One can well imagine that, without those payments, his youngest son's medical education, clearly so important to Alfonso, might have ended with his retirement. Formal-sector employment has also provided Alfonso with a small retirement benefit that supports him in conjunction with his lands back in his village and remittances from his daughter in the United States.

His daughter Francisca's experiences reflect an integration beyond the national economy to the international, unusual for this income group in Oaxaca city. It was possible in her case because of the intervention of anthropologists, a resource, of course, not available to every minimum wage family. Francisca also reflects the evolution of gender roles in Oaxaca. Even with Oaxaca's reintegration and Alfonso's formal-sector employment, his wife's leaving the family compelled Francisca to abandon school prematurely, just as traditional gender roles would dictate. Francisca, who was thirteen years old, was an excellent student and the first in her neighborhood, of either sex, to go beyond elementary school. In spite of her outstanding academic skills, she withdrew from school and became a full-time surrogate mother to her younger brothers. She cooked, washed, and sewed, scolded and congratulated her younger brothers and her father.

The fortuitous arrival of anthropologists provided her with a second chance. Otherwise, she most likely would never have returned to school.

Even with the language skills she developed in the United States, eco-nomic opportunities were severely limited in Oaxaca. She subsequently returned to the United States and became an executive housekeeper in a major hotel in one of the south's largest cities. She delayed marriage until she was in her mid thirties and chose her male friends with great care. Then, she only married because it would help her obtain permanent immigration status. In Oaxaca, she is an anomaly, but not a singular case. Oaxaca has an increasing number of young, professional and semiprofes-sional women for whom their natal family and career come before mar-riage. She now is a professional with a promising career.

Nevertheless, Francisca's experiences reveal that education for the minimum wage group (and the very poor) is risky in at least two ways: children may not complete their studies and thus all the investment will be lost; and, if they do finish or simply obtain advanced skills, they may have to leave Oaxaca to realize their worth. Her youngest brother is still in medical school and claims that he will remain in Oaxaca once his studies are completed. The two other brothers have not visibly benefited from Oaxaca's reintegration. One has left the city and the other maintains the family household.

Alfonso's story also reveals the paradoxical politics of Oaxaca's urban poor. He lives in an illegal squatter settlement and led the community's battle for services (Chapter 5 describes their struggle to get water). He also strongly backed the massive squatter invasion described in Chapter 5. Yet, under union and his boss's orders, he marched in the antisquatter demon-stration in the wake of the squatter invasion. Hoping to obtain better services, he has also worked closely with government officials, urging both Benito Juarez and his home village, Chiquihuitlán, to support PRI candi-dates. He has cooperated with the PRI, however, solely for instrumental reasons. The PRI, because of its affiliation with the government, has resources that the colonia is unlikely to obtain on its own. Although his Casa Brena job implied union membership, he completely ignores the union; the company's paternalism is more significant to him. When talking of working conditions and what improvements or benefits there are, he is more likely to mention the productivity prizes he has won and the company-sponsored yearly picnics and outings. In short, neither the government nor the unions they control are responsible for the lot of the urban poor. Whatever the poor receive, they must get through active struggle. Sometimes, for Alfonso, that active struggle means providing superficial support for the government and the union.

Alfonso's steady job and now his pension have undoubtedly eased the task of supporting his children until they finish their education. He has also achieved modest material gains in his life and considerably more than María Teresa and Elodia. He has more beds, a television set, ward-robe, couch, and a kerosene stove. Nevertheless, Alfonso has had to sacrifice improvements in his house in order to provide his children with as much education as possible. He claims his efforts are solely altruistic and he knows that his children's success is by no means assured. They do have better prospects than the children of the very poor, and Alfonso knows his children will do their best to take care of him even if their circumstances are only marginally better than their father's.

Javier and Lupe: An Aspiring Household

Javier and Lupe live in the INDECO site-and-services project mentioned in Chapter 2, which was designed for those with steady jobs. As did most households in the site-and-services project, Javier and Lupe moved onto a vacant lot. Their first task was to build a shack, in which they lived when we first knew them in 1974. The combination of Javier's stable employment and Lupe's home restaurant enabled them to add to their dwelling at a rate faster than most other members of the community. Within two years they had two brick rooms; today, they live in four large rooms, have a toilet and shower and a kitchen that opens to the outdoors and from which Lupe serves food to her clients. They have also been able to acquire a number of material possessions not common to members of the lower-income groups of Oaxaca. Lupe has a refrigerator she acquired before moving to the project. They purchased a gas stove, own a nice sofa and chair set, as well as a record player, 35mm camera, and various other smaller consumer goods. These goods not only make life more pleasant for the family, but they also provide a small source of income. Javier collects a small fee for making public announcements over his outdoor speaker system and for pictures he takes at parties with his camera. The stove and refrigerator make it possible for Lupe to sell cold drinks and food.

JAVIER: I was born in Cuicatlán, Oaxaca, on the fourth of February, 1930. Shortly after I was born, my father abandoned my mother, and my mother and I went to live with my grandmother until my mother died. I lived with my grandmother for twelve years. I helped her and my grandfather with the chores on the farm. I also went to school. My mother had made my grandmother promise she would send me to school. I went to four years of elementary school, which was the most available at Cuicatlán at that time. Finishing four years of elementary school in those days was like finishing all six years of elementary today. After my grandmother died, I went to live with some neighbors. They were very good people who had no children; so I became their child. I helped them with the work on the farm until Don Manuel, the man of the house, died. He had intended that I should inherit his land, because he had no children. But when he died, all of the uncles and nieces and nephews began to

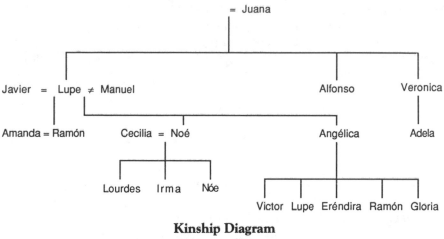

Kinship Diagram
Javier and Lupe

agitate for the land and drove me off it because I was not part of the family. So I went to work for myself as a laborer on a farm and in construction. I was twenty years old. I did all kinds of things. I picked fruit. In Cuicatlán there are a lot of mangos, and in the mango season I picked mangos. And we went to other areas to pick tomatoes when they needed to be picked. At that time, working in the fields from eight in the morning to two in the afternoon, I earned three pesos a day; but that was a lot. In those days one could get an egg for ten or fifteen centavos, and a cheese for a peso and a half. Food was cheap; so three pesos was plenty, especially for a single man. Economically, things were much better in those days. Salaries were low, but prices were much lower also.

When I was twenty-three years old, I went to Mexico City. Some cousins of mine came to Cuicatlán to get me. They said there was lots of work in Mexico City. They were working in a Jeep assembly plant and said they could find me work there. So I went with them. It was good. We made four to eight pesos a day, depending on where we worked; and living with my cousins, I did real well. There were five of us, and we paid two hundred pesos a month, including our utilities, and with the five of us, it came out real well. I worked there for about a year. I worked in the Jeep plant at first, and then the owners of the Jeep plant asked me to go to work in an air-conditioning factory they had. So I went there, and there they paid me eight pesos a day.

About a year after I had gone to Mexico City, I came home to Cuicatlán for the Easter celebrations. That is a very important celebration in Oaxaca, and a lot of people from Oaxaca go home at that time. The woman who had taken care of me after my grandmother died was very ill and wanted me to stay close. She suggested I go to Oaxaca City so that she could call me to come to be with her if she became very ill.

So I went to Oaxaca and did not return to Mexico City. It turned out that they were looking for people to work at Telégrafos, the telegraph office. The pay was twelve pesos a day for laborers. So I went to work there. It was temporary work. There were no fixed contracts, and we worked job by job. But I worked hard and my boss liked me, so I had fairly steady work. We worked all over the state. At first, our job was to put up telegraph lines along the rail lines that were being put in. So we had to push a pushcart along the rails to the site where we were working. This pushcart had no motor—we just pushed it—and it had the posts and the wire and everything on it.

Then in 1954 they sent me to work in Cuicatlán as an installer. That was real nice, because I was going back home to where I had lived before. But while I was in Cuicatlán—I hadn't been there very long—there was an order that came from the main office of the telegraph company asking if I would be willing to go to Ciudad Victoria and Tamaulipas because they needed help up there. I decided I ought to go, because if I wanted to stay with Telégrafos (I still was on a temporary contract), I ought to demonstrate that I really wanted to work and do the job.

So I went to Tamaulipas and was there from 1955 to 1959. It was a long time to be away from Oaxaca, but I learned a lot, and I got a chance to visit the border. I went to the United States a few times—just across the border. It was very cheap at that time.

Then, in 1959, I came back to Oaxaca, to Cuautla. I was made the head installer in Cuautla. Then in 1960 the telegraph office said that people who had completed elementary would have the opportunity, if they qualified, to go to Mexico City to get specialized training to become a more skilled installer or one who could run a crew. The head of the office in Cuautla, where I was working, suggested that I apply. So I did, and they took me, because even though I only had four years of elementary education, it was all that had been available at the time, and my bosses knew that I was a hard worker and would try very hard.

So I went to Mexico City in 1960, and I stayed there through most of 1961. First I went to the telegraph training school to learn the more advanced techniques of installing and repairing telegraph equipment. Then I had to go to a special school, where I became licensed in driving the motorized carts that we used on the rail lines to carry our equipment. These motorized carts had just come in. Then I had to go to a special three-month school for the new telephones that were being installed in some of the offices. When I finished they sent me back to Oaxaca, and I was sent to Ejutla and Ocotlán, where I worked for part of 1961 and 1962 and 1963. Then in October 1964 I was sent to Tamuzanchale [in San Luis

Potosí], where I was for two months working on a special assignment. But I got sick, so I had to return to Oaxaca. It was during 1963 that I met Lupe.

LUPE: I was born on the ninth of November in 1937 in Santa María Teresa, Tlacolula. I was the oldest of nine children, although six have died and only three are still living. Today, I only have one brother and one sister. I had to go to work early and never went to school. I went to work when I was seven years old and helped the family. We had no land in Santa María Teresa, so we all had to work at what we could. I was a maid. When I was nine, in 1946, my father decided to move to Tehuantepec, because his brother had told him he could get good work as a construction worker. So we all moved. It was a long trip. We walked from Santa María Teresa to Oaxaca, and then we spent the night in Oaxaca, and then we had to take a long bus ride from Oaxaca to Tehuantepec. The bus ride in those days was ten pesos each, and it was a lot of money for us. But my father had decided to move. When we got to Tehuantepec, I went to work for a lady who had a boarding house and a restaurant. She became my godmother, and I worked for her for a long time, first as a maid and then as a cook.

My father didn't make much money, but with my help and with that of my sister, who was also working for this woman, we were able to get along. I lived with my godmother and worked for her until I was fourteen years old. She gave me sixteen pesos a month and room and board. And she gave me other things. When I started working as a room-service maid, she gave me fifty pesos a month. And then when I got to be the cook, she gave me one hundred pesos a month. It wasn't much, but as I say, she was my godmother, and so she really gave me a lot of other things. She would buy me clothes and shoes and then give me some extra money when I needed it.

At the age of fourteen I decided to go back and live at home. My mother at that time was making tortillas to sell, and she said she needed help from everybody—both me and my sister. It was hard work, but we made more money. I had to get up at two in the morning. We had to start washing the corn, getting it ready so that by four in the morning we could be at the mill so the corn could be ground. By five we were making tortillas. We used to make twenty-five kilos of tortillas a day and sell them. It was hard work, but we could make a living in those days on that kind of income, and we were all together—my sister Veronica, my father, my mother, and I.

Two years later, when I was sixteen, I returned to work in the kitchen. My godmother came and asked my father if I would come back and work in the kitchen because she needed me. My father and mother said I could if I wanted to. I actually liked working in the kitchen, so I decided I would. Also, we needed a bit more money, and I thought I could help make it. We had money to buy things we needed and we owned a house; but whenever anybody got sick or we had to have a fiesta or anything, we had a hard time getting the money.

Then when I was seventeen, I got married to Manuel. My godmother, my mother, and my father didn't want me to marry Manuel, but I did anyway. He was a driver for the Dodge automobile dealership in Tehuantepec. As my mother, my godmother, my father, and my sister all suspected, it didn't work out. He was real lazy, drank a lot, and caroused around. Sometimes he would have money for the house, and sometimes he wouldn't. He wasn't Catholic; he was some kind of Protestant.

Manuel didn't want me to work, so we had to live on what he could bring in. But I started working at the house, anyway. I would take in washing and ironing. I had to work real hard to take care of my children. Finally, I decided it wasn't worth it—that if I had to work that hard, I might as well not put up with a husband. I just left him. That was after seven years. I had two children by then. Noé, who was six, and Angélica, who was four. I went back to my father and mother, and I worked with them making tortillas. Then I went back to work with my godmother, working in the kitchen and helping her in the restaurant.

It was there that I met the engineer who wanted to take me to Mexico to be a maid, and he asked me if I would go. I said yes, because he was going to pay me six hundred pesos a month, and that was a lot of money. So I left the children with my parents and went to Mexico. I was twenty-six years old.

I really liked Mexico City, except that I missed my children. I kept coming back to Oaxaca to visit them. One day I just decided I didn't want to go back. So I stayed in Tehuantepec for a while, and then I went to Oaxaca to look for work.

I was working on Calle Reforma; and one day when I was going down the street to do the morning shopping, I heard someone whistling at me. I turned around to see who was making those kinds of noises at me. I looked up, and it was Javier up on a pole whistling down at me. He was really silly looking. He asked me if I would go out with him. I said I didn't know, but he kept insisting and insisting and insisting. So we saw some of each other.

Then one day he asked me if I would live with him and be his wife, and I said, well, he had to know that I had children. But he wouldn't believe me. He said I couldn't have children. And one day he came to Tehuantepec and talked to my parents and asked them if I could live with him and be his wife. They said yes, and he promised to take care of my two children. He was really good to them, helping them as much as he could. Now my son's children and my daughter's children all call him grandfather, because he has been father and grandfather to them. Shortly after we were married—and we weren't married by the church; we were just married by the state—we went to Cuicatlán. He was sent to Cuicatlán. And it was while we were there that he told my brother he should come to Cuicatlán and be a baker there, because there was no baker and he could do real well. And he did. We had a nice family there.

I also started working when we were in Cuicatlán. I had always worked. Javier didn't really want me to work, but I did, because I had always worked and thought I should. So I opened a little restaurant on the weekends—I sold fish, *ceviche,* and fish cocktails. I would come down to Oaxaca on Friday, buy fish, and take them back to Cuicatlán to sell on Saturday, Sunday, and, if there were any left over, on Monday. It was then that I bought this refrigerator I have, so I could store the fish and keep them fresh. I did pretty well, and I really liked doing it. The money I got from it, I didn't really spend on myself. I sent it to Tehuantepec to help build the house we have down there. That's the house my son, Noé, is using now.

Then we moved back to Oaxaca into the Colonia Ferrocarrileros, and I couldn't really sell anything while we were there, because it just wouldn't work. We had our son Ramón then and taking care of him, in addition to the lack of space, just made having a restaurant too hard. Then in 1973, my cousin told me about this colonia being built out here by the government to help people who needed a house and didn't have a place to live. So we came out here and looked at this lot, liked it, and went to see if we could purchase it. And Javier did, and we've been here ever since.

My daughter, Angélica, moved in with us when we came here, and my mother has stayed with us at times. But she went back and forth between here and Tehuantepec. And my brother, Alfonso, who is a little slow, also came and lived with us. He helped us around the house—he's never gotten married.

My son, Noé, stayed in Tehuantepec. He went to high school and *preparatoria* and then was in the merchant marine academy. But he didn't like it. He said they didn't treat him well; they did all kinds of bad things to them. He's not that kind of boy. So he went back to Tehuantepec and found a job working for the federal agriculture and water commission and is doing well right now—he's married and has three children. We see them periodically.

My daughter, Angélica, has lived with us. We've got problems with her. She seems a bit lazy; I don't know what to do with her sometimes. But shortly after we moved in here, she ran off and stayed with a man for a while and had her first child. But this man wasn't very responsible; he was really lazy. Even the boy's mother told Angélica that she shouldn't have anything to do with him. But she did, and she had her child. Then she wouldn't work around here. I got really angry and sent her away, and she shouldn't have put those problems on Javier, either. I was very angry. So she went away. When she came back, she had another child. She's gotten a little better how, but we have to take care of them. Javier and I—we're getting old. We need to be able to have time for ourselves now, but now we have these grandchildren to take care of because the children's fathers won't have anything to do with them.

We also have my niece, Adela, who comes to stay with us sometimes. She is from Santa María Teresa, but when she finished high school, she came and lived with us for a year and then has come back several times. She was a big help. I wish Angélica were like her. I don't know. It's hard to raise children these days. When I was growing up, we all had to work hard and do what we had to do. But kids just run all over the place today. They just don't have any respect. But I must say, Javier has been a great deal of help to us during this whole time. He has treated everybody with a great deal of kindness.

And now that we're living here, we have our own house and we have our family. Ramón finished technical school and is working as a draftsman for the electric commission, and is renting a house just around the corner. He will have a child soon. Also in the colonia there are a lot of people who are together and work together. We are much better off than we were before, even though we have these extra children around. But if we are good to them, they will grow up and be kind to us in our old age.

JAVIER: Yes, I heard about this colonia from Lupe, and I thought at first that I didn't want to have anything to do with it, because they probably wanted a large down payment and high monthly payment. But Lupe suggested we come out and look at it; and since we were paying rent where we were, I did. It turned out we really liked the lot that was available, and the down payment was only two thousand pesos, and the monthly payments were six hundred pesos a month. I could manage that fine—I was paying six hundred pesos for rent where I was at the time. We moved out here immediately, because I didn't think we needed to be paying rent at one place and mortgage payments someplace else. At first we lived in a little bamboo shack on the back of the lot. Then I built the first room on the house. The first room was about five by three meters. And then we had the shack, which we used as a kitchen, and the first brick room, which we used to live and sleep in. Little by little we've been adding on, until today we have three rooms and an indoor kitchen. We also have a bathroom and a shower. We've done pretty well. It's been very nice here. Yes, we've had some problems with the children, but children are children, and they have to be taken care of. When I met Lupe, she had two children by another man, Noé and Angélica. He had made it impossible for her to live with him, so she left him. But children need to be taken care of. After all, the old couple who had taken care of me had been very kind to me and sent me to school. So I felt I should do the same. And we've had a very good time with the children, although now it's been a little more difficult. It really hurt me when Lupe sent Angélica off. It's true, she was not being a responsible mother, but then it wasn't the children's fault that their mother wasn't taking care of them the way she should.

What I want to do is raise these children so they will know how to work, and they will know that work is important. I don't want them to be taught to be lazy like a lot of children today. I want them to go to school. If the kids don't have an education, they won't be able to get anywhere. School is the only way they're going to get ahead.

In the last twenty years, food and clothing have gone up in price. Things are more expensive than they used to be. And although salaries are much higher, it's like a race between a bicycle and a car: the car is always ahead. The bicycle—and the salaries—don't even begin to catch up. For example, it used to be that three pesos would get you a nice cheese twenty centimeters across. Today, they charge you thirty pesos for the cheese, and it's only twelve centimeters across. Why don't they keep the size the same and just charge you more? At least you would know what you were getting. Bread is the same way. They keep raising the price and making it smaller. It isn't fair what's done to the workers.

The unions don't help at all. We really don't have a union to help us. The union probably does more to hurt the workers than anything else. It doesn't defend us. For example, I had to take a day off once, and they didn't discount that from my salary until almost a year later. By then my salary was much higher, but they discounted a whole day, anyway. When I tried to complain, they just told me not to make any trouble. For example, I am the shop steward for my area, and anytime anything happens and there's a problem and I take it to the general secretary of the union, he just says not to worry about it. I don't know what the union is for. It doesn't seem to help us at all.

So I want the kids to get educated so they won't have to depend on these kinds of things to help them. They've got to know how to work and work hard and have an education. Look at Ramón. We sent him to school and taught him to work hard and now he has a good job with the electric commission. However, I worry about him. Both he and his wife have good jobs, she works for the telephone company, but they spend much more than they earn. You look at their house and they have nothing. They should be living in a smaller place and saving for the future. I don't know what they are going to do if things get bad, or when Amanda has her baby and will have to quit work. But, I think we did our best with Ramón, we gave him a good education and found him a good job. The rest will be up to him.

I even want the granddaughters to study, because back when Lupe was growing up, girls didn't study very much. But now it's really important that they do, because if they don't, what will happen to them if they get a bad husband or something? They need to have an education to help them through. I don't know if we'll be able to do it, because family life and social life are much harder today, and Lupe and I are not getting any younger. We now have five grandchildren, two of whom live here with us. Although Angélica is here, she won't have a husband to help her. So we will have to do it.

Lupe and I are going to have to work hard because children just aren't raised right these days. They don't know who their parents are. Their parents are running off working or doing things and don't have time for children. It's not necessarily the parents' fault. It's the way things are these days. Everybody has to work. Father comes home and is real tired, and his son wants to know something or wants some help. The father says, "Not now, a little later." And a little later, the child is asleep or something else comes up. The mother comes home and says, "Oh, not now, I'm tired," and throws something together to eat. And then everybody goes to bed. It's just not a family life anymore. And at school it's not the same as it used to be. Teachers don't get help from the parents anymore. They can't educate the children. They can't teach them moral rules. If a teacher tries to discipline a child, the parent gets mad at the teacher. It wasn't like that in my day. When I was going to school, if the teacher came and said, "The child is not behaving," Don Manuel would say, "I give you permission to do anything you need to do to teach him proper manners." That doesn't happen anymore. But I hope we'll be able to do that. It's going to be hard for the children, but if we can give them the right kind of education, they'll be able to get through.

Javier and Lupe's origins are in places similar to those in our first two life histories: relatively isolated, rural agricultural communities. In contrast, however, Javier was pushed into formal education, rather than having to sneak into it as did María Teresa and Alfonso. He obtained all that was available in his village, four years of elementary schooling. It had little immediate payoff as he struggled at day labor during his teenage years, but then, rather than waiting for integration to come to Oaxaca, he migrated to Mexico City, where he found far more rewarding opportunities than either Elodia or Alfonso had discovered in their migrations to Oaxaca City. Javier worked for a multinational plant and earned good wages. In Oaxaca, he started working for the national telegraph company, which was expanding service throughout the nation. His hard work, education, and willingness to relocate (since he had no family at the time) allowed him to take advantage of opportunities offered by the expansion of the national political economy into rural areas. Oaxaca's reintegration thus provided Javier with job security, access to benefits, and socioeconomic mobility.

Oaxaca's reintegration has also affected his and Lupe's housing, since they live in a government-sponsored housing project. But unlike María Teresa, Elodia, and Alfonso, Javier and Lupe did not participate in the 1975 squatters' invasion and subsequent political activities. Nor do they articulate a radical political view of their conditions. Javier is simply cynical, especially about the union, in spite of his being a union steward. His political pragmatism is limited to informal ties developed through compadrazgo and *conocidos*. Being a member of the aspiring income group presented him with subsidized services through the INDECO project, available to numbers of the very poor and minimum wage groups only through political action.

His formal-sector job security, higher wages, and benefits have allowed him to build a substantial house relatively quickly and accumulate more material possessions than those in the lower-income groups. It has also aided the creation of a secondary income source from his wife's home restaurant. The restaurant provides the household with some supplementary income and a repository for the household's surplus labor and capital. The monetary returns are not tremendous. Rather, it reduces the cost of food, because they save something by buying in bulk and can eat the restaurant leftovers. Households from the two lower-income groups also frequently engage in petty commerce, but Javier and Lupe's mixed strategy (Javier's formal-sector job and Lupe's informal-sector restaurant) provide the combination of a stable income with access to benefits and the opportunity to use surplus labor for a small profit.

While Javier willingly relocated a number of times to take advantage of new economic opportunities, eventually his commitment to family drew him back, first to his village and then to Oaxaca City. His story demonstrates the profound importance of family to Oaxacans, and particularly how those of the aspiring income group are most capable of realizing family ideals. Although Javier's first approaches to Lupe appear to fit the macho mold (he whistled at her as she walked down the street), he is in reality warmly devoted to his family, including those Lupe brought into the family from her previous marriage. Javier feels a special obligation to care for Lupe's children because of the importance his grandmother and foster mother had in his early life. As for Lupe, while her family stayed together when she was growing up, she still had to work and experience the same harsh conditions as Elodia. She, like Elodia, had unfortunate experiences with men, and had to leave one husband before she happened upon Javier. Her marriage to Javier provided her with a devoted, faithful, and economically stable husband.

Under normal conditions Javier and Lupe would be entering the final stage of their domestic cycle in which their children are gone from home and they are enjoying the fruits of a comfortable retirement. However, Javier and Lupe have also lived in one version or another of an extended family ever since they moved to Oaxaca. Either Lupe's mother or brother, Alfonso, has always been with them helping with Lupe's restaurant or keeping the small store out front. Her niece, Adela, has also lived with them occasionally. Most importantly, Lupe's daughter, Angélica, has presented them with the job of raising two of their five grandchildren. Lupe's and Javier's dedication toward children (a value held by most Mexicans) is manifest in their determination to raise them as their own.

While they are devoted to their family, as with parents in any society they have had disappointments as well as successes in raising their family. When Javier retired his income fell, and with Lupe's restaurant less in demand in the consolidated colonia and Angélica's children for them to support, the family fell on hard times. Javier's eyes were damaged by his years of looking into the sun as he searched for broken telegraph lines, and Lupe has high blood pressure. Their hope is that the oldest grandchild will soon be able to work and help the family out. They are however, all keenly aware of Oaxaca's rising credentialism and the increasing need for formal education to obtain employment. Javier points out that it is not only formal schooling, but also the informal, moral training parents provide that allow children to prosper. The difficulties encountered by his step-daughter demonstrate that the way to a "proper" life is not always clear.

Abel: A Middle-Class/Elite Household

Abel is the youngest member of one of the city's wealthier families, a family typifying Oaxaca's most recent manifestation of an externally oriented elite. Unlike the locally oriented elite, he does not have family roots in the area's Spanish colonial past or the old commercial elite class. Rather, his father was a skilled technician who anticipated Mexico's post–World War II expansion. He moved from rural Oaxaca to the city to provide an education for his sons and thus prepare them for the new era. He saw to it that his sons were ready to take advantage of Mexico's growth when it did occur.

One of Abel's brothers is a medical doctor; one, a civil engineer; another was a captain in the military and now runs a business in Oaxaca; Abel runs an automobile service station that serves the external transportation business in both the public and private sectors.

Abel's living conditions reflect the success of his business. He recently moved to a new home in the northern part of the city. The house, started but not completed by one of the city's physicians, is a typical example of new upper-middle-class and elite housing in the city. It fronts the street with imposing wooden doors to the garage and front entrance. The garage has two cars, each less than five years old: a Dodge sedan for

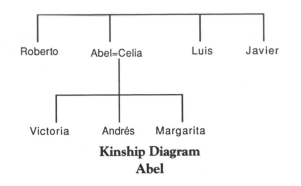

Kinship Diagram
Abel

his wife and a Jeep Wagoneer for himself. Inside the house there is a large kitchen, living room, dining room, family room, and patio. Upstairs there are four bedrooms (even though Abel's children live out of the city) and two baths. Flooring is either wood or polished concrete with new, coordinated furnishings in every room, including a stereo system and the latest kitchen appliances. The living area is dominated by a large china cabinet where Abel and his wife display the gifts they have received at special times in their life cycle, for example, their wedding and the baptisms of their children. Abel is particularly happy about the fact that he is on the same water system as the government's INFONAVIT development and therefore will have fewer water problems than friends who live farther into the heart of Oaxaca.

Abel enjoys the fruits of success. He is a frequent vacationer at the beach resorts of Mexico and during the late 1970s boom he paid cash for a second home in one of the fastest growing university cities of the southwestern United States. The house, a three-bedroom tract dwelling in a suburb of the city, is currently being used by his children as they attend college. It is Abel's intention to retire there when he gives up his current business.

ABEL: I was born in the city of Oaxaca in October 1928, approximately one year after my father came down from the northern mountains in order to educate the family. My father was a mechanic, or what today would be an engineer, working for one of the mining companies in the mountains. At that time, there were only four years of school in those places, and my father had to educate himself using a correspondence course from the United States. He decided to bring the family to Oaxaca in order to make it possible for us all to get a better education.

When we came down there were four children—all of them boys. About a year after they came down, I was born here, over on the street of Morelos where we were living at the time. When I was growing up, my father had to travel a lot in order to do his work. He went back to the mountains for a while, and after spending a few years there, he went to Taxco to work in the mines. He was there for ten years. Then after that, he went up to work in Durango for another ten years, and then he went to Chihuahua to work for five more years. But by then his lungs were giving out, because in those days they didn't use any kind of breathing devices or filters. And so my father, who had been a very strong man, came back to Oaxaca a weak and disabled man.

He did all that work in order to educate us kids so that we could do well in life. One of my brothers is now a doctor up in Guerrero and another is a civil engineer. My other brother was a pilot and captain in the military for several years and is now back in Oaxaca and has his own business. I was also studying medicine. In Mexico City, I went through two years of preparatory school in the medical program, but my marks weren't very good or not as good as my other brother. I was also the youngest. So my parents decided that since they probably couldn't afford to send everybody to school, and since my marks were the lowest, that my other brother would stay in school.

So I came back to Oaxaca in 1951 and went back to work at the service station up on García Vigil Street. I worked real hard, and the owner and I got along really well. I was his right-hand man. But then one day the owner was killed in an automobile accident. That was about 1953. And shortly thereafter, his family and his children told me they wanted me to turn over the shop to them. So I cleared up all the paper work and turned it over to them.

I then went to work for another gasoline station. All that time I—or I should say, we—were saving money to buy land to open our own service station. I had gotten married in October 1952. My wife, Celia, and I both worked and saved. Celia is also from Oaxaca and she has worked as hard as I have at getting our business going. We didn't have any children during that time. Then, because of people I met while running the first service station, in 1957 we bought this land here, where the service station is, right by the highway. We then worked for another two years to buy the things we needed to put in—an automobile lift and a lubrication pit—so we could begin work. In 1957 when we bought the land, it cost us thirty-five thousand pesos, and to put in the lift and the basic things we needed to be in business cost another twelve thousand pesos. All in all, it took about fifty thousand pesos to get started here. But we had saved, and we got some help from my family.

That's one of the things you find even today in Oaxaca. You find that the people who come from the outside are the ones who do most of the investing and are making this city grow. The old families of Oaxaca, or the Spaniards as we call them around here, don't really invest much. They save their money and put it in banks and let the banks do the investing for them. They don't want to take risks. That's one of the problems we have in Oaxaca. If the city is going to advance, we need some people here who are willing to invest their money and take risks—not silly risks, but calculated risks—things like the plastic container factory over by Tule or the plant to build the trailers out by Ocotlán. That trailer plant is part of a Mexico City firm, but it was started by Oaxaca money. It builds commercial trailers, everything from flatbeds to semis. It's a small plant by Mexico City standards. It employs somewhat less than two hundred workers, but that's very big and important here in Oaxaca. And it's been a big success for those who invested in it. That and the plastic factory are rather risky businesses, since they have to bring all the material down and transport the finished product out. But those people are making good money right now. You know, we don't even have our own eggs in Oaxaca. We have to import all those from Tehuacán. Why doesn't somebody open up a major egg-producing plant? It's hard to understand sometimes.

Celia and I, we don't have any of our money that isn't invested. It's all working in something, and very little of it is in the bank. If you look around, you'll find that the old families and the Spanish families who came in the mid 1930s own all the land and a lot of the commercial establishments, but nothing productive—nothing that brings in new money from the outside.

Anyway, Celia and I opened this business in 1959 with ourselves and two helpers. Today we have eight. My wife has worked here with me the whole time. A year after we opened up, our first child was born. That was Victoria, in 1960. A year later Andrés was born. Our third child, Margarita, was born in 1962. They're all just a little over a year apart. We planned our family, because we knew we had to save, and we couldn't afford to take care of them while we were getting the business started. Then we decided three was plenty, because we wanted to raise them and educate them well, and we didn't think that if we had more we would be able to do it. My brother who is a doctor also planned his family. He only has two children. My other brother, the pilot, has six. He's more of a macho than the rest of us. It's probably a good thing that we haven't had any more children, because things are getting much more difficult economically now.

All of our kids have gone to the United States for at least some of their university education. We bought a house so they could all live comfortably and my wife, Celia, moved up there to be with them while they were going to school. It was kind of difficult for me to see them all leave and go to the U.S. We are a very close family, but we felt that we had to do it for economic reasons, to give the children the most opportunities.

And, even though I'm alone, I'm not really alone. I still have my brothers and their families here. We see each other every day. One of my brothers owns a tire shop right next to my station and so we see each other in the course of our work. And on the weekends we are always together.

That's one of the things about Mexican families. They always stick together. Eat together, play together, have fun together. If it weren't for my family, I would be nowhere. Our father sacrificed so that we would get a good education and after that we each help each other out. My brothers helped me put the money together to get this business started and they helped me pay for the house in the United States. And, I, of course, help them when they need it.

All three of our children are in the United States now. The eldest, Victoria, was studying hotel management. She married a gringo and now she's a reservations manager in a Hyatt. The youngest, Margarita, is also in the United States studying to be a travel agent. Andrés is in the United States studying mechanics. He wants to open up his own service station, and we'll probably help him do that. But he's not going to do it here. He's going to Guadalajara, because he wants to open up a specialized shop, and you can't do that in Oaxaca. If you opened up a specialized shop in Oaxaca, you'd go broke, because there aren't enough cars. Andrés will have a much more difficult time opening his shop than I did. He'll probably need at least a million pesos to get his shop open.

We used to do much better than we do now, especially with the tourists. I used to be able to put together two to three hundred dollars a week, in dollars, from what I would bring in here from the automobile tourists who came through. But now it's much different. I'm lucky if I get a hundred dollars in U.S. dollars a month. What's happened is that the whole tourist industry has changed in Oaxaca. It used to be that we would get people coming down in their automobiles traveling around. But with the new emphasis on foreign tourists coming by airplane to the big hotels on package tours, we just don't get the kind of business we once did. It's good for the big hotel chains, but it doesn't do us medium-sized merchants very much good. That's one reason my son wants to open up his shop in Guadalajara.

Now Victoria, we may open our own hotel for her when she comes back. But we'll have to see how that goes—see how tourism is going in Oaxaca at the time and decide whether we want to invest in that. Tourism is a real problem here, because the people in Oaxaca are not used to dealing with outsiders. They still really don't know how to run good tourist facilities. You compare the best hotels in Oaxaca with the best hotels in Cancún, for example. In Cancún they're no more expensive than in Oaxaca, but they treat you a whole lot better. Margarita will have her own travel agency here in the city, because the travel agencies are going well, and we've been here long enough to have enough connections to help them.

But it's going to be tough, because things are getting much more expensive here in Oaxaca. Oaxaca is a really expensive city to live in. I travel a lot, and I can tell you that it's much more expensive in Oaxaca than in other places—even like Mexico City or Cancún, especially for the traveler. And that's one of the problems in Oaxaca. They're trying to make too much quick money off the tourist and not taking care of long-term trends.

However, I think my kids will do fine, because we've been able to educate them very well, and they've been able to go to the United States and learn English, and they interact very well with North Americans, which, if they're going to live in Oaxaca and make any money, they're going to have to do.

But we're going to have problems right here in Oaxaca because things are getting much more expensive, and most people are not willing—or can't—raise the wages of the workers as fast as prices are going up. The only solution is for the owners of establishments to make a little less money. And that would be all right, except that you don't see the government or anybody in the big establishments doing the same thing, and they're just causing the prices to keep going up and up faster and faster. At some point there's going to be a problem here, and I don't know when it's going to be. But I hope my children are well established so that they can take care of it when it comes.

Abel has benefited more than anyone else discussed in this chapter from Oaxaca's reintegration with the broader economy. As a mechanical engineer working for a mining company, Abel's father used his income and status to send his children to school in Mexico City. Abel and his brothers obtained much more education than María Teresa, Elodia, Alfonso, Javier, or Lupe, although Abel admits that he was not a particularly distinguished student. The intrafamily cooperation, along with Oaxaca's reintegration, allowed Abel to benefit from his brothers' education and turned him into a highly successful businessman.

Much like the small business person of North American legend, Abel feels he has pulled himself up by his bootstraps. His reconstruction of his own history tends to ignore a number of critical factors. Although he acknowledges that his family contributed to the capital that started the business, his brother helped by seeing to it that Abel got important contracts taking care of trucks for the ministry of tourism and the state police vehicles. His contacts with prominent Oaxacans, at least partially a result of family ties, provided him with the opportunity to purchase the propitious site for his business. And he was certainly much luckier in the timing of his business venture, which coincided with Oaxaca's reintegration with the national and international economies, than Alfonso had been with his weaving enterprise. Most important among all these factors was the location of the business. Situated on the Pan American Highway near two of the larger tourist hotels, he had ready access to Mexican and North American traffic when tourists started driving to Oaxaca in great numbers. In addition, the experience of his father working for a North

American mining firm gave Abel some inkling as to how North Americans like to see such service businesses run. He was there when the market opened and provided a service the clients recognized as similar to what they were used to back home. The result was a steady flow of U.S. dollars into Abel's hands.

Abel's experience with and benefits from Oaxaca's reintegration have oriented him to a much broader world. The profits from the business made it possible for him to purchase his house in the United States and send his children there to school. He also anticipates helping his son establish a business in a city, Guadalajara, that is more integrated with the national and international economies than is Oaxaca. Abel's experiences have also taught him the limits of integration. He recognizes that the more Oaxaca becomes integrated, the easier it is for large-scale, Mexico City capital to displace people like him. Air transport has already begun to dislodge him indirectly since fewer tourists come in cars. His experiences are reminiscent of what happened to local traditional artisans displaced by the importation of modern mass goods via the Pan American Highway.

Abel's household composition has been the most consistently nuclear of any of the families. He also explicitly gives credit to his wife in contributing her labor to the success of his business. They also delayed having their family in order to build resources. When he and his wife subsequently had children, they stopped at three. Yet, as already observed, the extended family's economic importance has not declined. While the household may be small, the extended family of all three brothers' nuclear families remains the most important social unit.

Abel appears to engage in the least political activity of anyone we have discussed. He has apparently stayed out of public life and done well. Yet, this impression is deceiving. His older brother, Roberto, fulfills the family's political needs. Roberto attended Mexico City's polytechnic university and became a civil engineer. He worked for several years on the construction of the metro system in Mexico City, after which he returned to Oaxaca as the director of a federal agency's state office. When a new federal administration came to power, Roberto left that post and started a private construction business. Roberto's capital came from some family friends who were officers in one of the branches of a national bank that had recently moved to the city. His first contracts were for public works contracted by a bureaucrat who had been his friend when Roberto held a public office. The construction business did well and Roberto became one of the technical advisers to the state office of the PRI. He helped Abel obtain contracts to service the trucks and automobiles of government agencies. Roberto is now in the process of refocusing his construction company. He believes the Oaxaca market is virtually saturated, and that the new opportunities are on the coast where a new highway and improved air links have opened the area to tourism. Roberto's ties with the government will provide him with the inside track when exploiting this new market.

Both men see the husbanding of resources in anticipation of future opportunities as an important quality present in the new Oaxacan entrepreneurial class, but lacking, they believe, in the old, locally oriented elite families. This may be ideological self-justification and their opinions are undoubtedly tempered by the 1980s economic calamity. In the midst of crisis, they must struggle to maintain what is a developed nation's middle-class life-style. Nevertheless, within Oaxaca they are undeniably much better off than anyone in the income groups below them and even in crisis they are unlikely to forfeit that advantage.

Conclusions

These four life histories reflect and refract not only the struggles and successes of the four families, but also the impact on families and individuals of the political, economic, cultural, and social forces we discussed in the previous chapters. The eloquence with which these people express themselves is not a product of our translation. Though many are uneducated, they are articulate about their problems and aware of the causes.

Like many of Oaxaca's mature, established families, that is, families that have children and even grandchildren, each of these four families migrated to the city. In spite of the diversity in the immediate conditions impelling migration, the themes of integration, employment, and family predominate in all four stories. The particular wheres and whys of migration, however, are more important than the simple fact of migration. These particularities differentiate the families into the four income groups. Elodia was sent by her mother to work and earn money. For many years, she moved back and forth between urban and rural settings. Alfonso came to escape a village where he saw no future, but his immediate goal was not simply to earn money. Javier moved throughout Mexico to advance his career, but returned to Oaxaca more for social than economic reasons. He wanted to be physically near those for whom he felt responsible. Abel had the least autonomy in his decision. His father wanted him and his brothers to obtain a better education, and even his incomplete education and bad grades propelled his career.

Those who migrated to urban centers outside of Oaxaca, Javier and Abel, did much better. Abel, who migrated for education to attend the university in Mexico City, did best of all. Abel's father had already achieved an occupation and income superior to the other three families. He passed that advantage onto his sons by providing them with more and better education than either of the other three families could provide.

The differences in the results of migration also result from the unequal economic development of Oaxaca and the nation. Because of its isolation and disengagement from the national economy, Oaxaca lagged in the provision of new formal-sector jobs. Throughout the 1940s, Oaxaca had no industry and the economic expansion of central Mexico bypassed the state. To obtain a modern, formal-sector job, one had to go to Mexico City, as did Javier. Alfonso considered following his brother to the United States, but family concerns kept him in Oaxaca. Abel was sent by his father to Mexico City where the best educational opportunities lie. María Teresa and Elodia were the most affected by Oaxaca's isolation. Domestic work and petty commerce were the sole economic opportunities available to uneducated, unskilled women. Elodia tried to escape Oaxaca, but she hardly fared better in the lowland hot country where she and her husband worked as unskilled agricultural laborers.

When Oaxaca began its reintegration with the national economy in the 1950s, new economic openings emerged. Both Javier and Abel benefited directly from Oaxaca's reintegration. As the national telegraph company expanded in Oaxaca, the demand for skilled workers outstripped the local supply. Javier, who did not have the credentials officially required (an elementary school diploma), advanced on the basis of his early unskilled work with the company. Abel, meanwhile, profited from the completion of the Pan American Highway linking Oaxaca to Mexico City. Abel's service station appealed greatly to North American tourists and he established a highly successful business.

The effects of Oaxaca's reintegration were not so dramatic for Alfonso, María Teresa, or Elodia. Alfonso did obtain a weaving job related to the tourist industry. Instead of being an independent artisan, however, he worked in a factory as a wage laborer. In the late 1940s, he attempted to become an independent artisan, but he proved to be ahead of the times and the business failed. He returned to the factory where his piece-rate pay averaged just above the minimum wage. Nevertheless, the work was steady and did offer fringe benefits not previously available. María Teresa and Elodia's employment opportunities have hardly been affected by Oaxaca's reintegration; uneducated, unskilled females still are relegated primarily to domestic work.

Each family's material living conditions reflect both Oaxaca's unequal reintegration with the national and international economies and the differences among the four income groups. Households of all income levels have more material goods than they would have had fifty years ago. Mass-produced consumer items have become widely available and many are affordable to even the poorest families. Plastic and metal have replaced fragile pottery for most kitchen uses. Shoes have replaced sandals and cover formerly bare feet. Virtually everyone has a kerosene or gas stove, a blender, a radio, and many have a television set.

While everyone has more than they would have had fifty years ago, there remain significant differences among the families of the four income groups. Alfonso's television set remains unusable because he does not have the money to fix it. María Teresa and Elodia have never owned one, while neither Javier nor Abel's family need worry about being without one. Abel is the only one able to afford an automobile, to have a telephone, employ servants, or have a house in the United States. Javier, Alfonso, and Elodia do not even dream of owning a house in the United States, while Abel's children and Alfonso's daughter have attended college there. Abel provided the sole support for his children, but Alfonso's daughter did it with the assistance of North American friends. Such opportunities are generally available only to those of the highest-income group. Among the three lower-income groups, the amount and kind of education is likely to distinguish them. Those of Javier's and Alfonso's group have a reasonable chance of having at least one son or daughter make it to the university level. They may also be able to place them in Mexico City schools, which are presumably of a higher quality. They have more education than their parents, but still not as much or of the same quality as children of the highest-income group.

While Abel's family clearly enjoys a higher standard of living than the others, even his family would only qualify as middle class by the standards of the developed world. He is certainly not rich by international standards. The services his house receives may be the best Oaxaca has to offer, but they remain those of the third world. His house receives usually polluted piped water, as does the rest of the city. His electricity is subject to frequent failures. Telephone connections are frequently impossible. The street in front of his house was only recently paved.

Besides demonstrating the structural similarities and differences among the four families, the life histories reveal the dynamic dimensions of each family's struggle to adapt. The most obvious dynamic element is place of residence. Not only have these families moved from rural origins to urban, but they have also moved among and within urban locales. Not a single one of these four families currently lives either where they were born and raised or even where they lived when they first moved to Oaxaca. Residential mobility punctuates their lives.

Equally important are their fluctuating social conditions, the variations in the structure of the household. We have argued that the most elemental social unit in Oaxaca is the family and household, and this chapter reveals how much more important it is than the individual. This chapter also discloses how the household's structure shifts constantly. Each of these households has experienced an episode when a relative from outside the immediate nuclear family resided within them.

Household size also fluctuates. María Teresa had an intact nuclear family until her husband died. After that she became the head of a household. During this time her daughters moved in and out of the household according to their income opportunities. They eventually established their own households and María Teresa moved in and out of those. For mutual economic and social support, the daughters, Elodia and Eustolia, linked their own households between two neighborhoods. Throughout, the family structure remained decidedly strong and stable, but household composition constantly changed.

Other families' household composition may not have fluctuated quite so much, but each has varied considerably. Alfonso moved back to his village once he became disabled and one of his sons became the head of the household. Javier accepted his wife's children from her former marriage and later incorporated the illegitimate children of one of his stepdaughters. Abel has had the most stable and nuclear household, although his children are all presently in the United States studying.

María Teresa's life history also reveals the difficulties and dynamic adaptation mechanisms confronted by female-headed households, at least those of the lowest-income group. Members of María Teresa's and Elodia's family have moved in and out of the work force in response to both needs and opportunities. All of María Teresa's and Elodia's jobs have been not only informal-sector jobs with no fringe benefits or security, but they have also been the least prestigious, the most demeaning, and the worst-remunerated employment in Oaxaca. They have sought to solidify their position by placing workers in the labor market as soon as feasible and have always experienced a tension between the delayed rewards of further education and the immediate benefit of a wage-earning job. Informal social networks have been the way they have found employment, and these networks have provided them with what little security they have. Elodia's husband has suffered in construction work because of a deficient informal social network, a lack of acquaintances who would not only help him find jobs but also provide opportunities for him to upgrade his skills. Elodia has used fictive kin to move from one job to another. When she finds herself without work, she asks one of her comadres for work. Only by these social networks and with cooperation within the family, with mother, sisters and later Elodia's own children, has this family survived.

The dynamic use of household labor is not limited to the poorest income group. Although largely self-taught, Alfonso's educational advantage over María Teresa opened up a few more opportunities. He found somewhat better jobs and eventually landed employment in Oaxaca's formal sector. Alfonso walked through numerous jobs, leaving most because of unacceptable working conditions, before he settled into the formal-sector weaving position that eventually disabled him. It appears that only one of his children will be able to remain in school until he obtains a professional degree. The other three all entered the labor force because they felt the need to contribute to the household income. The daughter still contributes through remittances from the United States, confirming the importance of second workers in a family. The eldest son augmented the household's income until he established his own independent household. The other child who dropped out of school has informally assumed the role of head of household by establishing his own family in his father's house.

Only Javier and Abel have had rather straightforward careers of upward mobility, Javier from unskilled to skilled worker and Abel from manager to owner. In both cases, the stability and upward mobility of their work freed other household members from the necessity of work. Nevertheless, reflecting the evolution of gender roles in Oaxaca, both wives have worked. Lupe, Javier's wife, has moved in and out of the labor market through self-employment and her restaurant operation, which has provided a supplemental rather than necessary income. Abel's wife, Celia, also contributed her labor to the family business. In these two income groups, it is seen, second workers can make a substantial contribution to a household's income.

Now that we have completed our discussion of inequality from the days of Oaxaca's prehistory until contemporary times, and from consideration of broad political, economic, and social forces down to the life histories of particular individuals, families, and households, it is time to reflect upon and draw conclusions from our investigation.

8

Conclusion

The most obvious conclusion of this ethnography is that Oaxaca City exhibits an ambiguous "in-betweenness." It is neither an important secondary city, comparable to Monterrey, for example, nor is it simply a somnolent, provincial town. It is neither a city of growth, nor one of utter inactivity. Moreover, Oaxaca is surely a city marked by social inequality, but apparently not as severely divided as other Mexican cities.

We feel, however, it is insufficient to conclude simply that Oaxaca is a city of contrasts. The task of these conclusions is to go beyond that simple observation to an integration of these and other empirical findings with the more general issue of socioeconomic inequality. We do so in two parts, as we did in the substantive chapters. First, we review Oaxaca's structure of socioeconomic inequality. Second, we explore Oaxacan's responses to inequality.

The Structure of Socioeconomic Inequality

Our findings based on the macro perspective examining the structure of Oaxaca's socioeconomic inequality can be summarized as having one constant, one cycle, and two trends:

The Constant

Oaxaca's economic base for more than two thousand years has been as a regional marketing and service center to the surrounding hinterland.

The Cycle

Population has recurringly grown and then declined in association with external political and economic links, imposed elites, and reversible increases in inequality. Because of Oaxaca's constant economic function, new and exploitative economic activities have never fundamentally transformed economic or social relations. As a result, externally based elites have been transitory, passing through in cycles, and social inequality in Oaxaca has been generally less sharp than other regions of Mexico.

The Trends

While Oaxaca's economic foundation has been primarily constant, the basis of inequality has shifted from heredity to economics.

The increasing power of the state during the contemporary era has increased the division of labor, social complexity, and the distribution of material goods. In particular, it has added new factions to the elite and improved the relative standing of those groups just below the elite.

The city of Oaxaca, and before it Monte Albán, has exhibited a remarkable constancy in its economic base and in socioeconomic inequality. For more than two millennia it has served in succession as a marketing and administrative center to the surrounding agricultural hinterland. Monte Albán was the center of early state formation in Mesoamerica, and Oaxaca has been an outpost city of a larger state (first the Aztecs, then Spain, and finally Mexico) for centuries. While the city and the region have experienced significant change in many respects, they have never lost this fundamental function as a regional center.

Far more than many regions of Mexico, the Oaxaca valley withstood the fundamental transformations wrought by Spanish colonialism. Most Indian villages successfully retained their access to land. Few haciendas arose and only a small part of the native population became thoroughly proletarianized.[1] Moreover, the native population had more than two thousand years experience with market-oriented production before the Spaniards' arrival. Spanish colonialism thus did not thoroughly revolutionize indigenous social relations. Society remained hierarchical as the Spaniards assumed the dominant positions and the Indian nobility became subordinate to them. The majority of the population continued market-oriented production primarily of agricultural goods on their own land. As a result, Oaxaca City assumed the role that Monte Albán (and a few other urban centers in the valley) had previously: as a marketing and administrative center. Unlike many Latin American cities, Oaxaca never fully became an "exploitative" or "parasitic" city peopled by wealthy landowners and their retinues living off the surplus of highly exploited rural workers.[2]

Instead of an unrelenting history of exploitation and dependence, Oaxaca has gone through cycles of integration into and isolation from the broader world. Each period of integration has produced a number of temporary, but significant consequences: the imposition of new economic activities at the behest of nonlocal elites, increased social differentiation, and tension between local and nonlocal elites. The end of each period of integration has tended to see a reverse of each of these consequences, as economic activity disappears, the nonlocal elites leave the area, and social differentiation declines.

In the two millennia of the prehispanic era, the Oaxaca Valley region went through a number of cycles of expansion and contraction. Although we have no information on the imposition of nonlocal elites, integration into a larger regional system usually produced more social stratification and more marked social inequality. In the half millennium of the postcolonial era, there have been four periods of Oaxacan integration into the broader world: the early colonial period, the cochineal era of the late colonial period, the Porfiriato of the late nineteenth century, and the contemporary period since 1950. The first three represent efforts at exploitative relationships that imposed new economic activities dedicated to enriching a nonlocal elite. Cynically, the same could be maintained for the last, the contemporary era, if one asserts that increased government activities, even though ostensibly for all Oaxacans, primarily benefit the largely nonlocal government bureaucrats.

Oaxaca's periods of integration appear to confirm the proposition that integration into the world system produces underdevelopment. During the early colonial era, Hernando Cortez, who never visited Oaxaca, attempted to establish agricultural enterprises for his own benefit. Spanish peninsular merchants constituted the primary beneficiaries of the cochineal era and foreign capitalists, mainly miners and manufacturers, principally profited during the Porfiriato. These periods of integration did, at least temporarily, affect Oaxaca's social fabric. Almost by definition, local society was more differentiated: there was a new elite faction, the nonlocals, and their newly imposed economic activities. The nonlocals directed the surplus to themselves and topped the local social hierarchy. They spent most of their wealth on luxury consumption or exported it to Mexico City and Spain. Sometimes infrastructure or the means of collective consumption increased, but such things as lavish churches or an opera house benefited the elite more than any other class. More important, the immense cochineal profits were not reinvested into diversified productive enterprises. During the cochineal era, weaving factories did multiply, but they were tied to cochineal production and when cochineal disappeared so did nearly all the looms. During the periods of integration, most native Oaxacans, those below the elite, continued living in much the same or even worse conditions than during Oaxaca's stretches of isolation. The new economic activities and new outside elites are superimposed upon the existing structure, adding a new layer of economic activities and social strata, related to but independent from the traditional ones.

Once the outside elites leave, their imposed economic activities cease, leaving the city's economic base and corresponding social structure relatively unchanged. In each case—after the local Spaniards deterred Cortez's efforts, the War for Independence disrupted the cochineal trade, and the Revolution interrupted the mining and manufacturing ventures—the nonlocal elites and their economic activities disappeared, leaving behind class structure and inequality as they had been previously, relatively undifferentiated. The city continued on much as before, much as if the nonlocals had never been there. The native rural population still maintained their land and the city still performed marketing and administrative functions. The traditional activities were transacted largely isolated from the world beyond Oaxaca.

The case of Oaxaca thus complicates the generalization that the advantages of colonial towns were transformed to attract new economic activities (Portes and Walton 1976). Oaxaca's geographical isolation, imposed by the surrounding mountains, deterred most investment. As soon as the geographically superior route from Mexico City to Acapulco was established in the late sixteenth century, the early advantage of Oaxaca evaporated. After that, Oaxaca attracted investment only when potential profits were extraordinarily high (as in cochineal) or when the state led investment (as in the Porfiriato and the contemporary period). Never did investment and growth become self-perpetuating.

Thus, Oaxaca was left no richer at the end of its periods of integration than it had been before. The class structure in Oaxaca on the eve of the contemporary era had more in common with its own colonial period than with the rest of Mexico in the 1940s. Unlike most parts of Mexico in the 1940s, Oaxaca had no large landed class, no large numbers of dispossessed peasants, no revolutionary heroes, no beneficiaries of the Revolution, and no seeds for industrialization. Instead, the local commercial elite maintained a system of low-level mercantilism.

While Oaxaca has undergone these cycles, there has been a trend transforming the bases of stratification. Colonialism may not have fundamentally altered the economic basis of Oaxaca, but it did recast the basis for social stratification. During both the prehispanic and early colonial periods, class was determined largely by heredity. For the prehispanic Indians, birth determined whether one was a noble or commoner. Similarly, during the early colonial era, birth determined one's social position: all white Spaniards were superior to Indians; within Indian society, the nobly born were superior to the commoners. Privileges, economic opportunities, residence, and dress styles were all largely determined by one's birth, at least in the early years of Spanish colonialism.

With time, however, the system changed. Criollos competed with peninsulares, mestizos tested the simple white/Indian dichotomy, and among Indians ethnic distinctiveness within the city gradually eroded. Moreover, while economic activities remained constant, social relations of production shifted from head taxes and forced labor to a thoroughly cash economy with free labor. By the end of the colonial era, economic position determined social status, rather than social status via birth determining economic position. And by the second half of the twentieth century, all signs of hereditary determination of social status had disappeared. Even the social divisions within the middle/elite class are governed by one's social relationship to the economic structure, as the elite is divided into merchants, agricultural exporters, and the newest class of government officials. At the other end of the social scale within the city, the contemporary era displays virtually no sign of ethnic Indian identity, as is common in large Latin American cities, or even an emerging, rediscovered ethnic identity, as has occurred in the United States. In the city, people's identity is Mexican, not Zapotec–Mexican or Mixtec–Mexican. Rather, economic characteristics—occupation, income, and relationship to the means of production—determine social status.

We hypothesize that the lack of ethnic identity, which contrasts with the importance of ethnicity in both the surrounding hinterland and larger Latin American cities, reflects the peculiar structural position of a secondary city such as Oaxaca. The "Mexicans" control resources within the city, while the homeland is so geographically close that it simultaneously provides an uncomfortable reminder of one's socioeconomic origins and convenient access to one's village for maintaining ties. Migrants from indigenous villages self-consciously manipulate their identity by behaving like Mexicans in the city and as indigenous people when in the village.[3]

The second trend and most recent imposition has been the state. We have attempted to demonstrate that the state has come to share the stage with the family as one of Oaxaca's two most important social institutions. In the prehispanic era, although the extent of state power is largely unknown, society went through epochs of increased militarization, imperialist expansion, and subsequent retrenchment. Throughout the colonial era and prerevolutionary period, the state had little effective local power. It was too distant and too weak; armies would invade and enforce allegiance, but afterward the central government in Mexico City generally ignored the region.

During most of the twentieth century, the state exhibited comparatively little interest in Oaxaca, certainly in comparison to the industrializing cities of the northern part of the country and even the agricultural regions of the central region, which were deeply affected by the agrarian reform thrust of the Revolution. The completion of the Pan American Highway, financed and constructed by the federal government, symbolically and concretely brought the federal government and the rest of the world to Oaxaca. The highway and later the airport (also federally financed and constructed) allowed tourism to increase and opened up the Oaxaca market to mass-produced items from outside the region. While the penetration of these items displaced the production of some local artisans, the local merchant elite profited from increases in both tourism and the sale of these goods. The merchant elite opened hotels and restaurants for tourists and acted as wholesalers and retailers for goods imported to the region.

An indirect but critical effect of the increased imposition of the state has been the creation of the formal sector. Although the fringe benefits that define the formal sector are financed by a tax on employers, they are provided by state agencies, most notably the health services of the *seguro social*. These benefits have created a new distinction among the poor between those whom we label the very poor and the minimum wage income groups. The minimum wage income group not only earns the official minimum wage, but is also much more likely to be in the formal sector and enjoy fringe benefits.

The most dramatic state involvement in the area followed the mid 1970s local challenges to state authority. Rather than simply exiting after reestablishing control (as it had always done in the past), the federal government followed up its military presence with an increased political and economic participation. Following a national trend of the 1960s and 1970s, which had in the past largely bypassed Oaxaca, federal expenditures in the region dramatically increased. Federal agencies, their employees, and their programs flowed into the state.

The case of Oaxaca is considerably more complex than most summaries of recent socioeconomic inequality in Mexico have noted (see Cockroft 1983; and Hellman 1983: 144). In Oaxaca, the past thirty years has not been an epoch marked by increased relative inequality and immiseration of the poor. On the other hand, the contemporary era has not seen steady economic progress for any group nor has there been an equal distribution of material gains and losses. For example, two classes benefited directly from increased state intervention: the aspiring income group, which consists largely of the skilled and lower-level professionals who obtained better jobs and higher wages because of the expanded federal presence, and the bureaucratic elite, who came into the city to manage the new programs and money. The local merchant elite has benefited, but has not been the primary beneficiary. Non-Oaxacan bureaucrats, with little local knowledge or experience, flowed into the city. Oaxacans who had left the city for advanced education also returned, but their new political positions oriented them, too, away from the city and toward the center of Mexico's power in Mexico City. While the merchant class remained the most important local economic group, its political power has gradually been eroded and replaced by the federal government.

All of this has produced a structure of inequality in which nearly everyone is poor, but more equally so than appears to be the case in other major Mexican and Latin American cities. Oaxaca has no dominant class of owners of modern capitalist enterprises nor is the petite bourgeoisie of the informal sector clearly distinguished from the merchant capitalists of the formal sector. The residential patterns and family and individual life histories also reveal that formal and informal workers differ only in their access to fringe benefits. Both their standards of living are low and the problems they confront and the solutions they devise for them are more similar than different. Everyone, regardless of income group, has experienced tremendous economic vacillations in the contemporary era, beginning notably with the first devaluation of the peso in 1976 and advancing dramatically with the 1980s economic crisis. Nevertheless, in the limited sense of possession of consumer goods, everyone in Oaxaca has improved in the contemporary era, and the aspiring income group has benefited relatively the most. In the broader sense of access to housing, stable employment, and decent wages, the record is much more mixed. Improvements have been made in every class, often only to be later reversed.

None of these improvements nor their subsequent reversals have occurred without the active struggle of Oaxacans themselves. Nor has the increased state presence been driven by either disembodied forces of modernization or the externally based federal government. At least in the case of Oaxaca, political disputes, rooted in and growing out of the structure of socioeconomic inequality, propelled the involvement of the state apparatus into the area. Only, or at least primarily, in response to local social protest did the state actively and fully intervene. While socioeconomic inequality is well entrenched, with roots before the arrival of European colonialism and modern capitalism or the contemporary state, the final portrait of Oaxaca, the presence and distribution of political, economic, and social benefits, can only be understood as the result of a process involving local forces in constant, dynamic interaction with external forces. The second set of our conclusions examines how Oaxacans have responded to this structure of socioeconomic inequality.

Oaxacans' Responses to the Structure of Inequality

Oaxacans' responses to the structure of socioeconomic inequality have been highly varied. They include the local elite's resistance to external control, the quiet, private struggles of families and households lobbying school administrators to admit their children; compadres trading information on job possibilities or asking one another for a bit of work; highly organized, efficient squatters' invasions; and the formation of an independent union, with resulting strikes, demonstrations, and repression.

What governs the choice of activity, its goals, who participates, when and how it is organized, and its success or failure? We believe the range of responses can be summarized by one constant, one cycle, and one trend.

The Constant

The family and household are the fundamental units and forces of adaptation. These are extended socially and figuratively through fictive kinship, the institution of compadrazgo.

The Cycle

The most notable and dramatic responses are the recurring center–periphery struggles. Most common among these have been intraelite struggles. Increasingly common in the contemporary era are working-class struggles against the state for access to the means of subsistence and collective consumption, that is, land, housing, and associated services.

The Trend

Increasingly the state is the initiator and object of responses, although as the most powerful force it has always been the ultimate arbiter of local disputes.

Other forms of organized response (neighborhood, class-based, and voluntary organizations) periodically arise and are significant in particular circumstances. As a general rule, Oaxacans respond with a strategy of instrumental, material pragmatism, a locally bounded and defined rationality: they choose activities that are goal directed, have reasonable chances of achieving the particular goal, and implicitly take into account structural features. Table 8.1 summarizes the various response patterns.

Table 8.1
Response Patterns

Level of Social Organization	Structural Causes	Social Class of Initiators	Opposition	Goals	Preconditions for Success
Intraclass	State centralization of power	Local elite	External elite	Local elite control	Central state's lack of effective power
Neighborhood	Lack of free market in housing Unequal distribution of income	Working classes (3 lowest income groups)	State	Land/Services	Tolerant regime Federal or ambiguous title Strong internal organization
Interclass	Power of alliances Regime's revolutionary heritage	Usually 2 lowest income groups	Employers	Improved working conditions Transportation	Tolerant regime (early 1970s) Weak state
Family/Household	Untrustworthiness of nonkin	All levels	Diffused external to household	Dependent on income group	Dependent on income group

The first column indicates what kind of social groups are involved, for example, those within a particular social class such as elites or neighborhood organizations. The second column attempts to identify the most important underlying factors producing the response. The next column indicates who immediately initiates the response. While the general argument of this book is that broad structural factors ultimately cause Oaxacans' responses to socioeconomic inequality, this column identifies the social group that is the proximate cause, those who initiate a particular response. The next column identifies to whom the response is directed and who presumably can address and resolve the problem by meeting the initiators' desired goals. The last column identifies factors that are preconditions for initiators' success in their response.

Confirming the observation that regional elites tend to oppose structural change (see Hardoy 1972; 1975), the most notable responses throughout the past four hundred fifty years since the arrival of the Spaniards have been the repeated struggles of the local merchant elite against the central state. In the prehispanic era, although the extent of state power is largely unknown, society went through epochs of increased militarization, imperialist expansion, and subsequent retrenchment. The local elite's battles have been historically successful when the state is incapable of exerting an effective presence. When the Spaniards arrived, the new Spanish elite first ignored the wishes of Cortez to have them settle elsewhere. Two hundred and fifty years later the local elite ignored the Crown's efforts to reform the alcalde system and redirect a greater proportion of cochineal profits to Spain. In both cases, the power of colonial Spain was comparatively weak and the periphery prevailed. Similarly, the nineteenth-century social and economic reforms of Presidents Juárez and Díaz, which so thoroughly transformed most of Mexico, left Oaxaca relatively unchanged.

In the current century, local-elite success at resisting central control has been due more to the central state's temporary disinterest in Oaxaca than the state's lack of power to enforce its will. After the central state subjugated Oaxaca's sovereignty movement during the revolutionary era, the central government ignored the region for nearly half a century. During the contemporary era, the local merchant elite has again struggled to maintain its control. The 1950 to 1952 dispute pitted this group against the state's emerging agricultural export interests. The merchants won the battle and then allowed the economic penetration of the region via improved state-financed and -constructed communication links. Indirectly, this increased responses to social inequality and particularly social strife within the city, as cityward migration escalated and disputes arose over working conditions and access to land, housing, and associated services. The most obvious and the most disruptive responses were organized at the level of interclass conflicts and in the neighborhoods.

A combination of structural forces common throughout urban Latin

America has led to the formation of neighborhood organizations: low wages, a shortage of low-cost housing, and government tolerance of and even participation in squatters' invasions. A shortage of affordable housing is universal in capitalist underdeveloped cities and even existed in nineteenth-century London (Roberts 1978: 148). Oaxaca, with over 60 percent of its land area and houses having once been squatter settlements, epitomizes the ubiquitous third-world solution to the housing problem. As in other Latin American cities (see, for example, Castells 1983; and Portes and Walton 1976, 1981), the state, rather than private landholders, are the opposition: the goal is land and associated services, not a more radical restructuring of private property. Strong squatter organization, as occurred in the 1975 invasion, helps advance the cause. A climate of government tolerance, as occurred generally in Mexico during the Echeverría presidency (1970–76) and during the Oaxacan gubernatorial terms of Bravo Ahuja (1968–70) and Gómez Sandoval (1970–74), further promotes the likelihood of success.

Two aspects of Oaxaca's neighborhoods and their organizations appear different from that reported in other parts of Latin America. First, the thrust and function of squatter settlements appears more narrowly focused on providing housing. Oaxacan squatter settlements, unlike those in other parts of urban Latin America, do not support a significant amount of informal production or subsistence activities that would further lower the social wages assumed by capital or the state, that is, both direct wages and indirect costs of maintaining and reproducing the labor force (Portes 1985). The relatively small differences between Oaxaca's formal and informal sectors are one factor that might contribute to this condition. Secondly, Oaxaca's geographic compactness also means that businesses, whether formal or informal, can locate wherever they please, although the city center has significantly better infrastructure than most squatter settlements (for example, telephone service, "purified" water, and transportation links) and access to the broader market that flows through it. The importance of subsistence production in squatter settlements is similarly unimportant in Oaxaca. The income generated and the proportion of subsistence produced is minimal compared to that gained through wages and work. Thus, Oaxaca demonstrates that a weak formal sector in a geographically compact city renders unimportant the function of squatter settlements as a locus of informal economic activity lowering social reproduction costs.

Nevertheless, Oaxaca squatter settlements do fulfill the same general function of lowering the costs of the reproduction of labor power by decreasing the social wage assumed by capital or the state (Portes and Walton 1976). If it were not for squatter settlements either local wages or the state's local investment in public housing would have to be higher to provide shelter for the majority of the population.

While the squatter neighborhoods in Oaxaca apparently contain less informal economic activity than in other Latin American cities, the mobilization around housing appears to be greater. It incorporates all levels of the local population: first, obviously, the squatters themselves are involved, including people from all three of the lower-income groups, not just the very poor or simply those of the informal sector as some have emphasized (Portes 1985: 31). Second, bureaucrats and politicians, representatives of the state, participate as they on occasion organize invasions and eventually extend services to the settlements. Third, even middle/elite neighborhoods have become involved, as when they organize opposition to a housing project.

Examining neighborhood organizations clearly reveals the trend toward increased state involvement as the initiator and object of responses. In Oaxaca's 1975 land invasions, for example, a federal bureaucrat initiated the invasion and the landowners responded via the state, which quickly and effectively suppressed the invasion. The state followed suppression with a partial solution: a small, government-funded, site-and-services project. Beginning in the late 1970s the state initiated activity by attempting to systematically incorporate squatter settlements. The most notable effort and failure was CORETT, which attempted to recognize and regularize land tenure. The intended beneficiaries, the squatters, saw no advantage to state-sponsored regularization. The squatters already had de facto control and exercised property rights as if they had legal control as well. In the early 1980s the state, via the PRI, tried to coopt squatter communities by offering access to resources in return for political fealty. While this project got more support than CORETT, it hardly produced die-hard PRI loyalists. Community leaders quite self-consciously recognized and debated the advantages and expectations of cooperating with the PRI.

Also beginning in the late 1970s, the state provided subsidized housing. Although the housing projects are small compared to the squatter settlements, they cost much more and are the only housing policy that, because of the location of one project, elicited an organized middle-class backlash. The housing projects also failed to produce the community solidarity and support for the state that bureaucrats had expected. The recipients viewed the state much more as a private contractor. They complained about the quality and size of houses. When asked to support public projects, the residents of a site-and-services project refused with the exception of those projects they themselves initiated and controlled.

The trend of an increasing central state presence can also be seen in the interclass responses that have characterized Oaxacan political activity. As in the case of intraclass battles, they are most common when the central state is either not effectively present, such as the revolutionary period's decrease in the length of the working week, or when there is a tolerant regime, such as during the 1970s when independent unions were allowed to organize. The opposition in both cases was composed of the particular employers of the workers. Although this sometimes was the local state, more frequently the employers were private. Local authorities managed most local political disputes that occurred in the 1960s and early 1970s. In some, they were even behind-the-scenes organizers. But the most serious disputes of the mid 1970s, the large 1975 land invasion and the 1977 university disturbances, commanded direct intervention by federal authorities. The presence of federal troops and the imposition of a military governor symbolically marked the end of the local merchant elite's political control. Following the withdrawal of federal troops was the arrival of federal bureaucrats and federal programs. The local elite grumbled about the changes, but there was little they could do; the federal government had become both the ultimate and the immediate arbiter of local disputes. The state can and does suppress some popular movements while it attempts to incorporate, frequently in a patronizing fashion, the remainder (Castells 1983).

Yet the state has experienced difficulties incorporating popular movements at all levels. The above-mentioned difficulties the PRI encountered in incorporating squatters are also seen in its attempt to form unions. Government-affiliated, PRI unions, ostensibly for workers, are despised and little used by their members. Most workers view the unions more as representatives of the PRI's, that is, the state's, interests rather than those of the workers. Instead of relying on formal voluntary organizations affiliated with the state for the protection of their interests, workers trust real and fictive kin relationships, particularly those within the family and household.

We have argued that the most fundamental adaptation to inequality in Oaxaca is within the family and household. The family and household are held together by bonds of trust and reciprocity that frequently find individuals sacrificing their own needs and ends for those of the family. For example, Davíd, who became an architect and whose story began Chapter 6, still lived with his family after finishing his education because he wanted to repay his debt to them. Javier, who works for the telegraph company and whose life history we told in Chapter 7, has incorporated his stepdaughter and her illegitimate children into his family and household because it is simply the morally correct thing to do. Alejandro, the macho lover of Cristina whom we discussed in Chapter 6, has apprenticed two of Cristina's children by her now-deceased husband so that they may earn a living. While Cristina maintains that Alejandro himself does not sufficiently contribute materially to her household, he has undoubtedly helped Cristina and the rest of her family. The early migration history of María Teresa's and Elodia's family also reveals how the family remains the most significant social unit even when the household is forced to split up.

Nevertheless, not all families respond in the same way to Oaxaca's inequality. The effect of varying structural characteristics on the family and household are seen, for example, in gender relations. Women, especially relatively uneducated and unskilled ones, have few economic opportunities anywhere. Cities may have a few more possibilities than rural villages, but not many more. Not surprisingly, the highest proportion of female-headed households is among the very poor. Somewhat more surprisingly, the middle/elite has the second highest proportion of female heads of households. The structural advantages of higher-class position allow middle/elite female heads of households to avoid the bind common among the lower classes of finding a man, who may be a domineering macho, simply for economic security.

The most notable family and household response to structural conditions is in household demography. The very poor, and especially female-headed households among this group, react to economic insecurity by maintaining the smallest households. Household size increases as household income rises. The one exception is the middle/elite, who maintain smaller households by having fewer children, but have a higher proportion of extended-family households. It appears as if a primary advantage of higher income is the ability for the family to realize the ideal of staying together, remaining within a single household.

Another example of family and household responses to structural conditions is in housing. A common ideal is for children to build housing on the same lot as their parents. Then, although the children maintain a physically separate house, they remain part of the same household. Lots, of course, are not always big enough to permit this, so other solutions must be found. In the 1975 squatters' invasion, families with children who were close to or already had started their own families were the most likely to participate. Here, an explicit political act, one that ran the risk and the reality of suppression, was motivated by family concerns delimited by the structural condition of a housing shortage.

The more constant, common strategy is the creation of significant dyadic relationships, most likely cemented through compadrazgo. The ties of compadrazgo tend to make such relationships familylike, and to contain recognized, expected reciprocal responsibilities that cannot be ignored easily. Compadrazgo ties help obtain access to a variety of resources that households need and desire: access to schools with limited enrollments, promotions within organizations, jobs when one needs work. In short, compadrazgo itself is a strategy that families and households use to adapt to structural conditions. It extends the family and household and fills in where voluntary organizations, including interclass movements, fail.

All these strategies reflect the constant struggle of the family and household to adapt to Oaxaca's structure of socioeconomic inequality. Laid on top of this constant is the cycle of center–periphery struggles and the trend of the state's increasing prominence. The state and the family are indirectly competing to fill the void created by the recent evolution in the structure of socioeconomic inequality. The state's activities, such as road building, have supported population growth without economic development. The inability of the local elite to satisfy local social demands has boosted the role of the central state. Nevertheless, the state neither initiates nor controls all political activity. Notwithstanding the state's tremendously increased role in housing and employment conditions, it is not the sole power. Local forces, both of the elite and among the masses, can and do resist state power. Neighborhood organizations extract some resources usually without being entirely coopted. They create and implement their own, rather than the PRI's or a government agency's, projects. Independent unions gain benefits before they are suppressed. Households resist the state's land regularization program. After being dispossessed of squatters' rights, they force the provision of a site-and-services project. And most important, individual families constantly labor to provide for themselves. Most notably, they do so by altering their demographic profile and by extending themselves through incorporation of extended family members, migration, and the creation of fictive kin ties.

In short, in spite of the state's increased presence, Oaxacans continue to affect significantly the local pattern of socioeconomic inequality, working within the imposed parameters of a dependent city of only secondary (or perhaps less) importance within a dependent nation. This relative unimportance has helped preserve Oaxaca's constant primary economic function as a marketing and administrative center and insulate it from both the extreme advances and devastations that have characterized most of urban Mexico for the past half a millennium.

Notes

Chapter 1: Introduction

1. A full discussion of Oaxaca's prehistory can be found in Winter 1989. The most complete discussion of Monte Albán is in Blanton 1978.

2. For a full discussion of Oaxaca's climate, see Aceves 1976.

3. A full discussion of these issues is presented in Gulick 1989. See especially chaps. 1, 2, and 3.

4. See, for example, Collins 1980; Eames and Goode 1977; Fox 1972, 1977; and Press 1979.

5. The political economy literature on third-world cities is extensive. See for overviews Portes and Walton 1976, 1981.

6. Each of these areas has its own extensive bibliography. See especially Alonso 1980; Castells 1977; Cornelius 1975; Lomnitz 1977; Perlman 1976; Portes and Walton 1976; and Smith 1990.

7. Stepick 1974 discusses the methodological and epistemological impediments to a formal analysis of rationality among Oaxaca's urban poor. For a more general discussion of the difficulties, see Plattner 1974.

8. Other publications based on these data include: Hackenberg, Murphy, and Selby 1984; Hendricks and Murphy 1981; Kowalewski, Murphy, and Cabrera 1984; Lorenzen, Murphy, and Selby 1989; Murphy 1983, 1987; Murphy et al. 1987, 1990; Murphy and Selby 1979, 1981, 1985; Murphy, Stepick, and Castañeda 1984; Selby et al. 1987; Selby and Murphy 1982; Selby, Murphy, and Lorenzen 1990; Stepick and Murphy 1979, 1980; Winter, Morris, and Murphy 1990.

Chapter 2: A Social History of Oaxaca

1. For a discussion of the people of the Mixteca, see Spores 1967, 1984.

2. With the conquest, the Zapotec, Mixtec, and Aztec peoples began their transformation from distinct ethnic groups into one class—Indian.

229

3. An *encomienda* was a grant of an Indian town or towns to a Spaniard giving him the right to extract tribute and labor from them (Simpson 1966). Whitecotton (1977) argues that the *encomienda* was not a significant institution in the valley of Oaxaca, although it had some importance in the surrounding mountains.

4. In the 1980s, Santa Cruz Huatulco and the entire Pacific coast of Oaxaca, after being abandoned for four hundred years, were being developed as a major ocean resort area.

5. While the Spaniards never discovered mines in Oaxaca as rich as those in Zacatecas or San Luis Potosí, in 1580 they did discover some valuable ones that brought a rush of people searching for a quick and easy fortune. They forced the Indians to work without pay through the *repartimiento* system, in which the government authorized drafts of Indian labor to serve on public works projects, in mines, and on private estates. *Repartimientos* provided most of New Spain's labor in the sixteenth and early seventeenth centuries. When these were insufficient in Oaxaca, Spaniards resorted to direct threats of violence. Thousands died, and the abuses became so infamous the Crown sent an investigator to Oaxaca in 1617. When he called for Indians to present their complaints, more than eight thousand appeared. Small-scale mining has continued sporadically until today. At various times mines have been reopened with an infusion of new capital or infrastructure, only to be abandoned once again when the market declined.

6. In 1548, Oaxaca began a silk industry centered in the northern mountains of the Mixteca Alta (see Map 2.1). It was so immediately successful that the viceroy expressed concern that the Indians would abandon producing food and dedicate themselves exclusively to silk worms. Yet, initially, most of the benefits of the silk industry accrued neither to Oaxaca nor to the Indians. In the beginning the virgin silk was not processed in Oaxaca, but shipped to Mexico City, which had a monopoly on processing. In 1552, however, Oaxaca received permission to weave silk, and a brisk industry quickly developed. Indians, especially women, served as laborers under the direction of Spanish overlords and traders. The Indians were treated so badly that they eventually retaliated by cutting down the trees and killing the worms. By 1570 the industry was dead. Weaving, however, had become an integral component of Oaxaca's economy and would rise and fall in importance over the next four centuries.

7. Borah and Cook (1960, 1963) show a similar process for central Mexico.

8. Their prehispanic experience with legal forms provided the Indians with an important tool for dealing with the local Spaniards. Oaxaca Indians often set out on foot to Mexico City, the seat of colonial government, to defend their rights to a small piece of land. In the 1790s one Indian from the valley village of Mitla mortgaged all his belongings and sailed to Spain to appeal directly to the king on behalf of his town. At other times, the natives defended their lands more violently. When the Spaniards tried to survey the land, the villagers invariably resisted, sometimes throwing rocks at the surveyors or stealing the measuring rope. In several cases they massed in front of the inspectors and refused to let them proceed. At times protests became outright revolts. In 1531, not long after the arrival of the Spanish, Indians throughout the mountainous region north of the valley mounted a revolt that required massive military force to defeat. Again, in 1570, a revolt convulsed the Mixe and Villa Alta regions in the same area. Not

all disputes were "anti-imperialist" outbreaks between Indians and Spaniards. Land disputes between Indian communities frequently arose and occasionally resulted in violence. A dispute among four Indian villages in 1726 produced a brief but pitched battle with inhabitants wielding clubs, spears, knives, and firearms against each other (Taylor 1972: 107, 201). These disputes continue to the present day (Dennis 1973, 1979, 1987).

9. This analysis is based on the work of William B. Taylor's *Landlord and Peasant in Colonial Oaxaca* (Stanford: Stanford University Press, 1972).

10. Political divisions in the state mirrored those at the national level, particularly the battle between conservatives and liberals. The conservatives sought to minimize the changes wrought by Independence and wished to establish a centralized government akin to those in Europe. The liberals sought to "modernize" Mexico and create a liberal capitalist state with a federal government much like that in the United States. The critical issue dividing the two groups, however, concerned the proper relationship between church and state. While conservatives strove to maintain the political prerogatives that the Catholic Church had enjoyed under Spanish rule, liberals challenged the temporal power of the Church and sought to divest the institution of its special privileges. Because of contemporary political events in Europe, including Napoleon's occupation of Spain, allegiances were quite complicated, and numerous factions participated in the struggle. These are treated in various histories of Mexico, for example, Fehrenbach 1983; Miller 1985; and Parkes 1969.

11. For an early history of the institute, see Universidad Autónoma Benito Juárez de Oaxaca (1990). One hundred and fifty years later, the institute, renamed the Autonomous University of Benito Juárez, became the locus of a direct challenge to the ruling political authorities and the impetus for the military occupation of the city by federal troops. See Chapter 5.

12. Upon resuming control of the nation in 1855, the liberals embarked upon a revolutionary cause: the complete separation of church and state. The liberals viewed the Church as an impediment to progress and economic prosperity. They believed that the vast landholdings of the Church would be far more productive if placed in individual hands. The implementation of these ideas came to be known as the Reform and the 1858–64 bloody response, the War of Reform. The Reform began in 1855 with the Ley Juárez, which eliminated the jurisdiction of ecclesiastical and military courts in civil and criminal cases. In 1856, the Ley Lerdo required corporations to sell all their lands and urban property. The 1857 constitution contained these and other more far-reaching provisions: education was to be secular and not controlled by the Church, nuns and priests were to be given the opportunity to renounce their vows, and Roman Catholicism was not to be the sole or official religion of the nation. Reaction was quick and strong. Pope Pius IX decreed that all who accepted the Mexican constitution would be excommunicated, and the clergy and military united to defend their privileges. The liberals responded by pronouncing even more dramatic restrictions on the Church. Cemeteries were nationalized, tithes abolished, monasteries suppressed, novitiates in nunneries prohibited, and marriage became a civil rather than a religious ceremony.

13. For a full account of the effects of the Reform in Oaxaca, see C. Berry 1967, 1981.

14. Worcester and Schaeffer, vol. II, 1971: 225. For a discussion of Díaz and his regime, see Beals 1971; and Gil 1977. Cosío Villegas (1963) has a good discussion of relations between Díaz and the United States.

15. For a discussion of railroads in Oaxaca during the Porfiriato, see Chassen (1990).

16. A rail link that bypassed the Oaxaca Valley connected the Gulf of Mexico with the Pacific through the Isthmus of Tehuantepec in 1894. The completion of the Pacific port of Salina Cruz in 1907 initiated a seven-year boom there that lasted until the completion of the Panama Canal in 1914.

17. Coatsworth's *Growth against Development* (1981) presents a comprehensive discussion of the links between railroads and development during the Porfiriato.

18. For a full discussion of the impact of coffee production on the political economy of this region, see Greenberg 1981, 1987, 1989; and Hernández Díaz 1987.

19. Accounts of the Revolution in Oaxaca from various perspectives can be found in Esparza 1985; Garner 1988; Martínez Vásquez 1985; Meixuerio Hernández 1989; Rojas 1965; Romero Frizzi 1990c; Ruíz Cervantes 1986.

20. For a discussion of Lawrence's time in Oaxaca, see Parmenter 1984.

21. Mexico was one of the few nations that welcomed Spanish Republican refugees. See Drucker-Brown 1982: 27.

22. A good discussion of twentieth-century politics can be found in Raat and Beezley, 1986. See especially Brown, "The Calles-Cárdenas Connection," and LaFrance, "Mexico since Cárdenas."

Chapter 3: People and Places

1. A citywide study of water quality in 1990 demonstrated that none of the water delivered to residents in the city met U.S. standards.

2. The Federal Electric Commission calculates that it loses 25 to 35 percent of its power to illegal hookups in Mexico City alone.

3. It has since been sold to Stouffer Hotels.

4. See the film, *Pelota Mixteca*, A. D. Murphy, R. Camp, and T. Cohen. Greeley: Educational Material Service, University of Northern Colorado, 1987.

5. For a description of the Mesoamerican cargo system, see Cancian 1965. Although Cancian's description is of the system as it pertains to the Maya of Chiapas, the general system was the same throughout Mesoamerica.

6. *Colonias populares* have numerous alternative names in other locales for example, *barrios, pueblos jovenes,* and *favelas.* See Butterworth and Chance 1981; Chance 1971; and Murphy 1987.

7. The amount of time required to establish possession can vary. See Greenberg 1989; Rees 1989.

8. See Nolasco 1981; and Murphy and Stepick 1978. Mangin (1967) and Turner (1977) describe this process in other parts of Latin America.

9. See the film *When Will Our Turn Come: The Urban Poor of Oaxaca,* M. J. Higgins, R. Camp, and J. Payne. Greeley: Educational Materials Service, University of Northern Colorado, 1982.

10. See Prince and Murphy (1990) and Ward (1984) for a discussion of INDECO and site-and-services projects in Mexico.

Chapter 4: Contemporary Economics

1. The crisis was exacerbated by falling petroleum prices in the mid 1980s.

2. Subsistence agriculture today only partially supports peasant families in the Oaxaca Valley (see Clarke 1986). Complementary activities include commercial agriculture on irrigated lands, handicrafts, and migration to work (either daily migration to Oaxaca City or more permanent migration to more distant places, including the United States).

3. Since prehispanic times, various villages in the valley have specialized in particular crafts, and the jewelry and stoneware of the prehispanic Zapotecs and Mixtecs are world renowned. The handicrafts of Oaxaca's artisans have had a national reputation since the nineteenth century. As with all Oaxaca's economic sectors, artisanry, however, suffered during the Mexican Revolution. Following the first national exhibition of Oaxacan artisan goods in Mexico City in 1922 and another exhibition in San Antonio, Texas, Oaxaca's handicraft reputation and market spread. The Great Depression and World War II boosted local production as the availability of consumer goods from the industrial world declined. Ever since the arrival of the Spaniards, who reordered the traditional relationships of production, villages have been evolving different roles in response to new economic demands and changing technology. One village, for example, used to weave serapes from cloth made of hair derived as a by-product from the curing of animal skins. A new curing process introduced in the late 1940s, however, dissolved the hairs on the skins and thus eliminated the weaver's raw materials. The village is now exclusively a farming community. The products of a number of other villages have been displaced by cheaper and frequently more durable manufactured goods. Much of the cloth for clothing and blankets is no longer locally produced. Plastic and enameled aluminum have largely replaced ceramics. Many farming and other tools now come from Mexico City or other industrial regions. Yet numerous handicrafts and local products persist either because they remain cheaper or because of an appreciation of their aesthetic qualities. Basket weaving, ceramics, textiles, and stone and iron work are tourist favorites, while locally produced wood and furniture products and locally processed foods are preferred by many residents. For further discussion of the role of crafts, see Bailón Corres 1980; Cook 1982, 1984; Nahmad, González, and Rees 1988; and Stephen 1987.

4. In the late 1960s, the Mexican government, viewing artisan handicrafts as a way to stem the rural exodus and increase tourist revenues, formed several organizations to promote handicraft production throughout Mexico and the rest of the world. These organizations include the Fondo Nacional para el Fomento de las Artesanias (National Fund for the Promotion of Artisanry) (FONART), the Fondo Nacional para las Actividades Sociales (National Fund for Social Activities) (FONAPAS), and the Department of Artisanry of the Directorate for Socioeconomic Development. In Oaxaca City they maintain some retail outlets

and assist in the export of artisan goods. Nevertheless, the private sector dominates in both local retailing and export.

5. In the INDECO survey of 1977, the preponderance of migrants in government jobs was clear. For example, if one considered only fairly young households in which childbearing had begun but was probably not complete (see Chapter 5), among migrant household heads who had arrived in the city between 1974 and 1977, 26 percent held government jobs. In contrast, only 19 percent of native resident heads of household in this group held government jobs (Hendricks and Murphy 1981).

6. El Tule residents claim that pollutants from the factory are killing the tule tree, a mammoth two thousand-year-old tree, perhaps the largest of its kind, that is their main source of tourist income.

7. For a full discussion of the formal/informal sector literature, see de Soto 1986; Lorenzen 1986, chap. 1; Portes 1983; Portes and Sassen-Koob 1987; Schmink 1984; Smith 1990; and vol. 4, no. 2 (1990) of the journal *City and Society*.

8. The small permanent stalls in marketplaces provided a difficult classification problem. Their profits are not large, they frequently rely on family labor, and they do not require much capital to establish—all characteristics that would place them in the informal sector. On the other hand, they are permanently established, with most having been in existence more than five years, they pay taxes to municipal authorities, and some even belong to formal organizations representing their interests—characteristics of formal sector firms. Because of the importance of being regulated by the government and their incorporation into organizations, we consider them members of the formal sector.

9. For an excellent and more thorough discussion of this kind of relationship, see Lomnitz 1977.

10. Geographers generally use relative population to define a nation's "secondary" cities. The concept refers to cities that are not important on a national scale, but have central-place functions within a limited region (Rondinelli 1983). For the purposes of its activities, INDECO defined all the cities of fifty thousand or more inhabitants (excluding Mexico City, Monterrey, Puebla, and Guadalajara) as the secondary cities of Mexico. Ultimately the study gathered data from nine cities and one region within Mexico City: Mexicali, Mérida, San Luis Potosí, Querétaro, Tampico, Villahermosa, Mazatlán, Reynosa, Oaxaca, and Venustiano Carranza in Mexico City. For a comparison of household strategies in the ten cities, see Kim 1987; Lorenzen 1986; and Selby, Murphy, and Lorenzen 1990.

Chapter 5: Community-Level Adaptation

1. The 1968 student revolts are often cited as an important turning point in opposition to the PRI-dominated Mexican regime. The 1968 student movement began as an insignificant street fight between students from two high schools in Mexico City. Overreaction by the police transformed it into a violent confrontation that rocked society. As host to the 1968 summer Olympics, Mexico wanted

to project the image of a successful institutionalized revolution that had transformed a backward corrupt society into a progressive, developing democracy. There could be little tolerance of public dissent that might draw the attention of the international media. The authorities moved quickly and forcefully to quell protests. They also moved violently and under the gaze of those whom they were trying to impress, the international media. Thus a small, insignificant event was transformed into a national disturbance. Mass rallies occurred almost daily, with the largest drawing 300,000. For the first time in recent Mexican history, an incumbent president was publicly criticized. At numerous rallies, the loudest cheering came after speeches attacking the government for having sold out to U.S. interests. Despite its supposed autonomy, the national university, along with other schools, was occupied by the army. Violence escalated, and soon scores of students were arrested or killed. On October 2, as thousands peacefully listened to a rally in Mexico City's Plaza of the Three Cultures (Plaza de las Tres Culturas), situated in a large housing project, five thousand soldiers surrounded the plaza and a helicopter dropped flares into the crowd. Moments later troop carriers arrived, blocking the plaza's exits. The soldiers jumped down and began shooting into the crowd. The *New York Times* estimated between 200 and 325 dead. For a vivid account of the events of October 2, see Poniatowska (1975). The long-term effects were somewhat contradictory. The massacre destroyed the students' solidarity and, for the moment, the student movement. Many fled to the hills to carry on a small, largely ineffectual guerrilla movement. The federal government absorbed the remaining leaders into the bureaucracy. Ironically in the conservative provinces, such as Oaxaca, the student movement survived and flourished.

2. For a detailed discussion from the perspective of COCEO of political movements in the 1970s, see Lozano 1984 and Ruíz Cervantes (1984). Santibañez Orozco (1982) and Yescas Martínez (1982) have less detailed and less ideological discussions.

3. The CNOP is one of PRI's three national sections. The other two are the Confederación de Trabajadores Mexicanos (CTM), which represents labor, and the Confederación Nacional Campesina (CNC), representing peasants. CNOP incorporates the middle classes and the popular sector with control in the hands of professional bureaucrats. It is largely a broker's organization and support is measured by the number of persons the government can supply for public demonstrations. Padgett (1976) describes its general functions, while Vélez-Ibañez (1983) discusses it within the specific context of colonias populares in Mexico City.

4. An integral and important component of Mexico's 1917 constitution is land reform motivated by and intended for rural peasants. The wording is sufficiently vague, however, that Mexican leftists have frequently claimed it applies to the urban poor, too. The Mexican government has never shared this view.

5. In this context, several survey teams of CORETT, the government mechanism to regularize land tenure were shot at in the ejidos and villages surrounding Oaxaca when they attempted to carry out their surveys. The government assigned soldiers to protect these teams, thus sparking further unrest in the city.

6. A branch of COCEO in the Isthmus of Tehuantepec (COCEI) did have

success for a few years in Juchitán, until 1983 when the government finally succeeded in temporarily displacing it. A graphic description of COCEI is presented in Doniz 1983; see also Bustamante et al. 1984, chap. 9, and Martínez López 1985.

7. This increased presence in Oaxaca coincided with Mexico's oil boom and an increased federal penetration throughout the nation.

8. Even while the water pipe was being laid less than 50 percent of Benito Juarez's residents participated in the project. Most of the nonparticipants lived at one end of the colonia, far from the water tank. They claimed that the colonia's leaders, who lived close to the tank, unduly benefited from the project. The colonia leaders replied that the water department had determined the tank's position. After completion of the water tank, even fewer residents actively participated in tequios, which returned to the project of building streets. Out of a colonia of nearly one hundred households, less than ten regularly appeared for the Sunday morning tequio ritual. Those at the far end only showed up when the tequio was working on the road immediately adjacent to their own lot. The rest of the time they criticized the corruption and self-interest of the colonia's leadership. They eventually coalesced among themselves and forced an election. The leaders had not called a new election in fifteen years and the opposition never came to the colonia meetings to challenge them. One charismatic figure finally organized them to demand a new election. The opposition won the new election and now holds the official positions within the colonia. A different 10 percent then showed up for the weekly tequio work parties.

9. For a discussion of tequios in Oaxaca's colonias, see Murphy 1973.

10. For a discussion of the relationship between INDECO and a colonia popular in Oaxaca, see Higgins 1974.

11. Anthropological works dealing with rural Oaxaca are innumerable. See Varese 1983 for a general discussion of ethnicity and rural Oaxaca. Romero Frizzi 1974 offers an extensive bibliography now, unfortunately, slightly out of date. Barabas and Bartolomé 1986 offers a good collection of articles.

12. For a discussion of voluntary associations in Latin American cities, see Butterworth and Chance 1981, chap. 7. Butterworth 1962 provides a discussion of voluntary associations of Oaxacans in Mexico City.

13. The Mexican public school system has been a prime factor in the Mexicanization of the indigenous population of Oaxaca. See Gibaja 1986. Schoolchildren spend a great deal of time learning Mexican history and culture and receive a not subtle message about how much better that culture is than the indigenous culture. The importance of dress in identifying an individual's place in the culture is seen in the census, where wearing shoes, eating bread, and speaking Spanish are used as signs of modernity. When an individual moves to the city the message is, "Dress and act like a modern Mexican if you want to get along in the system." A major proponent of the role of education in the assimilation of Indians into Mexican society has been Aguirre Beltrán 1979. His views and those of the state have been opposed by some Mexican anthropologists. See Warman et al. 1970. In Oaxaca, opposition to the states' use of education as a tool for the destruction of indigenous culture was a major factor in an opposition movement among rural schoolteachers in the late 1970s and 1980s. See Yescas and Zafra 1985.

Chapter 6: Family and Household

1. In Mexico, nominal military service is compulsory for all men. With free room and board and the possibility of financing further education, a career in the military can be attractive to the urban poor.

2. Per capita units could also be employed, but we believe these units would overemphasize the cost of children. For a full discussion of the use of per-adult equivalent income measures and age differentiation of household members, see Kuznets 1976. For a fuller discussion of its application to Oaxaca, see Murphy 1979.

3. This arrangement also worked to the advantage of Isác's boss in Oaxaca. He had a trusted friend in Mexico City whom he could call at a moment's notice to handle problems arising in the central office. One could argue that Isác's eventual incorporation into the national bureaucracy gives Oaxaca's elite more leverage in the national decision-making apparatus.

Chapter 7: Four Households

1. Dennis 1987: 39–42 describes typical land tenure patterns in Oaxaca.

Chapter 8: Conclusion

1. We remind the reader that this statement is not absolutely true. There were and are some regions of the state and valley where the native population has been dispossessed of their land and has become proletarianized. These regions, however, are atypical within the Oaxaca Valley context. See Bartolomé and Barabas 1982; Greenberg, 1981, 1989; Hernández Díaz 1987; Santibañez Orozco 1982; Yescas Martínez 1982; and Zafra 1982.

2. This does not imply that Indians in Oaxaca's hinterland were unexploited and totally unaffected by the Spanish presence. They labored strenuously to meet their tribute and other tax demands while the European-introduced diseases decimated their numbers.

3. A discussion of ethnicity from this theoretical perspective can be found in Worsley 1983.

Further Reading

The purpose of this bibliographic essay is to provide novice and advanced readers with a guide to some of the literature that was important to us in our studies of Oaxaca and in establishing the theoretical foundations of this book. It is not intended to be exhaustive, but simply to guide the reader interested in learning more about urban anthropology, Mexico, and Oaxaca.

Theoretical Issues

Political Economy

Eric Wolf's *Europe and the People Without History* (1982) is a history of the impact of European expansion on non-European peoples and the transformation that contact caused in local political, social, and economic structures. Wolf argues that European expansion created a world economy that placed disparate local peoples at the mercy of international market forces. The most relevant chapters from Wolf for our book on Oaxaca are chapter 1: "Introduction," chapter 3: "Modes of Production," and chapter 5: "Iberians in America." Our description of Oaxaca in the colonial period closely parallels his discussion of broader geographical areas. Portes and Walton's *Urban Latin America* (1976) also provides a context for understanding Oaxaca's posthispanic development. Their *Labor, Class, and the International System* (1981) focuses more specifically on labor markets, especially the structure of occupations, wages, and the relation between the labor force in the third and first worlds. Two major themes important to our work are the manner in which low wages in the third world subsidize wages for industrial workers in the first world, and the need for third world countries to invest scarce resources in exotic technologies in order to retain skilled individuals who have been trained in the first world. This is relevant to Oaxaca in two ways: first, because it addresses the issue of the structure of the labor force, which we deal with in the book, but also because it emphasizes the wide context in which the local labor force exists.

Manuel Castells is a Spanish sociologist of the French structuralist school that emerged in and after the social movement of 1968 in France. In *The Urban Question: A Marxist Approach* (1977), he describes his view of the nature of the city as the place where capital accumulation takes place most efficiently in industrial capitalism. The state helps make accumulation more efficient by providing urban services (transportation, electricity, water, and the like) that are "collectively consumed." He also reviews the history of industrial cities and underdeveloped cities, the state, popular culture, political movements, and class structure. This is a major work in modern theories of urbanization. Later works by Castells (1983) include data from Latin America, and have described more completely the role of political movements, women, the state in urbanization, and the North American economy.

Our collaboration with urban geographers early in our careers led us to an appreciation of the spatial dimensions of class and the distribution of resources in the city of Oaxaca and its environment. Particular volumes that have been important to us in developing our analysis are David Harvey's *Social Justice and the City* (1973) and David M. Smith's *Where the Grass is Greener* (1979). Harvey is an urban geographer who in this classic work argued that more than simple market forces were involved in the distribution of resources in an urban setting. His is one of the first attempts to apply a materialist analysis to the physical distribution of resources in an urban setting. David Smith takes the analysis to a wider plane and looks at the distribution of resources: within cities, between cities and their hinterland, and in nation–states. The value of urban geography in developing a holistic approach to the study of cities is demonstrated by Colin G. Clarke's *Kingston, Jamaica: Urban Development and Social Change, 1692–1962* (1975). Clarke has done for Kingston what we have tried to accomplish in our description of Oaxaca. Milton Santos's *The Shared Space* (1979) is an application of Wallerstein's core–periphery analysis to an urban context. Santos demonstrates how such an analysis can be fruitfully applied to a segmented urban space. Finally, Ian Scott, in *Urban and Spatial Development in Mexico* (1982), uses World Bank data in a spatial analysis of urban poverty in Mexico. He demonstrates how unregulated growth has led to a spatial disequilibrium concentrating resources in one location and retarding the nation's growth.

Urban Studies

Studies of urbanization in the modern world abound. Alan Gilbert and Josef Gugler, in *Cities, Poverty, and Development: Urbanization in the Third World* (1982), provide a good introduction to the issues discussed here. A more advanced treatment of many of the same issues is found in *Urbanization in the World-Economy* (1985), edited by Michael Timberlake. Reflecting our association with urban geographers, we found Brian Berry's *Comparative Urbanization: Divergent Paths in the Twentieth Century* (1981) very helpful. Especially pertinent to our work were chapter 1: "Nineteenth-Century Industrial Urbanization" and chapter 2: "Transformation During Diffusion: Third World Urbanization."

Urbanization in Latin America: Approaches and Issues (1975), edited by Jorge E. Hardoy, is a classic dealing with most of the important urban issues facing Latin America today. *Latin American Urbanization* (1981), by Douglas Butterworth and John K. Chance, is a good application of the general approach used in this book to the process of urbanization in Latin America. The book is especially strong when dealing with questions of migration. It was important for us because of its heavy use of examples from Mexico and Oaxaca. Paul Singer, a Brazilian urban sociologist not published in English, has added a Latin American perspective to the debate on urban political economy, insisting on the importance of specific historical and social factors, including social class, in the study of urbanization in the third world. Although he is heavily influenced by Brazil's history, which is quite different from Mexico's, his critique of dependency theory, *La economía política de la urbanización* (1975), is especially important. Finally, we must mention Bryan Roberts's *Cities of Peasants: The Political Economy of Urbanization in the Third World* (1978). This short book was critical in directing our early analysis of our Oaxaca material. Although over a decade old, this book is a must for any student of today's urban society.

Urban Anthropology

In 1977, Prentice Hall published two textbooks in urban anthropology. Both were particularly important in the formation of the theories underlying this book. The first, *Anthropology and the City: An Introduction to Urban Anthropology* (1977), by Edwin Eames and Judith Goode, addresses the historic trends in urban anthropology. It details the various levels of analysis undertaken by anthropologists in cities and provides a significant bibliography of work through 1977. In its concluding sections, it strongly argues that anthropology should view cities as important units of analysis and study, moving away from simply studying populations within a city to a view of the city as a significant player in human events.

The second text, Richard G. Fox's *Urban Anthropology: Cities in Their Cultural Settings* (1977), studies the relationship between particular cities and their political, historic, and economic contexts. While it is possible to argue with the particular typology of cities he develops, and with the forces he sees as significant in determining a city's type, the book provides significant food for thought for the urban anthropologist.

For the anthropologist wondering how to move to the city to begin work, we recommend Ulf Hannerz's *Exploring the City: Inquiries Toward an Urban Anthropology* (1980). This book chronicles the methodological and theoretical perspectives of the most important urban anthropologists. Although it should not be used as a cookbook of how to work in the field, it is an excellent manual for advanced undergraduate and graduate students who want some insight into how to begin working in a complex social setting.

We cannot fail to mention four classic volumes that were important to us in our early study of urban process in Latin America and which we feel are still of value to the beginning and advanced student. *Two Cities of Latin America: A Comparative Description of Social Classes* (1964), by Andrew H. Whiteford, was one of the first attempts at a systematic comparative study of class structure in two Latin American cities. Although the book is dated, the material is still important baseline data for an understanding of change in modern Latin America. In addition, Whiteford paved the way in demonstrating to anthropologists that urban society was not the same everywhere south of the Río Grande. In 1968 the Southern Anthropological Society held one of the first sets of symposia dedicated to the question of urban anthropology. The papers from those symposia were published in *Urban Anthropology: Research Perspectives and Strategies* (1968), Elizabeth M. Eddy, ed. Of special interest to us is the paper by Anthony Leeds in which he alerted anthropologists to the importance of the multiplicity of variables present in an urban system. William Mangin's classic collection, *Peasants in Cities: Readings in the Anthropology of Urbanization* (1970), is still required reading for those who wish to understand the nature of squatter settlements in Latin America and the early theoretical thinking about them on the part of social scientists and planners. Last but not least is the collection edited by Aidan Southall, *Urban Anthropology: Cross-Cultural Studies of Urbanization* (1973). This book is a collection of classic empirical and theoretical papers not to be missed by a modern student of urban anthropology.

Finally, John Gulick's *The Humanity of Cities: An Introduction to Urban Societies* (1989) represents a grand synthesis of many of the debates in urban studies in general and urban anthropology in particular.

Households

The issue of the appropriateness of the household as a unit of analysis reappeared in the mid 1970s. A comprehensive review of the arguments can be found in Marianne Schmink's review article "Household Economic Strategies" (1984). In our development of the household as a unit of analysis for life in Oaxaca three works were especially useful. Simon Kuznets's "Demographic Aspects of the Size Distribution of Income: An Exploratory Essay" (1976) discusses the appropriateness of households as a discrete unit of analysis in economic and social analysis. *Households: Comparative and Historical Studies of the Domestic Group* (1984), edited by Robert McC. Netting, Richard R. Wilk, and Eric J. Arnould, presents seventeen studies of the use of households in social science. Of particular theoretical interest are the chapters by Wilk and Netting, "Households: Changing Forms and Functions"; Hammel, "On the *** of Studying Household Form and Function"; and Carter, "Household Histories." The papers in *Households and the World-Economy* (1984), edited by Joan Smith, Immanuel Wallerstein, and Hans-Dieter Evers, approach the question of the household as a unit of study from the perspective of world systems theory. We found the chapters by Diana Wong, "The Limits of Using the Household as a Unit of Analysis," and Georg Stauth, "Households, Modes of Living, and Production Systems," most useful to our work. Wong focuses our attention on the fact that households are not tightly bounded units, while Stauth discusses the role of households as units of labor production in the modern world capitalist system. Olivia Harris's work (1981) criticizes various treatments of the concept of household from a feminist perspective. She challenges treatments of households as universals and as isolates, except with reference to work-force reproduction. She criticizes the work of Meillassoux (1981), who defines the household as the place where the reproduction of workers and the production of new workers takes place.

Mexico

Histories of Mexico

Political and social histories of Mexico by historians, ethnohistorians, and anthropologists abound. However, in our opinion, two of the earliest are still the best. For an introduction to the region one can do no better than Eric Wolf's *Sons of the Shaking Earth* (1959). A short, well-written panorama of Mexico, this book begins with a study of Mexico's geography and concludes with the development of Mexico's various regional cultures. A recommended companion is Lesley Byrd Simpson's *Many Mexicos* (1964). Again, one of the early general histories and introductions to Mexican culture, this remains a classic in its field that has yet to be bettered. The importance of this book is indicated by the fact that even though the original edition was completed in 1941, it is continuously updated and reprinted by the University of California Press. For those who have not read it, we recommend Michael Coe's *Mexico* (1962) as an introduction to prehispanic Mexico. While some of the details of interpretation may have changed since this book was first written, it remains one of the most accessible introductions to Mexico before the arrival of the Spaniards.

Three general histories of Mexico were particularly helpful to us in our work and we recommend them to both the beginning and advanced student. Henry Bramford Parkes's *A History of Mexico* (1969) remains one of the best synthetic histories of Mexico we have read. First published in 1938, and revised several times through 1969, it is weak in its coverage of the period since the 1940s. A more recent volume we found to be a good companion to Parkes is Robert Ryal Miller's *Mexico: A History* (1985). We found Miller's narrative of political, economic, and social forces most compelling and recommend the volume to both the new and experienced student of Mexico. *The Course of Mexican History* (1987), by Meyer and Sherman, has become the standard general history of Mexico.

The Political Economy of Mexico

Mexico's economic situation is the subject of various books. Susan Eckstein's *The Poverty of Revolution: The State and the Urban Poor in Mexico* (1977) was important in helping us to understand the relationship between the state and poverty, not just in Mexico but in the third world in general. Alain de Janvry's *The Agrarian Question and Reformism in Latin America* (1981) helped us understand the relationship between rural economic policy and what we saw happening in Mexico's urban areas. The Mexican crisis is discussed by many writers. General discussions are provided by González Casanova and Aguilar Camín (1986) and Rivera Ríos (1986). Valenzuela F. (1986) presents a very economistic view of Mexico in the 1980s.

Mexico's dependence on the United States as a consumer of its goods and supplier of major technology is well known. The effects of this dependence on Mexico's political economy are well documented by Daniel Levy and Gabriel Székely in *Mexico: Paradoxes of Stability and Change* (1983). This book is easy to read and well suited for classroom use.

Although controversial in some of its aspects, Alan Riding's *Distant Neigh-*

bors (1986) is a good introduction to Mexico's current political and social structure. In reading the book it should be remembered that Riding is a journalist and
while he speaks excellent Spanish and knows Latin culture, he spent most of his
time in Mexico City with politicians and the elite. Pastor and Castañeda's book,
Limits to Friendship (1988), is a more scholarly and less impressionistic discussion
of the same issues.

Demography and Urbanization in Mexico

The classic work on Mexican urban demographics, which we have used
heavily in the formation of this manuscript, is Luís Unikel's *El desarrollo urbano
de México* (1976). Based on 1940, 1950, 1960, and 1970 census material, the
book is an excellent compilation and comparison of demographics and standards
of living in the major urban areas of the country. Unikel's untimely death
probably means the comparable study for the 1980 census will not be made.
However, the census division of the Secretaría de Programación y Presupuesto
has begun to publish a series of works based on Mexico's somewhat uneven census
material. There are general studies of housing, labor, migration, and income, in
addition to general demographic studies for each state in the nation. *Cuatro
ciudades: El proceso de urbanización dependiente* (1981), by Margarita Nolasco, is a
comparative study of Coatzacoalcos, Puebla, Oaxaca, and Ixtapalapa based on
interviews and survey data from the 1970s. Using a more economic analysis,
Selby, Murphy, and Lorenzen, in *The Mexican Urban Household: Organizing for
Self-Defense* (1990), compare life for the majority of citizens in ten urban areas of
Mexico: Mexicali, Mérida, San Luis Potosí, Querétaro, Tampico, Villahermosa,
Mazatlán, Reynosa, Oaxaca, and the Delegación Venustiano Carranza in Mexico
City.

For studies of specific cities, one should begin with Balán, Browning, and
Jelin's *Men in a Developing Society: Geographic and Social Mobility in Monterrey,
Mexico* (1973). This is classic study of one of Mexico's major cities and it should
be read by any serious student of Mexico. A good companion book to Balán et al.
would be Jorge Montaño's *Los pobres de la ciudad en los asentamientos espontáneos*
(1976), which provides a look at squatter settlements and political movements in
Monterrey and Mexico City. Jorge Alonso is the editor of *Lucha urbana y acumula-
ción de capital* (1980), which enters into the debate about the nature of the
adaptations of the poor in Mexico City with Larissa Lomnitz's *Networks and
Marginality: Life in a Mexican Shantytown* (1977). Brígida García, Humberto
Muñoz, and Orlandina de Oliveira's *Hogares y trabajadores en la Ciudad de México*
(1982) presents data on households in Mexico City. *Rituals of Marginality: Politics,
Process, and Culture Change in Central Urban Mexico, 1969–1974* (1983), by
Carlos G. Vélez-Ibañez, was especially important in helping us orient our analysis
of how the poor adapt to urban Mexico.

Finally, the student of urban Mexico cannot ignore the classic works by
Oscar Lewis. Despite disagreements over the question of the existence or not of a
"culture of poverty," *The Children of Sánchez: Autobiography of a Mexican Family*
(1961) remains one of the classic descriptions of urban life in the face of extreme
poverty. No reader of this book can fail to see the influence of Lewis's *Five Families:
Mexican Case Studies in the Culture of Poverty* (1959) on our work.

Since the early 1970s important studies of urbanization in Mexico have been published by Mexican researchers. Most of these treat the problems associated with urban growth in Mexico City, the oil regions, and the border with the United States, for example, Jorge Legorreta's *El proceso de urbanización en ciudades petroleras* (1983), Nolasco and Acevedo's *Los niños de la frontera* (1985), as well as Carrillo and Hernández (1985), Hiernaux (1986), and Iglesias (1985). The best anthropological and sociological account of the effects of the 1980s crisis can be found in de la Peña, Durán, Escobar, and Alba (1990).

Oaxaca

Prehispanic Oaxaca

Although compiled in the early 1960s, *Ancient Oaxaca: Discoveries in Mexican Archaeology and History* (1966), edited by John Paddock, remains the classic work in Oaxacan archaeology and should be read by any serious student of the region. In developing our understanding of the historic matrix in which the city of Oaxaca is imbedded, the work of the Valley of Oaxaca Settlement Pattern Project has been particularly important. The most significant work for us was *Ancient Mesoamerica: A Comparison of Change in Three Regions* (1981), by Richard E. Blanton, Stephen A. Kowalewski, Gary Feinman, and Jill Appel. In this volume the valley of Oaxaca and Monte Albán, the ancient capital, are placed in a regional perspective similar to the approach we have attempted for the modern city. Additional works by the Valley of Oaxaca Settlement Pattern Project important to placing the valley in a historic context are *Monte Albán: Settlement Patterns at the Ancient Zapotec Capital* (1978), by Richard Blanton, and *The Valley of Oaxaca Settlement Project*, Report no. 3 (1988), by Stephen A. Kowalewski, Richard E. Blanton, Laura Finsten, and Gary Feinman. In "The Economic Systems of Ancient Oaxaca: A Regional Perspective" (1983), Stephen A. Kowalewski and Laura Finsten discuss changes in Oaxaca's relationship to the outside world in the preconquest period and how those changes affected the valley's internal organization. For those interested in a detailed description of the archaeological sites in the valley of Oaxaca, a comprehensive report is available in *The Cloud People* (1982), edited by Kent Flannery and Joyce Marcus. Flannery's *Guilá Naquitz* (1986) is a beautiful work, describing life in prehistoric Oaxaca. Marcus Winter's *Oaxaca: The Archaeological Record* (1989) presents a more popular discussion, while Winter's recent compilation provides a number of excellent articles (1990).

For more detailed histories of Oaxaca's ethnic groups, we recommend Ronald Spores' *Mixtec Kings and Their People* (1967) and Joseph Whitecotton's *The Zapotecs* (1977).

Colonial Oaxaca

Colonial Oaxaca is receiving more and more attention by scholars. A book of particular interest to us in developing this study was William Taylor's *Landlord and Peasant in Colonial Oaxaca* (1972). This is a detailed study of the relationships between Indians and Spaniards in the colonial period. Taylor documents the efforts by Indian communities to hold their land in the face of encroachment by the Spaniards and shows how the successful battles by Indians set the stage for much of Oaxaca's current ethnic structure. In *Race and Class in Colonial Oaxaca* (1978), John Chance reviews the ethnic structure that developed in the valley after the Spanish conquest. Marcello Carmagnani's *El regreso de los dioses* (1988) addresses the same issues for the state of Oaxaca. Brian Hamnett's *Politics and Trade in Southern Mexico, 1750–1821* (1971) demonstrates how the economic connections between the city and the wider world economy through trade in cochineal subjected the city to economic fluctuations based on events in Europe. Kate Young's case study of the effects of cochineal on Zapotec families (1978) provides a useful complement. The collection *Lecturas históricas del estado de Oaxaca: Época colonial* (1986), edited by María de los Angeles Romero Frizzi, is perhaps the most comprehensive volume on Oaxaca's colonial period, while her work on the colonial Mixteca alta (1990d) provides an excellent case study of colonial regional economics.

Numerous recent works have addressed the long-neglected nineteenth century in Oaxaca. Critical to us has been Charles Berry's *The Reform in Oaxaca, 1856–76* (1981). Maria de los Angeles Romero Frizzi's (1990b) edited collection contains an excellent set of articles. Pastor (1987) has an excellent analysis of the late colonial and early independence period in the Mixteca.

The Porfiriato and the Revolutionary Period

A number of recent works have established the development of Oaxaca during the Porfiriato. Most outstanding are those by Chassen (1990) and the edited collection by Romero Frizzi (1990c). Arellanes Meixueiro (1990) covers the development of organized labor from the Porfiriato through the revolutionary period (1870–1930). The classic analysis of Oaxaca and the Revolution is Waterbury (1975). A number of more detailed analyses have recently appeared including Garner (1988), Martínez Medina (1985), Meixueiro Hernández (1989), Ruíz Cervantes (1985), and Sánchez Silva (1985, 1990).

Contemporary Oaxaca

The earliest study of the spatial distribution of classes in the city of Oaxaca is Butterworth's study of its neighborhoods, "Squatters or Suburbanites? The growth of Shantytowns in Oaxaca, Mexico," in *Latin American Modernization Problems,* ed. R. E. Scott (1973). In this paper, Butterworth and his colleagues undertake an analysis and classification of the various low-income neighborhoods found in the outlying regions of the city. Murphy's 1979 study of the city of Oaxaca, *Urbanization, Development and Household Adaptive Strategies in Oaxaca, a Secondary City of Mexico,* provides a comprehensive study of the city based on a systematic sample of the city's households. A briefer study of Oaxaca's neighborhood types is available in Murphy (1987).

Unfortunately there are few studies of neighborhoods in Oaxaca City. Michael Higgins's *Somos gente humilde: Etnografía de una colonia urbana pobre de Oaxaca* (1974) and *Somos Tocayos: Anthropology of Urbanism and Poverty* (1983) are based on his work in the Colonia Linda Vista. "Haciendo Colonia: The

Making of a Community Near Oaxaca, Mexico," by Zack Prince, is a study of organization in a government-sponsored community on the city's outskirts.

Two additional works on population distribution in the city of Oaxaca are available in Spanish. José I. Aguilar Medina's *La ciudad de Oaxaca: El hombre y la urbe* (1980) is a detailed study of the people living in the central part of the city. The book is based on a 1976 survey by the Instituto Nacional de Antropología e História under the direction of María Luisa Acevedo Conde. A condensed version of the same study can be found in Margarita Nolasco's *Cuatro ciudades: El proceso de urbanización dependiente* (1981).

The economy of Oaxaca City and its environs has been discussed by Ralph Beals in *The Peasant Marketing System of Oaxaca, Mexico* (1975) and Cook and Diskin in *Markets in Oaxaca* (1976). Beals' study is a classic economic approach to the market system of Oaxaca. Cook and Diskin take a more materialistic and Marxist view of the economic structures of Oaxaca. While we lean toward the analysis in Cook and Diskin, we feel that both volumes are necessary if one is to understand fully what is happening in the valley. Contreras (1987) focuses on Oaxaca's commercial elite. María Luisa Acevedo Conde's *Desempleo y subempleo rural en los valles centrales de Oaxaca* (1982) is a recent study of employment conditions in the area immediately surrounding the city of Oaxaca. This study is important for this book because the Valles Centrales is the region of origin for most of the migrants in the city. Lynn Stephen, in her recent dissertation "Weaving Changes: Economic Development and Gender Roles in Zapotec Ritual and Production" (1987), shows how changes in subsistence patterns in Teotitlán del Valle have affected not only production in the village but ritual patterns in the village and migration patterns to Oaxaca City and the United States. Teotitlán is of interest because of its long tradition as an artisan village and because it is the source of the blankets that draw many tourists to Oaxaca City.

Also in the valley, Selby's *Zapotec Deviance* (1974) describes the social organization of a Zapotec valley community. *The Myth of Ritual* (1986), by El Guindi and Hernández, is an ethnography of another valley community. Parsons's *Mitla: Town of the Souls* (1936) is a classic ethnography of an important valley Zapotec community. Julio de la Fuente's *Yalalag* (1977) is also a classic ethnography of mountain Zapotecs. Nahmad et al. (1988) describe indigenous technologies and their environmental impact for several valley communities.

Farther out from the city, James Greenberg, in *Santiago's Sword: Chatino Peasant Economics and Religion* (1981) and *Blood Ties* (1989), and Jorge Hernández Díaz, in *El café amargo: Diferenciación y cambio social entre los chatinos* (1987), demonstrate how penetration by the world economy, in the form of coffee, into the Chatino region has affected its politics, religion, and social organization.

The collection of essays edited by Aubrey Williams, *Social, Political, and Economic Life in Contemporary Oaxaca* (1979), provides an overview of conditions in the city and state from the mid 1960s through the mid 1970s. A contemporary account of Oaxaca City's power structure can be found in *La composición del poder, Oaxaca 1968–1984* (1987), edited by Miguel Basañez E. Basañez and his group do a very good job of tracing family relations between the various companies in Oaxaca as well as their connection to the world economy. Scott Cook's two volumes, *Zapotec Stoneworkers: The Dynamics of Rural Simple Commodity Production in Modern Mexican Capitalism* (1982) and *Peasant Capitalist Industry: Piecework and Enterprise in Southern Mexican Brickyards* (1984), provide excellent studies of the development of simple commodity production in response to the demands of the market in Oaxaca City.

Finally, we must mention two more general histories of Oaxaca that have helped us place much of the detail in a perspective. Dalton Palomo et al. provide a good overview of Oaxacan history in their two-volume *Historia de Oaxaca: Libro de texto para la primera enseñanza* (1980a, 1980b). While written for use in schools, each of the authors is a well-respected scholar whose interpretations and detail can be relied upon. A more detailed history of a more restricted period can be found in Iturribarría's *Historia de Oaxaca* (1935, 1939a, 1939b); these three volumes offer detailed insight into Oaxaca during much of the period between Independence and the rise of Porfirio Díaz. Iturribarría's *Oaxaca en la historia* (1955) is a general history of Oaxaca from prehispanic times through World War II. In this book Iturribarría offers us a glimpse of life in the city just prior to the major changes that occurred after the introduction of the Pan American Highway.

More recently Dalton Palomo has published a multivolume set, to which *Oaxaca, una historia compartida* (1990b) provides a good general introduction. The remaining volumes offer a mix of analytical articles and copies of original documents (1990c, d, e, and f). Romero Frizzi's multivolume set (1990a, b, and c) contains an excellent collection of analytical articles.

Our understanding of Oaxaca's more recent political history was helped by the publication of *Oaxaca, una lucha reciente: 1960–1983* (1984), by Bustamante et al., which chronicles the rise of COCEI in Oaxaca and its impact on the state's political establishment. Raúl Benítez Zenteno has compiled a series of studies from the Instituto de Investigación Sociológicos de la Universidad Autónoma Benito Juárez de Oaxaca, *Sociedad y política en Oaxaca 1980: 15 estudios de caso* (1982), which provides a detailed analysis of many of the events discussed in this book. Also noteworthy are Martínez Lopez (1985), Arellanes Meixueiro, Martínez Vasquez, and Ruíz Cervantes (1988), Díaz Montes (1989). Less rigorous works include Paddock (1990a, 1990b), Ramírez Bohorquez (1989), Gonzalez Santiago (1985), and Altamirano Ramírez (1990). Garza Cuarón (1987) reflects Oaxaca's relative isolation through a linguistic study of the city in the 1960s. These works are part of a growing body of literature dealing with the city and state of Oaxaca being published in Mexico. We have included as much of that work as possible in our bibliography in order to make it more accessible to North American researchers.

References

Acevedo Conde, María Luisa.
1982. *Desempleo y subempleo rural en los valles centrales de Oaxaca.* Mexico, D.F.: Instituto Nacional de Antropología e Historia.
Aceves de la Mora, José Luís.
1944. *El agua en la ciudad de Oaxaca: Monografía histórica.* Oaxaca: Publicaciones del Gobierno del Estado.
1976. *Climatología del estado de Oaxaca.* Oaxaca: Ediciones INDECO.
1988. *Compilación bibliográfica sobre flora oaxaqueña.* Mexico, D.F.: Instituto Politécnico Nacional.
Acuña, René, ed.
1984. *Relaciones geográficas del siglo XVI: Antequera.* Vol. 1. Mexico, D.F.: Instituto de Investigaciones Antropológicas, Universidad Nacional Autónoma de Mexico.
Aguilar Medina, José Iñigo.
1980. *La ciudad de Oaxaca: El hombre y la urbe.* Mexico, D.F.: Instituto Nacional de Antropología e Historia.
Aguirre Beltrán, Gonzalo.
1979. *Regions of Refuge.* Washington, D.C.: Society for Applied Anthropology.
Alonso, Jorge, ed.
1980. *Lucha urbana y acumulación de capital.* Mexico: Ediciones Casa Chata.
Altamirano Ramírez, Hugo.
1990. *Casos y casos curiosas de Oaxaca.* Oaxaca: Carteles Editores, Colección Obra Negra.
Aranda, Josefina.
1990. Género, familia y división del trabajo en Santo Tomás Jalieza. *Estudios Sociológicos* 8, no. 22 (jan–abr.): 3–22.
Arellanes Meixueiro, Anselmo.
1990. *Los trabajos y los guías: Mutualismo y sindicalismo en Oaxaco, 1870–1930.* Oaxaca: Instituto Tecnológico de Oaxaca.

Arellanes Meixueiro, Anselmo, Victor Raúl Martínez Vásquez, and Francisco José Ruíz Cervantes.
1988. *Oaxaca en el siglo XX: Testimonios de historia oral.* Oaxaca: Ediciones Meridiano 100.
Bailón Corres, Moisés J.
1980. Artesanías y capital commercial en los valles centrales de Oaxaca. In *Sociedad y política en Oaxaca,* ed. Raúl Zenteno, 83–109. Oaxaca: Instituto de Investigaciones Sociológicas, Universidad Autónoma Benito Juárez de Oaxaca.
1990. Los problemas de Morro Mazatán: la lucha por el control de una agencia municipal en el Estado de Oaxaca. *Estudios Sociológicos* 8, no. 22 (jan.–abr.): 67–87.
Bailón Corres, Moisés J., and Seriog Zermeño.
1987. *Juchitán: Límites de una experiencia democrática.* Mexico, D.F.: Universidad Autónoma Nacional de México.
Balán, Jorge, Harley Browning, and Elizabeth Jelin.
1973. *Men in a Developing Society: Geographic and Social Mobility in Monterrey, Mexico.* Austin: University of Texas Press.
Balán, Jorge, and Elizabeth Jelin.
1980. *Taller sobre las condiciónes de vida de los sectores populares urbanos: Informe sobre sus resultados.* Documento de Trabajo no. 5. Mexico City: Population Council.
Barabas, Alicia Mabel, and Miguel Bartolomé.
1986. *Etnicidad y pluralismo cultural: La dinámica étnica en Oaxaca.* Consejo Nacional para Cultura y los Artes, Mexico, D.F.: Instituto Nacional de Antropología e Historia.
Bartolomé, Miguel Alberto.
1979. *Narrativa y etnicidad entre los Chatinos de Oaxaca.* Mexico, D.F.: SEP-INAH, Cuadernos de los Centros Regionales.
Bartolomé, Miguel Alberto, and Alicia Mabel Barabas.
1982. *Tierra de la palabra: Historia y etnografía de los Chatinos de Oaxaca.* Centro Regional de Oaxaca, Etnología, Colección Científica, no. 108. Mexico City: Instituto Nacional de Antropología e Historia.
1986. Los migrantes étnicos de Oaxaca. *Mexico Indígena* 13 (nov.–dic.): 23–25.
Basañez, Miguel E., ed.
1987. *La composición del poder, Oaxaca 1968–1984.* Mexico, D.F.: Instituto Nacional de Administración Pública.
Beals, Carleton.
1971. *Porfirio Díaz, Dictator of Mexico.* Westport, Conn.: Greenwood Press.
Beals, Ralph L.
1975. *The Peasant Marketing System of Oaxaca, Mexico.* Berkeley: University of California Press.
1979. "Some Social and Economic Implications of an Open Peasant Marketing System." In *Social, Political, and Economic Life in Contemporary Oaxaca,* ed. A. Williams, 23–41. Vanderbilt Publications in Anthropology, no. 24. Nashville, Tenn.

Bender, D.
1967. "A Refinement of the Concept of Household: Co-residence and Domestic Functions." *American Anthropologist* 69: 493–504.
Benítez Zenteno, Raúl.
1975. Desarrollo científico, el papel de las ciencias sociales y el centro de sociología de Oaxaca. *Revista Mexicana de Sociología* 37, no. 2 (abr.–jun.): 523–29.
Benítez Zenteno, Raúl, ed.
1982. *Sociedad y política en Oaxaca 1980: 15 estudios de caso.* Oaxaca: Instituto de Investigaciones Sociológicas, Universidad Autónoma Benito Juárez de Oaxaca.
Berg, Richard Lewis, Jr.
1974. *El impacto de la economía moderna sobre la economía tradicional de Zoogocho, Oaxaca y su area circundante.* Mexico, D.F.: Instituto Nacional Indigenista.
Berlín, Heinrich, Gonzálo de Balsalobre, and Diego de Hevia y Valdés.
1988. *Idolatría y superstición entre los Indios de Oaxaca.* Mexico, D.F.: Ediciones Toledo.
Berry, Brian.
1981. *Comparative Urbanization: Divergent Paths in the Twentieth Century.* New York: St. Martin's Press.
Berry, Charles R.
1967. *The Reform in the Central District of Oaxaca, 1856–1867: A Case Study.* Ann Arbor, Mich.: University Microfilms International.
1981. *The Reform in Oaxaca, 1856–76: A Microhistory of the Liberal Revolution.* Lincoln: University of Nebraska Press.
Bevan, Bernard.
1987. *Los Chinantecos y su habitat.* Mexico, D.F.: Instituto Nacional Indigenista.
Blanton, Richard E.
1978. *Monte Albán: Settlement Patterns at the Ancient Zapotec Capital.* New York: Academic Press.
Blanton, Richard E., Stephen A. Kowalewski, Gary Feinman, and Jill Appel.
1981. *Ancient Mesoamerica: A Comparison of Change in Three Regions.* Cambridge: Cambridge University Press.
1982. *Monte Albán's Hinterland, Part I: The Prehispanic Settlement Patterns of the Central and Southern Parts of the Valley of Oaxaca, Mexico.* Memoirs of the Museum of Anthropology, no. 15. Ann Arbor: University of Michigan.
Boege, Eckart.
1988. *Los Mazatecos ante la nación.* Mexico: Siglo Veintiuno.
Borah, W., and S. F. Cook.
1960. *The Population of Central Mexico in 1548. Iberoamericana,* no. 43. Berkeley: University of California Press.
1963. *The Aboriginal Population of Central Mexico on the Eve of the Conquest. Iberoamericana,* no. 45. Berkeley: University of California Press.

Bradomín, José María.
 1980. *Monografía del estado de Oaxaca.* 2d ed. Mexico, D.F.: Oaxaca La Impresora Azteca.
 1987. *Historia antigua de Oaxaca.* 2d ed. Oaxaca: Talleres de la Editorial Tradición.
Brito de Martí, Esperanza, ed.
 1982. *Almanaque de Oaxaca.* Oaxaca: Gobierno del Estado de Oaxaca.
Bustamante V., R., P. Cuauhtemoc González, F. J. Ruíz, C. M. Lozano, S. Millan E., and F. A. Gomezjara.
 1978. *Oaxaca, una lucha reciente: 1960–1978.* Mexico: Ediciones Nueva Sociología.
 1984. *Oaxaca, una lucha reciente: 1960–1983.* Mexico: Ediciones Nueva Sociología.
Butterworth, D.
 1962. "A Study of the Urbanization Process among Mixtec Migrants from Tilantongo in Mexico City." *America Indígena* 22: 257–74.
 1973. "Squatters or Suburbanites? The Growth of Shantytowns in Oaxaca, Mexico." In *Latin American Modernization Problems,* ed. R. E. Scott, 208–32. Urbana: University of Illinois Press.
Butterworth, Douglas, and John K. Chance.
 1981. *Latin American Urbanization.* Cambridge: Cambridge University Press.
Cadena Kima-Chang, Susana, and Susana Suárez Paniagua.
 1988. *Los Chontales ante una nueva expectativa de cambio: El petróleo.* Mexico, D.F.: Instituto Nacional Indigenista.
Cancian, Frank.
 1965. *Economics and Prestige in a Maya Community: The Religious Cargo System in Zinacantan.* Stanford, Calif.: Stanford University Press.
Carmagnani, Marcello.
 1988. *El regreso de los dioses: El proceso de reconstitutción de la identidad etnica en Oaxaca: Siglos XVII y XVIII.* Mexico, D.F.: Fondo de Cultural Económica.
Carrillo, Jorge, and Alberto Hernández.
 1985. *Mujeres fronterizas en la industria maquiladora.* Mexico: SEP, Centro de Estudios de la Frontera Norte.
Carter, Anthony T.
 1984. "Household Histories." In *Households: Comparative and Historical Studies of the Domestic Group,* ed. Robert McC. Netting, Richard R. Wilk, and Erik J. Arnould, 44–83. Berkeley: University of California Press.
Castells, Manuel.
 1977. *The Urban Question: A Marxist Approach.* London: Edward Arnold.
 1983. *The City and the Grass Roots: A Cross-cultural Theory of Urban Social Movements.* Berkeley: University of California Press.
Centro de Investigaciones y Estudios en Antropología Social (CIESAS)—Oaxaca.
 1989. *Primeros jornadas sobre estudios antropológicos Mixtecos y Mixes.* Notebook no. 1. Oaxaca: CIESAS.
Chance, John K.
 1971. "Kinship and Urban Residence: Household and Family Organization in a Suburb of Oaxaca, Mexico." *Journal of the Steward Anthropological Society* 2, no. 2: 122–47.
 1975. "The Colonial Latin American City: Preindustrial or Capitalist."

Urban Anthropology 4, no. 3: 211–28.

1976. "The Urban Indian in Colonial Oaxaca." *American Ethnologist* 3, no. 4: 603–32.

1978. *Race and Class in Colonial Oaxaca.* Stanford, Calif.: Stanford University Press.

1981. "The Ecology of Race and Class in Late Colonial Oaxaca." In *Studies of Spanish American Population History,* ed. David J. Robinson. Boulder, Colo.: Westview Press: 93–117.

1989. *Conquest of the Sierra: Spaniards and Indians in Colonial Oaxaca.* Norman: University of Oklahoma Press.

Chance, J. K., and W. B. Taylor.

1977. "Estate and Class in a Colonial City: Oaxaca in 1792." *Comparative Studies in Society and History* 19, no. 4 (Oct.): 454–87.

1979. "Estate and Class: A Reply." *Comparative Studies in Society and History* 21, no. 3: 434–42.

Chassen, Francie R.

1990. *Regiones y ferrocarriles en la Oaxaca Porfirista.* Oaxaca: Obra Negra.

Chevalier, François.

1963. *Land and Society in Colonial Mexico: The Great Hacienda.* Berkeley: University of California Press.

Clarke, Colin G.

1975. *Kingston, Jamaica: Urban Development and Social Change, 1692–1962.* Berkeley: University of California Press.

1986. "Livelihood Systems, Settlements, and Levels of Living in 'Los Valles Centrales de Oaxaca,' Mexico." Research Paper no. 37. Oxford: School of Geography, University of Oxford.

Coatsworth, John H.

1981. *Growth against Development: The Economic Impact of Railroads in Porfirian Mexico.* DeKalb: Northern Illinois University Press.

Cockcroft, James D.

1983. *Mexico.* New York: Monthly Review Press.

Coe, Michael D.

1962. *Mexico.* New York: Praeger.

Collins, Thomas W., ed.

1980. *Cities in a Larger Context.* Athens: University of Georgia.

Consejo Nacional de Población.

1987. *Indicadores sobre fecundidad, marginación y ruralidad a nivel municipal: Oaxaca.* Mexico, D.F.: Consejo Nacional de Población.

Contreras, Enrique.

1987. Participación económica y política del comercio organizado de Oaxaca, 109–42. In Guillermo Boils, coordinator, *México: Problemas urbanos regionales.* Mexico, D. F.: García Valdés editores.

Cook, Scott.

1982. *Zapotec Stoneworkers: The Dynamics of Rural Simple Commodity Production in Modern Mexican Capitalism.* Washington, D.C.: University Press of America.

1984. *Peasant Capitalist Industry: Piecework and Enterprise in Southern Mexican Brickyards.* Washington, D.C.: University Press of America.

Cook, Scott, and Martin Diskin, eds.

1976. *Markets in Oaxaca.* Austin: University of Texas Press.

Cornelius, Wayne.
1975. *Politics and the Migrant Poor in Mexico City.* Stanford, Calif.: Stanford University Press.
Corona, Rodolfo.
1979. *Cuantificación del nivel de la mortalidad en Oaxaca, 1970.* Oaxaca: Centro de Sociología, Universidad Autónoma de Benito Juárez de Oaxaca.
Cosío Villegas, Daniel.
1963. *The United States versus Porfirio Díaz.* Lincoln: University of Nebraska Press.
Culturas Populares, Dirección General de.
1982. Ciclo de vida entre los Mixes (español). *Cuadernos de Trabajo, Acayucan,* no. 30. Mexico, D.F.: Dirección General de Culturas Populares, Secretaría de Educación Pública.
Dalton Palomo, Margarita.
1990a. La organización política, las mujeres y el Estado: el Caso de Oaxaca. *Estudios Sociológicos* 8, no. 22 (jan.–abr.): 39–66.
1990b. *Oaxaca, una historia compartida.* Oaxaca: Gobierno del Estado de Oaxaca.
1990c. *Oaxaca, textos de su historia,* vol. 1. Oaxaca: Gobierno del Estado de Oaxaca.
1990d. *Oaxaca, textos de su historia,* vol. 2. Oaxaca: Gobierno del Estado de Oaxaca.
1990e. *Oaxaca, textos de su historia,* vol. 3. Oaxaca: Gobierno del Estado de Oaxaca.
1990f. *Oaxaca, textos de su historia,* vol. 4. Oaxaca: Gobierno del Estado de Oaxaca.
Dalton Palomo, Margarita, Reyna Moguel Viveros, and Marcus Winter.
1980a. *Historia de Oaxaca: Libro de texto para la primera enseñanza.* Vol 1. Oaxaca: Centro de Sociología, Instituto de Investigaciones Sociológicas de la Universidad Autónoma Benito Juárez de Oaxaca.
1980b. *Historia de Oaxaca: Libro de texto para la primera enseñanza.* Vol. 2. Oaxaca: Centro de Sociología, Instituto de Investigaciones Sociológicas de la Universidad Autónoma Benito Juárez de Oaxaca.
de Janvry, Alain.
1981. *The Agrarian Question and Reformism in Latin America.* Baltimore, Md.: Johns Hopkins University Press.
de la Cruz, Victor.
1981. *Las guerras entre aztecas y zapotecas.* Juchitán, Oaxaca: H. Ayuntamiento Popular.
1983a. *En torno a las islas del mar oceano.* Juchitán, Oaxaca: H. Ayuntamiento Popular de Juchitán.
1983b. *La rebelión de Che Gorio Melendre.* Juchitán, Oaxaca: Publicaciones del H. Ayuntamiento Popular de Juchitán.
1989. *La educación en las épocas prehispanica y colonial en Oaxaca.* Oaxaca: Centro de Investigaciones y Estudios en Antropología Social (CIESAS). Oaxaca y GADE, A. C., cuaderno 2.

de la Fuente, Julío.
    1977. *Yalalag: Un pueblo zapoteco serrano.* Mexico, D.F.: Instituto Nacional Indigenista.
de la Peña, Guillermo, Juan Manuel Durán, Agustín Escobar, and Javier García de Alba, eds.
    1990. *Crisis, conflicto y sobrevivencia: Estudios sobre la sociedad urbana de México.* Guadalajara, Mexico: Universidad de Guadalajara and Centro de Investigaciones y Estudios Superiores en Antropología Social.
de Soto, Hernando.
    1986. *El otro sendero: La revolucíon informal.* Lima: Editorial El Barranco.
Dennis, Phillip A.
    1973. *An Inter-Village Land Feud in the Valley of Oaxaca, Mexico.* Ann Arbor, Mich.: University Microfilms International.
    1979. "Inter-Village Conflicts and the Origin of the State." In *Social, Political, and Economic Life in Contemporary Oaxaca,* ed. A. Williams, 43–66. Vanderbilt Publications in Anthropology, no. 24. Nashville, Tenn.
    1987. *Intervillage Conflict in Oaxaca.* New Brunswick, N.J.: Rutgers University Press.
Díaz Montes, Fausto.
    1987. *Los conflictos municipales: Problemática municipal de Oaxaca.* Cuadernos de Investigación, pp. 36–55. Oaxaca: Instituto de Investigaciones Sociológicas, Universidad Autónoma Benito Juárez de Oaxaca.
    1989. *Elecciones municipales, conflicto y negociación: Oaxaca 1986, los conflictos municipales en Oaxaca.* Oaxaca: Instituto de Investigaciones Sociológicas, Universidad Autónoma Benito Juárez de Oaxaca.
Doniz, Rafael.
    1983. *Fotografías del H. Ayuntamiento Popular de Juchitán.* Juchitán, Oaxaca: H. Ayuntamiento Popular de Juchitán.
Dotson, Floyd.
    1953. "A Note on Participation in Voluntary Associations in a Mexican City." *American Sociological Review* 18: 308–86.
Drucker, Susan.
    1963. *Cambio de indumentaria: La estructura social y el abandono de la vestimenta indigena en la villa de Santiago Jimaltipec.* Mexico, D.F.: Instituto Nacional Indigenista.
Drucker-Brown, Susan, ed.
    1982. *Malinowski in Mexico: The Economics of a Mexican Market System.* London: Routledge & Kegan Paul.
Eames, Edwin, and Judith Goode.
    1977. *Anthropology and the City: An Introduction to Urban Anthropology.* Englewood Cliffs, N.J.: Prentice-Hall.
Eckstein, Susan.
    1976. "The Rise and Demise of Research on Latin American Urban Poverty." *Studies in Comparative International Development* 11, no. 2: 107–26.
    1977. *The Poverty of Revolution: The State and the Urban Poor in Mexico.* Princeton, N.J.: Princeton University Press.

Eddy, Elizabeth, M. ed.
   1968. *Urban Anthropology: Research Perspectives and Strategies.* Athens: University of Georgia Press.

El Guindi, Fadwa, and Abel Hernández.
   1986. *The Myth of Ritual: A Native's Ethnography of Zapotec Life-Crisis Rituals.* Tucson: University of Arizona Press.

Esparza, Manuel.
   1979. "The Poor 'Visitors': An Aspect of Oaxacan Tourism." In *Social, Political, and Economic Life in Contemporary Oaxaca,* ed. A. Williams, 143–60. Vanderbilt Publications in Anthropology, no. 24. Nashville, Tenn.
   1985. *Gillow durante el porfiriato y la revolución en Oaxaca (1887–1922).* Oaxaca: Secretaría de administración del Gobierno del Estado de Oaxaca.

Esparza, Manuel, and Jennifer Holderman.
   1975. *Estudio de un caso. Estudios de Antropología e Historia,* no. 4. Oaxaca: Centro Regional, SEP-INAH.

Falcone, F. S.
   1977. "Juárez, B. versus Díaz Brothers: Politics in Oaxaca, 1867–1871." *Americas* 33, no. 4: 630–51.

Fehrenbach, T. R.
   1983. *Fire and Blood: A History of Modern Mexico.* New York: Bonanza Books.

Felix, David.
   1983. "Income Distribution and the Quality of Life in Latin America: Patterns, Trends, and Policy Implications." *Latin American Research Review* 18, no. 2: 3–33.

Flanet, Véronique.
   1977. *Viviré, si Dios quiere: Un estudio de la violencia en la Mixteca de la costa.* Mexico, D.F.: Instituto Nacional Indigenista.

Flannery, Kent, ed.
   1986. *Guilá Naquitz: Archaic Foraging and Early Agriculture in Oaxaca, Mexico.* New York: Academic Press.

Flannery, Kent, and Joyce Marcus, eds.
   1982. *The Cloud People.* Albuquerque: University of New Mexico Press.

Foster, Brian.
   1984. "Family Structure and the Generation of Thai Social Exchange Networks." In *Households: Comparative and Historical Studies of the Domestic Group,* ed. Robert McC. Netting, Richard R. Wilk, and Eric J. Arnould, 84–105. Berkeley: University of California Press.

Foster, Donald W.
   1971. "Tequio in Urban Mexico: A Case from Oaxaca City." *Journal of the Steward Anthropological Society* 2, no. 2: 148–79.

Fox, Richard G.
   1972. "Rationale and Romance in Urban Anthropology." *Urban Anthropology* 1:205–33.
   1977. *Urban Anthropology: Cities in Their Cultural Settings.* Englewood Cliffs, N.J.: Prentice-Hall.

García, Brígida, Humberto Muñoz, and Orlandina de Oliveira.
1982. *Hogares y trabajadores en la Ciudad de México.* Mexico, D.F.: El Colegio de Mexico.

Garner, P.
1985. "Federalism and Caudillismo in the Mexican Revolution—The Genesis of the Oaxaca Sovereignty Movement (1915–20)." *Journal of Latin American Studies* 17 (May): 111–442.
1988. *La revolución en la provincia: Soberanía estatal y caudillismo en las montañas de Oaxaca (1919–1920).* Mexico, D.F.: Fondo de Cultura Económica.

Garza Cuarón, Beatriz.
1987. *El español hablado en la ciudad de Oaxaca, Mexico.* Mexico, D.F.: El colegio de México.

Gay, José Antonio.
1881a. [1978]. *Historia de Oaxaca.* Vol. 1. Reproducción facsímilar. Oaxaca: Ediciones del Gobierno Constitucional del Estado de Oaxaca.
1881b. [1978]. *Historia de Oaxaca.* Vol. 2. Reproducción facsímilar. Oaxaca: Ediciones del Gobierno Constitucional del Estado de Oaxaca.
1982. *Historia de Oaxaca.* Mexico, D.F.: Editorial Porrúa, S.A.

Gerhard, Peter.
1960. *Pirates on the West Coast of New Spain, 1575–1742.* Glendale, Calif.: Arthur H. Clark Company.

Gibaja, Regina C.
1986. *El mundo simbólico de la escuela.* Oaxaca: Universidad Autónoma Benito Juárez de Oaxaca.

Gibson, Charles.
1964. *The Aztecs under Spanish Rule: A History of the Indians of the Valley of Mexico, 1519—1810.* Stanford, Calif.: Stanford University Press.

Gil, Carlos B., ed.
1977. *The Age of Porfirio Díaz: Selected Readings.* Albuquerque: University of New Mexico Press.

Gilbert, Alan, and Josef Gugler.
1982. *Cities, Poverty, and Development: Urbanization in the Third World.* Oxford: Oxford University Press.

González Casanova, Pablo.
1970 [1965]. *Democracy in Mexico.* Oxford: Oxford University Press.

González Casanova, Pablo, and Héctor Aguilar Camín, eds.
1986. *México ante la crisis.* 2d ed. Mexico, D.F.: Siglo Veintiuno.

González Martínez, Alfonso.
1986. *Relación de Santa María Chimalapa.* Colección Agua Quemado. Oaxaca: Gobierno del Estado de Oaxaca, Casa de la Cultura.

González Pacheco, Cuauhtemoc.
1984. La lucha de clases en Oaxaca: 1960–1970. In *Oaxaca, una lucha reciente: 1960–1983,* ed. Bustamante, et al. Mexico: Ediciones Nueva Sociología.

González Santiago, Moises.
1985. *La fiesta de lunes del cerro y la guelaguetza.* Oaxaca: Proveedora Escolar.

González Villanueva, Pedro, S.D.B.
   1989. *El sacrifio mixe: Rumbos para una antropología religiosa indígena.* Mexico, D.F.: Centro de Estudios Pastorales y Antropológicos de la Prelatura Misepolitanta.
Graedon, Teresa L.
   1976. "Health and Nutrition Status in an Urban Community of Southern Mexico." Ph.D. diss., University of Michigan.
Greenberg, James.
   1981. *Santiago's Sword: Chatino Peasant Economics and Religion.* Berkeley: University of California Press.
   1987. *Religión y economía de los chatinos.* Serie de Anthropología Social, no. 77. Mexico, D.F.: Instituto Nacional Indigenista.
   1989. *Blood Ties: Life and Violence in Rural Mexico.* Tucson: University of Arizona Press.
Gulick, John.
   1989. *The Humanity of Cities: An Introduction to Urban Societies.* Granby, Mass.: Bergin and Garvey.
Hackenberg, R., A. D. Murphy, and H. A. Selby.
   1984. "The Urban Household in Dependent Development." In *Households: Comparative and Historical Studies of the Domestic Group,* ed. Robert McC. Netting et al., 187–216. Berkeley: University of California Press.
Hammel, E. A.
   1984. "On the *** of Studying Household Form and Function." In *Households: Comparative and Historical Studies of the Domestic Group,* ed. Robert McC. Netting, et al., 29–43. Berkeley: University of California Press.
Hamnett, Brian R.
   1971. *Politics and Trade in Southern Mexico, 1750–1821.* Cambridge Latin American Studies, no. 12. Cambridge: Cambridge University Press.
Hannerz, Ulf.
   1980. *Exploring the City: Inquiries Toward an Urban Anthropology.* New York: Columbia University Press.
Haraven, Tamara K., ed.
   1978. *Transitions: The Family and Life Course in Historical Perspectives.* New York: Academic Press.
Hardoy, Jorge E.
   1972. "Urbanization Policies and Urban Reform in Latin America." In *Latin American Urban Research,* ed. Guillermo Guisse and J. E. Hardoy, vol. 2, 19–44. Beverly Hills, Calif.: Sage Publications.
   1975. *Urbanization in Latin America: Approaches and Issues.* Garden City, N.Y.: Anchor Books.
Harris, Olivia.
   1981. "Households as Natural Units." In *Of Marriage and the Market,* ed. Kate Young, Carol Wolkowitz, and Roslyn McCullagh, 49–68. London: CSE Books.
Harvey, David.
   1973. *Social Justice and the City.* Baltimore: Johns Hopkins University Press.

Hayner, Norman S.
   1944. "City of Old Mexico." *Sociology and Social Research* 29, no. 2.
   1948. "Differential Social Change in a Mexican Town." *Social Forces* 26, no. 4: 381–90.
Hellman, Judith Adler
   1983. *Mexico in Crisis.* 2d ed. New York: Holmes & Meier.
   1988. "Continuity and Change in Mexico." *Latin American Research Review* 23, no. 2: 133–44.
Hendricks, Janet, and Arthur D. Murphy.
   1981. "From Poverty to Poverty: The Adaptation of Young Migrant Households in Oaxaca, Mexico." *Urban Anthropology* 10, no. 1: 53–70.
Hernández Díaz, Gilberto.
   1988. *El convento de Santo Domingo de Guzmán de Oaxaca: Fundación del siglo XVI.* Mexico: Serie Monumentos 2.
Hernández Díaz, Jorge.
   1987. *El café amargo: Diferenciación y cambio social entre los chatinos.* Oaxaca: Instituto de Investigaciones Sociológicas, Universidad Autónoma Benito Juárez de Oaxaca.
Hernández Ramos, Dionisio.
   1986. *Poemas de un cuarto solitario y dos leyendas.* Colección Siete Venado. Oaxaca: Gobierno del Estado de Oaxaca, Casa de la Cultura.
Hiernaux, Daniel.
   1986. *Urbanización y autoconstrucción de vivienda en Tijuana.* Mexico, D.F.: Centro de Ecodesarrollo.
Higgins, Cheleen Mahar.
   1975. "Integrative Aspects of Folk and Western Medicine among the Urban Poor of Oaxaca." *Anthropological Quarterly* 48, no. 1 (Jan.): 31–37.
Higgins, Michael James.
   1972. "The Internal Stratification System of a Mexican Colonia." *Journal of the Steward Anthropological Society* 3, no. 1 (Fall): 19–38.
   1974. *Somos gente humilde: Etnografía de una colonia urbana pobre de Oaxaca.* Mexico, D.F.: Instituto Nacional Indigenista.
   1979. "Social Relationships among the Urban Poor of Oaxaca." In *Social, Political, and Economic Life in Contemporary Oaxaca,* ed. A. Williams, 103–41. Vanderbilt Publications in Anthropology, no. 24. Nashville, Tenn.
   1983. *Somos Tocayos: Anthropology of Urbanism and Poverty.* New York: University Press of America.
Higgins, M., R. Camp, and J. Payne.
   1982. *When Will Our Turn Come: The Urban Poor of Oaxaca.* Greeley: Educational Materials Service, University of Northern Colorado.
Humphries, Jane.
   1982. "The Family and Economy: Notes toward a Relative Autonomy Approach." Paper presented at the Conference on Demographic Research in Latin America: Linking Individual, Household and Societal Variables, sponsored by the Social Sciences Research Council, Ixtapan de la Sal, Mexico, 23–27 August.

Iglesias, Norma.
　　1985. *La flor más bella de la maquiladora.* Mexico, D.F.: SEP, Centro de Estudios de la Frontera Norte.
INEGI, Secretaría de Programación y Presupuesto.
　　1984a. *X censo general de población y vivienda, 1980: Estado de Oaxaca.* 3 vols. Mexico, D.F.: Secretaría de Programación y Presupuesto.
　　1984b. *X censo general de población y vivienda, 1980: Resumen general abreviado.* Mexico, D.F.: Secretaría de Programación y Presupuesto.
　　1985. *Anuario de estadísticas Estatales, 1985.* Mexico, D.F.: Dirección General de Estadística, Secretaría de Programación y Presupuesto.
Iturribarría, Jorge Fernando.
　　1935. *Historia de Oaxaca.* Vol 1, *1821–1854: De la consumación de la independencia a la iniciación de la reforma.* Mexico, D.F.: Ediciones E.R.B.
　　1939a. *Historia de Oaxaca.* Vol. 2, *1855 a 1861: La reforma–la guerra de tres años.* Oaxaca: Imprenta del Gobierno del Estado de Oaxaca.
　　1939b. *Historia de Oaxaca.* Vol. 3, *1861 a 1867: La intervención, el imperio y la restauración de la república.* Oaxaca: Imprenta del Gobierno del Estado de Oaxaca.
　　1955. *Oaxaca en la historia: De la época precolombina a los tiempos actuales.* Mexico, D.F.: Editorial Stilo.
Jelin, Elizabeth.
　　1982. *Pan y afectos: la organización doméstica en la producción.* Buenos Aires: CEDES.
Kim, Myung-Hye.
　　1987. "Female Labor Force Participation and Household Reproduction in Urban Mexico." Ph.D. dissertation, University of Texas, Austin.
Kowalewski, Stephen A., Richard E. Blanton, Laura Finsten, and Gary Feinman.
　　1988. *The Valley of Oaxaca Settlement Project.* Report no. 3. Ann Arbor: Museum of Anthropology, University of Michigan.
Kowalewski, Stephen A., Gary Feinman, Laura Finsten, and Richard E. Blanton, Linda M. Nichols.
　　1989. *Monte Alban's Hinterland, Part II: Prehispanic Settlement Patterns in Tlacolula, Etla, and Ocotlan, the Valley of Oaxaca, Mexico.* 2 vol. Museum of Anthropology, Technical Reports, no. 23. Ann Arbor: Museum of Anthropology, University of Michigan.
Kowalewski, Stephen A., and Laura Finsten.
　　1983. "The Economic Systems of Ancient Oaxaca: A Regional Perspective." *Current Anthropology* 24, no. 4: 413–41.
Kowalewski, Stephen A., Arthur D. Murphy, and Ignacio Cabrera.
　　1984. "3500 Years of Housing in Oaxaca." *Ekistics* 307: 354–59.
Kuznets, Simon.
　　1976. "Demographic Aspects of Size Distribution of Income: An Exploratory Essay." In *Economic Development and Cultural Change* 25, no. 1: 1–99.
Lawrence, D. H.
　　1982. *Mornings in Mexico.* Reprint of original edition. Layton, Utah: Gibbs M. Smith.

Leeds, Anthony.
1968. "The Anthropology of Cities: Some Methodological Issues." In *Urban Anthropology: Research Perspectives and Strategies*, ed. Elizabeth Eddy, 31–47. Athens, Ga.: Southern Anthropological Society.

Legorreta, Jorge.
1983. *El proceso de urbanización en ciudades petroleras*. Mexico, D.F.: Centro de Ecodesarrollo.

Levy, Daniel, and Gabriel Székely.
1983. *Mexico: Paradoxes of Stability and Change*. Boulder, Colo.: Westview Press.

Lewis, Oscar.
1959. *Five Families: Mexican Case Studies in the Culture of Poverty*. New York: Wiley.
1961. *The Children of Sánchez: Autobiography of a Mexican Family*. New York: Random House.

Lomnitz, Larissa Adler.
1977. *Networks and Marginality: Life in a Mexican Shantytown*. New York: Academic Press.

Lorenzen, Stephen A.
1986. "Earnings and Consumption Strategies in Urban Mexico." Ph.D. diss., Department of Economics, University of Texas at Austin.

Lorenzen, Stephen A., Arthur D. Murphy, and Henry A. Selby.
1989. "Household Budgetary Strategies in Urban Mexico: Mediating the Income-Consumption Nexus." In *Problems and Issues in the Study of Consumption*. Monographs in Economic Anthropology, ed. Benjamin Orlove and Henry Rutz, no. 6. Lanham, Md.: University Press of America.

Lozano, Miguel.
1984. Oaxaca: Una experiencia de lucha. In *Oaxaca, una lucha reciente: 1960–1983*, ed. Bustamante et al. Oaxaca: Ediciones Nueva Sociológica.

Malinowski, Bronislaw, and Julio de la Fuente.
1982. *Malinowski in Mexico: The Economics of a Mexican Market System*. Boston, Mass.: Routledge and Kegan Paul.

Mangin, William, ed.
1967. "Latin American Squatter Settlements: A Problem and a Solution." *Latin American Research Review* 3: 65–98.
1970. *Peasants in Cities: Readings in the Anthropology of Urbanization*. Boston, Mass.: Houghton Mifflin.

Manso de Contreras, Christobál.
1987. *La rebelión de Tehuantepec*. 2d ed. Juchitán, Oaxaca: Ediciones Toledo.

Martínez López, Felipe.
1982. El movimiento oaxaqueño de 1951. In *Sociedad y política en Oaxaca 1980: 15 estudios de caso*, ed. Raúl Benítez Zenteno. Oaxaca: Instituto de Investigaciones Sociológicas, Universidad Autónoma Benito Juárez de Oaxaca.
1985. *El crépusculo del poder: Juchitán, Oax. 1980–1982*. Oaxaca: Instituto de Investigaciones Sociológicas, Universidad Autónoma Benito Juárez de Oaxaca.

Martínez Medina, Héctor G.
    1985. *Los movimientos revolucionarios Maderistas en Oaxaca.* Oaxaca: Instituto de Administración Pública de Oaxaca.
Martínez Vásquez, Victor Raúl.
    1985. *La revolución en Oaxaca 1900–1930.* Oaxaca: Instituto de Administración Pública de Oaxaca.
McCan, Robert, and Stuart B. Schwartz.
    1983. "Measuring Marriage Patterns: Percentages, Cohen's Kappa, and Log-Linear Models." *Comparative Studies in Society and History* 25, no. 4: 711–20.
McCan, Robert, Stuart B. Schwartz, and Arturo Grubessich.
    1979. "Race and Class in Colonial Latin America: A Critique." *Contemporary Studies in Society and History* 23, no. 1 (July): 421–33.
Medina Aguilar, José I.
    1976. *La ciudad de Oaxaca: El hombre y la urbe.* Mexico, D.F.: Secretaría de Educación Pública, Instituto Nacional de Antropología e Historia.
Meillassoux, Claude.
    1981. *Maidens, Meal and Money.* Cambridge: Cambridge University Press.
Meixueiro Hernández, Everardo.
    1989. *Guillermo Meixueiro Delgado: Un caudillo de la soberanía de Oaxaca.* Oaxaca: Talleres de Lásser Plus.
Méndez Martínez, Enrique.
    1979. *Indice de documentos relativos a los pueblos del estado de Oaxaca.* Colección Científica no. 67. Mexico, D.F.: Secretaría de Educación Pública, Instituto Nacional de Antropología e Historia.
Meyer, Michael C., and William L. Sherman.
    1987. *The Course of Mexican History.* 3d ed. New York: Oxford University Press.
Miller, Robert Ryal.
    1985. *Mexico: A History.* Norman: University of Oklahoma Press.
Mogel, Reyna.
    1979. *Regionalizaciones para el estado de Oaxaca: Análisis comparativo.* Oaxaca: Centro de Sociología, Universidad Autónoma de Benito Juárez de Oaxaca.
Montaño, Jorge.
    1976. *Los pobres de la ciudad en los asentamientos espontáneos.* Mexico, D.F.: Siglo Veintiuno.
Morris, Earl W.
    1991. "Household, Kin and Nonkin Sources of Assistance in Home Building: The Case of the City of Oaxaca." *Urban Anthropology* 20, no. 1: 49–66.
Mullen, Robert J.
    1975. *Dominican Architecture in Sixteenth-Century Oaxaca.* Phoenix: Center for Latin American Studies, Arizona State University.
Muñoz Muñoz, Carlos.
    1977. *Crónica de Santa María Chimalapa.* San Luis Potosí: Ediciones Molina.

Murphy, Arthur D.
1973. "A Quantitative Model of Goals and Values in Coquito Sector, San Juan, Oaxaca, Oaxaca." Master's thesis, University of Chicago.
1979. *Urbanization, Development, and Household Adaptive Strategies in Oaxaca, a Secondary City of Mexico.* Ann Arbor, Mich.: University Microfilms International.
1983. "The Economic Groups of Oaxaca." In *Somos Tocayos: The Anthropology of Urbanism and Poverty,*" ed. Michael J. Higgins. Lanham, Md.: University Press of America.
1987. "Studying Housing Areas in a Developing Nation: Lessons from Oaxaca City Mexico." *Housing and Society* 14, no. 2: 143–60.
1991. "City in Crisis: Introduction and Overview." *Urban Anthropology* 20, no. 1: 1–14.
Murphy, A. D., R. Camp, and T. Cohen.
1987. *Pelota Mixteca.* Greeley: Educational Material Service, University of Northern Colorado. Film.
Murphy, Arthur D., Ignacio Cabrera F., Henry A. Selby, and Ignacio Ruíz Love.
1987. "The Mexican Urban Household Project: A Collaboration Between 'la area técnica y la area social.'" In *Collaborative Research and Social Change,* ed. Donald D. Stull and Jean J. Schensul, 159–77. Boulder, Colo.: Westview.
Murphy, Arthur D., Martha W. Rees, Karen French, Earl W. Morris, and Mary Winter.
1990. "Informal Sector and the Crisis in Oaxaca, Mexico: A Comparison of Households 1977–1987." In *Making Out and Making Do: The Informal Economy in Cross-cultural Perspective.* Monographs in Economic Anthropology, ed. Estellie Smith, no. 8. Lanham, Md.: University Press of America.
Murphy, Arthur D., and Henry A. Selby.
1979. La vivienda en la ciudad de Oaxaca. CIDIV 2, no. 9: 42–79.
1981. "A Comparison of Household Income and Budgetary Patterns in Four Mexican Cities." *Urban Anthropology* 10, no. 3: 247–67.
1985. "Poverty and the Domestic Cycle in Oaxaca." *Urban Anthropology* 14, no. 4: 347–65.
Murphy, Arthur D., and Alex Stepick.
1978. "Economic and Social Integration among Urban Peasants." *Human Organization* 37, no. 4: 394–97.
1991. "Oaxaca's Cycles of Conquest." *Urban Anthropology* 20, no. 1: 99–107.
Murphy, Arthur D., Alex Stepick, and Aída Castañeda.
1984. La articulación de una ciudad intermedia con la economía mexicana y el efecto sobre los niveles de vida: El caso de Oaxaca. *Revista de la Sociedad Interamericana de Planificación* 18, no. 71: 115–28.
Musalem Merhy, Guadalupe.
1990. Población y vida cotidiana. Los niños del portal: Estategías de sobrevivencia. *Oaxaca, Población y Futuro* 1, no. (abr.–jun.): 3–4.

Nahmad, Salomón.
   1990. Reflexiones sobre la identidad étnica de los mixes. Un proyecto de investigación por los propios sujetos. *Estudios Sociológicos* 8, no. 22 (jan.–abr.): 23–39.
Nahmad, Salomón, Alvaro González, and Martha Rees.
   1988. *Tecnologías indígenas y medio ambiente*. Mexico, D.F.: Centro de Ecodesarrollo.
Netting, Robert McC., Richard R. Wilk, and Eric J. Arnould, eds.
   1984. *Households: Comparative and Historical Studies of the Domestic Group*. Berkeley: University of California Press.
Nolasco, Margarita.
   1981. *Cuatro ciudades: El proceso de urbanización dependiente*. Mexico, D.F.: Instituto Nacional de Antropología e Historia.
Nolasco, Margarita, and María Luisa Acevedo.
   1985. *Los niños de la frontera*. Mexico: Océano and Centro de Ecodesarrollo.
Oaxaca, Gobierno del Estado de.
   1883. *Cuadros sinópticos de los pueblos, haciendas y ranchos del estado libre y soberano de Oaxaca: Anexo numero 50 a la memoria administrativa presentada al H. Congeso del mismo el 17 de setiembre de 1883*. 2 vols. Oaxaca: Imprenta del Estado.
   1980. *Plan estatal de desarrollo, 1980–1986*. Oaxaca: Gobierno del Estado.
   1982. *Manual de estadísticas básicas del Estado de Oaxaca, 1982*. 3 vols. Mexico, D.F.: Gobierno del Estado de Oaxaca and Secretaría de Programación y Presupuesto.
   1985. *Los gobernantes de Oaxaca*. Mexico, D.F.: J. R. Fortson y Compañía.
Olivera, Mercedes, and Ma. de los Angeles Romero.
   1973. La estructura política de Oaxaca en el siglo XVI. *Revista Mexicana de Sociología* 35, no. 2 (abr.–jun.): 227–87.
Ornelas López, José Luz.
   1985. *Movimiento campesino y desarrollo regional en Tuxtepec: Tres invasiones de tierra en El Mirador, Loma Bonita*. Cuadernos de Investigación. Oaxaca: Instituto de Investigaciones Sociológicas, Universidad Autónoma Benito Juárez de Oaxaca.
   1987. *Los municipios indígenas*. Cuadernos de Investigación, pp. 1–35. Oaxaca: Instituto de Investigaciones Sociológicas, Universidad Autónoma Benito Juárez de Oaxaca.
Pacheco Vasquez, Pedro D., Earl W. Morris, Mary Winter, and Arthur D. Murphy.
   1991. "Neighborhood Type, Housing and Housing Characteristics in Oaxaca." *Urban Anthropology* 20, no. 1: 31–48.
Paddock, John, ed.
   1966. *Ancient Oaxaca: Discoveries in Mexican Archaeology and History*. Stanford, Calif.: Stanford University Press.
   1990a. *De Oaxaca, I*. Oaxaca: Casa de la Cultura Oaxaqueña.
   1990b. *De Oaxaca, II*. Oaxaca: Casa de la Cultura Oaxaqueña.

Padgett, L. Vincent.
    1976. *The Mexican Political System.* 2d ed. Boston, Mass.: Houghton Mifflin.
Parkes, Henry Bramford.
    1969. *A History of Mexico.* Boston, Mass.: Houghton Mifflin.
Parmenter, Ross.
    1984. *Lawrence in Oaxaca: A Quest for the Novelist in Mexico.* Salt Lake City, Utah: Gibbs M. Smith.
Parsons, Elsie Clews.
    1936. *Mitla: Town of the Souls.* Chicago, Ill.: University of Chicago Press.
Pastor, Robert A., and Jorge G. Castañeda.
    1988. *Limits to Friendship: The United States and Mexico.* New York: Alfred A. Knopf.
Pastor, Rodolfo.
    1987. *Campesinos y reformas: La mixteca, 1700–1856.* Mexico, D.F.: El Colegio de México.
Pastor, Rodolfo, Lief Anderson, Erika Berra, Flor Hurtado, Josefina MacGregor, and Guillermo Zermeño.
    1979. *Fluctuaciones económicas en Oaxaca durante el siglo XVIII.* Mexico, D.F.: El Colegio de Mexico.
Perelló, Sergio.
    1989. *Reparto agrario en Oaxaca, 1915–1987.* Oaxaca: Instituto de Investigaciones Sociológicas, Universidad Autónoma Benito Juárez de Oaxaca.
Perlman, Janice E.
    1976. *The Myth of Marginality: Urban Poverty and Politics in Rio de Janeiro.* Berkeley: University of California Press.
Pieyre de Mandiargues, André.
    1985. *La noche de Tehuantepec.* Juchitán, Oaxaca: Editorial Guchachireza.
Plattner, Stuart.
    1974. "Formal Models and Formalist Economic Anthropology: The Problem of Maximization." *Reviews in Anthropology* 1:572–82.
Poniatowska, Elena.
    1975. *Massacre in Mexico.* New York: Viking Press.
Portes, Alejandro.
    1983. "The Informal Sector: Definition, Controversy, and Relation to National Development." *Review* 7, no. 1 (Summer): 151–74.
    1985. "Latin American Class Structures." *Latin American Research Review* 20: 7–39.
Portes, Alejandro, and Saskia Sassen-Koob.
    1987. "Marketing it Underground: Comparative Material on Informal Sector in Western Market Economies." *American Journal of Sociology* 93:30–61.
Portes, Alejandro, and John Walton.
    1976. *Urban Latin America: The Political Condition from Above and Below.* Austin: University of Texas Press.
    1981. *Labor, Class, and the International System.* New York: Academic Press.

Press, Irwin.
    1979. *The City as Context: Urbanism and Behavioral Constraints in Seville.*
    Urbana: University of Illinois Press.
Prince, Zack.
    1988. "Haciendo Colonia: The Making of a Community Near Oaxaca,
    Mexico." Master's thesis, Baylor University.
Prince, Zack, and Arthur D. Murphy.
    1990. "Generative and Regulative Organization in Site and Services Hous-
    ing Projects: A Case from Oaxaca, Mexico." *City and Society* 4, no. 2.
Raat, W. Dirk, and William H. Beezley, eds.
    1986. *Twentieth-Century Mexico.* Lincoln: University of Nebraska Press.
Ramírez Bohorquez, Everardo.
    1989. *Itinerario crítico de mi ciudad: Oaxaca.* Oaxaca: H. Ayuntamiento
    Constitucional, 1986–1989.
Rees, Martha W.
    1989. "Losing Ground in Ajusco: Mexico City's Urban Expansion, 1977–
    1981." Ph.D. Diss., University of Colorado, Boulder.
Rees, Martha W., Arthur D. Murphy, Earl W. Morris, and Mary Winter.
    1991. "Migrants to and in Oaxaca City." *Urban Anthropology* 20, no. 1: 15–
    30.
Reina, Leticia, ed.
    1988. *Historia de la cuestión agraria mexicana: Estado de Oaxaca.* 2 vols.
    Mexico: Juan Pablos Editor.
Riding, Alan.
    1986. *Distant Neighbors: A Portrait of the Mexicans.* New York: Vintage.
Rivera Ríos, Miguel Angel.
    1986. *Crisis y reorganización del capitalismo mexicano, 1960–1985.* Mexico,
    D.F.: Ediciones Era.
Roberts, Bryan.
    1973. *Organizing Strangers.* Austin: University of Texas Press.
    1978. *Cities of Peasants: The Political Economy of Urbanization in the Third
    World.* New York: Edward Arnold.
Rodrigo Alvarez, Luís.
    1983. *Geografía general del Estado de Oaxaca.* Oaxaca: Edición del Gobierno
    del Estado de Oaxaca.
Rodríguez, Roberto, and Imelda García.
    1985. *Los pescadores de Oaxaca y Guerrero.* Mexico, D.F.: Centro de Inves-
    tigaciones y Estudios Superiores en Antropología Social.
Rodríguez Canto, Adolfo, Gabriel Naraváez Carvajal, Antonio Hernández
Mendo, Jorge Romero Peñaloza, Bernardo C. Solano Solano, Francisco L. Anaya
Arrazola, Nicolás Dillanes Ramírez, José de los Santos Castro C.
    1989. *Caracterización de la producción agrícola de la región costa de Oaxaca.*
    Chapingo, Mexico: Universidad Autónoma Chapingo.
Rojas, Basilio.
    1965. *Un gran rebelde: Manuel García Vigil.* Mexico, D.F.: Editorial Luz.
Romero Frizzi, María de los Angeles.
    1973. La estructura política de Oaxaca en el siglo XVI. *Revista Mexicana de
    Sociología* 35, no. 2: 227–87.

1974. *Bibliografía antropológica del estado de Oaxaca.* Oaxaca: Dirección de Centros Regionales, Centro Regional de Oaxaca, Instituto Nacional de Antropología e Historia.

Romero Frizzi, María de los Angeles, ed.

1986. *Lecturas históricas del estado de Oaxaca: Época colonial.* Mexico, D.F.: Instituto Nacional de Antropología e Historia.

1990a. *Lecturas históricas del estado de Oaxaca.* Vol. 2, *Época colonial.* 2d ed. Mexico, D.F.: Instituto Nacional de Antropología e Historia.

1990b. *Lecturas históricas del estado de Oaxaca.* Vol. 3, *Siglo XIX.* Mexico, D.F.: Instituto Nacional de Antropología e Historia.

1990c. *Lecturas históricas del estado de Oaxaca.* Vol. 4, *1877–1930.* Mexico, D.F.: Instituto Nacional de Antropología e Historia.

1990d. *Economía y vida de los Españolas en la Mixteca alta, 1519–1720.* Mexico, D.F.: Instituto Nacional de Antropología e Historia.

Rondinelli, Dennis A.

1983. *Secondary Cities in Developing Countries: Policies for Diffusing Urbanization.* Beverly Hills, Calif.: Sage Publications.

Rosas Solaeguí, Guillermo.

1978. *La vida de Oaxaca: En el carnet del recuerdo.* Oaxaca: Lito Offset de Oaxaca.

Ruíz Cervantes, Francisco José.

1984. La lucha de clases en Oaxaca: 1971–1977. In *Oaxaca, una lucha reciente: 1960–1983,* ed. Bustamante et al. Mexico: Ediciones Nueva Sociología.

1985. *La revolución en Oaxaca 1900–1930: Dos gobiernos en Oaxaca: De la soberanía a la administración preconstitucional.* Oaxaca: Instituto de Administración Pública de Oaxaca.

1986. *La revolución en Oaxaca: El movimiento de la Soberanía (1915–1920).* Oaxaca: Instituto de Investigaciones Sociales. Fondo de la Cultura Económica, Mexico.

Salazár, Godofredo.

1982. *Producción y comercialización de la grana cochinilla de Oaxaca y condición social de los indígenas en la época de la colonia.* Oaxaca: Imprenta Ríos.

Saldaña, Angel, José Valderrey, Chepi Crisanto, Jorge Hernández Díaz, Enrique Marroquín Zaleta, and Raúl Macin.

1987. *De sectas a sectas: Una aproximación al estudio de un fenómeno apasionante.* Claves Latinoamericanas. Oaxaca: Instituto de Investigaciones Sociológicas, Universidad Autónoma Benito Juárez de Oaxaca.

Sánchez López, Alberto.

1989. *Oaxaca: Tierra de maguey y mezcal.* Oaxaca: Instituto Tecnológico de Oaxaca.

Sánchez Silva, Carlos.

1985. *La revolución en Oaxaca, 1900–1930. Empresarios y comerciantes en Oaxaca (1919).* Oaxaca: Instituto de Administración Pública de Oaxaca.

1990. *Los oaxaqueños que se llevó la revolución.* Oaxaca: Carteles Editores, Colección Obra Negra.

Santibañez Orozco, Porfirio.
1982. Oaxaca: la crisis de 1977. In *Sociedad y política en Oaxaca 1980: 15 estudios de caso*, ed. Raúl Benítez Zenteno, 309–30. Oaxaca: Instituto de Investigaciones Sociológicas, Universidad Autónoma Benito Juárez de Oaxaca.

Santos, Milton.
1979 [1975]. *The Shared Space: The Two Circuits of the Urban Economy in Underdeveloped Countries*. London: Methuen.

Schmink, Marianne.
1984. "Household Economic Strategies," *Latin American Research Review* 19: 87–100.

Schnore, L.
1967. "On the Spatial Structure of Cities in the Two Americas." In *The Study of Urbanization*, ed. P. Houser and L. Schnore, 347–98. New York: John Wiley and Sons.

Scott, Ian.
1982. *Urban and Spatial Development in Mexico*. Baltimore, Md.: Johns Hopkins University Press.

Scott, R. E., ed.
1973. *Latin American Modernization Problems*. Urbana: University of Illinois Press.

Seed, P., and P. F. Rust.
1983. "Estate and Class in Colonial Oaxaca Revisited." *Comparative Studies in Society and History* 25, no. 4: 703–10.

Selby, Henry A.
1974. *Zapotec Deviance: The Convergence of Folk and Modern Society*. Austin: University of Texas Press.
1991. "The Oaxacan Urban Household and the Crisis." *Urban Anthropology* 20, no. 1: 87–98.

Selby, Henry A., and Arthur D. Murphy.
1982. *The Mexican Urban Household and the Decision to Migrate to the United States*. ISHI Occasional Papers in Social Change, no. 4. Philadelphia: Institute for the Study of Human Issues.

Selby, Henry A., Arthur D. Murphy, Ignacio Cabrera Fernández, and Aída Castañeda R. C.
1987. "Battling Urban Poverty from Below: A Profile of the Poor in Two Mexican Cities." *American Anthropologist* 89, no. 2: 419–24.

Selby, Henry A., Arthur Murphy, and Steve Lorenzen.
1990. *The Mexican Urban Household: Organizing for Self-Defense*. Austin: University of Texas Press.

Simpson, Lesley Byrd.
1964 [1941]. *Many Mexicos*. 2d rev. ed. Berkeley: University of California Press.
1966. *The Encomienda in New Spain: The Beginning of Spanish Mexico*. Berkeley: University of California Press.

Singer, Milton.
1968. "The Indian Joint Family in Modern Industry." In *Structure and Change in Indian Society*. Chicago: Aldine.

Singer, Paul.
1975 [1973]. *La economía política de la urbanización.* Mexico: Siglo Veintiuno.

Smith, David M.
1979. *Where the Grass is Greener.* Baltimore, Md.: Johns Hopkins University Press.

Smith, Joan, Immanuel Wallerstein, and Hans-Dieter Evers, eds.
1984. *Households and the World-Economy.* Beverly Hills, Calif.: Sage Publications.

Smith, M. Estellie, ed.
1990. *Perspectives on the Informal Economy.* Monographs in Economic Anthropology, no. 8. Lanham, Md.: University Press of America and Society for Economic Anthropology.

Smith, Michael P.
1980. "Critical Theory and Urban Political Theory." *Comparative Urban Research* 7, no. 3: 5–23.

Sorroza, Carlos.
1990. Cambios agroproductivos y crisis alimentaria en Oaxaca (1940–1985). *Estudios Sociológicos* 8, no. 22 (jan.–abr.): 87–116.

Southall, Aidan.
1973. *Urban Anthropology: Cross-Cultural Studies of Urbanization.* New York: Oxford University Press.

Spores, Ronald.
1967. *Mixtec Kings and Their People.* Norman: University of Oklahoma Press.
1984. *The Mixtecs in Ancient and Colonial Times.* Norman: University of Oklahoma Press.

Stauth, Georg.
1984. "Households, Modes of Living, and Production Systems." In *Households and the World-Economy,* ed. Joan Smith, Immanuel Wallerstein, and Hans-Dieter Evers, 90–100. Beverly Hills, Calif.: Sage Publications.

Stephen, Lynn.
1987. "Weaving Changes: Economic Development and Gender Roles in Zapotec Ritual and Production." Ph.D. Diss., Brandeis University.

Stepick, Alex.
1974. "The Rationality of the Urban Poor." Ph.D. Diss., University of California, Irvine.
1978. "Values and Migration Decision-Making." In *Urbanization in the Americas, Selected Papers,* ed. N. S. Kinzer and R. P. Schaedel. The Hague, Netherlands: Mouton Press.

Stepick, Alex, and Gary Hendrix.
1974. "Predicting Behavior from Values." *Southwestern Anthropology Association Newsletter,* February.

Stepick, Alex, and Michael Higgins.
1980. "Somos gente humilde: Failed urban social movement?" Serie de Conferencias, no. 6, Centro Regional de Oaxaca, Mexico, Instituto Nacional de Antropología e Historia, Oaxaca, Mexico, Summer.

Stepick, Alex, and Arthur D. Murphy.
1979. "Housing and Government Intervention among the Urban Poor." *Ekistics* 46, no. 279 (Nov.–Dec.).
1980. "Comparing Squatter Settlements and Government Self-Help Projects as Housing Solutions in Oaxaca, Mexico." *Human Organization* 39, no. 4: 339–43.

Stepick, Alex, and Carol Dutton Stepick.
1979. "Cultural Interdependencies of Chronic Health Problems: Oaxaca, Mexico." In *Transcultural Nursing Care: The Adolescent and Middle Years,* ed. Madeleine Leininger. Salt Lake City: University of Utah.

Stepick, Carol Dutton.
1979. "Health and Poverty of the Urban Poor in Oaxaca, Mexico." Master's thesis, Cornell University.

Tabulse, Elias, ed.
1979. *Fluctuaciones económicas en Oaxaca durante el siglo XVIII.* Mexico, D.F.: El Colegio de Mexico.

Tamayo, Jorge L.
1956. *Oaxaca en el siglo XX: Apuntes históricos y análisis político.* Mexico, D.F.: Editorial Porrúa.

Taylor, William B.
1972. *Landlord and Peasant in Colonial Oaxaca.* Stanford, Calif.: Stanford University Press.
1979. *Drinking, Homicide, and Rebellion in Colonial Mexican Villages.* Stanford, Calif.: Stanford University Press.

Timberlake, Michael, ed.
1985. *Urbanization in the World-Economy.* Orlando, Fla.: Academic Press.

Toussaint, Manuel.
1983. *Oaxaca y Tasco.* Mexico, D.F.: Fondo de Cultura Ecónomica and Secretaría de Educación Pública.

Turner, John F. C.
1977. *Housing by People: Towards Autonomy in Building Environments.* New York: Pantheon Books.

UABJO (Universidad Autónoma Benito Juárez de Oaxaca)
1990. *El Instituto de ciencias y artes del estado: Los años de formación.* Oaxaca: Universidad Autónoma Benito Juárez de Oaxaca.

Unikel, Luís.
1976. *El desarrollo urbano de México.* Mexico, D.F.: El Colegio de Mexico.

Uzzell, Douglas.
1976. "Ethnography of Migration: Breaking out of the Bi-Polar Myth." In *New Approaches to the Study of Migration,* ed. David Guillet and Douglas Uzzell, 45–54. Houston, Tex.: Rice University Press.

Valenzuela F., José.
1986. *El capitalismo mexicano en los ochenta.* Mexico, D.F.: Ediciones Era.

Varese, Stefano.
1983. *Proyectos etnicos y proyectos nacionales.* Mexico, D.F.: El Fondo de Cultura Económica, SEP.

Vélez-Ibañez, Carlos G.
1983. *Rituals of Marginality: Politics, Process, and Culture Change in Central Urban Mexico, 1969–1974.* Berkeley: University of California Press.

Ward, P. M.
1984. "Mexico: Beyond Sites and Services." In *Low-income Housing in the Developing World: The Role of Sites and Services and Settlement Upgrading,* ed. G. K. Payne, 149–58. New York: John Wiley and Sons.

Warman, Arturo, Margarita Nolasco Armas, Guillermo Bonfil, Mercedes Olivera de Bazquez, and Enrique Valencia.
1970. *De eso que llaman antropología Mexicana.* Mexico: C.P AENAH.

Waterbury, Ronald.
1970. "Urbanization and Traditional Market Systems." In *The Social Anthropology of Latin America,* ed. Harry Hoijer and Walter Goldschmidt, 126–53. Los Angeles: Latin American Center, University of California.
1975. "Non-revolutionary Peasants: Oaxaca Compared to Morelos in the Mexican Revolution." *Comparative Studies in Society and History* 17, no. 4 (Oct.): 410–42.

Whitecotton, Joseph W.
1977. *The Zapotecs: Princes, Priests, and Peasants.* Norman: University of Oklahoma Press.

Whiteford, Andrew H.
1964. *Two Cities of Latin America: A Comparative Description of Social Classes.* Garden City, N.Y.: Doubleday-Anchor.

Wilk, Richard R., and Robert McC. Netting.
1984. "Households: Changing Forms and Functions." In *Households: Comparative and Historical Studies of the Domestic Group,* ed. Robert McC. Netting et al., 1–28. Berkeley: University of California Press.

Williams, Aubrey, ed.
1979. *Social, Political, and Economic Life in Contemporary Oaxaca.* Vanderbilt Publications in Anthropology, no. 24. Nashville, Tenn.

Winter, Marcus C.
1989. *Oaxaca: The Archaeological Record.* Mexico, D.F.: Editorial Minutiae Mexicana.

Winter, Marcus C., ed.
1990. *Lecturas históricas del Estado de Oaxaca.* Vol. 1, *Epoca prehispánica.* Mexico, D.F.: Instituto Nacional de Antropología e Historia.

Winter, Mary.
1991. "Interhousehold Exchange of Goods and Services in the City of Oaxaca." *Urban Anthropology* 20, no. 1: 67–86.

Winter, Mary, Earl W. Morris, and Arthur D. Murphy.
1990. "Planning and Implementation in the Informal Sector: Evidence from Oaxaca, Mexico." *City and Society* 4, no. 2: 131–43.

Wolf, Eric.
1959. *Sons of the Shaking Earth.* Chicago, Ill.: University of Chicago Press.
1982. *Europe and the People without History.* Berkeley: University of California Press.

Wolf, E., and S. Mintz.
.1957. "Haciendas and Plantations in Middle America and the Antilles." *Social and Economic Studies* 6, no. 3: 380–412.

Wong, Diana.
1984. "The Limits of Using the Household as a Unit of Analysis." In *Households and the World-Economy*, ed. Joan Smith, Immanuel Wallerstein, and Hans-Dieter Evers, 56–63. Beverly Hills, Calif.: Sage Publications.

Worcester, Donald E., and Wendell G. Schaeffer.
1971. *The Growth and Culture of Latin America.* Vol. 2, *The Continuing Struggle for Independence.* 2d ed. New York: Oxford University Press.

Worsley, Peter.
1983. *The Three Worlds: Culture and World Development.* Chicago: University of Chicago Press.

Yescas Martínez, Isidoro.
1982. La coalición obrero-campesino-estudiantil de Oaxaca: 1972–1974. In *Sociedad y política en Oaxaca 1980: 15 estudios de caso*, ed. Raúl Benítez Zenteno, 289–308. Oaxaca: Instituto de Investigaciones Sociológicas, Universidad Autónoma Benito Juárez de Oaxaca.

Yescas Martínez, Isidoro, and Gloria Zafra.
1985. *La insurgencía magisterial en Oaxaca, 1980.* Oaxaca: Instituto de Investigaciones Sociológicas de la Universidad Autónoma Benito Juárez de Oaxaca.

Yescas Peralta, Pedro.
1958. Estructura social de la ciudad de Oaxaca. *Revista Mexicana de Sociología* 20, no. 3: 767–80.

Young, Kate.
1978. "Modes of Appropriation and the Sexual Division of Labour: A Case Study from Oaxaca, Mexico." In *Feminism and Materialism*, ed. Annette Kuhn and AnnMarie Wolpe, 124–54. London: Routledge and Kegan Paul.

Zafra, Gloria.
1982. Problemática agraria en Oaxaca. In *Sociedad y política en Oaxaca 1980: 15 estudios de caso*, ed. Raúl Benítez Zenteno. Oaxaca: Instituto de Investigaciones Sociológicas, Universidad Autónoma Benito Juárez de Oaxaca.

Index

273